CANADIAN

LIVRES CANADIENS POUR LA JEUNESSE

4th EDITION

Canadian Books for Young People

Livres canadiens pour la jeunesse

4th Edition

Edited by
André Gagnon
and
Ann Gagnon

UNIVERSITY OF TORONTO PRESS
Toronto   Buffalo   London

© University of Toronto Press 1988
Toronto Buffalo London
Printed in Canada
ISBN 0-8020-6662-3

Canadian Cataloguing in Publication Data
Main entry under title:

Canadian books for young people = Livres
canadiens pour la jeunesse

"Revision and expansion of Canadian books for Children/
Livres canadiens pour enfants," English or French; includes
English and French publications.
Includes index.

ISBN 0-8020-6662-3 pa.
1. Children's literature, Canadian – Bibliography. I. André
Gagnon and Ann Gagnon. II. Title: Livres canadiens pour
la jeunesse.

Z1378.C32 1988   028.52   C77-001754-1E

This book has been published with the assistance of the
Ontario Ministry of Culture and Communications.

Cet ouvrage a été publié avec l'aide du ministère de
la Culture et des Communications de l'Ontario.

Contents

Foreword vii
Avant-propos viii

BOARD BOOKS 3

PICTURE BOOKS 5

FOLKLORE 18

SOCIAL SCIENCES 22
Transportation and Communications; Politics and Government; Law;
Social Services; Customs and Beliefs; Holidays

SCIENCE 25
Physical Sciences; Natural History; Plants and Flowers; Animals;
Birds; Health; Mathematics

APPLIED SCIENCE 31
Technology; Food and Cookery

THE ARTS 32
Art; Music; Dance

SPORTS AND RECREATION 35
Games; Hobbies and Crafts; Sports; Outdoor Life; Youth Organizations

LANGUAGE AND LITERATURE 38
Language; Anthologies; Poetry; Plays

FICTION 43
Realistic Fiction; Historical Fiction; Fantasy; Science Fiction;
Short Story Collections

GEOGRAPHY AND TRAVEL 63
Description and Travel; Maps

BIOGRAPHY 65

HISTORY 68
Archaeology; Native Peoples; Canadian History; Pioneer Life

REFERENCE 73

MAGAZINES FOR YOUNG PEOPLE 75

PUBLISHERS' SERIES 77

AWARD BOOKS 86

PROFESSIONAL MEDIA 92
Professional Tools; Literary History & Criticism;
Storytelling; Periodicals

LIVRES CARTONNES 101

ALBUMS 103

BANDES DESSINEES 110

LEGENDES 111

RELIGION 113

SCIENCES SOCIALES 114

SCIENCES PURES 115

TECHNIQUES (SCIENCES APPLIQUEES) 117

LES ARTS 119
Arts decoratifs, mineurs et graphiques; Musique;
Loisirs: spectacles, jeux, sports

LANGUAGE ET LITTERATURE 120
Anthologies; Poésie; Theatre

ROMANS 123

GEOGRAPHIE ET VOYAGES 137

BIOGRAPHIES 138

HISTOIRE 139

REFERENCE 140

REVUES 141

COLLECTIONS 142

PRIX DE LITTERATURE DE JEUNESSE 145

LITTERATURE PROFESSIONNELLE 148
Outils Professionnels; Periodiques

AUTHORS / AUTEURS 151

TITLES / TITRES 161

ILLUSTRATORS / ILLUSTRATEURS 183

Foreword

Since the publication of the third edition of *Canadian Books for Young People/Livres canadiens pour la jeunesse* in 1980, the production of books in French and in English for children and young adults has continued to grow. Noticeable advances have been made in the quality of literary content and format, especially in the areas of picture books and informational books. A significant number of titles for young adults has been published and this growing body of worthy literature has led to the establishment of an annual award. Unfortunately, titles still tend to go out of print quickly.

Due to the number of titles published in the years between the third and fourth editions, it has been necessary to impose a limit on the number of titles included in the fourth edition. While attempting to provide a representative sample of the wealth of books that have been published and are currently in print, the editors have also attempted to maintain the selection criteria used in previous editions by choosing the most informative, relevant, and excellent books for young people.

Titles for young people from pre-school age to age eighteen have been included; the extended upper age limit reflects recent attention paid to the young adult reader. Suggested reading levels for each title have been assigned. The English-language titles are designated as suitable for *younger* (pre-school through age seven), *middle* (ages seven to ten), *older* (ages ten to thirteen), and *young adult* (ages thirteen to eighteen). French-language titles are similarly labelled: *tout-petits* (pre-school through age seven), *debutants* (ages seven to nine), *moyens* (ages nine to twelve), *grands* (ages twelve to fourteen), and *aînés* (ages thirteen to eighteen). These reading levels are guidelines only. The individual child must be considered.

We would like to express our appreciation to Bessie Egan of the Winnipeg Public Library and Joye Hardman of the Calgary Public Library who contributed to the annotation of English-language titles and Micheline Persaud of the Ottawa Public Library who assisted in the selection and annotation of French-language titles. We wish to acknowledge the work of the previous editor, Irma McDonough-Milnes, the continued financial support of the Ontario Ministry of Culture and Communications and all those who have contributed to earlier editions. The generous support and cooperation of the Regina Public Library has made this project possible. We thank the Board, Chief Librarian Ronald Yeo, and the staff, particularly those in the Central Children's Library. Special thanks are due to Kim Jahnke of the Regina Public Library for word processing. Finally, we wish to thank Harald Bohne and the staff of the University of Toronto Press, in particular, Kieran Simpson.

ANDRE GAGNON
ANN GAGNON

Avant-propos

Depuis la publication de la troisième édition de *Canadian Books for Young People/Livres canadiens pour la jeunesse* en 1980, le nombre de livres pour enfants et adolescents en français et en anglais a continué à augmenter à un rythme accéléré. Des progrès remarquables ont été accomplis du point de vue de la qualité littéraire et de la présentation, particulièrement avec les albums et les livres documentaires. La publication d'un plus grand nombre de livres pour les adolescents a suscité la création d'un prix littéraire décerné annuellement.

Le nombre de parutions depuis la publication de la troisième édition a rendu nécessaire une limite aux nombres de livres à inclure dans cette quatrième édition. Tout en essayant de choisir une sélection représentative parmi les nombreux livres présentement disponibles sur le marché, les éditeurs ont tenté de maintenir les critères de sélection établis dans les éditions précédentes tout en choisissant les livres les meilleurs, les plus instructifs, et les mieux adaptés aux besoins des jeunes.

On trouvera des livres s'adressant à des enfants d'âge préscolaire jusqu'aux jeunes de dix-huit ans. L'extension du niveau d'âge jusqu'à dix-huit ans reflète l'attention récente que les éditeurs ont portée aux livres pour les adolescents. La catégorie de lecteurs que vise chaque titre a été précisée. Les livres anglais portent les indications *younger* (les enfants d'âge préscolaire jusqu'à sept ans), *middle* (les enfants de sept à dix ans, *older* (les enfants de dix à treize ans), et *young adult* (les jeunes de treize à dix-huit ans). Des indications semblables accompagnent les titres français. *Tout-petits* désigne les enfants d'âge préscolaire jusqu'à sept ans; *débutants,* les enfants de sept à neuf ans; *moyens,* les enfants de neuf à douze ans; *grands,* les enfants de douze à quatorze ans; *aînés,* les enfants de treize à dix-huit ans. Ces indications ne sont données qu'à titre indicatif. Il est important de considérer l'intérêt individuel de chaque enfant.

Nous voudrions exprimer notre reconnaissance à Bessie Egan de la bibliothèque municipale de Winnipeg et Joye Hardman de la bibliothèque municipale de Calgary qui ont contribué aux annotations des titres anglais, ainsi qu'à Micheline Persaud de la bibliothèque municipale d'Ottawa qui a assisté à la sélection et l'annotation des titres français. Nous voudrions signaler le travail accompli par Irma McDonough-Milnes, l'éditeur des trois premières éditions, et remercier tous ceux qui ont contribué aux éditions précédentes, de même que le ministère de la Culture et des Communications de l'Ontario pour l'appui financier qu'il continue d'offrir. Ce projet a été rendu possible grâce à la coopération et au support généreux de la bibliothèque municipale de Régina. Nous tenons à remercier les membres du conseil d'administration de la bibliothèque municipale de Régina, Ronald Yeo, le directeur, et tous les employés, particulièrement ceux de la bibliothèque centrale des enfants. Un merci spécial à Kim Jahnke de la bibliothèque municipale de Régina pour son travail de traitement de texte. Finallement, nos remerciements s'adressent à Harald Bohne et aux employés des Presses de l'Université de Toronto, et tout particulièrement à Kieran Simpson.

ANDRE GAGNON ANN GAGNON

BOARD BOOKS

Anastasiu, Stéphane. The Farmyard. Ill. by Stéphane Anastasiu. Lorimer, 1985. 16 pp. $3.95 boards [0-88862-820-X].
Cartoonish farm animals are found in this accordion-style board book. Inset pictures and vocabulary appear on the flip side. Translation of *La basse-cour. Younger.*

Anastasiu, Stéphane. My house. Ill. by Stéphane Anastasiu. Lorimer, 1984. 16 pp. $3.95 boards [0-88862-765-3].
This accordion-style wordless board book shows the inside of a house on one side and an illustrated vocabulary on the other. Translation of *Chez moi. Younger.*

Assathiany, Sylvie and Pelletier, Louise. The Bad day. Ill. by Philippe Béha. Lorimer, 1985. 14 pp. $3.95 boards [0-88862-778-5].
A little bear comes to grips with his bad day. Translation of *Quand ça va mal. Younger.*

Assathiany, Sylvie and Pelletier, Louise. Don't cut my hair. Ill. by Philippe Béha. Lorimer, 1984. 14 pp. $3.95 boards [0-88862-771-8].
Dominique has long hair and a vivid imagination. Translation of *Mes cheveux. Younger.*

Assathiany, Sylvie and Pelletier, Louise. Grandma's visit. Ill. by Philippe Béha. Lorimer, 1985. 14 pp. $3.95 boards [0-88862-775-0].
Grandma's visits every Wednesday are very special for Little Bear. Translation of *Grand-maman. Younger.*

Assathiany, Sylvie and Pelletier, Louise. I love my babysitter. Ill. by Philippe Béha. Lorimer, 1984. 14 pp. $3.95 boards [0-88862-768-8].
A little boy enjoys spending the day with his babysitter. Translation of *J'aime Claire. Younger.*

Assathiany, Sylvie and Pelletier, Louise. Little Bear can't sleep. Ill. by Philippe Béha. Lorimer, 1984. 14 pp. $3.95 boards [0-88862-769-6].
Little Bear overcomes his night-time fears and sleeps in his own bed. Translation of *Dors petit ours. Younger.*

Assathiany, Sylvie and Pelletier, Louise. My baby sister. Ill. by Philippe Béha. Lorimer, 1985. 14 pp. $3.95 boards [0-88862-776-9].
Little Bear enjoys having a baby sister because it means that he can be a big brother. Translation of *Mon bébé-soeur. Younger.*

Assathiany, Sylvie and Pelletier, Louise. Peepee in the potty. Ill. by Philippe Béha. Lorimer, 1984. 14 pp. $3.95 boards [0-88862-770-X].
Since beginning to use her potty, Catherine no longer needs to wear diapers. Translation of *Pipi dans le pot. Younger.*

Assathiany, Sylvie and Pelletier, Louise. Where is my dummy? Ill. by Philippe Béha. Lorimer, 1985. 14 pp. $3.95 boards [0-88862-777-7].
Little Bear grows up and no longer needs his pacifier when he goes to bed. Translation of *Où est ma tétine? Younger.*

Béha, Philippe. The Sea. Ill. by Philippe Béha. Lorimer, 1985. 16 pp. $3.95 boards [0-88862-817-X].
Different marine animals are shown on one side of this accordion-style wordless board book. On the flip side, are the names and pictures of some of the animals. Translation of *La mer. Younger.*

4 BOARD BOOKS

Béha, Philippe. The Tree. Ill. by Philippe Béha. Lorimer, 1984. 16 pp. $3.95 boards [0-88862-763-7].
This accordion-style wordless board book shows a tree from top to bottom on one side and, on the flip side, items on the tree are illustrated beside the vocabulary list. Translation of *L'arbre*. *Younger.*

Côté, Marie-Josée. My street. Ill. by Marie-Josée Côté. Lorimer, 1984. 16 pp. $3.95 boards [0-88862-766-1].
Daily activities of the residents of *My street* are highlighted on this accordion-style wordless board book. An illustrated vocabulary list appears on the flip side. Translation of *Ma rue*. *Younger.*

Fall. Ill. by Sylvie Talbot. Lorimer, 1986. 16 pp. $3.95 boards [0-88862-827-7].
Text and illustrations show activities and characteristics of fall. Translation of *Automne*. *Younger.*

Gay, Marie-Louise. The Garden. Ill. by Marie-Louise Gay. Lorimer, 1985. 16 pp. $3.95 boards [0-88862-819-6].
Animals and plants in a garden are shown on one side of this accordion-style wordless board book and, on the other side, an illustrated vocabulary list appears. Translation of *Le potager*. *Younger.*

Khalsa, Dayal Kaur. The Baabee books. Series I. Ill. by Dayal Kaur Khalsa. Tundra, 1983. $14.95 for a set of four; boards [0-88776-149-6].
Four books with coloured illustrations to 'help the infant grasp the concept of how symbols and pictures stand for things.' Accordion-folded to stand or hang. *Younger.*

Khalsa, Dayal Kaur. The Baabee books. Series II. Ill. by Dayal Kaur Khalsa. Tundra, 1983. $12.95 for a set of four; boards [0-88776-149-6].
Toddlers will recognize the familiar situations such as taking a bath, playing, going out, and going to sleep in these bright and boldly-illustrated board books. *Younger.*

Khalsa, Dayal Kaur. The Baabee books. Series III. Ill. by Dayal Kaur Khalsa. Tundra, 1984. Happy birthday, Baabee. $2.95 boards [0-88776-144-5]; Merry Christmas, Baabee. $2.95 boards [0-88776-144-5]; Bon voyage, Baabee. $2.95 boards [0-88776-146-1]; Welcome, twins. $2.95 boards [0-88776-147-X].
Child and parent will be able to discuss familiar objects in situations that young children experience. *Younger.*

Levert, Mireille. The Train. Ill. by Mireille Levert. Lorimer, 1984. 16 pp. $3.95 boards [0-88862-764-5].
One side of this accordion-style board book shows the interior of a passenger train and the other side provides an illustrated vocabulary list. Translation of *Le train*. *Younger.*

Pratt, Pierre. The Fridge. Ill. by Pierre Pratt. Lorimer, 1985. 16 pp. $3.95 boards [0-88862-818-8].
The inside of a refrigerator is shown on one side of this accordion-style wordless board book. An illustrated vocabulary list appears on the flip side. Translation of *Le frigo*. *Younger.*

Spring. Ill. by Sylvie Talbot. Lorimer, 1986. 16 pp. $3.95 boards [0-88862-825-0].
Text and illustrations show activities and characteristics of spring. Translation of *Printemps*. *Younger.*

Summer. Ill. by Sylvie Talbot. Lorimer, 1986. 16 pp. $3.95 boards [0-88862-826-9].
Text and illustrations show activities and characteristics of summer. Translation of *Eté*. *Younger.*

Winter. Ill. by Sylvie Talbot. Lorimer, 1986. 16 pp. $3.95 boards [0-88862-828-5].
Text and illustrations show activities and characteristics of winter. Translation of *Hiver*. *Younger.*

PICTURE BOOKS

see also
PUBLISHERS' SERIES
Kids of Canada Series

Alderson, Sue Ann. Bonnie McSmithers (you're driving me dithers). Ill. by Fiona Garrick. Tree Frog, 1974. 53 pp. $7.95 hardcover [0-88967-052-8]; $4.95 paper [0-88967-008-0].
A lively little girl gets into mischief and her mother goes 'blithery blathery out of her mind.' *Younger.*

Alderson, Sue Ann. Bonnie McSmithers is at it again!. Ill. by Fiona Garrick. Tree Frog, 1980. 41 pp. $4.95 paper [0-88967-028-5].
This time Bonnie makes pancakes for breakfast with a little Too Much Salt but no help from Mommy. *Younger.*

Alderson, Sue Ann. Hurry up, Bonnie. Ill. by Fiona Garrick. Tree Frog, 1977. 43 pp. $7.95 hardcover [0-88967-024-2]; $4.95 paper [0-88967-023-4].
Intrepid, self-directed Bonnie keeps her mother hopping – this time on a trip to get the paper. *Younger.*

Alderson, Sue Ann. Ida and the wool smugglers. Ill. by Ann Blades. Groundwood, 1987. 32 pp. $11.95 hardcover [0-88894-790-9].
A charming story about the growth of initiative and self-confidence in a child of the west coast island sheep farms. Appropriately illustrated in the familiar style of this award-winning illustrator. *Younger.*

Andrews, Jan. Very last first time. Ill. by Ian Wallace. Groundwood, 1985. 32 pp. $10.95 hardcover [0-88899-043-X].
Distinguished illustrations depict the coming-of-age ritual of a young Inuit girl, Eva Padlyut, as she walks alone on the ocean floor collecting mussels. *Younger.*

Anfousse, Ginette. The Bath. Ill. by Ginette Anfousse. Tr. by Mayer Romaner. NC Press, 1981. 22 pp. $2.50 paper [0-919601-68-5].
Jojo must take a second bath after eating chocolate and playing in the mud. Translation of *Le savon. Younger.*

Anfousse, Ginette. Chicken pox. Ill. by Ginette Anfousse. Tr. by Mayer Romaner. NC Press, 1978. 22 pp. $2.50 paper [0-919601-80-4].
Jojo gets the chicken pox and finds a way to bring Pichou into her bedroom to play with her. Translation of *La varicelle. Younger.*

Anfousse, Ginette. The Fight. Ill. by Ginette Anfousse. Tr. by Mayer Romaner. NC Press, 1978. 22 pp. $2.50 paper [0-919601-30-8].
Jojo and CloClo Tremblay have a terrible fight. Translation of *La chicane. Younger.*

Anfousse, Ginette. Hide and seek. Ill. by Ginette Anfousse. Tr. by Mayer Romaner. NC Press, 1978. 22 pp. $2.50 paper [0-919601-78-2].
Jojo and Pichou invite the reader to play hide-and-seek with them. Translation of *La cachette. Younger.*

Anfousse, Ginette. My friend Pichou. Ill. by Ginette Anfousse. Tr. by Mayer Romaner. NC Press, 1978. 22 pp. $2.50 paper [0-919601-08-1].
Jojo introduces Pichou, her honest-to-goodness-baby-aardvark-who-really-eats-ants. Translation of *Mon ami Pichou. Younger.*

Anfousse, Ginette. Winter: the bogey-man-twice-seven. Ill. by Ginette Anfousse. Tr. by Mayer Romaner. NC Press, 1981. 22 pp. $2.50 paper [0-919601-70-7].

A humorous story about a little girl who sees the bogey-man-twice-seven. Translation of *L'hiver ou le bonhomme sept heures. Younger.*

Arnold, Rist. I like birds. Ill. by Rist Arnold. Tundra, 1977. 30 pp. $2.95 hardcover [0-88776-043-0].

A cunning counting book in five languages with the months of the year and a simple narrative added. *Younger.*

Aska, Warabé. Who goes to the park. Ill. by Warabé Aska. Tundra, 1984. 32 pp. $17.95 hardcover [0-88776-162-3]; $9.95 paper [0-88776-187-9].

Simple poetry and full-colour paintings celebrate Toronto's High Park. *Younger, middle.*

Aska, Warabé. Who hides in the park/Les mystères du parc. Ill. by Warabé Aska. Tundra, 1986. 32 pp. $14.95 hardcover [0-88776-182-88]; $9.95 paper [0-88776-186-0].

A magical excursion through Vancouver's Stanley Park. Aska's art readily conveys the legend, the mystery, and the reality that have come together through the decades in this natural landmark. With a brief introductory text presented simultaneously in English, French, and Japanese. *Younger, middle.*

Bianchi, John. The Bungalo boys: last of the tree ranchers. Ill. by John Bianchi. Bungalo, 1986. 24 pp. $12.95 hardcover [0-921285-02-7]; $4.95 paper [0-921285-00-0].

The tree-ranching Bungalo Boys capture the tree-rustling Beaver Gang. *Younger.*

Blades, Ann. By the sea: an alphabet book. Ill. by Ann Blades. Kids Can, 1985. 32 pp. $12.95 hardcover [0-919964-74-5]; $6.95 paper [0-919964-64-8].

A visual alphabet book that depicts seashore activities, animals, and people enjoying themselves. *Younger.*

Blades, Ann. Mary of Mile 18. Ill. by Ann Blades. Tundra, 1971. 40 pp. $7.95 paper [0-88776-059-7].

The author-artist taught in a backwoods Mennonite community in British Columbia and here shows and tells Mary's story. *Younger.*

Bodger, Joan. Belinda's ball. Ill. by Mark Thurman. Oxford, 1981. 40 pp. $9.95 hardcover [0-19-540378-9].

A concept book that encourages participation by the reader and is based on Piaget's psychological theories. *Younger.*

Borden, Darryl. Yeah, I'm just a kid. Ill. by Lynn Smith. Annick, 1983. 26 pp. $10.95 hardcover [0-920236-78-2]; $4.95 paper [0-920236-76-6].

This story emphasizes the many things that children can do. Intriguing collage illustrations. *Younger.*

Bourgeois, Paulette. Big Sarah's little boots. Ill. by Brenda Clark. Kids Can, 1987. 32 pp. $10.95 hardcover [0-921103-11-5].

When Sarah outgrows her little yellow boots that go SQUISH and KERSPLAT!, she gets new yellow boots that go WHOOSH! *Younger.*

Bourgeois, Paulette. Franklin in the dark. Ill. by Brenda Clark. Kids Can, 1986. 32 pp. $10.95 hardcover [0-919964-93-1].

Franklin, the turtle, overcomes his fear of the dark and learns to sleep in his shell. *Younger.*

Buchanan, Joan. It's a good thing. Ill. by Barbara Di Lella. Annick, 1984. 32 pp. $12.95 hardcover [0-920236-72-3]; $4.95 paper [0-920236-65-0].

Text and illustration depict the fond interplay of older and younger sister, each of whom in her own way takes care of the other. *Younger.*

Calleja, Gina. Tobo hates purple. Ill. by Gina Calleja. Annick, 1983. 29 pp. $4.95 paper [0-920236-43-X].

A young boy decides that he likes being purple better than any of the other colours that he tries to be. *Younger.*

Carrier, Roch. The Hockey sweater. Ill. by Sheldon Cohen. Tr. by Sheila Fischman. Tundra, 1984. 24 pp. $14.95 hardcover [0-88776-169-0]; $6.95 paper [0-88776-174-7].

The story of what happens to a young boy who receives a Toronto Maple Leafs' sweater instead of the Montreal Canadiens' sweater that he really wants. Translation of *Le chandail de hockey. Younger, middle.*

Chase, Edith. The New baby calf. Ill. by Barbara Reid. North Winds, 1984. 30 pp. $9.95 hardcover [0-590-71456-2].Scholastic-TAB, 1984. $3.95 paper [0-590-71405-8]; $22.95 Big Book [0-590-71404-X].

Buttercup's new calf explores his farmyard world described through plasticine illustrations. *Younger.*

Children of La Loche and friends. Byron and his balloon/Byrón chu bets'i balloón: an English-Chipewyan counting book. Ed. by David C. May. Tree Frog, 1984. 30 pp. $11.95 hardcover [0-88967-075-7].

A rhyming text and pictures by grade one children are combined in this effective bilingual counting book. *Younger.*

Chislett, Gail. Busy nights. Ill. by Barbara Di Lella. Annick, 1985. 22 pp. $12.95 hardcover [0-920303-20-X]; $4.95 paper [0-920303-22-6].

A crack in the wall of Bram's bedroom is a source of all kinds of imaginary happenings. *Younger.*

Chislett, Gail. Pardon me, Mom. Ill. by Joanne Fitzgerald. Annick, 1986. 23 pp. $12.95 hardcover [0-920303-69-2]; $4.95 paper [0-920303-68-4].

A humorous look at a young boy's selective hearing when his mother calls him to breakfast. *Younger.*

Chislett, Gail. The Rude visitors. Ill. by Barbara Di Lella. Annick, 1984. 32 pp. $12.95 hardcover [0-920236-74-X]; $4.95 paper [0-920236-69-3].

A series of imaginary visitors that includes a hippo, a rabbit, a cow, and an elephant causes Bram a lot of problems. *Younger.*

Clark, Joan. The Leopard and the lily. Ill. by Velma Foster. Oolichan, 1984. 42 pp. $9.95 paper [0-88982-078-3].

A modern fable about a very old leopard and a very frail girl, both near death, who are touched by the beauty of a single white lily. *Middle.*

Cleaver, Elizabeth. ABC. Ill. by Elizabeth Cleaver. Oxford, 1984. 56 pp. $5.95 hardcover [0-19-540466-1].

A beautifully-illustrated ABC that is just the perfect size for little hands. *Younger.*

Climo, Lindee. Clyde. Ill. by Lindee Climo. Tundra, 1986. 24 pp. $11.95 hardcover [0-88776-185-2].

When Clyde the horse thinks that he has been replaced by a tractor, he imagines all the ways in which he could make himself more attractive to his farmer. Lively illustrations convey all Clyde's fantastical new views of himself. *Younger.*

Corrigan, Kathy. Emily Umily. Ill. by Vlasta Van Kampen. Annick, 1984. 32 pp. $12.95 hardcover [0-920236-96-0]; $4.95 paper [0-920236-99-5].

Emily learns how to overcome her habit of saying 'um' in this humorous picture book. *Younger.*

Davis, Ascher. My Grandma the monster. Ill. by Ann Powell. Women's, 1985. 32 pp. $3.95 paper [0-88961-099-1].

The years between grandmother and granddaughter vanish when grandmother admits that she used to play monsters. *Younger.*

Day, Shirley. Ruthie's big tree. Ill. by Shirley Day. Annick, 1982. 30 pp. $12.95 hardcover [0-920236-33-2]; $4.95 paper [0-920236-35-9].

Ruthie leads the other children in a protest when old man Tester decides to have the Tree Service cut down their favourite weeping willow tree. *Younger.*

Day, Shirley. Waldo's back yard. Ill. by Shirley Day. Annick, 1984. 32 pp. $12.95 hardcover [0-920236-90-1]; $4.95 paper [0-920236-73-1].

Irascible Mr. Tester discovers that Waldo and Elizabeth, two children who have worn a path right across his beautiful green grass, are actually very good neighbours. *Younger.*

Downie, Mary Alice. Dragon on parade. Ill. by Mary Lynn Baker. Irwin, 1974. 44 pp. $2.95 paper [0-88778-106-3].

Lazy summer holidays in Bayfield, Ontario and three sisters who dress up as a dragon in the Lions Club parade. Integral, intimate drawings. *Younger, middle.*

Downie, Mary Alice. Jenny Greenteeth. Ill. by Barbara Reid. Kids Can, 1984. 38 pp. $5.95 paper [0-919964-58-3].

A revised text and humorous illustrations enliven this tale of Jenny Greenteeth and her new toothbrush. *Younger.*

Drawson, Blair. I like hats. Ill. by Blair Drawson. Scholastic-TAB, 1979. 24 pp. $2.95 paper [0-590-71485-6].

A very small book with a slight story line about a little girl and the different hats she wears. Bright, humorous illustrations. *Younger.*

Dumas, Jacqueline. And I'm never coming back. Ill. by Iris Paabo. Annick, 1986. 23 pp. $12.95 hardcover [0-920303-64-1]; $4.95 paper [0-920303-65-X].

A young child in the throes of a bad day decides to run away and discovers that her sympathetic mother is prepared to accompany her. *Younger.*

Eyvindson, Peter. Kyle's bath. Ill. by Wendy Wolsak. Pemmican, 1984. 32 pp. $4.75 paper [0-919143-05-9].

Kyle devises a humorous plan that will excuse him from ever having to take baths. *Younger.*

Eyvindson, Peter. Old enough. Ill. by Wendy Wolsak. Pemmican, 1986. 24 pp. $4.00 paper [0-919143-41-5].

A father who is too busy with work to play with his own son finds he has time enough to play with his grandson. Line drawings with interesting details to show the passage of time. *Younger.*

Fairfield, Lesley. Let's eat!/Allons manger! Ill. by Lesley Fairfield. Tr. by Françoise Marois. Kids Can, 1982. 32 pp. $3.95 paper [0-919964-43-5].

A thematic grouping of nouns, supported by humorous related scenes, introduces young readers to basic vocabulary. A bilingual picture book in English and French. *Younger.*

Fairfield, Lesley. Let's go!/Allons-y. Ill. by Lesley Fairfield. Tr. by Martine Connat. Kids Can, 1983. 32 pp. $4.95 paper [0-919964-37-0].
A bilingual book that introduces children to words associated with special places. *Younger, middle.*

Fairfield, Lesley. My first French-English word book. Ill. by Lesley Fairfield. Kids Can, 1987. 48 pp. $5.95 paper [0-921103-03-4].
A compilation of Lesley Fairfield's bilingual word books: *What's the word/Cherchez le mot, Let's go/Allons-y, Let's eat/Allons manger. Younger.*

Fairfield, Lesley. What's the word/Cherchez le mot. Ill. by Lesley Fairfield. Tr. by Françoise Marois. Kids Can, 1981. 32 pp. $3.95 paper [0-919964-39-7].
English and French captions accompany line drawings of familiar words used in daily experience. *Younger.*

Fernandes, Eugenie. A Difficult day. Ill. by Eugenie Fernandes. Kids Can, 1987 (rev.ed.). 32 pp. $10.95 hardcover [0-919964-54-0].
Melinda has a difficult day but her mother is there with milk and cookies and, soon, the difficult day is forgotten. *Younger.*

Fernandes, Eugenie. The Little boy who cried himself to sea. Ill. by Eugenie Fernandes. Kids Can, 1982. 32 pp. $4.95 paper [0-919964-42-7].
A very gentle story with simple childlike line drawings for children who do not want to have a nap. *Younger.*

Foon, Dennis. The Short tree and the bird that could not sing. Ill. by John Bianchi. Douglas & McIntyre, 1986. 32 pp. $10.95 hardcover [0-88899-046-4].
A tree and a non-musical bird become more tolerant of one another in this fun-filled story. *Younger.*

Gagnon, Cécile. Snowfeather. Ill. by Suzanne Duranceau. Tr. by Valerie Hepburn Craig. Lorimer, 1981. 16 pp. $12.95 hardcover [0-88862-525-1]; $4.95 paper [0-88862-524-3].
The snowman that Stephanie makes, comes to life and walks away, so she makes a snowdog and a snowhouse to tempt him back. Translation of *Plumeneige. Younger.*

Galloway, Priscilla. Good times, bad times, Mummy and me. Ill. by Lissa Calvert. Women's, 1980. 32 pp. $5.95 paper [0-88961-066-5].
A little girl describes the good and bad times that she shares with her mother. *Younger.*

Galloway, Priscilla. Jennifer has two daddies. Ill. by Ana Auml. Women's, 1985. 32 pp. $4.95 paper [0-88961-095-9].
Jennifer learns to appreciate the time she spends with her father and her stepfather. *Middle.*

Galloway, Priscilla. When you were little and I was big. Ill. by Heather Collins. Annick, 1984. 32 pp. $12.95 hardcover [0-920236-84-7]; $4.95 paper [0-920236-71-5].
A picture story of role reversal where the little girl becomes the mother who tells her daughter about the wonderful things she does for her. *Younger.*

Garrett, Jennifer. The Queen who stole the sky. Ill. by Linda Hendry. North Winds, 1986. 29 pp. $12.95 hardcover [0-590-71524-0]; $4.95 paper [0-590-71523-2].
When she tricks Queen Tallyrat into returning the sky, Tabatha becomes the village heroine. *Younger.*

Gay, Marie-Louise. Moonbeam on a cat's ear. Ill. by Marie-Louise Gay. Stoddart, 1986. 32 pp. $9.95 hardcover [0-7737-2053-7].
An imaginative story about Rosie and Toby who discover a way to steal the moon right out of the sky. *Younger.*

Gay, Marie-Louise. Rainy day magic. Ill. by Marie-Louise Gay. Stoddart, 1987. 32 pp. $12.95 hardcover [0-7737-2112-6].
Two children have a wonderful, imaginative adventure during a rainy day. *Younger.*

Gill, Gail. There's an alligator under my bed. Ill. by Veronika Martenova Charles. Three Trees, 1984. 24 pp. $11.95 hardcover [0-88823-087-7]; $4.95 paper [0-88823-089-3].
Kevin gets rid of the alligator that lives under his bed with the help of his hockey stick. *Younger.*

Gilman, Phoebe. The Balloon tree. Ill. by Phoebe Gilman. North Winds, 1984. 32 pp. $14.95 hardcover [0-590-71410-4].
An original fairy tale about an innovative princess who lives in a kingdom that is filled with balloons. *Younger.*

Gilman, Phoebe. Jillian Jiggs. Ill. by Phoebe Gilman. North Winds, 1985. 36 pp. $10.95 hardcover [0-590-71548-8]; $3.95 paper [0-590-71515-1].
Jillian has boundless energy and a wonderful imagination but has a hard time keeping her room clean. *Younger.*

Gilman, Phoebe. Little Blue Ben. Ill. by Phoebe Gilman. North Winds, 1986. 40 pp. $9.95 hardcover [0-590-71692-1].
In an effort to avoid a lunch of blue eggs prepared by Blue Hen, Blue Cat and Little Blue Ben play a game of hide-and-seek. *Younger.*

Goman, Joan R. Rebecca's Nancy: a story of a little Mennonite girl. Ill. by Joan R. Goman. Scholastic-TAB, 1982. 56 pp. $2.50 paper [0-590-71149-0].
Losing Nancy was a calamity for Rebecca, but finding her favourite doll made life right again. Cunning collages. *Younger.*

Green, Carrolle. The Too busy day. Ill. by Leonard Aguanno. Annick, 1985. 23 pp. $12.95 hardcover [0-920303-34-X]; $4.95 paper [0-920303-35-8].
Allyson's too busy day turns out to be fun when a surprise picnic ends the day. *Younger.*

Green, John F. There's a dragon in my closet. Ill. by Linda Hendry. North Winds, 1987. $13.95 hardcover [0-590-71705-7]; $3.00 paper [0-590-71704-9].
Jonathan uses a library book to help him cope with the dragon in his closet. *Younger.*

Hadden Mole, Elsie. A Christmas tree from Puddin' Stone Hill. Ill. by Sylvia Hahn. Penumbra, 1985. 31 pp. $6.95 paper [0-920806-74-0].
With the help of Black Cat, Timmy brings home a perfect Christmas tree. *Younger.*

Hammond, Franklin. Ten little ducks. Ill. by Franklin Hammond. Groundwood, 1987. 24 pp. $9.95 hardcover [0-88899-052-9].
Ten little ducks squish, squirt, swoosh, slurp, and snuggle through their daily activities in a gaily-illustrated counting book for the very young. *Younger.*

Handman, Fran. The Upside-down king of Minnikin. Ill. by Robin Baird Lewis. Annick, 1983. 32 pp. $12.95 hardcover [0-920236-52-9]; $4.95 paper [0-920236-46-4].
King Millikin of Minnikin insists that his subjects walk on their hands and then wonders why the people do not applaud him any more. Light-hearted, cartoonish illustrations complement the text. *Younger.*

Harris, Dorothy Joan. Four seasons for Toby. Ill. by Vlasta Van Kampen. North Winds, 1987. 28 pp. $10.95 hardcover [0-509-71677-8].
Toby, the turtle, sets out in search of spring and learns something about each season before he returns to his starting point. *Younger.*

Harris, Dorothy Joan. Goodnight Jeffrey. Ill. by Nancy Hannans. Warne, 1983. 32 pp. $13.95 hardcover [0-7232-6224-1].
Jeffrey knows that he will not be able to go to sleep until he has gathered together his favourite things from around his room. *Younger.*

Harris, Dorothy Joan. The House mouse. Ill. by Barbara Cooney. Warne, 1973. 48 pp. $2.95 paper [0-7232-6096-6].
Four-year-old Jonathan has secret meetings with a mouse who lives in his doll's house. *Younger, middle.*

Harrison, Ted. A Northern alphabet. Ill. by Ted Harrison. Tundra, 1982. 30 pp. $12.95 hardcover [0-88776-133-X].
Each page features a letter and a scene from northern Canada, framed by a border of northern place names beginning with the letter. *Younger.*

Haseley, Dennis. The Cave of snores. Ill. by Eric Beddows. Fitzhenry & Whiteside, 1987. 38 pp. $15.95 hardcover [0-88902-933-4].
In the cave of snores a shepherd boy finds the sound to keep his flock safe from wolves and thieves. *Younger.*

Hasler, Eveline. Winter magic. Ill. by Michèle Lemieux. Methuen, 1985. 32 pp. $9.95 hardcover [0-416-51520-7].
Monty, the big white cat, takes Peter into the fantasy and magic that is winter. Illustrations alive with the glow of winter convey the wonders Peter discovers. *Younger.*

Hazbry, Nancy. How to get rid of bad dreams. Ill. by Roy Condy. Scholastic-TAB, 1983. 32 pp. $3.95 paper [0-590-71174-1].
Antidotes for dreams of ghosts, monsters, dragons, and the like. *Younger.*

Hearn, Emily. Good morning Franny, goodnight Franny. Ill. by Mark Thurman. Women's, 1984. 32 pp. $4.95 paper [0-88961-087-8].
After Franny's friend Ting unexpectedly disappears, Franny finds that Ting has written a message for her on the pavement in the park. *Younger.*

Hearn, Emily. Race you Franny. Ill. by Mark Thurman. Women's, 1986. 32 pp. $4.95 paper [0-88961-104-1].
Expressive coloured drawings help to show that Franny's wheel-chair doesn't prevent her from delivering papers or being a friend. *Younger.*

Hearn, Emily. Woosh! I hear a sound. Ill. by Heather Collins. Annick, 1983. 28 pp. $12.95 hardcover [0-920236-58-8]; $4.95 paper [0-920236-59-6].
A small child investigates the sources of several household sounds. Presented in a question and answer format. *Younger.*

Hutchins, Hazel J. Ben's snow song: a winter picnic. Ill. by Lisa Smith. Annick, 1987. 24 pp. $12.95 hardcover [0-920303-91-9]; $4.95 paper [0-920303-90-0].
Words glide over pages, like skis on snow, in this cheerfully-illustrated story of a family outing. *Younger.*

Hutchins, Hazel J. Leanna builds a genie trap. Ill. by Catharine O'Neill. Annick, 1986. 24 pp. $12.95 hardcover [0-920303-54-5]; $4.95 paper [0-920303-55-2].

With determination – and ultimately with kindness – Leanna pursues the 'genie' that collects so many of her family's lost treasures. Half-page, lively illustrations complement the text and often tell a story of their own. *Younger.*

Kassian, Olena. Flip the dolphin saves the day. Ill. by Olena Kassian. Greey de Pencier, 1984. 24 pp. $2.00 paper [0-919872-91-3].

Flip was smaller than the other dolphins, but he was happy just as he was. *Younger.*

Kassian, Olena. Slip the otter finds a home. Ill. by Olena Kassian. Greey de Pencier, 1984. 24 pp. $2.00 paper [0-919872-90-5].

Slip is forced to find a new home when the river can no longer support the growing number of otters. *Younger.*

Kellerhals-Stewart, Heather. Cricket Christmas. Ill. by Lucya Yaryomich. Borealis, 1978. 26 pp. $5.95 paper [0-919594-70-0].

A graceful, simple story about Stalky the cricket who performed a miracle on Christmas Eve. *Younger, middle.*

Khalsa, Dayal Kaur. I want a dog. Ill. by Dayal Kaur Khalsa. Tundra, 1987. 32 pp. $14.95 hardcover [0-88776-196-8].

Through entertaining words and amusing pictures, the author-illustrator tells about a little girl whose ingenuity almost turns a rollerskate into a dog. *Younger.*

Khalsa, Dayal Kaur. Tales of a gambling grandma. Ill. by Dayal Kaur Khalsa. Tundra, 1986. 32 pp. $14.95 hardcover [0-88776-179-8].

Anna lovingly records days spent with her grandmother. In story and colourful, lively paintings, Anna shares the wisdom that was her grandma's. *Middle.*

Kilbourne, Frances. Overnight adventure. Ill. by Ann Powell. Women's, 1977. 30 pp. $7.95 hardcover [0-88961-054-1]; $4.95 paper [0-88961-047-9].

This adventure-without-words involves two self-sufficient youngsters through a night in the backyard tent. *Younger.*

Kilbourne, Frances. The Recyclers. Ill. by Ann Powell. Women's, 1979. 28 pp. $9.50 hardcover [0-88961-059-2]; $4.95 paper [0-88961-060-6].

This wordless story follows two youngsters who collect neighbourhood cast-offs and recycle them for new uses. *Younger.*

Kovalski, Maryann. Brenda and Edward. Ill. by Maryann Kovalski. Kids Can, 1984. 32 pp. $14.95 hardcover [0-919964-77-X]; $6.95 paper [0-919964-59-1].

Two dogs, Brenda and Edward, live in domestic bliss until the day they are accidentally separated. *Younger.*

Kovalski, Maryann. The Wheels on the bus. Ill. by Maryann Kovalski. Kids Can, 1987. 32 pp. $10.95 hardcover [0-921103-09-3].

Grandma teaches Jenny and Joanna a song that her Granny taught her, in this adaption of the traditional song. Humorous illustrations. *Younger.*

LaRouche, Adelle. Binky and the bamboo brush. Ill. by Adelle LaRouche. Gage, 1981. 48 pp. $6.95 hardcover [0-7715-9561-1].

Not until Grandfather gives him an old, treasured bamboo brush that makes wonderful pictures and Chinese characters does Binky come to enjoy his daily trek to Chinese school in Vancouver's Chinatown. *Younger.*

Lasker, David. The Boy who loved music. Ill. by Joe Lasker. Viking, 1979. 47 pp. $13.95 hardcover [0-670-18385-7].

Karl plays the horn in Joseph Hayden's chamber orchestra whose patron is Prince Nicolaus Esterhazy. Apposite water colours grace this period story. *Younger.*

Lemieux, Michèle. What is that noise? Ill. by Michèle Lemieux. Methuen, 1984. 30 pp. $9.95 hardcover [0-416-49450-1].

All summer long, Bear searches for the source of a thumping noise – the sound of his own beating heart. *Younger.*

Levchuk, Helen. The Dingles. Ill. by John Bianchi. Groundwood, 1985. 24 pp. $6.95 paper [0-88899-044-8].

When a fierce wind strikes the backyard and carries chairs and flowerpots over the fence, Doris Dingle knows just the way to rescue the three cats she loves with all her heart. *Younger.*

Lewis, Robin Baird. Aunt Armadillo. Ill. by Robin Baird Lewis. Annick, 1985. 20 pp. $12.95 hardcover [0-920303-38-2]; $4.95 paper [0-920303-39-0].

Always in the company of her armadillos, the young narrator's adored, eccentric aunt pleases countless acquaintances and relatives alike with her passion for children's books. *Younger.*

Loewen, Iris. My mom is so unusual. Ill. by Alan Pakarnyk. Pemmican, 1986. 24 pp. $4.00 paper [0-919143-37-7].

A young girl describes her mother who is unconventional but loving. *Younger.*

Lottridge, Celia. One watermelon seed. Ill. by Karen Patkau. Oxford, 1986. 24 pp. $9.95 hardcover [0-19-540473-4].

A counting book that tells the story of Max and Josephine who plant their garden and harvest, among other things, twenty pumpkins, thirty eggplants, and hundreds of kernels of popcorn. Vibrant collage shows off the bounty of this garden. *Younger.*

MacKay, Jed. The Big secret. Ill. by Heather Collins. Annick, 1984. 32 pp. $12.95 hardcover [0-920236-88-X]; $4.95 paper [0-920236-89-8].

Mario's adopted family and all his friends and neighbours surprise him with a party on the first anniversary of his joining the family. *Younger.*

Marcus, Susan. Casey visits the doctor. Ill. by Deborah Drew-Brook. CBC, 1981. 32 pp. $3.95 paper [0-88794-101-X].

Casey and Mr. Dressup visit Dr. Jane for Casey's annual check-up. *Younger.*

Michailiuk, George. Wayne's wagon. Ill. by George Michailiuk. Zenovia, 1983. 33 pp. $9.95 hardcover [0-88991-037-5].

Wayne builds a wagon and becomes the envy of his friends. This well-designed picture book was hand set and privately printed. *Younger.*

Michailiuk, Richard. The Wind. Ill. by Richard Michailiuk. Zenovia, 1983. 32 pp. $9.95 hardcover [0-88991-036-7].

A simple description of the wind's activities. Colour block prints decorate a private press book. *Younger.*

Mintzberg, Yvette. Sally, where are you? Ill. by Yvette Mintzberg. Heinemann, 1986. 28 pp. $5.95 hardcover [0-434-95158-7].

A picture puzzle book in which narrator and reader together try to find the playful and elusive Sally. Brightly-coloured illustrations, with the simplest of lines, capture the drama and mood of the dialogue. *Younger.*

Moak, Allen. A Big city ABC. Ill. by Allan Moak. Tundra, 1984. 32 pp. $11.95 hardcover [0-88776-161-5].

Vibrant illustrations depict scenes familiar to a child in Toronto and appealing to a child anywhere in Canada. *Younger.*

Morgan, Allen. Barnaby and Mr. Ling. Ill. by Franklin Hammond. Annick, 1984. 30 pp. $10.95 hardcover [0-920236-70-7]; $4.95 paper [0-920236-67-7].

An elephant and a peanut man run away from the circus and make their dreams come true. *Younger.*

Morgan, Allen. Christopher and the dream dragon. Ill. by Brenda Clark. Kids Can, 1984. 32 pp. $5.95 paper [0-919964-60-5].

When Christopher needs a dream, he rides his special closet elevator to the clouds. In this magic world he also finds out why the moon changes shape. *Younger.*

Morgan, Allen. Christopher and the elevator closet. Ill. by Franklin Hammond. Kids Can, 1981. 48 pp. $9.95 hardcover [0-919964-72-9]; $4.95 paper [0-919964-40-0].

When Christopher rides his elevator closet up into the clouds, he discovers the sources of rain and lightning. A book for beginning readers. *Younger.*

Morgan, Allen. Matthew and the midnight money van. Ill. by Michael Martchenko. Annick, 1987. 21 pp. $12.95 hardcover [0-920303-75-7]; $4.95 paper [0-920303-72-2].

Matthew discovers an imaginative way of getting a Mother's Day present for his mother. *Younger.*

Morgan, Allen. Matthew and the midnight tow truck. Ill. by Michael Martchenko. Annick, 1984. 32 pp. $12.95 hardcover [0-920303-00-5]; $4.95 paper [0-920303-01-3].

A magical adventure at midnight with a tow truck driver who restores equilibrium to Matthew's world. *Younger.*

Morgan, Allen. Matthew and the midnight turkeys. Ill. by Michael Martchenko. Annick, 1985. 24 pp. $12.95 hardcover [0-920303-36-6]; $4.95 paper [0-920303-37-4].

When Matthew sets a trap near his mother's flower bed, he catches more silly turkeys than he dreamed possible. Another magical midnight adventure for this young boy. *Younger.*

Morgan, Allen. Molly and Mr. Maloney. Ill. by Maryann Kovalski. Kids Can, 1981. 48 pp. $4.95 paper [0-919964-41-9].

Three charmingly-illustrated stories about Molly, her friend Mr. Maloney, and his pet raccoon in an I-Can-Read format. *Younger.*

Morgan, Allen. Nicole's boat. Ill. by Jirina Marton. Annick, 1986. 24 pp. $12.95 hardcover [0-920303-60-9]; $4.95 paper [0-920303-61-7].

A rhythmic text and softly-coloured, childlike illustrations capture the pleasure of Nicole's evening sail into the 'sea of night.' *Younger.*

Morgan, Allen. Sadie and the snowman. Ill. by Brenda Clark. Kids Can, 1985. 32 pp. $14.95 hardcover [0-919964-86-9]; $6.95 paper [0-919964-78-8].

All winter long Sadie rolls snowballs again and again so that her snowman will last for a long, long time. Realistic watercolour illustrations depict mood, setting, and characters. *Younger.*

Morgan, Nicola. Pride of lions. Ill. by Nicola Morgan. Fitzhenry & Whiteside, 1987. 34 pp. $13.95 hardcover [0-88902-838-9].

The names of animal groups are depicted in clever and colourful illustrations that are full of playful puns. *Younger.*

Muir, Mary Jane. Gynn. Ill. by Mary Jane Muir. North Winds, 1985. 32 pp. $9.95 hardcover [0-590-71546-1]; $3.95 paper [0-590-71513-5].

A gentle story about the life and death of a pet guinea pig. *Younger.*

Munsch, Robert. The Dark. Ill. by Sami Suomalainen. Annick, 1984 (rev.ed.). 32 pp. $4.95 paper [0-920303-85-5].

A repetitive text and colourful illustrations tell the story of the 'Dark' that drops out of Jule Ann's cookie jar and eats up all the shadows it can find. *Younger.*

Munsch, Robert. David's father. Ill. by Michael Martchenko. Annick, 1983. 30 pp. $12.95 hardcover [0-920236-62-6]; $4.95 paper [0-920236-64-2].

Julie becomes friends with a new boy in the neighbourhood and discovers that David's father is a giant. *Younger.*

Munsch, Robert. 50 below zero. Ill. by Michael Martchenko. Annick, 1986. 24 pp. $12.95 hardcover [0-920236-86-3]; $4.95 paper [0-920236-91-X].

A rhythmic text, complete with sound effects, and full-colour, cartoonlike illustrations delineate the lengths to which Jason goes in order to rescue his sleep-walking father. A story alive with eccentricity and humour. *Younger.*

Munsch, Robert. I have to go! Ill. by Michael Martchenko. Annick, 1986. 24 pp. $12.95 hardcover [0-920303-77-3]; $4.95 paper [0-920303-74-9].

Andrew is always asked if he has to go to the bathroom and he answers yes at the most inopportune moments. *Younger.*

Munsch, Robert. Jonathan cleaned up – then he heard a sound, or blackberry subway jam. Ill. by Michael Martchenko. Annick, 1981. 30 pp. $12.95 hardcover [0-920236-22-8]; $4.95 paper [0-920236-20-2].

When his living room wall slides open and an assortment of people troop through his apartment, Jonathan goes to City Hall to find out why his address on Yonge Street has become a subway stop. *Younger.*

Munsch, Robert. Millicent and the wind. Ill. by Suzanne Duranceau. Annick, 1984. 26 pp. $12.95 hardcover [0-920236-98-7]; $4.95 paper [0-920236-93-6].

A descriptive text and muted full-colour illustrations depict Millicent's unusual life on the mountainside, her friendship with the wind, and her longing for more young companions. *Younger.*

Munsch, Robert. Mortimer. Ill. by Michael Martchenko. Annick, 1985 (rev.ed.). 24 pp. $12.95 hardcover [0-920303-12-9]; $4.95 paper [0-920303-11-0].

A repetitive text, flavoured with sound effects and a catchy chant, tells the story of the imperturbable Mortimer who refuses to fall asleep. Colourful illustrations also capture the humour of the text. *Younger.*

Munsch, Robert. Mud puddle. Ill. by Sami Suomalainen. Annick, 1982 (rev.ed.). 32 pp. $12.95 hardcover [0-920236-47-2]; $4.95 paper [0-920236-28-6].

Whenever Jule Ann, freshly bathed and dressed in clean clothes, ventures into her backyard, the watchful mud puddle jumps on her with predictable results. *Younger.*

Munsch, Robert. Murmel, murmel, murmel. Ill. by Michael Martchenko. Annick, 1982. 32 pp. $12.95 hardcover [0-920236-29-4]; $4.95 paper [0-920236-31-6].

When five-year-old Robin discovers a baby in her sand-box, she immediately sets out to find someone responsible to care for him. *Younger.*

Munsch, Robert. The Paperbag princess. Ill. by Michael Martchenko. Annick, 1980. 32 pp. $10.95 hardcover [0-920236-82-0]; $4.95 paper [0-920236-16-2].

As Elizabeth, dressed in a dirty paper bag, rescues Prince Ronald from the dragon, she comes to her own understanding of loyalty and royalty. A modern fairy tale told and illustrated with lively and colourful humour. *Younger, middle.*

Munsch, Robert. Thomas' snowsuit. Ill. by Michael Martchenko. Annick, 1985. 24 pp. $12.95 hardcover [0-920303-32-3]; $4.95 paper [0-920303-33-1].

Text and illustration depict the nonsense-cum-havoc that ensue when young Thomas refuses to don his new brown snowsuit. *Younger.*

Munsil, Janet. Dinner at Auntie Rose's. Ill. by Scot Ritchie. Annick, 1984. 32 pp. $12.95 hardcover [0-920303-66-9]; $4.95 paper [0-920303-63-4].

Faced with so many manners to practise, food she doesn't like, and her cousin Jeremy, Lucy knows that dinner at her aunt's will be a trial. How she faces the ordeal is told and illustrated with humour and empathy. *Younger.*

Murphy, Joanne Brisson. Feelings. Ill. by Heather Collins. Black Moss, 1985. 27 pp. $5.95 paper [0-88753-129-6].
A young boy explores the world of emotions and feels good about himself. *Younger.*

Murphy, Joanne Brisson. Please don't interrupt. Ill. by Maureen Paxton. Black Moss, 1986. 16 pp. $5.95 paper [0-88753-143-1].
Katy learns how difficult it is to speak to her mother and grandmother without interrupting. *Younger.*

nichol, b.p. Once: a lullaby. Ill. by Anita Lobel. Greenwillow, 1986. 24 pp. $17.95 hardcover [0-688-04284-8].
Repetition of refrain and detail of drawings lend a soothing pattern to this beautifully-presented picture book. Musical notation by Adam Lobel. *Younger.*

nichol, b.p. To the end of the block. Ill. by Shirley Day. Black Moss, 1984. 24 pp. $4.95 paper [0-88753-119-0].
A very short and simple story-poem about an endless walk. Charming illustrations. *Younger.*

Obed, Ellen Bryan. Little Snowshoe. Ill. by William Ritchie. Breakwater, 1984. 30 pp. $5.95 paper [0-919519-29-6].
Little Snowshoe, a lovable rabbit, gets into mischief in this enjoyable picture book. *Younger.*

Oickle, Don. Edgar Potato. Ill. by Sue Skaalen. Ragweed, 1985. 31 pp. $5.95 paper [0-920304-49-4].
After a lonely life in the field, Edgar discovers that being the biggest potato on Prince Edward Island has rewards. *Younger.*

Oppenheim, Joanne. Have you seen birds? Ill. by Barbara Reid. North Winds, 1986. 32 pp. $13.95 hardcover [0-590-71596-8]. Scholastic-TAB, 1986. $4.95 paper [0-590-71577-1]; $22.95 Big Book [0-590-71576-3].
A variety of birds are brought to life through distinguished plasticine illustrations and lyrical prose. *Younger.*

Pachano, Jane and Ozores, J. Rabbit. James Bay Cree ABC in song and picture. Ill. by J. Eitzen, R. Menarick, and M. Orr. James Bay Cree Cultural Education Centre, 1983. 57 pp. $12.75 paper [0-920791-10-7].
A unique alphabet book that provides insight into Native culture. *Younger, middle.*

Paré, Roger. A Friend just like you. Ill. by Roger Paré. Annick, 1984. 24 pp. $12.95 hardcover [0-920303-04-8]; $4.95 paper [0-920303-05-6].
A jolly cat lists the reasons why he likes his friend. Translation of *Plaisir de chats. Younger.*

Pasternak, Carol and Sutterfield, Allen. Stone soup. Ill. by Hedy Campbell. Women's, 1975 (rev.ed.). 32 pp. $4.95 paper [0-88961-014-2].
An inner city school class makes a stone soup that brings multinational children closer together. Imaginative collages. *Younger, middle.*

Pittman, Al. One wonderful fine day for a sculpin named Sam. Ill. by Shawn Steffler. Breakwater, 1983. 32 pp. $8.95 hardcover [0-919948-86-3].
A very lonely day takes a happy turn when Sam meets a beautiful young sculpin named Sara. Brightly-coloured illustrations add emphasis to Sam's story. *Younger.*

Poulin, Stéphane. Ah! belle cité!/A Beautiful city ABC. Ill. by Stéphane Poulin. Tundra, 1985. 32 pp. $11.95 hardcover [0-88776-175-5].
A dual language picture puzzle alphabet book. Colourful, descriptive illustrations introduce twenty-six scenes in Montreal. *Younger.*

Poulin, Stéphane. Can you catch Josephine? Ill. by Stéphane Poulin. Tundra, 1987. 24 pp. $12.95 hardcover [0-88776-198-4].
In a second story about a mischievous cat, the reader follows Josephine who, in turn, has followed her young owner to school. Coloured illustrations give clever clues to Josephine's whereabouts. Translation of *Peux-tu attraper Joséphine? Younger.*

Poulin, Stéphane. Have you seen Josephine? Ill. by Stéphane Poulin. Tundra, 1986. 24 pp. $12.95 hardcover [0-88776-180-1].
A young boy follows his cat to learn where the cat mysteriously disappears to once a week. Translation of *As-tu vu Joséphine? Younger.*

Quinlan, Patricia. My dad takes care of me. Ill. by Vlasta Van Kampen. Annick, 1987. 21 pp. $12.95 hardcover [0-920303-79-X]; $4.95 paper [0-920303-76-5].
A young boy, whose father has lost his job, describes what life is like around his house and decides that he is glad that his father is at home to take care of things. *Younger.*

Ramsay, Marion. No ordinary pig. Ill. by Ina K. Lee. Borealis, 1980. 24 pp. $13.95 hardcover [0-88887-091-4]; $6.95 paper [0-88887-044-2].
Not only can Little Albert Porker hoe turnips, pick beans, and shell peas, he can drive a train. *Younger.*

Reid, Barbara. Sing a song of Mother Goose. Ill. by Barbara Reid. North Winds, 1987. 40 pp. $15.95 hardcover [0-590-71381-2]; $5.95 paper [0-590-71381-7]; $22.95 Big Book [0-590-71380-9].

Delicate and detailed plasticine illustrations decorate familiar nursery rhymes. *Younger.*

Richards, Jack. Johann's gift to Christmas. Ill. by Len Norris. Douglas & McIntyre, 1980. 32 pp. $3.95 paper [0-88894-289-3].

About a musical mouse and his involvement in the writing of a Christmas carol, 'Silent Night.' *Younger, middle.*

Richards, Nancy Wilcox. Farmer Joe's hot day. Ill. by Werner Zimmerman. North Winds, 1987. 24 pp. $13.95 hardcover [0-590-71717-0].

Farmer Joe's clever wife helps him to cope with being hot and tired on a summer day. Playful illustrations. *Younger.*

Roache, Gordon. A Halifax ABC. Ill. by Gordon Roache. Tundra, 1987. 32 pp. $14.95 hardcover [0-88776-183-6].

The artist uses the alphabet to unify these personal glimpses of the Halifax that he and his family know. End-notes explain significant landmarks and historical events. *Younger.*

Robart, Rose. The Cake that Mack ate. Ill. by Maryann Kovalski. Kids Can, 1986. 24 pp. $10.95 hardcover [0-919964-96-6].

A cumulative text describes the circumstances leading up to an unexpected treat for Mack the dog. Accompanied by clear, colourful illustrations that capture the laughter and rhythm in the story. *Younger.*

Rosser, Eric. Snow babies. Ill. by Olena Kassian. Greey de Pencier, 1985. 24 pp. $1.75 paper [0-920775-01-2].

A story of the early lives of birds and animals of the Arctic. *Younger.*

Rothstein, Etho. Jill and the big cat. Ill. by Maureen Paxton. Black Moss, 1984. 42 pp. $4.95 paper [0-88753-112-1].

Jill, a beautiful dog, is frightened by a cat, but learns a good trick to use on other cats. *Younger.*

Roussan, Jacques de. Au-delà du soleil/ Beyond the sun. Ill. by Jacques de Roussan. Tundra, 1977. 28 pp. $2.95 hardcover [0-88776-031-7].

A bilingual picture book about space flight. Eye-catching illustrations allow the imagination to soar. *Younger.*

Roussan, Jacques de. If I came from Mars/Si j'étais Martien. Ill. by Jacques de Roussan. Tundra, 1977. 28 pp. $2.95 hardcover [0-88776-032-5].

Peter takes an imaginary trip from Mars to look at the Earth and decides 'how happy the people who live on it must be!' *Younger.*

Saltman, Judith. Goldie by the sea. Ill. by Kim LaFave. Groundwood, 1987. 32 pp. $11.95 hardcover [0-88899-060-X].

Invigorating and imaginative language and drawings tell the story of a child who persists in her determination to draw the ocean as it really looks. *Younger.*

Sarrazin, Johan. Tootle. Ill. by Aislin. Tundra, 1984. 24 pp. $9.95 hardcover [0-88776-168-2].

Tootle the dog wonders when he will be able to walk like the people that he sees. *Younger.*

Shaw, Barbara. Kiki of Kingfisher Cove: a tale of a Nova Scotia cat. Ill. by Barbara Shaw. Lancelot, 1977. 40 pp. $1.50 paper [0-88999-067-0].

Authentic Nova Scotian fishing village life in words and pictures. *Younger.*

Sillers, Pat. Ringtail. Ill. by Karen Patkau. Oxford, 1987. 24 pp. $12.50 hardcover [0-19-540585-4].

A racoon named Ringtail, who lives in a city ravine, hunts from dusk to dawn for fun and food. *Younger.*

Simmie, Lois. What holds up the moon? Ill. by Anne Simmie. Coteau, 1987. 32 pp. $13.95 hardcover [0-919926-71-1]; $6.95 paper [0-919926-71-1].

A child asks everyone she knows, 'What holds up the moon?' *Younger.*

Speare, Jean E. A Candle for Christmas. Ill. by Ann Blades. Douglas & McIntyre, 1986. 32 pp. $10.95 hardcover [0-88894-783-6].

Tomas dreams that the candle he left on the windowsill grows large enough to light his parents' way home from his uncle's farm on Christmas Eve. Text and illustration depict scenes of family love and community warmth. *Younger.*

Stafford, Terry. Amie and Anika. Ill. by Terry Stafford. Children's Studio, 1983. 33 pp. $6.95 paper [0-9691404-0-1].

Amie takes a very positive approach to being a big sister when baby Anika is born. *Younger.*

Staunton, Ted. Puddleman. Ill. by Maryann Kovalski. Kids Can, 1983. 32 pp. $4.95 paper [0-919964-51-6].

Michael, alias Puddleman, enjoys the mud until it keeps him from his peanut butter sandwich. *Younger.*

Staunton, Ted. Simon's surprise. Ill. by Sylvie Daigneault. Kids Can, 1986. 32 pp. $10.95 hardcover [0-919964-97-4].

Early Saturday morning, using every rag and brush he can find, Simon realizes his dream of being big enough to wash and polish the family car. Full-colour illustrations provide a lively perspective on Simon's enthusiasm and his parents' surprise. *Younger.*

Staunton, Ted. Taking care of Crumley. Ill. by Tina Holdcroft. Kids Can, 1984. 32 pp. $14.95 hardcover [0-919964-75-3]; $6.95 paper [0-919964-55-9].

With the help of his friend Maggie, Cyril takes care of that bully, Crumley. *Younger.*

Stinson, Kathy. The Bare naked book. Ill. by Heather Collins. Annick, 1986. 31 pp. $12.95 hardcover [0-920303-52-8]; $4.95 paper [0-920303-53-6].

A lyrical sound poem about parts of the body that is accompanied by colourful illustrations that depict the anatomy in an array of shapes, sizes, and movements. *Younger.*

Stinson, Kathy. Big or little? Ill. by Robin Baird Lewis. Annick, 1983. 28 pp. $12.95 hardcover [0-920236-30-8]; $4.95 paper [0-920236-32-4].

An active pre-school child recalls the many daily activities and feelings that show that sometimes he is little and at the same time he is growing up. *Younger.*

Stinson, Kathy. Mom and Dad don't live together anymore. Ill. by Nancy Lou Reynolds. Annick, 1984. 32 pp. $12.95 hardcover [0-920236-92-8]; $4.95 paper [0-920236-87-1].

In quiet tones a young girl reviews what impact her parents' separation has on her daily life. She puzzles over happiness that comes – or does not come – when people are apart and together. *Younger.*

Stinson, Kathy. Red is best. Ill. by Robin Baird Lewis. Annick, 1982. 26 pp. $12.95 hardcover [0-920236-24-3]; $4.95 paper [0-920236-26-X].

Presented as an engaging dialogue between mother and child, this picture book story leaves little doubt that red is Kelly's favourite colour. *Younger.*

Stinson, Kathy. Those green things. Ill. by Mary McLoughlin. Annick, 1985. 24 pp. $12.95 hardcover [0-920303-40-4]; $4.95 paper [0-920236-41-2].

A story that positions the imaginative young narrator's interpretation of various green household objects against her mother's rather realistic view. Told in question and answer format. *Younger.*

Stren, Patti. Hug me. Ill. by Patti Stren. Harper, 1984. 32 pp. $4.95 paper [0-88902-974-1].

Line drawings illustrate a small-size book about a porcupine in search of love. *Younger, middle.*

Swede, George. Dudley and the birdman. Ill. by Mary McLoughlin. Three Trees, 1985. 24 pp. $11.95 hardcover [0-88823-104-6]; $4.95 paper [0-88823-102-4].

When Dudley meets the old man who captures birds to preserve their songs through the winter months, he knows exactly what to do with the second tape recorder given to him for his birthday. *Younger.*

Tappage, Mary Augusta. The Big tree and the little tree. Ill. by Terry Gallagher. Ed. by Jean E. Speare. Pemmican, 1986. 32 pp. $16.00 Big Book [0-919143-23-7]; $6.95 paper [0-919143-21-0].

A young tree and an older tree settle their differences in this story which is an excerpt from an earlier book *The Days of Augusta (1973)*. *Younger.*

Thompson, Richard. Jenny's neighbours. Ill. by Kathryn E. Shoemaker. Annick, 1987. 21 pp. $12.95 hardcover [0-920303-73-0]; $4.95 paper [0-920303-70-6].

Two little girls play house and create an imaginative world that is filled with story-book characters. *Younger.*

Thompson, Richard. Sky full of babies. Ill. by Eugenie Fernandes. Annick, 1987. 24 pp. $12.95 hardcover [0-920303-93-5]; $4.95 paper [0-920303-92-7].

Illustrations that are full of movement accompany this story in which Jesse takes her father on a ride through space. *Younger.*

Thurman, Mark. City scrapes. Ill. by Mark Thurman. NC Press, 1983. 22 pp. $10.95 hardcover [0-920053-14-9]; $4.95 paper [0-920053-14-9].

Douglas, the elephant, and Albert, the alligator, go on a shopping spree and enjoy themselves. *Younger.*

Thurman, Mark. The Elephant's cold. Ill. by Mark Thurman. NC Press, 1981. 23 pp. $10.95 hardcover [0-920053-47-5]; $4.95 paper [0-920053-68-8].

Douglas's friends argue about the best way to cure his cold in this cheerful, colourful, and soothing story. *Younger.*

Thurman, Mark. The Lie that grew and grew. Ill. by Mark Thurman. NC Press, 1981. 22 pp. $10.95 hardcover [0-920053-54-8]; $4.95 paper [0-920053-86-6].

Douglas the elephant admits that he has lied to his friends. *Younger.*

Thurman, Mark. Old friends, new friends. Ill. by Mark Thurman. NC Press, 1985. 24 pp. $10.95 hardcover [0-920053-60-2]; $4.95 paper [0-920053-58-0].

Until he meets them, Douglas is jealous of the new friends with whom Albert shares time. *Younger.*

Thurman, Mark. Two pals on an adventure. Ill. by Mark Thurman. NC Press, 1982. 22 pp. $10.95 hardcover [0-920053-84-X]; $4.95 paper [0-920053-52-1].

With visions of untold excitement and mystery, Douglas, the elephant, and Albert, the alligator, set off from home on a journey of discovery. *Younger.*

Thurman, Mark. You bug me. Ill. by Mark Thurman. NC Press, 1984. 22 pp. $10.95 hardcover [0-920053-13-0]; $4.95 paper [0-920053-03-3].

Douglas, the elephant, and Albert, the alligator, make up after a rip-roaring fight. *Younger.*

Van Kampen, Vlasta. ABC/123: the Canadian alphabet and counting book. Ill. by Vlasta Van Kampen. Hurtig, 1982. 47 pp. $5.95 hardcover [0-88830-223-1].

Busy black and white illustrations decorate the letters of the alphabet and numbers one to ten. *Younger.*

Von Königslöw, Andrea Wayne. Toilet tales. Ill. by Andrea Wayne von Königslöw. Annick, 1985. 24 pp. $12.95 hardcover [0-920303-14-5]; $4.95 paper [0-920303-13-7].

A humorous story about animals who should definitely not use toilets. *Younger.*

Wallace, Ian. Chin Chiang and the dragon's dance. Ill. by Ian Wallace. Groundwood, 1984. 32 pp. $10.95 hardcover [0-88899-020-0].

Richly-detailed, coloured illustrations complement the story of Chin Chiang who overcomes self-doubt to dance in the New Year's parade. *Younger, middle.*

Wallace, Ian. Morgan the Magnificent. Ill. by Ian Wallace. Groundwood, 1987. 32 pp. $11.95 hardcover [0-88899-056-1].

Morgan achieves her dream of becoming a high-wire artist in the circus. Illustrated in detailed watercolours. *Younger.*

Wallace, Ian. The Sparrow's song. Ill. by Ian Wallace. Viking Kestrel, 1986. 32 pp. $12.95 hardcover [0-670-81453-9].

Watercolour paintings of the Niagara Falls landscape in the early twentieth century evoke the special summer Katie and her brother Charles nurtured an orphaned song sparrow. *Younger, middle.*

Wallace, Ian and Wood, Angela. The Sandwich. Ill. by Ian Wallace. Kids Can, 1985 (rev. ed.). 41 pp. $4.95 paper [0-919964-02-8].

Vincenzo's favourite sandwich of provolone and mortadella offends his friends' sense of smell until they taste it and enjoy it too. *Younger.*

Waterton, Betty. Mustard. Ill. by Barbara Reid. Scholatic-TAB, 1983. 38 pp. $2.95 paper [0-590-71175-X].

Not until he rescues a kitten from the sea does Miss Goldfinch see her way to finding a home for the large yellow whiskery pup left on her porch. Mustard's friendly, mischievous, and helpful nature is evident in story and pictures alike. *Younger.*

Waterton, Betty. Orff, 27 dragons (and a snarkel!). Ill. by Karen Kulyk. Annick, 1984. 32 pp. $12.95 hardcover [0-920303-02-1]; $4.95 paper [0-920303-03-X].

Orff was a dragon who dared to be different. *Younger.*

Waterton, Betty. Pettranella. Ill. by Ann Blades. Douglas & McIntyre, 1980. 30 pp. $5.95 paper [0-88894-406-3].

The joys and hardships of emigrating to and homesteading in Canada are conveyed through the experiences of Pettranella and her parents. Text and full-colour illustrations depict the little girl's springtime delight to find the seeds she carried from her grandmother's garden to her new homeland are in full bloom. *Younger, middle.*

Waterton, Betty. A Salmon for Simon. Ill. by Ann Blades. Douglas & McIntyre, 1978. 28 pp. $9.95 hardcover [0-88894-168-4]; $3.95 paper [0-88894-533-7].

Simon finally catches a salmon only to free it again. Blades's drawings are award-winning. *Younger, middle.*

Wheeler, Bernelda. A Friend called 'Chum'. Ill. by Andy Stout. Pemmican, 1984. 30 pp. $5.75 paper [0-919143-13-X].

A Native, rural setting is used in this story about a young girl who has a bad day and mistreats her pet dog. *Younger.*

Wheeler, Bernelda. I can't have bannock, but the beaver has a dam. Ill. by Herman Bekkering. Pemmican, 1984. 32 pp. $5.75 paper [0-919143-11-3].

When a beaver fells a tree, the power lines go out and the oven won't heat to make bannock. Cumulative questions and answers between a young Indian boy and his mother tell this realistic story. Illustrated with soft charcoal drawings. *Younger.*

Wheeler, Bernelda. Where did you get your moccasins? Ill. by Herman Bekkering. Pemmican, 1986. 26 pp. $5.75 paper [0-919143-15-6].

An interracial story about a young boy who tells his classmates where his moccasins came from. *Younger.*

Whitaker, Muriel. Pernilla in the perilous forest. Ill. by Jetske Ironside. Oberon, 1979. 24 pp. $11.95 hardcover [0-88750-312-8].

Pernilla braves the seven deadly sins to find a horse to eat sugar from her hand and lay its head in her lap. *Middle.*

Wilson, Barbara. ABC & 123. Ill. by Gisèle Daigle. Porcépic, 1980. 38 pp. $4.95 paper [0-88878-165-2].

An ingenious bilingual alphabet and counting book that demonstrates the similarities in our official languages. *Younger.*

Wolfson, Steve. Monster cheese. Ill. by Bill Johnson. Coteau, 1985. 32 pp. $11.95 hardcover [0-919926-44-4]; $5.95 paper [0-919926-43-6].

When Sam sneezes, too much of the secret ingredient falls into the cheese tub. Line drawings help to tell this story of a runaway cheese. *Younger.*

Wynne-Jones, Tim. I'll make you small. Ill. by Maryann Kovalski. Groundwood, 1986. 32 pp. $10.95 hardcover [0-88899-045-6].

When Roland discovers the room full of toys in the house next door, he begins to understand his eccentric neighbour, Mr. Swanskin, whose constant threat is 'I'll make you small.' *Younger.*

Wynne-Jones, Tim. Zoom at sea. Ill. by Ken Nutt. Groundwood, 1983. 32 pp. $9.95 hardcover [0-88899-021-9].

Pencil drawings illustrate the story of an adventurous cat who, with the help of the mysterious Maria, experiences a day at sea. *Younger.*

Wynne-Jones, Tim. Zoom away. Ill. by Ken Nutt. Groundwood, 1985. 32 pp. $9.95 hardcover [0-88899-042-1].

In a second illustrated adventure, Zoom and Maria journey to the North Pole. *Younger.*

Zinnemann-Hope, Pam. Find your coat Ned. Ill. by Kady MacDonald Denton. Walker, 1987. 36 pp. $4.95 hardcover [0-7445-06271].

Ned's search for his lost coat causes all kinds of chaos. *Younger.*

Zinnemann-Hope, Pam. Let's go shopping Ned. Ill. by Kady MacDonald Denton. Walker, 1986. 26 pp. $4.95 hardcover [0-7445-0629-8].

An easy-to-read book about Ned and Fred who are on a shopping trip with Dad. Lively and colourful illustrations. *Younger.*

Zinnemann-Hope, Pam. Let's play ball Ned. Ill. by Kady MacDonald Denton. Walker, 1987. 36 pp. $4.95 hardcover [0-7445-0627-1].

Ned's decison to play ball indoors turns out to be very unwise indeed. *Younger.*

Zinnemann-Hope, Pam. Time for bed Ned. Ill. by Kady MacDonald Denton. Walker, 1986. 26 pp. $4.95 hardcover [0-7445-0626-3].

Written in simple, rhythmic words aimed at the earliest reader and illustrated with bright and charming pictures, this tale is about Ned who is not inclined to go to bed. *Younger.*

Zola, Meguido. My kind of pup. Ill. by Wendy Wolsak. Pemmican, 1985. 32 pp. $4.75 paper [0-919143-19-9].

An Indian boy imagines what his kind of pup will be like. *Younger.*

Zola, Meguido and **Dereume, Angela.** Nobody. Ill. by Wendy Wolsak. Pemmican, 1983. 32 pp. $4.75 paper [0-919143-38-5].

'Nobody's always up to something. Nobody's always into everything.' A story suited to every family and illustrated with Canadian Indian characters. *Younger.*

FOLKLORE

see also
PUBLISHERS' SERIES
Kon-Skelowh/We Are the People Series

Anderson, Anne. Legends of Wesakecha. Cree, 1976 (rev.ed.). 44 pp. $5.50 paper [0-919864-28-7].
Cree legends of the great trickster and hero, in authentic tellings. *Older.*

Aubry, Claude. The Magic fiddler and other legends of French Canada. Ill. by Saul Field. Tr. by Alice Kane. Irwin, 1968. 98 pp. $6.95 paper [0-7720-1440-X].
Ten French-Canadian folktales artfully retold and illustrated; included are *La Corriveau, Le loup-garou* and *La chasse-galerie* among others. Translation of *Le violon magique et autres légendes du Canada français. Older, young adult.*

Barbeau, Marius. The Golden phoenix, and other fairy tales from Quebec. Retold by Michael Hornyanksy. Ill. by Arthur Price. Oxford, 1980. 144 pp. $6.95 paper [0-19-540345-2].
A reprinting of the 1958 award-winning edition of eight French-Canadian folktales retold by Michael Hornyansky, including *The Princess of Tomboso, The Fairy quite contrary,* and *Scurvyhead. Middle, older.*

Barkhouse, Joyce. The Witch of Port LaJoye. Ill. by Daphne Irving. Ragweed, 1983. 48 pp. $8.95 paper [0-920304-26-5].
A legend set in the early 1700s about a bubbling spring, a magical stone, and a young Basque woman who learns the healing powers of the Micmac much to the dismay of the settlers who think that she is a witch. *Middle, older.*

Cameron, Anne. How Raven freed the moon. Ill. by Tara Miller. Harbour, 1985. 32 pp. $4.95 paper [0-920080-67-9].
Raven, transformed into a beautiful baby, tricks the old fisherwoman and her daughter into freeing the Moon. *Younger, middle.*

Cameron, Anne. How the Loon lost her voice. Ill. by Tara Miller. Harbour, 1985. 32 pp. $4.95 paper [0-920080-55-3].
Loon's lonely cry, Bear's long winter sleep, Deer's moulting antlers, and Raven's love of shiny objects all come from trying to free the daylight. *Younger, middle.*

Clark, Ella E. Indian legends of Canada. McClelland & Stewart, 1981. 177 pp. $9.95 paper [0-7710-2122-4].
Brief, simple retellings of Canadian Indian legends, grouped generically. *Older, young adult.*

Cleaver, Elizabeth. The Enchanted caribou. Ill. by Elizabeth Cleaver. Oxford, 1985. 30 pp. $8.95 hardcover [0-19-540492-0].
An old Inuit tale with shadow puppet illustrations and instructions for making a shadow-puppet theatre combined to form a distinguished picture book. *Middle, older.*

Cleaver, Nancy. How the chipmunk got its stripes. Ill. by Laszlo Gal. Scholastic-TAB, 1975. 28 pp. $2.50 paper [0-590-71121-0].
Algonkian pourquoi legend simply and wittily told, simply and strikingly illustrated. *Younger.*

Collins, Meghan. The Willow maiden. Ill. by Laszlo Gal. Groundwood, 1985. 38 pp. $12.95 hardcover [0-88899-039-1].
A romantic fairy tale about mystery and magic enhanced by exquisite full-colour paintings. *Middle.*

Creighton, Helen. Bluenose ghosts. McGraw, 1976 (rev.ed.). 280 pp. $11.50 paper [0-077709-8].
Excellent collection of supernatural tales and folklore from Nova Scotia. *Older, young adult.*

Downie, Mary Alice. The Wicked fairy-wife. Ill. by Kim Price. Kids Can, 1983. 32 pp. $5.95 paper [0-919964-53-2].
Jean-Paul sets out to avenge his mother's misfortunes in this French-Canadian folktale. *Middle.*

D'Oyley, Enid F. Animal fables and other tales retold. Ill. by Larissa Kauperman. Williams-Wallace, 1982. 40 pp. $5.95 paper [0-88795-020-5].
Retellings of African tales about the spider, leopard, tortoise, and monkey that have survived in the New World. *Middle.*

Elbl, Martin and **Wink, J.T.** Tales from the Amazon. Ill. by Gerda Neubacher. Hayes, 1986. 32 pp. $9.95 hardcover [0-88625-127-3].
Three Amazon Indian tales are gracefully adapted and illustrated with full-colour paintings. *Middle.*

Finnigan, Joan. Look! The land is growing giants: a very Canadian legend. Ill. by Richard Pelham. Tundra, 1983. 40 pp. $14.95 hardcover [0-88776-151-8].
A retelling of the Canadian legend of Joe Montferrand (the giant lumberjack from the Ottawa Valley), accompanied by black and white sketches. *Middle, older.*

Fowke, Edith. Folktales of French Canada. Ill. by Henri Julien. NC Press, 1981 (rev.ed.). $6.95 paper [0-919601-76-6].
Jokes, anecdotes, legends, animal tales, and folk tales selected from translations that 'adhere as closely as possible to the way the original narrators told the stories.' *Older, young adult.*

Fowke, Edith. Tales told in Canada. Doubleday, 1986. 174 pp. $12.95 hardcover [0-385-25109-2]; $14.95 paper [0-385-25041-X].
Organized and annotated in a way that will appeal to the serious folklorist, this collection of tales told in English or available in English translation will also interest the general reader. Includes myths, animal tales, supernatural tales, romantic tales, jokes and anecdotes, formula tales, legends, and personal experience narratives. *Young adult.*

Fox, Mary Lou. Why the beaver has a broad tale. Ill. by Martin Panamik. Highway Book Shop, 1974. 24 pp. $1.50 paper [0-88954-049-7].
An Ojibwe pourquoi legend told in English and Ojibwe by an elder of the Wikwemikong Reserve on Manitoulin Island. *Younger.*

Franko, Ivan. Fox Mykta. Ill. by William Kurelek. Tr. by Bohdan Melynk. Tundra. 1978. 152 pp. $4.95 paper [0-88776-112-7].
Translation of the nineteenth century Ukrainian poet's version of the mediaeval Reynard the Fox tales, illustrated by a Ukrainian-Canadian artist. *Older, young adult.*

Gautreau, Evalyn. Tale spinners in a spruce tipi. Borealis, 1981. 72 pp. $16.95 hardcover [0-88887-075-2]; $8.95 paper [0-88887-061-2].
These literary retellings of myths and legends of the Dogrib Indians retain the spirit of the original tales. *Older, young adult.*

Brothers Grimm. Lucky Hans. Retold by Margaret Greaves. Ill. by Michèle Lemieux. Methuen, 1986. 16 pp. $7.95 hardcover [0-416-54910-1].
Lucky Hans begins with a lump of silver and, after a series of exchanges, ends up with nothing at all. Only then does he feel free. *Younger.*

Hamilton, Mary. A New world bestiary. Ill. by Kim LaFave. Douglas & McIntyre, 1985. 40 pp. $9.95 hardcover [0-88994-485-3].
A visual interpretation of strange and frightening creatures that were seen by early explorers of the New World. *Older.*

Harber, Frances. My king has donkey ears. Ill. by Maryann Kovalski. North Winds, 1986. 28 pp. $13.95 hardcover [0-590-71522-4].
A magnificent king of Old Korea learns to cope with his donkey ears. *Middle.*

Harris, Christie. Mouse Woman and the mischief-makers. Ill. by Douglas Tait. McClelland & Stewart, 1977. 115 pp. $13.95 hardcover [0-7710-4022-9]; $7.95 paper [0-7710-4021-0].
This second volume of North West Indian lore about Mouse Woman, who was a narnauk, a supernatural being, includes seven more stories. *Middle, older.*

Harris, Christie. Mouse Woman and the muddleheads. Ill. by Douglas Tait. McClelland & Stewart, 1979. 131 pp. $13.95 hardcover [0-7710-3984-0].
Seven further adventures of the tiny narnauk whose special charges are muddleheaded young people whom she helps to choose the proper way to do things. *Middle, older.*

Harris, Christie. Mouse Woman and the vanished princesses. Ill. by Douglas Tait. McClelland & Stewart, 1976. 155 pp. $13.95 hardcover [0-7710-4023-7].
Mouse Woman, that tiny busybody, is the central figure in these six Indian tales. *Middle, older.*

Harris, Christie. Once more upon a totem. Ill. by Douglas Tait. McClelland & Stewart, 1978. 195 pp. $6.95 paper [0-7710-3992-1].

Three short traditional tales told by North West Coast Indians, retold and placed in their social context, by a sympathetic author. *Middle, older.*

Harris, Christie. The Trouble with adventurers. Ill. by Douglas Tait. McClelland & Stewart, 1982. 162 pp. $12.95 hardcover [0-7710-3997-2].

Retellings of five traditional stories and one true story about the adventurous people who lived on the Northwest Pacific coast. *Middle, older.*

Hewitt, Garnet. Ytek and the Arctic orchid: an Inuit legend. Ill. by Heather Woodall. Douglas & McIntyre, 1981. 38 pp. $6.95 paper [0-88894-405-5].

Dramatic illustrations punctuate this tale of a youthful shaman's search for caribou to feed his starving people. *Middle.*

Hill, Kay. Glooscap and his magic: legends of the Wabanaki Indians. Ill. by Robert Frankenberg. McClelland & Stewart, 1963. 189 pp. $6.95 paper [0-7710-4117-9].

Hill, Kay. More Glooscap stories. Ill. by John Hamberger. McClelland & Stewart, 1978. 178 pp. $9.95 paper [0-7710-4089-X].

Two volumes of Micmac legends about the great chief Glooscap who guided his people in living wisely and well. *Older.*

Ilmokari, Irina. Finnish fairy tales and stories for children. Borealis, 1981. 52 pp. $18.95 hardcover [0-88887-942-3]; $6.95 paper [0-88887-944-X].

A project started during the International Year of the Child culminated in this collection of six tales translated from the original Finnish and illustrated by Finnish-Canadian young people. The translations are rhythmic and rich. *Middle.*

Johnston, Basil. Tales the elders told: Ojibway legends. Ill. by Shirley Cheechoo. Royal Ontario Museum, 1981. 63 pp. $8.95 hardcover [0-88854-261-5].

An Ojibway historian and a Cree artist have created an attractive and entertaining collection of nine tales. *Younger, middle.*

Johnston, Patronella. Tales of Nokomis. Ill. by Francis Kagige. Musson, 1975. 64 pp. $4.95 paper [0-7737-1008-6].

Sixteen simply-told Ojibway legends stunningly illustrated in colour. *Middle, older.*

Kong, Shiu L. and Wong, Elizabeth K. Fables and legends from ancient China. Ill. by Michele Nidenoff and Wong Ying. Kensington Educational, 1985. 99 pp. $15.00 hardcover [0-9692005-0-2].

Eighteen fables and legends, some dating back three thousand years, are presented in a lively, witty, flowing translation. *Middle.*

Kong, Shiu and Wong, Elizabeth. The Magic pears. Ill. by Wong Ying. Kensington Educational, 1986. 100 pp. $15.00 hardcover [0-9692005-3-6].

Twenty classic folktales, including creation myths, legends, fables, and anecdotes, present a perceptive overview of many subjects and periods in Chinese history. *Middle, older.*

Lunn, Janet. The Twelve dancing princesses. Ill. by Laszlo Gal. Methuen, 1979. 32 pp. $6.95 paper [0-458-98540-6].

A graceful retelling of an old French tale also retold by the Grimm Brothers, with illustrations enchanting and romantic. *Middle.*

MacEwen, Gwendolyn. The Honey drum: seven tales from Arab lands. Mosaic, 1983. 77 pp. $10.95 hardcover [0-88962-228-0]; $5.95 paper [0-88962-227-2].

An unusual collection that contains two original tales and five that are derived from oral and written tales well-known in the Arab world. *Middle.*

Maloney, Margaret Crawford. The Goodman of Ballengiech. Ill. by Laszlo Gal. Methuen, 1987. 32 pp. $14.95 hardcover [0-458-81120-3].

James V, King of Scotland, travels about his kingdom disguised as a commoner in order to gain a better understanding of his subjects. *Middle.*

Maloney, Margaret Crawford. The Little mermaid. Ill. by Laszlo Gal. Methuen, 1983. 32 pp. $12.95 hardcover [0-458-95110-2].

Andersen's wonder tale is retold with poignancy; elegant and ethereal illustrations augment the feeling of timeless tradition. *Middle.*

Martin, Eva. Canadian fairy tales. Ill. by Laszlo Gal. Groundwood, 1984. 124 pp. $15.95 hardcover [0-88899-030-8].

A collection of twelve Canadian fairy tales is enhanced by twelve ornate illustrations. *Middle, older.*

Metayer, Maurice. Tales from the igloo. Ill. by Agnes Nanogak. Hurtig, 1975. 127 pp. $6.95 paper [0-88830-088-3].

Twenty-two stories from the Copper Eskimo, illustrated in rich colours by an Eskimo artist. *Older.*

Morriseau, Norval. Legends of my people, the great Ojibway. Ed. by Selwyn Dewdney. McGraw, 1977. 130 pp. $9.95 paper [0-07-077714-4].

Beliefs, tales, and lore of the Ojibway nation of Lake Nipigon and Thunder Bay District. *Older, young adult.*

Muller, Robin. The Lucky old woman. Ill. by Robin Muller. Kids Can, 1987. 30 pp. $10.95 hardcover [0-921103-07-7].

A poor, hard-working old woman who encounters the Grumpleteaser finds a pot of gold, loses everything she owns, and still decides that she is the luckiest person alive. *Younger.*

Muller, Robin. Mollie Whuppie and the giant. Ill. by Robin Muller. North Winds, 1982. 44 pp. $10.95 hardcover [0-590-71106-7]; $3.95 paper [0-590-71170-9].

Resourceful, clever Mollie Whuppie, the youngest of three sisters, repeatedly outmanoeuvres the fierce giant of the woods. Expressive black and white illustrations capture the many moods and characters of this traditional tale. *Younger, middle.*

Muller, Robin. The Sorcerer's apprentice. Ill. by Robin Muller. Kids Can, 1985. 30 pp. $12.95 hardcover [0-919964-80-X]; $6.95 paper [0-919964-84-2].

Robin, an ingenious young orphan, pits his courage and kindness against the evil dreams of the sorcerer for whom he works. Full-colour, detailed illustrations match the power of this traditional tale. *Younger, middle.*

Muller, Robin. Tatterhood. Ill. by Robin Muller. North Winds, 1984. 40 pp. $14.95 hardcover [0-590-71411-2]; $5.95 paper [0-590-71446-5].

Tatterhood saves her darling younger sister from witches and finds handsome husbands for both of them. Engaging illustrations. *Younger, middle.*

Nanogak, Agnes. More tales from the igloo. Ill. by Agnes Nanogak. Hurtig, 1986. 116 pp. $12.95 hardcover [0-88830-301-7].

'The stories Nanogak tells here ... are concerned with the problems of everyday life, they are legends that have some basis in historical facts and events.' *Older.*

Robinson, Gail. Raven the trickster: legends of the North American Indians. Ill. by Joanna Troughton. Chatto & Windus, 1981. 124 pp. $12.95 hardcover [0-7011-2600-0].

Raven is a supernatural creature of significance to the people of the Northwest Pacific Coast. These stories show that Raven, like all tricksters, can be mischievous and cruel. *Middle.*

San Souci, Robert D. The Enchanted tapestry. Ill. by Laszlo Gal. Groundwood, 1987. 32 pp. $14.95 hardcover [0-88899-050-2].

Only LiJu, the youngest of the weaver's three sons, has the courage to recover his mother's stolen tapestry. Retold in graceful prose with delicate illustrations. *Younger, middle.*

Schwarz, Herbert T. Elik and other stories. Ill. by Mona Ohoveluk. McClelland & Stewart, 1970. 79 pp. $16.95 hardcover [0-7710-7976-1].

Legends retold by living Eskimos and rendered into English by an author who includes biographies of the story-tellers. *Young adult.*

Scribe, Murdo. Murdo's story: a legend from northern Manitoba. Ill. by Terry Gallagher. Pemmican, 1985. 44 pp. $16.00 Big Book [0-919143-09-1]; $6.95 paper [0-919143-07-5].

A legend explaining how the animal and bird worlds came to share summer and winter and how the Big Dipper first appeared in the northern sky. *Younger.*

Spray, Carole. The Mare's egg: a new world folk tale. Ill. by Kim LaFave. Camden, 1981. 56 pp. $11.95 hardcover [0-920656-06-4]; $6.95 paper [0-920656-25-0].

A humorous Canadian tale about a young man who buys a pumpkin that he hopes will hatch into a mare. *Younger, middle.*

Spray, Carole. Will o' the wisp: folk tales and legends from New Brunswick. Brunswick, 1979. 132 pp. $5.95 paper [0-88790-106-9].

Folk tales and legends, yarns and tall tales about devilish bears and red-haired ghosts, buried treasure and legendary curses, collected in New Brunswick from English language sources. *Older, young adult.*

Symchych, Victoria and **Vesey, Olga.** The Flying ship ... and other Ukrainian folk tales. Ill. by Peter Kuch. Holt, 1975. 93 pp. $12.95 hardcover [0-03-929950-3].

Both the colourful drawings and the simple translations impart an authentic flavour to these Ukrainian folk tales retold for Canadian children. *Middle.*

Toye, William. The Fire stealer. Ill. by Elizabeth Cleaver. Oxford, 1979. 24 pp. $6.95 paper [0-19-540515-3].

Scintillating collage pictures interpret this Ojibway legend of how humans received the gift of fire. *Younger, middle.*

Toye, William. How summer came to Canada. Ill. by Elizabeth Cleaver. Oxford, 1978. 32 pp. $7.95 paper [0-19-540290-1].

Micmac legend explains the occurrence of the seasons in simple words and dramatic collages. *Younger.*

Toye, William. The Loon's necklace. Ill. by Elizabeth Cleaver. Oxford, 1977. 24 pp. $10.95 hardcover [0-19-540278-2].

A simple retelling of a Tsimshian legend beautifully illustrated by a prize-winning artist. *Younger.*

Toye, William. The Mountain goats of Temlaham. Ill. by Elizabeth Cleaver. Oxford, 1969. 32 pp. $7.95 paper [0-19-540320-7].
Tsimshian Indian legend recreated simply and dramatically. *Younger.*

Trueman, Stuart. Tall tales and true tales from down east. McClelland & Stewart, 1983. 171 pp. $11.95 paper [0-7710-8635-0].
Readable and amusing retellings of New Brunswick tall tales and historical events that will have a popular following. *Older, young adult.*

Wallas, James and **Whitaker, Pamela.** Kwakiutl legends. Hancock, 1981. 210 pp. $14.95 hardcover [0-88839-094-7].
Short, easily-read retellings of Kwakiutl legends and prayers. Glossary and notes. *Middle.*

White, Ellen. Kwulasulwut: stories from the Coast Salish. Theytus, 1981. 64 pp. $9.95 hardcover [0-919441-04-1].
Through a mixture of traditional tales and original stories, Kwulasulwut, a Salish Indian, gives insight into the Salish way of life. *Middle.*

SOCIAL SCIENCES

TRANSPORTATION AND COMMUNICATIONS

Berton, Pierre. The Great railway. McClelland & Stewart, 1971. 2 vols. 336 pp. $59.50 (boxed) [0-7710-1328-0].
Pictorial history of the CPR is a condensation of the author's *The National dream* and *The Last Spike. Older, young adult.*

Collins, David H. Wings across time: the story of Air Canada. Griffin, 1978. 94 pp. $10.95 paper [0-88760-090-5].
Uncritical history of Air Canada from its beginnings in 1937 to 1977 describes the progress made by the company to serve Canadians in peace and war. *Older.*

Collins, Robert. A Voice from afar; the history of telecommunications in Canada. McGraw, 1977. 304 pp. $19.95 hardcover [0-07-082536-X].
An illustrated history of telephones, cables, microwave, high-frequency radio, and Anik satellites. Chronology, extensive bibliography, and index. *Older, young adult.*

Custode, Michael. Ancient ships on American shores. Ill. by Michael Custode. Three Trees, 1986. 24 pp. $12.95 hardcover [0-88823-113-X]; $5.95 paper [0-88823-115-6].
Depicts the people who landed on the shores of America before Christopher Columbus, with information about the ships they sailed. *Middle.*

Guillet, Edwin C. Pioneer travel in Upper Canada. Univ. of Toronto, 1966. 241 pp. $7.50 paper [0-8020-6052-8].
Various modes of travel and how they affected the development of Upper Canada. *Middle, older.*

Mika, Helma and Mika, Nick. Railways of Canada: a pictorial history. McGraw, 1978. 176 pp. $12.95 paper [0-07-082815-6].
A pictorial and chronological survey of the development of railways from the Champlain and St. Lawrence Railroad to the Canadian National Railways. *Older, young adult.*

POLITICS AND GOVERNMENT

The Arms, flags and emblems of Canada. Canada. Secretary of State; Deneau, 1984. 65 pp. $6.95 paper [0-88879-030-9].
Comprehensive, informative guide to the significance and uses of Canadian arms, flags, and emblems. *Older, young adult.*

Carleton, Alex. Here's how it happens. Gage, 1978. 86 pp. $5.75 paper [0-7715-8507-1].
How municipal, provincial, and federal governments work in Canada. *Middle.*

Kahn, Charles and **Howard, Richard.** Government and you. McClelland & Stewart, 1984 (rev.ed.). 144 pp. $9.50 paper [0-7710-4514-X].
An examination of the function of government at all levels: local, provincial, federal, international. *Older.*

Mackay, Claire. Pay cheques & picket lines: all about unions in Canada. Kids Can, 1987. 96 pp. $19.95 hardcover [0-921103-32-8]; $12.95 paper [0-921103-34-3].
An examination of the history and present role of unions in Canada, presented in terms that young people can understand. *Older.*

Stanley, George F.G. The Story of Canada's flag. McGraw, 1965. 96 pp. $8.95 [0-7700-0197-1].
How it was designed, how it was chosen, how it is to be used. *Older.*

LAW

Harvey, Wendy and **Watson-Russell, Anne.** So, you have to go to court!: a child's guide to testifying as a witness in child abuse cases. Butterworths, 1986. 41 pp. $6.95 paper [0-409-80519-X].
Addressed particularly to children who may have been victims of child abuse, this guide covers everything that may happen to a child in court from preliminary questioning to the day in court. *Middle.*

Horwood, Harold and **Butts, Ed.** Pirates & outlaws of Canada 1610-1932. Doubleday, 1984. 260 pp. $19.95 hardcover [0-385-18373-9].
A fascinating 'record of some of the Canadians who, during the past four centuries, have lived outside of the law.' *Young adult.*

Wilson, Jeffery and **Tomlinson, Mary.** Children and the law. Butterworths, 1986. 2nd ed. 505 pp. $75.00 hardcover [0-409-87762-X].
Lacking a set of legal rules for children or a children's legal code in Canada the authors present 'a collection of our existing laws affecting, in various degrees, the interest of children.' *Adult.*

SOCIAL SERVICES

see also
PUBLISHERS' SERIES
In Your Community

Blakely, Cindy and **Drinkwater, Suzanne.** The Look out book!: a child's guide to street safety. Ill. by Barbara Klunder. Viking Kestrel, 1986. 34 pp. $9.95 hardcover [0-670-81205-6].
Illustrated guidelines to keep children safe at home, at school, and at play. Endorsed by the Block Parent Program. *Younger.*

Darrach, Jim. Fingerprinting: a science at your fingertips. Irwin, 1977. 30 pp. $3.95 hardcover [0-7725-5117-0].
Attractive, succinct yet comprehensive study of fingerprinting. *Middle.*

Foon, Dennis and **Knight, Brenda.** Am I the only one?: a young people's book about sex abuse. Douglas & McIntyre, 1985. 68 pp. $9.95 paper [0-88894-486-1].
A series of personal experiences from kids who have been sexually abused and who eventually tell someone about what has happened to them. *Middle, older.*

Horrall, Stanley. The Pictorial history of the Royal Canadian Mounted Police. McGraw, 1973. 256 pp. $25.95 hardcover [0-07-077366-1].
Factual history of the Royal Canadian Mounted Police from 1873-1973,liberally illustrated. *Older.*

Schuessler, Karl and **Schuessler, Mary.** School on wheels: reading and teaching the isolated children of the North. Boston Mills, 1986. 66 pp. $9.95 paper [0-919783-46-5].
In 1926 Fred and Cela Sloman began a forty-year career in a railway car that was their home and school to children of northern settlements. *Older.*

CUSTOMS AND BELIEFS

Johnson, Philip E. 'Goodbye mom, goodbye.' Ill. by David Peacock. Welch, 1987. 31 pp. $9.95 hardcover [1-55011-032-2].
A family story about the death of a mother explores the different emotions that are experienced by different family members. *Middle, older.*

Lafortune, Claude. Good news in paper. Canadian Bible Society, 1978. 112 pp. $5.95 hardcover [0-88834-058-3].

Attractive cut-paper colour illustrations bring life to this simplified retelling of Bible stories. Translation of *L'évangile en papier. Middle.*

HOLIDAYS

see also
PUBLISHERS' SERIES
Special Days Series

A Canadian yuletide treasury. Irwin, 1982. 156 pp. $8.95 paper [0-7720-1392-6].

A collection of stories, poems, reminiscences, and recipes to celebrate Christmas. *All ages.*

"Crean, ed. The Fireside book of Canadian Christmas. Fitzhenry & Whiteside, 1986. 220 pp. $24.95 hardcover [0-88902-990-3].

A collection of historical and contemporary stories and poems about Christmas written by many well-known Canadians. *Young adult.*

Harper, Kenn, ed. Christmas in the big igloo. Ill. by John Allerston. Outcrop, 1983. 54 pp. $14.95 hardcover [0-919315-07-0].

Recollections of Christmas celebrations in the Canadian Arctic. Simple, eloquent drawings illustrate the stories. *Older, young adult.*

Kurelek, William. A Northern nativity. Ill. by William Kurelek. Tundra, 1976. 48 pp. $14.95 hardcover [0-88776-071-6]; $5.95 paper [0-88776-099-6].

A multi-ethnic interpretation of the universal meaning of Christmas that has been beautifully illustrated by an award-winning illustrator.

Newman, Fran and **Boulanger, Claudette.** Hooray for today. Scholastic-TAB, 1979. 52 pp. $9.95 hardcover [0-590-07623-X]; Posters and teacher's guide $19.95.

A short note, an appropriate quote, and a full-page colour painting on twenty-four days special to Canadians, starting with Canada Day and including Octoberfest and Chinese New Year. *Older.*

Owens, Judy. Hallowe'en fun. Ill. by Kathryn Cole and Terry Brooks. Scholastic-TAB, 1977. 32 pp. $3.25 paper [0-590-71047-8].

Gaily-illustrated paperback offers games, decorations, and costumes for celebrating Hallowe'en. *Younger, middle.*

Parry, Caroline. Let's celebrate! Ill. by Paul Barker, Chris Hayes, Linda Hendry, Sharon Matthews, and Roslyn Schwartz. Kids Can, 1987. 256 pp. $24.95 hardcover [0-921103-38-7]; $14.95 paper [0-921103-40-9].

More than 250 social, religious, cultural, and traditional holidays are described, with activities to enhance the celebrations. *All ages.*

SCIENCE

PHYSICAL SCIENCES

Bailey, Lydia. The Big bang: the creation of the universe. Ill. by Nancie Warner. Annick, 1982. 32 pp. $6.95 hardcover [0-920236-41-3]; $3.95 paper [0-920236-39-1].
Full-colour paintings and simple text are combined to form a scientific explanation of how the universe was created. *Younger.*

Bosak, Susan S. Science is.... Ill. by Anthony Gower. Youth Science Foundation, 1986. 406 pp. $19.95 looseleaf binder [0-921181-00-0].
Science activities varying in complexity from simple to more complex. The activity sheets are arranged in a three-ring binder. Includes a subject and activity title index. *Middle, older.*

Dickinson, Terence. Exploring the night sky: the equinox astronomy guide for beginners. Ill. by John Bianchi. Camden, 1987. 72 pp. $15.95 hardcover [0-920656-64-1]; $9.95 paper [0-920656-66-8].
Attractive illustrations add to this description of aspects of the universe and introduction to stargazing. *Middle.*

Dickinson, Terence. Night watch: the equinox guide to viewing the universe. Camden, 1983. 160 pp. $19.95 spiral bound paper [0-920656-29-9].
A guide for the amateur astronomer contains information on equipment, a star atlas, plus photographs and diagrams. *Older, young adult.*

Dickinson, Terence. The Universe ... and beyond. Ill. by Adolf Schaller. Camden, 1986. 168 pp. $29.95 hardcover [0-920656-50-1]; $22.95 paper [0-920656-48-X].
Scientific data and speculation on the Earth, moon, planets, other solar systems, and the Milky Way has been illustrated with photographs, diagrams, and drawings. *Older, young adult.*

Gross, Renie. Dinosaur country: unearthing the Badlands' prehistoric past. Western Producer Prairie, 1985. 128 pp. $12.95 paper [0-888333-121-5].
The Badlands of southern Alberta is the location of one of the world's most important dinosaur sites. This volume describes dinosaurs as they lived and explains how dinosaur study has developed. *Young adult.*

Hornstein, Reuben A. The Weather book. McClelland & Stewart, 1980. 95 pp. $9.95 paper [0-7710-4216-7].
Lore, legend, and scientific facts about weather help the layman to forecast his own weather. *Young adult.*

Lai, Elizabeth and **Schwalbe, Monica**, eds. Science activities for young people. Ill. by Lori Richards. Hummingbird, 1983. 74 pp. $9.95 paper [0-919952-19-4].
Experiments and information about electricity, stalactites, crystals, soil erosion, and more. Line drawings supplement instructions. *Middle, older.*

Penrose, Gordon. Dr. Zed's dazzling book of science activities. Ill. by Linda Bucholtz-Ross. Greey de Pencier, 1982. 48 pp. $5.95 paper [0-919872-78-6].
As in the earlier *Dr. Zed's brilliant book of science experiments*, the experiments found here are illustrated, tested, and encourage discovery. *Middle, older.*

Professor Kurius. The Super science discovery book: easy-to-do experiments that really work! Ill. by Jacques Goldstyn. Tr. by Susan Le Pan. Grosvenor, 1984. 105 pp. $13.95 hardcover [0-919959-07-5]; $9.95 paper [0-919959-12-1].
A collection of over one hundred science experiments with easy-to-follow instructions and cartoonish illustrations. Translation of *Le petit débrouillard. Middle, older.*

Rowe, Erna Dirks and Daniel, Alan. Flying and swimming creatures from the time of the dinosaurs. Scholastic-TAB, 1980. 33 pp. $9.95 hardcover [0-590-71049-4]; $2.75 paper [0-590-71050-8]. Paperback title: *Strange creatures from the time of the dinosaurs.* Scholastic-TAB, 1981. 33 pp. $4.50 paper [0-590-72151-8].
An identification book that juxtaposes realistic drawings of each creature with cartoon-like pictures that show comparisons in modern settings. *Younger.*

Rowe, Erna. Giant dinosaurs. Ill. by Merle Smith. Scholastic-TAB, 1977 (rev.ed.). 32 pp. $3.50 paper. No ISBN.
Facts about seven dinosaurs simply stated and humorously illustrated. *Younger, middle.*

Scienceworks: an Ontario Science Centre book of experiments. Ill. by Tina Holdcroft. Kids Can, 1984. 86 pp. $19.95 hardcover [0-919964-81-8]; $9.95 paper [0-919964-61-3].
A wide-ranging assortment of clearly-presented experiments designed to answer the 'how' and 'why' from pure and applied science. Equipment required to carry out the activities can readily be found at home. *Middle, older.*

Vowles, Andrew. The Hayes book of amazing experiments you can do at home. Ill. by Tim O'Halloran and Terry Winik. Hayes, 1985. 32 pp. $5.95 paper [0-88625-073-0].
Introductory and entertaining experiments that explain such phenomena as static electricity, inertia, and sound. *Middle.*

NATURAL HISTORY

Blood, Don and Hall, Tom W. Rocky Mountain wildlife. Ill. by Susan Im Baumgarten. Hancock, 1976. 130 pp. $35.00 hardcover [0-919654-37-1].
Describes climate, vegetation, and fauna of the Rocky Mountains and contains full descriptions of animals found there. Lavishly illustrated. *Older.*

Brooks, Bill. Wildlife of Canada. Hounslow, 1976. 96 pp. $17.95 hardcover [0-88882-010-0].
Striking full-colour pictures of Canadian birds and animals that will encourage their conservation. *All ages.*

Bruemmer, Fred. The Arctic. Ill. by Fred Bruemmer. Optimum, 1982. 224 pp. $19.95 paper [0-88890-147-X].
Spectacular photographs enhance a detailed text. *Young adult.*

Bruemmer, Fred. Arctic animals: a celebration of survival. Ill. by Fred Bruemmer. McClelland & Stewart, 1986. 160 pp. $29.95 hardcover [0-7710-1717-0].
Stunning photographs and fact-filled text provide a fascinating view of birds and animals of the Arctic. *Older, young adult.*

Gilroy, Doug. Parkland portraits: some natural history of the prairie parklands. Western Producer Prairie, 1979. 127 pp. $24.95 hardcover [0-88833-019-7]; $14.95 paper [0-88833-031-6].
Flora and fauna beautifully photographed in colour and carefully captioned. *Older, young adult.*

Gilroy, Doug. Prairie wildlife: the best of Doug Gilroy's nature photography. Western Producer Prairie, 1985. 122 pp. $14.95 paper [0-88833-155-X].
Remarkable photographs show the magnificent colour of plants, animals, and birds in their natural habitats. Annotations give information on each subject and indicate the circumstances for taking each photograph. *All ages.*

Hosie, R.C. Native trees of Canada. Fitzhenry & Whiteside, 1979. 383 pp. $22.95 hardcover [0-88902-572-X]; $14.95 paper [0-88902-558-4].
The definitive work on indigenous trees, not ones introduced to our country, well illustrated. *Young adult.*

Karstad, Aleta. Canadian nature notebook. McGraw, 1979. 144 pp. $14.95 hardcover [0-07-082782-6].
A field naturalist-artist collects material from twenty-five communities of animals and plants and records their relationships in an easily-understood text and meticulously-detailed drawings. *Older, young adult.*

Owl's question and answer book #1. Greey de Pencier, 1983. 45 pp. $6.95 hardcover [0-919872-82-4].

Owl's question and answer book #2. Greey de Pencier, 1983. 45 pp. $6.95 hardcover [0-919872-83-2].
These books give answers to the thousands of questions most often asked by readers of OWL magazine. *Middle.*

Pavlick, Leon E. Red pines on the ridge. Ill. by Lissa Calvert. Braemar, 1985. 35 pp. $12.95 hardcover [0-919749-07-0].
The story of the red pine, common to southwestern Manitoba, is told from the perspective of the tree. Evocative illustrations. *Middle.*

Van Camp, J.L. Fifty trees of Canada east of the Rockies. Irwin, 1952. 64 pp. $2.95 paper [0-7725-1099-7].
Brief, illustrated notes. *Middle, older.*

PLANTS AND FLOWERS

Ferguson, Mary and Saunders, Richard. Canadian wildflowers. Van Nostrand, 1976. 192 pp. $19.95 hardcover [0-442-29859-5].
A treasury of native flowers beautifully illustrated and clearly described. *All ages.*

Fitzharris, Tim. Wildflowers of Canada. Oxford, 1986. pp. $29.95 hardcover [0-19-540566-8].
A beautiful photographic guide. *Older, young adult.*

Porsild, A.E. Rocky Mountain wild flowers. Ill. by Dagny Tande Lid. National Museums of Canada, 1979. 454 pp. $9.95 paper [0-660-00073-3].
Well-arranged and illustrated with minutely-detailed water-colours. This will introduce children to a wide variety of mountain flora. *Older.*

Suzuki, David and Hehner, Barbara. Looking at plants. Stoddart, 1985. 96 pp. $8.95 paper [0-7737-5039-8].
Experiments and activities help to show the construction of plants and their role in nature. *Middle.*

Trelawny, John G. Wildflowers of the Yukon and Northwestern Canada, including adjacent Alaska. Gray's, 1983. 214 pp. $19.95 paper [0-88826-097-0].
An illustrated glossary and a key to species using flower colour and shape supplement this useful guide to northern flora. *Older.*

Vance, F.R.; Jowsey, J.R.; and McLean, J.S. Wildflowers across the prairies. Western Producer Prairie, 1984 (rev.ed.). 214 pp. $17.95 paper [0-88833-131-2].
This useful guide to 270 species of western wildflowers includes a glossary and coloured photos. *Older.*

ANIMALS

see also
PUBLISHERS' SERIES
Natural History Notebook Series
Nature's Children Series
Zoo Book Series

Climo, Lindee. Chester's barn. Ill. by Lindee Climo. Tundra, 1982. 32 pp. $12.95 hardcover [0-88776-132-1]; $7.95 paper [0-88776-155-0].
A descriptive story of the animals and day-to-day events in a Prince Edward Island barn; expressive illustrations. *Younger.*

Dagg, Anne Innis. Mammals of Ontario. Ill. by Roslyn A. Alexander. Otter, 1974. 159 pp. $12.00 hardcover [0-9690963-1-3]; $6.50 paper [0-9690963-2-1].
Scientific data, short items of research, and excellent drawings familiarize readers with all common animals from the vole to the ringed seal. *Older.*

Dingwall, Laima and Slaight, Annabel, eds. The Kids' cat book. Greey de Pencier, 1984. 96 pp. $6.95 paper [0-919872-89-1].
Stories, facts, drawings, and photographs about all kinds of domestic and wild cats. Tips on care of a pet cat. *Younger, middle.*

Dingwall, Laima and Slaight, Annabel, eds. The Kids' dog book. Greey de Pencier, 1984. 96 pp. $6.95 paper [0-919872-88-3].
A variety of fascinating facts and entertaining stories, games, and riddles about dogs, compiled by the editors of OWL magazine and illustrated with photographs and drawings. *Younger, middle.*

Forsyth, Adrian. Mammals of the Canadian wild. Camden, 1985. 351 pp. $29.95 hardcover [0-920656-40-4].
Identification, habits, and behaviours of mammals native to Canada and the northern United States are accompanied by photographs that have captured the creatures in their natural habitats and pursuits. *Older, young adult.*

Foster, Janet. The Wilds of Whip-poor-will Farm: true animal stories. Ill. by Olena Kassian. Greey de Pencier, 1982. 112 pp. $7.95 paper [0-919872-79-4].
When Janet and John Foster build a log cabin on their farm, they become well-acquainted with their animal neighbours. *Middle.*

Froom, Barbara. The Amphibians of Canada. McClelland & Stewart, 1982. 120 pp. $14.95 paper [0-7710-3207-2].
An informative book about frogs, toads, and salamanders. *Older.*

Froom, Barbara. The Snakes of Canada. McClelland & Stewart, 1977. 128 pp. $14.95 paper [0-7710-3186-6].
Illustrations, description, folklore, and geographic habitat. *Older.*

Froom, Barbara. The Turtles of Canada. McClelland & Stewart, 1978. 120 pp. $9.95 paper [0-7710-3182-3].
This companion to *The Snakes of Canada* is another excellent, readable guide, well illustrated. *Older.*

Jesseau, Patricia. Willow: the story of an Arabian foal. Ill. by Jeannette Lightwood. Penumbra, 1985. 24 pp. $6.95 paper [0-920806-70-8].

Gentle pencil drawings enhance this story of the first summer in the life of an exceptional Arabian horse. *Younger.*

Little, Harry Lee. Rima: the monkey's child. Ill. by H.G. Glyde. Univ. of Alberta, 1983. 123 pp. $14.95 hardcover [0-88864-040-4].

An orphaned spider monkey is adopted by a family in the Mexican rainforest. *Middle, older.*

MacEwan, Grant. Heavy horses: highlights of their history. Western Producer Prairie, 1986. 150 pp. $24.95 hardcover [0-88833-209-2].

History and development of familiar breeds of horses in Canada. *Older.*

Mowat, Farley. Never cry wolf. Seal, 1982. 242 pp. $3.95 paper [0-7704-2137-7].

Fascinating account of a man's attempt to study the wolf through a summer of daily observations. *Older, young adult.*

Mowat, Farley. A Whale for the killing. McClelland & Stewart, 1977. 239 pp. $16.95 hardcover [0-7710-6600-7].

An attempt to save a trapped whale on the Newfoundland coast results in a crusade to save this endangered species. *Young adult.*

Ripley, Catherine. Night and day. Ill. by Debi Perna and Brenda Clark. Greey de Pencier, 1985. 24 pp. $2.00 paper [0-920775-00-4].

A day in the lives of the animals who inhabit the meadow, the woods, and the pond. *Younger.*

Russell, Andy. Adventures with wild animals. Ill. by Harry Savage. Hurtig, 1981. 183 pp. $4.95 paper [0-88830-199-5].

Elks, otters, and friendly owls are among the wild animals that live through the author's pen. *Young adult.*

Scott, W.B. Freshwater fishes of eastern Canada. Univ. of Toronto, 1967. 2nd ed. 137 pp. $10.95 paper [0-8020-6074-9].

Detailed reference work with complete descriptions. *Older, young adult.*

Seton, Ernest Thompson. Animal tracks and hunter signs. Macmillan, 1978. 160 pp. $5.95 paper [0-7705-1672-6].

Habits and behaviour of animals as revealed by their trails. *Middle, older.*

Shuh, John Hennigar. Crabs wear their skeletons on the outside. Ill. by Nancy Stobie. Nova Scotia Museum, 1979. 40 pp. $3.00 paper [0-919680-17-8].

A simple explanation of this crustacean's life cycle carefully illustrated with line drawings. *Younger.*

Smith, David Allenby. Sharptooth: a year of the beaver. Ill. by Bob Kebic. Irwin, 1978. 54 pp. $4.95 paper [0-88778-180-2].

Two beavers follow the natural round as integral components of the Canadian ecology. *Middle, older.*

Suzuki, David and **Hehner, Barbara.** Looking at insects. Ill. by Robert Tuckerman. Stoddart, 1986. 96 pp. $8.95 paper [0-7737-5062-2].

An informative guide to the world of insects. The book includes facts about the history and life of several species, a look at common lore, and many experiments that encourage further investigation. *Younger, middle.*

Trueman, Stuart. The Wild life I've led. Ill. by Stuart Trueman. McClelland & Stewart, 1976. 160 pp. $19.95 hardcover [0-7710-8600-8].

Encounters with a bull moose in mating season, a bat in a bedroom, and other animals, told with a chuckle by a winner of the Stephen Leacock Memorial Medal for Humour. *Older, young adult.*

The Whale Research Group. Getting along: fish, whales, and fishermen. Ill. by Don Wright. Breakwater, 1984. 88 pp. $6.50 paper [0-919519-78-4].

A book of information, lessons, and activities to increase understanding of the marine environment and its problems. *Middle, older.*

Wooding, Frederick. The Book of Canadian fishes. McGraw, 1973. 2nd ed. 303 pp. $9.95 paper [0-07-077635-0].

A comprehensive illustrated catalogue. *Older, young adult.*

Wooding, Frederick H. Wild mammals of Canada. McGraw, 1982. 272 pp. $34.95 hardcover [0-07-082973-X].

This informative narrative describes the physical characteristics, habits, and behaviour of more than 150 species of wild mammals. Line drawings and photographs. *Older, young adult.*

Woods, Shirley E. The Squirrels of Canada. National Museum of Natural Sciences, 1980. 199 pp. $29.95 hardcover [0-660-10344-3].

More than twenty species of squirrels are described in this identification book. *Older.*

Wrigley, Robert E. Mammals in North America. Ill. by Dwayne Harty. Hyperion, 1986. 325 pp. $49.95 hardcover [0-920534-33-3].

Stories and paintings of animals in their daily lives are supplemented by detailed scientific information. Organized by geographical habitat. *Older, young adult.*

BIRDS

Angell, Tony. Owls. Douglas & McIntyre, 1980. 80 pp. $9.95 paper [0-88894-252-4].

Sixty beautiful drawings and short informative descriptions of the eighteen North American species, by an owl lover. *Middle, older.*

Dobson, Clive. Feeding wild birds in winter. Ill. by Clive Dobson. Firefly, 1981. 128 pp. $8.95 paper [0-920668-17-8].

This excellent guide identifies birds, lists suitable food, provides plans for feeders, and suggests solutions to problems. Beautiful pencil drawings. *Middle to young adult.*

Godfrey, W. Earl. The Birds of Canada. Ill. by John A. Crosby and S.D. MacDonald. National Museums of Canada, 1986 (rev.ed.). 595 pp. $39.95 hardcover [0-660-10758-9].

'The revised edition includes all bird species known to occur, or to have occurred, in Canada and its coastal waters within a limit of 320 km off shore, up to December 1984, a total of 578 species.' Maps and colour plates. *Older, young adult.*

Hancock, David A. and Hancock, Susan. Guide to western wildlife. Hancock, 1977. 33 pp. $3.00 paper [0-919654-81-9].

A brief text and attractive illustrations serve as an introduction to animals and birds. *Middle, older.*

Loates, Glen and James, Ross. Glen Loates birds of North America. Prentice, 1979. 116 pp. $29.95 hardcover [0-13-357103-3].

Sketches and coloured plates of twenty-four North American birds in folio format show off Glen Loates's precision and artistry. *Older, young adult.*

McKeever, Katherine. Granny's gang: life with the most unusual family of owls. Ill. by Olena Kassian. Greey de Pencier, 1984. 96 pp. $8.95 paper [0-919872-96-4].

A series of stories about owls who live in an Owl Rehabilitation Research Foundation in Southern Ontario. *Middle, older.*

Rising, Trudy and Rising, Jim. Canadian songbirds and their ways. Ill. by Kathryn Devos-Miller. Tundra, 1982. 176 pp. $39.95 hardcover [0-88776-124-0].

An introduction and identification guide to songbirds, plus an explanation of their annual cycles. *Older, young adult.*

Salt, W.Ray and Salt, Jim R. The Birds of Alberta with their ranges in Saskatchewan and Manitoba. Hurtig, 1976. 498 pp. $19.95 hardcover [0-88830-108-1].

Beautiful colour photographs, clear and well-detailed, enhance an accurate and informative text. 'The birds give the impression that they have flown onto the pages and are merely resting before flying off again.' *Older.*

Speirs, J. Murray. Birds of Ontario: Volumes I and II. Natural Heritage/Natural History, 1985. Vol.I, $49.95 hardcover [0-920474-38-1]; Vol.II, $24.95 hardcover [0-920474-39-4].

Two excellent books for bird lovers. Volume I shows colour plates of birds in their habitats with a brief annotation given for each bird mentioned. Volume II summarizes the status of each species using maps to record the average population from 1968-1977. Documented observations and bird-banding information are also included. *Older.*

HEALTH

Cairo, Shelley; Cairo, Jasmine; and Cairo, Tara. Our brother has Down's Syndrome. Ill. by Irene McNeil. Annick, 1985. 23 pp. $12.95 hardcover [0-920303-30-7]; $4.95 paper [0-920303-31-5].

A photographic essay told from a child's point of view. *Younger.*

Corby, Lynda and Clark, Patti. You're someBODY: how to be a slim kid. Fifth, 1985. 96 pp. $10.95 paper [0-920079-13-X].

Designed with charts for personal use, this book provides an assortment of facts, figures, and suggestions to help a child plan a nutritious diet. *Middle, older.*

Davis, Calvin Lewis. Insect alert: a layman's guide to insect safety. Davis Publications, Box 66, Oshawa ON, <s>L1H 4G0 $3.25 paper [0-9690922-2-9].

This useful guide gives a general description of seventeen insects plus symptoms of known allergic reactions to bites and stings, danger signs, emergency treatment, and safety precautions. *Older.*

Doan, Helen and Morse, Janice M. Every girl: learning about menstruation. Stoddart, 1985. 84 pp. $7.95 paper [0-7737-5027-4].

A reassuring handbook that answers questions a girl might have about the onset of menstruation. *Middle, older.*

Dunlop, Marilyn. Understanding cancer: an invaluable book for cancer patients and their families. Irwin, 1985. 197 pp. $9.95 paper [0-7725-1507-7].

Emotional and physiological aspects of the detection and treatment of cancer are discussed. Symptoms of individual cancers are outlined. Glossary and directory of where to find help. *Young adult.*

Fine, Judylaine. Afraid to ask: a book about cancer. Kids Can, 1984. 168 pp. $19.95 hardcover [0-919964-79-6]; $12.95 paper [0-919964-56-7].

A straightforward explanation about the biology of the disease and the emotional problems it entails. *Older, young adult.*

Leibel, B.S. and **Wrenshall, G.A.** Insulin. Canadian Diabetic Association, 1971. 45 pp. $1.00 hardcover. No ISBN.

History of diabetes, and the discovery of insulin – a Canadian accomplishment. *Middle.*

Levine, Dr. Saul and **Wilcox, Dr. Kathleen.** Dear Doctor: teenagers ask about.... Kids Can, 1986. 239 pp. $9.95 paper [0-919964-85-0].

In response to letters from young people the authors address such adolescent concerns as nutrition, sexuality, relationships, and drugs. *Older, young adult.*

Razzell, Mary. The secret code of DNA. Ill. by J.O. Pennanen. Penumbra, 1986. 32 pp. $6.95 paper [0-920806-83-X].

A clear and well-written explanation of the DNA molecule as well as a discussion on ways to improve the genes. *Older.*

Steen, David. Aerobic fun for kids. Fitzhenry & Whiteside, 1982. 128 pp. $7.95 paper [0-88902-581-9].

Aerobic exercises for children to do individually, in pairs, or in groups, with an emphasis on individual achievement rather than competition. Illustrated with explanatory photographs or diagrams. *Middle, older.*

Suzuki, David. David Suzuki talks about AIDS. Stoddart, 1987. 96 pp. $4.95 paper [0-7736-7153-6].

This excellent introduction to the AIDS virus will answer questions that young adults might have on the topic. *Older, young adult.*

Suzuki, David and **Hehner, Barbara.** Looking at senses. Ill. by Peter Grau. Stoddart, 1986. 96 pp. $8.95 paper [0-7737-5078-9].

Clearly-presented experiments and intriguing facts invite readers to explore the senses. *Younger, middle.*

Wright, R.H. A Nose is for smelling. Ill. by Barbara Hodgson. Douglas & McIntyre, 1983. 75 pp. $7.95 paper [0-88894-337-7].

An explanation of the sense of smell and how it works, rather sparsely illustrated. *Middle.*

MATHEMATICS

Black, Gerald J. Thinking metric for Canadians. Ill. by Robert Brown. Doubleday, 1975. 93 pp. $1.95 paper. No ISBN.

Advanced guide to the history of the metric system, its various components, and their uses. *All ages.*

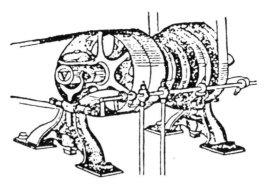

APPLIED SCIENCE

TECHNOLOGY

Girard, Suzanne and **Willing, Kathlene R.** The Primary computer dictionary. Ill. by Melanie Hayes. Highway Book Shop, 1983. 55 pp. $6.95 paper [0-88954-293-7].
Fifty computer-related terms accompanied by simple definitions and descriptive line drawings introduce young children to computers. *Middle.*

Willing, Kathlene R. and **Girard, Suzanne.** The Junior computer dictionary. Ill. by Melanie Hayes. Highway Book Shop, 1984. 68 pp. $8.95 paper [0-88954-302-X].
One hundred and one computer-related words are accompanied by simple definitions and descriptive line drawings. *Older.*

FOOD AND COOKERY

Bourgeois, Paulette. The Amazing apple book. Ill. by Linda Hendry. Kids Can, 1987. 63 pp. $8.95 paper [0-921103-42-5].
History, folklore, and facts about apples are presented in a lively, readable format. Directions for apple crafts and snacks are also included. *Middle.*

Clubb, Angela. Fun in the kitchen. Ill. by Paddy Benham. Irwin, 1984. 135 pp. $12.95 paper [0-7725-1508-5].
Recipes for snacks, sweets, and treats for adults and children to make together. Extensive holiday suggestions. *Adult.*

Daniels, Betty Ternier. The Prairie kid's cook book. Handprinted and ill. by Wanda Hanley. Prairitopian Enterprises, 1983. 96 pp. $6.00 paper [0-9691259-1-7].
A handprinted cookbook of nutritious recipes all of whose ingredients can be grown in the Prairie Provinces. *Middle, older.*

Ferrier, Shannon. Kids in the kitchen. Ill. by Hans Zander. Lorimer 1978. 32 pp. $12.95 hardcover [0-88862-225-2]; $6.95 spiral bound [0-88862-230-9].
An introduction to cooking with natural foods and the metric system for both boys and girls. Amusing line drawings illustrate the instructions. *Middle, older.*

Ferrier, Shannon and **Shuttleworth, Tamara.** The Kids' bakebook. Ill. by Hans Zander. Lorimer, 1984. 78 pp. $13.00 hardcover [0-88862-761-0]; $7.95 spiral bound [0-88862-760-2].
An introduction to baking cookies, cakes, muffins, biscuits, quick breads, and yeast breads. Metric and imperial measurements. Level of difficulty indicated for each recipe. *Middle, older.*

Ferrier, Shannon and **Shuttleworth, Tamara.** The KidsFood cookbook. Ill. by Sheila Shapira. Lorimer, 1982. 64 pp. $13.95 hardcover [0-88862-596-0]; $7.95 spiral bound [0-88862-595-2].
Metric recipes for favourite 'first foods.' Recipes are labelled easy, medium, hard, and adult supervision. *Middle, older.*

Ferrier, Shannon and **Shuttleworth, Tamara.** More kids in the kitchen: metric munchies for junior cooks. Ill. by Sheila Shapira. Lorimer, 1980. 64 pp. $13.00 hardcover [0-88862-386-0]; $7.95 spiral bound [0-88862-385-2].
Easy-to-follow recipes with suggestions for planning a well-balanced meal. Level of difficulty indicated. *Middle, older.*

Fine, Diane and **Teale, Ria.** The Cookie bookie. Ill. by Diane Fine. NC Press, 1983. 120 pp. $9.95 paper [0-919601-96-0].

Over forty recipes for cookies made from tasty, wholesome ingredients. Simple, point-form instructions. *Older*.

Foodworks: an Ontario Science Centre book. Ill. by Linda Hendry. Kids Can, 1986. 93 pp. $19.95 hardcover [0-919964-90-7]; $9.95 paper [0-919964-91-5].

Fascinating facts about food with projects, experiments, and some puzzles that have surprising answers. *Middle, older*.

Franklyn, Mary Eliza. Pepper makes me sneeze. Petheric, 1978. 120 pp. $4.95 paper [0-919380-25-5].

Indigo Proboscis gives helpful hints, reminders, bits of local history, and food notes in this cookbook featuring Nova Scotia recipes easy for young people to cook. *Older*.

Linton, Marilyn. Just desserts and other treats for kids to make. Ill. by Barbara Reid. Kids Can, 1986. 64 pp. $7.95 spiral bound [0-921103-02-6].

Ingredients, utensils, and directions are clearly presented. Interesting facts and clever line drawings are included. *Middle, older*.

Linton, Marilyn. The Maple syrup book. Ill. by Lesley Fairfield. Kids Can, 1983. 48 pp. $8.95 paper [0-919964-52-4].

History, legends, recipes, facts, and activities explore the wonders of maple trees, sap, and syrup. *Middle*.

Macdonald, Kate. The Anne of Green Gables cookbook. Ill. by Barbara Di Lella. Oxford, 1985. 48 pp. $9.95 hardcover [0-19-540496-3].

An assortment of recipes inspired by L.M. Montgomery's Anne series. Cooking tips and thoughtfully-presented directions make this an accessible 'how-to-do-it' title. *Middle*.

Mendelson, Susan. Let me in the kitchen!: a cookbook for kids & other first-timers. Ill. by Carol Sedgewick. Douglas & McIntyre, 1982. 96 pp. $9.95 spiral bound [0-88894-345-8].

Appealing and practical recipes for breakfasts, lunches, salads, and desserts, with a special section for holiday treats. Amusing illustrations and some explanatory drawings. Metric and imperial measurements. *Middle, older*.

THE ARTS

ART

see also
PUBLISHERS' SERIES
Canadian Artists Series

Boulton, Roger. Canada coast to coast. Oxford, 1982. 198 pp. $24.95 hardcover [0-19-540388-6].

Descriptive colour photographs of Canada by celebrated photographers arranged in a geographical sequence from east to west coasts. *All ages*.

Fulford, Robert. An Introduction to the arts in Canada. Copp, 1977. 135 pp. $5.95 hardcover [0-7730-4029-3]; $4.95 paper [0-7730-4028-5].

Brief survey of music, theatre, painting and sculpture, dance, film, architecture, broadcasting, native art, and literature in Canada. *Older*.

Kurelek, William and Murray, Joan. Kurelek's vision of Canada. Ill. by William Kurelek. Hurtig, 1983. 80 pp. $19.95 hardcover [0-88830-254-1].

A selection of paintings from the works of William Kurelek, depicting the artist's view of Canadians in a variety of landscapes. *Older*.

Morrison, A.L. My Island pictures: the story of Prince Edward Island. Ill. by A.L. Morrison. Ragweed, 1980. 78 pp. $19.95 hardcover [0-920304-05-2]; $9.95 paper [0-920304-06-0].

A self-described folk artist, the author-illustrator has painted scenes from Prince Edward Island's history and countryside. *Middle.*

Murray, Joan and **Harris, Lawren.** The Best of the Group of Seven. Hurtig, 1984. 95 pp. $19.95 hardcover [0-88830-265-7].

A selection of outstanding works by members of the Group of Seven: F.H. Carmichael, A.J. Casson, L.L. FitzGerald, L. Harris, E. Holgate, A.Y. Jackson, F.H. Johnston, A. Lismer, J.E.H. MacDonald, T. Thomson, F.H. Varley. *Young adult.*

Murray, Joan. The Best of Tom Thomson. Ill. by Tom Thomson. Hurtig, 1986. 90 pp. $22.95 hardcover [0-88830-299-1].

A chronological collection of paintings by Tom Thomson, with commentary and a biographical essay. *Young adult.*

Steltzer, Ulli. Indian artists at work. Douglas & McIntyre, 1976. 163 pp. $13.95 hardcover [0-88894-116-1].

Dedicated West Coast native artists pictured at work on the knitting, weaving, and carving that distinguish their creative bent. *Older.*

MUSIC

Barber, Lois. Twelve days of Christmas north. Ill. by Carl Chaplin. Northern Times, 1984. 28 pp. $5.95 paper [0-920390-04-8].

In this northern version of a favourite Christmas song 'three bull moose, six beavers swimming and a blue grouse in a spruce tree' among other forest denizens capture an authentic Canadian feeling. Green monochromes and clever design add to this ingenious rendition. *Younger.*

Cass-Beggs, Barbara. Canadian folk songs for the very young. Douglas & McIntyre, 1975. 48 pp. $6.95 paper [0-88894-266-4].

Humorous drawings, simple musical notation, and pertinent comments embellish thirty-two Canadian folk songs. *Younger, middle.*

Cass-Beggs, Barbara. Your baby needs music. Douglas & McIntyre, 1978. 144 pp. $9.95 hardcover [0-88894-213-3]; $6.95 paper [0-88894-278-8].

Using music with children from birth to two years; why, how, and a selection of songs, fingerplays, and singing games to choose from. *Younger, middle.*

Creighton, Helen. Songs and ballads from Nova Scotia. General, 1966. 333 pp. $7.50 paper [0-7736-1017-0].

One hundred and fifty folk songs from eastern Canada. *All ages.*

Fowke, Edith. The Penguin book of Canadian folk songs. Penguin, 1973. 224 pp. $6.95 paper [0-14-070842-1].

Songs that evoke the history, the land, and the people of Canada. Guitar chords. *All ages.*

Fowke, Edith. Sally go round the sun. Ill. by Carlos Marchiori. McClelland & Stewart, 1969. 160 pp. $19.95 hardcover [0-7710-3165-3].

Sandlot, street-corner, and playroom poetry that Canadian children chant as they play. *Younger, middle.*

Fowke, Edith (literary ed.) and **Johnston, Richard** (music ed.). Folk songs of Canada. Ill. by Elizabeth Wilkes Hoey. Waterloo Music, 1978. 198 pp. Vol. I $12.95 hardcover [0-88909-006-8]; choral ed. $6.95 paper [0-88909-004-1]. Vol. II $12.95 hardcover [0-88909-010-6]; choral ed. $6.95 paper [0-88909-008-4].

Songs of French and English Canada: variants of traditional folksongs and popular songs. *All ages.*

Fowke, Edith and **Mills, Alan.** Singing our history. Doubleday, 1984 (rev.ed.). 249 pp. $15.95 paper [0-385-19499-4].

A revised and expanded edition of *Canada's story in song. All ages.*

Fowke, Edith (trans.) and **Johnston, Richard** (arr.). Folk songs of Quebec (Chansons de Québec). Ill. by Elizabeth Wilkes Hoey. Waterloo Music, 1957. 207 pp. $6.95 Library edition [0-88909-011-4].

Familiar French-Canadian folk songs, in French and English, collected by Canada's foremost authority in the field. *All ages.*

Glatt, Louise. What to do until the music teacher comes. Ill. by Kitty Cockburn. Berandol Music, 1978. 94 pp. $7.95 paper. No ISBN.

A sensitive introduction to using music as an integral part of a young child's life. There are chapters on listening, games, instruments, songs, and recommended books and records. *Middle to young adult.*

Magadini, Peter. Music we can see and hear. Ill. by Carole Precious. Frederick Harris, 1982. 69 pp. $9.95 paper [0-88797-162-8].

The author provides a complete music programme consisting of a series of musical concepts and activities that have proven to be successful with children. *All ages.*

Manny, Louise, ed. Songs of Miramichi. Brunswick, 1968. 330 pp. $12.50 hardcover [0-88790-02204].

Over one hundred songs handed down by the early European settlers in the 'land of the Micmacs,' New Brunswick's Miramichi river country. *Older, young adult.*

Raffi. Baby Beluga book. Ill. by Jane Fernandes, Franklin Hammond, Vladyana Krykarka, Maryann Kovalski, Barbara Reid, and James Tughan. McClelland & Stewart, 1983. 48 pp. $15.95 hardcover [0-7710-77261-9]; $9.95 paper [0-7710-7260-0].

Songs, games, stories, and activities based on Raffi's recording *Baby Beluga*. Musical notation and chords accompany most of the selections. *Younger, middle.*

Raffi. The Raffi singable songbook. Ill. by Joyce Yamamoto. Chappell Music, 1981. 106 pp. $12.95 spiral bound. No ISBN.

Words and music for many of the songs found on three Raffi albums: *Singable songs for the very young, More singable songs,* and *The Corner grocery store.* Guitar and ukelele chords provided. *Younger, middle.*

Rubin, Mark. The Orchestra. Ill. by Alan Daniel. Groundwood, 1984. 48 pp. $7.95 paper [0-88899-067-7].

An inviting picture book that provides music appreciation and an introduction to musical instruments. *Younger, middle.*

Sharon, Lois & Bram. Elephant jam. Piano arrangements by Frank Metis. McGraw, 1980. 128 pp. $13.95 paper [0-07-092398-1].

A collection of songs, games, rhymes, fingerplays, and suggestions for working with children from a talented musical trio. *All ages.*

Sharon, Lois & Bram. Sharon, Lois & Bram's Mother Goose. Ill. by Maryann Kovalski. Douglas & McIntyre, 1985. 95 pp. $12.95 paper [0-88894-487-X].

A collection of traditional nursery rhymes and songs accompanied by musical notation and fingerplays. Evocative, softly-toned illustrations detail the nonsense of the rhymes. *Younger.*

DANCE

Hoffman, E.T.A. The Nutcracker. Retold by Veronica Tennant. Ill. by Toller Cranston. McClelland & Stewart, 1985. 49 pp. $19.95 hardcover [0-7710-2316-2].

Both the lively text and the dramatic illustrations in this retelling of a Christmas tradition stimulate the eye, ear, and imagination. *Middle.*

Pecknold, Adrian. Mime: the step beyond words. NC Press, 1982. 144 pp. $12.95 paper [0-920053-46-7].

Step-by-step instructions and photographs explain the basic techniques of mime. *Young adult.*

Ptak, Andrew. The Ballet book: a young dancer's guide. Key Porter, 1984. 128 pp. $19.95 hardcover [0-919493-45-9].

An introduction to the study of ballet, including biographical notes on some famous dancers and synopses of famous ballets. *Older.*

Stravinsky, Igor; Benois, Alexandre; and **Cleaver, Elizabeth** (adapter). Petrouchka. Ill. by Elizabeth Cleaver. Macmillan, 1980. 30 pp. $12.95 hardcover [0-7705-1877-X].

Vibrant collage art and a simple text suited to young children are combined to retell the haunting story of Petrouchka, a puppet with a soul who falls in love with a ballerina. Based on the ballet. *Younger, middle.*

SPORTS AND RECREATION

GAMES

Anderson, Valerie and **Bereiter, Carl.** Thinking games. Ill. by Rod Della-Vedova. O.I.S.E., 1975. Vol. 1 80 pp. $7.75 paper [0-7744-0118-4]; Vol. 2 79 pp. $7.75 paper [0-7744-0119-2].
Children are involved in thinking, problem solving, and group participation while they enjoy playing games of varying difficulty. Vol.1 is for ages five to nine; vol.2 is for ages nine and older. *Middle, older.*

Gryski, Camilla. Cat's cradle, owl's eyes: a book of string games. Ill. by Tom Sankey. Kids Can, 1983. 80 pp. $9.95 paper [0-919964-49-4].
The simple 'Cup and Saucer' to the more complex 'Apache Door' will keep the reader's interest and enthusiasm. *Middle.*

Gryski, Camilla. Many stars and more string games. Ill. by Tom Sankey. Kids Can, 1985. 80 pp. $9.95 paper [0-919964-66-4].
More challenges and fun with string games, including 'The Ghost Dance' and a solo 'Cat's Cradle', are explained with easy-to-follow diagrams. *Middle.*

Gryski, Camilla. Super string games. Ill. by Tom Sankey. Kids Can, 1987. 80 pp. $19.95 hardcover [0-921103-44-1]; $9.95 paper [0-921103-01-8].
Twenty-six traditional string games are presented to challenge readers who enjoyed the earlier, and easier, *Cat's cradle* and *Many stars*. *Middle, older.*

Kalbfleisch, Susan. Skip to it! the new skipping book. Ill. by Laurie McGugan. Kids Can, 1985. 128 pp. $9.95 paper [0-919964-65-6].
The author describes how to warm up before exercising, how to skip, and how to perform easy and advanced tricks. Clear black and white drawings of skipping figures support the instructions. *Middle.*

Pearse, Jack. Campfire programs. Camp Tawingo Publications, 1986. 203 pp. $8.75 paper [0-921155-01-8].
Songs, games, skits, and storytelling suggestions to enhance a campfire program. *Older, young adult.*

Pearse, Jack; McCutcheon, Jane; and **Laughton, Barrie.** Clouds on the clothesline & 200 other great games. Camp Tawingo Publications, 1986. 225 pp. $9.75 paper No ISBN.
Nature, campcraft, water, evening, indoor, outdoor, and activity games intended for use by youth groups and campers. *Middle to young adult.*

Weber, Ken. Mental gymnastics for trivia freaks and puzzle nuts. Methuen, 1984. 151 pp. $9.95 paper [0-458-97950-3].
A variety of visual, verbal, and numerical games test the reader's skill and memory. Answers provided. *Older.*

HOBBIES AND CRAFTS

Coombs, Ernie and **Tanaka, Shelley.** 50 more things to make and do: year-round activities from Mr. Dressup. CBC, 1984. 62 pp. $6.95 paper [0-88794-131-1].
A sequel to *Mr. Dressup's book of things to make and do* that will provide seasonal activities for children. *Younger, middle.*

Coombs, Ernie and **Tanaka, Shelley.** Mr. Dressup's book of things to make and do. CBC, 1982. 64 pp. $6.95 paper [0-88794-106-0].
A fun-filled book for parents and teachers to share with children. *Younger.*

Downie, Mary Alice and **Gilliland, Jillian Hulme**. Seeds and weeds: a book of country crafts. Scholastic-TAB, 1981. 112 pp. $8.95 paper [0-590-71054-0].
Plants, flowers, and other natural materials are used to make a variety of crafts, gifts, and decorations. Instructions are also given for drying, pressing, and preserving flowers. *Middle, older.*

Fales, Douglas. A Kite on the wind. Borealis, 1973. 16 pp. $4.95 paper [0-919594-11-5].
Introduction to different kinds of kites and directions for the construction of one simple kite. *Older.*

Fitzharris, Tim. The Adventure of nature photography. Hurtig, 1983. 216 pp. $27.95 hardcover [0-88830-250-9]; $19.95 paper [0-88830-237-1].
A detailed guide to equipment, background, and subjects of still and live nature photography. *Older, young adult.*

Franklyn, Mary Eliza. Costume guide and suggestions, 1848-1868. Petheric, 1978. 24 pp. $1.25 paper [0-919380-26-3].
Prepared for the Joseph Howe Festival in Halifax this short guide gives enough information to create a costume. *Middle.*

Gilliland, Jillian Hulme and **Downie, Mary Alice**. Stones and cones. Scholastic-TAB, 1984. 65 pp. $2.95 paper [0-590-712217-7].
Simple directions and drawings explain how to make animals, holiday decorations, and toys from plants, seeds, stones, and other natural materials. *Middle.*

Haas, Rudi and **Blohm, Hans**. Egg-carton zoo. Oxford, 1986. 64 pp. $9.95 paper [0-19-540513-7].
Children and adults alike will enjoy making animals by following the clear directions contained in this appealing craft book. *Middle, older.*

Hearn, John. The Young collector. Ill. by Ian Leventhal. Groundwood, 1983. 124 pp. $9.95 paper [0-88899-026-X].
Hearn's suggestions for collections range from the more common comics, rocks, hockey cards, and model trains to the more unusual buttons, fishing lures, and cacti. Each chapter offers advice on where to find various treasures and how to house them. *Middle, older.*

Hehner, Barbara, ed. Free stuff for kids. 5th ed. Stoddart, 1987. 112 pp. $5.95 paper [0-7737-5115-7].
Mailing instructions and addresses for ordering interesting and informative items, some with fees of no more than $1.50. *Middle.*

Irvine, Joan. How to make pop-ups. Ill. by Barbara Reid. Kids Can, 1987. 93 pp. $9.95 paper [0-921103-36-0].
Instructions for making intriguing and imaginative pop-up cards, games, and decorations. *Middle, older.*

Rousseau-Darnell, L. Darnell stamps of Canada catalogue. Darnell, 1986. 216 pp. $7.95 paper [0-2-920734-01-6].
An illustrated reference work on Canadian stamps, with information for collectors. *Older.*

SPORTS

Cutler, Michael. Great hockey masks/Grands masques de hockey. Tundra, 1983. 32 pp. $7.95 paper [0-88776-152-6].
Painted masks have become a distinctive and very individual part of a goalie's equipment. *All ages.*

McFarlane, Brian. Brian McFarlane's NHL hockey. McClelland & Stewart, 1983. 128 pp. $12.95 paper [0-7710-5430-0].
Questions and answers about Canadian hockey and its heroes, as well as information about other NHL greats. *Older.*

Petrie, Francis J. Roll out the barrel: the story of Niagara's daredevils. Boston Mills, 1985. 62 pp. $4.95 paper [0-919783-38-4].
An account, based on newspaper articles written for the Niagara Falls *Evening Review,* of the men and women who have gone over the Niagara Falls. *Older.*

Watt, Tom. How to play hockey. Ill. by Bob Berger. Doubleday, 1974. 176 pp. $3.95 paper. No ISBN.
A well-illustrated, comprehensive guide for young players and their coaches. *Middle, older.*

Wilkins, Charles. Hockey: the illustrated history. Ed. by Dan Diamond. Doubleday, 1985. 192 pp. $24.95 hardcover [0-385-23329-9].
Captioned photographs, quotations, and some commentary comprise this record of hockey in Canada from the early 1900s to the present day. *Middle to young adult.*

OUTDOOR LIFE

Canada. Dept. of Indian Affairs and Northern Development. Northern survival. Fitzhenry & Whiteside, 1979 (rev.ed.). 93 pp. $6.95 paper [0-88902-555-X].
Survival techniques in the wildernesss include providing heat, shelter, food, first aid. Emphasizes Arctic conditions. *Older, young adult.*

Leaden, Bruce W. Bicycle camping in Canada. Queenston, 1984. 170 pp. $12.95 paper [0-919866-95-6].

Tips on bicycle maintenance, personal kit and packing, and itinerary for touring in Canada. *Older, young adult.*

Knap, Jerome. The Complete outdoorsman's handbook: a guide to outdoor living and wilderness survival. Pagurian, 1974. 192 pp. $8.95 hardcover [0-88932-041-1]; $4.95 paper [0-919362-62-4].

Basic skills for outdoor survival include axemanship, cooking, skiing, first aid, and foraging. This book encourages an outdoor ethic that ensures man's harmony with nature. *Young adult.*

Morrow, Patrick. Beyond Everest: quest for the seven summits. Camden, 1986. 176 pp. $19.95 paper [0-920656-46-3].

Candid narration and clear colour photographs describe the exhilarating climbs of the world's magnificent mountain peaks. *Young adult.*

YOUTH ORGANIZATIONS

Boy Scouts of Canada. National Council. Fieldbook for Canadian Scouting. Boy Scouts of Canada, 1986. 432 pp. $9.95 paper [0-919062-54-7].

Valuable information about campcraft, water activities, conservation, personal fitness, and many other aspects of outdoor life. *Middle, older.*

McCarrick, Ismay. Brownies around the world, Book 1. Ill. by Eric Ford and Frances Shadbolt. Girl Guides of Canada, 1982 (rev.ed.). 55 pp. $3.75 paper [0-919220-02-9].

McCarrick, Ismay. Brownies around the world, Book 2. Ill. by Frances Shadbolt. Girl Guides of Canada, 1979 (rev.ed.). 63 pp. $3.75 paper [0-919220-03-7].

McCarrick, Ismay. Brownies around the world, Book 3. Ill. by Frances Shadbolt. Girl Guides of Canada, 1981. 61 pp. $3.75 paper [0-919220-14-2].

McCarrick, Ismay. Brownies around the world, Book 4. Ill. by Frances Shadbolt. Girl Guides of Canada, 1981. 63 pp. $3.75 paper [0-919220-15-0].

A continuing series about Brownies in forty-nine countries throughout the world. *Middle.*

Milks, Robert E. 75 years of Scouting in Canada. Boy Scouts of Canada, 1981. 102 pp. $10.00 hardcover. No ISBN.

An informal history of Scouting in Canada, with personal reminiscences. *Young adult.*

Robinson, Marita. Celebration: 75 years of challenge and change. Grosvenor, 1984. 115 pp. $19.95 hardcover [0-919959-05-9].

In recognition of the seventy-fifth anniversary of the Girl Guides of Canada, this book records the history and development of the organization from 1908 to the present day. Illustrated with photographs. *Older, young adult.*

LANGUAGE AND LITERATURE

LANGUAGE

Colter, Rob. Grammar to go. Anansi, 1981 (rev.ed.). 176 pp. $4.95 paper [0-88784-077-9].
'An informal guide to correct usage' lists common errors and confusions and sets the reader straight about such challenges as when to use accept/except, obtuse/abstruse, loath/loathe. *Older, young adult.*

O'Byrne, Lorainne. What is it?: a gallery of historic phrases. Boston Mills, 1977. 48 pp. $3.00 paper [0-919822-19-3].
Delightful introduction to the craft origins of common sayings, like: strike while the iron is hot, from the smithy. *Middle, older.*

ANTHOLOGIES

see also
PUBLISHERS' SERIES
Zap Series

Achimoona. Introduced by Maria Campbell. Illustrated. Fifth, 1985. 98 pp. $19.95 hardcover [0-920079-18-0]; $9.95 paper [0-920079-16-4].
A collection of eleven stories by native authors is enhanced by full-colour paintings done by native artists. *Older.*

Downie, Mary Alice; Greene, Elizabeth; and Thompson, M.A., eds. The Window of dreams: new Canadian writing for children. Methuen, 1986. 256 pp. $19.95 hardcover [0-458-80390-1].
An anthology of thirty stories and poems by some well-known authors and some new authors whose work is introduced in this collection. *Middle, older.*

McArthur, Wenda and **Ursell, Geoffrey,** eds. Prairie jungle: songs, poems and stories for children. Ill. by Denis Nokony. Coteau, 1985. 105 pp. $7.95 paper [0-919926-45-2].

Represented among this selection of poetry, songs, and stories are such Western Canadians as Lois Simmie, Connie Kaldor, and Diana J. Wieler. A contemporary collection. *Middle, older.*

POETRY

Colombo, John Robert, ed. Poems of the Inuit. Oberon, 1981. 117 pp. $23.95 hardcover [0-88750-403-5].
Eighty poems originally transcribed and translated by cultural anthropologists are arranged in nine sections which correspond to a day in the life of the traditional Inuit: The World, Human Nature, Making Songs, Day and Night, Incantations, Wild Things, The Hunt, Life and Death. Notes and bibliography included. *Young adult.*

Dawe, Tom. Landwash days: Newfoundland folklore, sketches and verse for youngsters. Ill. by Tom Dawe. Newfoundland Book, 1980. 56 pp. $4.95 paper [0-920508-15-4].
For each of the fish, birds, and fishing phenomena included in this collection, the author provides an explanation of traditions plus an original poem. *Middle, older.*

Dear mom, dear dad: poems for everyone. Ill. by Valerie Sinclair. Annick, 1982. 48 pp. $4.95 paper [0-919984-14-2].
Poems written by young Canadians across the country that reflect their need for love, freedom, independence, understanding, and acceptance. *Older, young adult.*

Desbarats, Peter. The Night the city sang. Ill. by Frank Newfeld. McClelland & Stewart, 1977. 24 pp. $16.95 hardcover [0-7710-2685-4].
Three rollicking poems that evoke the spirit of Christmas with unsentimental delight. *Middle, older.*

Downie, Mary Alice and **Robertson, Barbara**, comps. The New wind has wings. Ill. by Elizabeth Cleaver. Oxford, 1984. 112 pp. $15.95 hardcover [0-19-540431-9]; $9.95 paper [0-19-540432-7].

A new edition of Canadian poetry with new collage illustrations. *Middle, older.*

Dunn, Sonja and **Pamenter, Lou.** Butterscotch dreams: chants for fun and learning. Pembroke, 1987. 111 pp. $9.95 paper [0-921217-07-2].

Original chants – 'sound poems with many rhythmical possibilities' – are arranged in themes with suggestions for expression and use. *All ages.*

Field, Eugene. Wynken, Blynken and Nod. Ill. by Ron Berg. North Winds, 1985. 22 pp. $21.95 Big Book [0-590-71588-7]; $15.95 hardcover [0-590-71597-6]; $3.95 paper [0-590-71589-5].

A favourite bedtime poem has been beautifully illustrated with full-colour drawings. *Younger.*

Fitch, Sheree. Toes in my nose. Ill. by Molly Lamb Bobak. Doubleday, 1987. 47 pp. $12.95 hardcover [0-385-25106-8].

A collection of thirty-six poems about childlike favourites such as the *Watermelon Man, William Worm*, and many others. *Younger, middle.*

Fleischman, Paul. I am Phoenix: poems for two voices. Ill. by Ken Nutt. Harper, 1985. Available from Fitzhenry & Whiteside. 51 pp. $16.95 hardcover [0-06-012881-9].

These fifteen poems about birds are intended to be read aloud by two voices, each taking one of two parts. Each poem is enhanced with exquisite pencil drawings by an award-winning Canadian illustrator. *Middle to young adult.*

Hahn, Sylvia. Shadow cat. Ill. by Sylvia Hahn. Penumbra, 1983. 16 pp. $4.95 paper [0-920806-49-X].

This slim volume of six poems about cats is strikingly illustrated with wood engravings. *Middle, older.*

Heidbreder, Robert. Don't eat spiders. Ill. by Karen Patkau. Oxford, 1985. 48 pp. $9.95 hardcover [0-19-540497-1].

Effective collage illustrations add colour and interest to this collection of poems that focus on topics familiar to children and places found in Canada. *Middle.*

Hogan, Homer, ed. Listen! Songs and poems of Canada. Methuen, 1972. 166 pp. $6.95 paper [0-458-90900-9].

Modern Canadian songs and poems that speak to young people. *Older, young adult.*

Kouhi, Elizabeth. North country spring: a book of verse for children. Ill. by Robert Rickels. Penumbra, 1980. 52 pp. $6.95 paper [0-920806-10-4].

The poet evokes peaceful and exhilarating images of nature in Canada's north country not only in spring but throughout the year. *Middle.*

Lane, John. What are uncles for? Ill. by Silas White and Jeremy Twigg. Harbour, 1984. 45 pp. $5.95 paper [0-920080-76-6].

Conversations between four-year-old Michael and Uncle Johnny are captured in this collection of poems. Illustrated with children's drawings. *Younger, middle.*

Layton, Irving. A Spider danced a cosy jig. Ed. by Elspeth Cameron. Ill. by Miro Malish. Stoddart, 1984. 30 pp. $9.95 hardcover [0-7737-0079-X].

Layton takes a humorous look at the animal kingdom through his collection of adult-oriented poems. *Older, young adult.*

Lear, Edward. The Owl and the pussycat. Ill. by Ron Berg. North Winds, 1984. 24 pp. $21.95 Big Book [0-590-71406-6]; $14.95 hardcover [0-590-71457-0]; $3.95 paper [0-590-71407-4].

Rich and vibrant illustrations by Berg suggest new dimensions for this well-loved poem. *Younger, middle.*

Lear, Edward. The Owl and the pussycat. Ill. by Erica Rutherford. Tundra, 1986. 24 pp. $12.95 hardcover [0-88776-181-X].

Vibrant tones and simple lines set an intriguing new flavour and mood for Lear's nonsense verse. *Younger.*

Lee, Dennis. Alligator pie. Ill. by Frank Newfeld. Macmillan, 1974. 64 pp. $10.95 hardcover [0-7715-9591-3]; $6.95 paper [0-7715-9566-2].

Silly, funny, surprising poems that grew from a poet's search for a Canadian *Mother Goose*. Marvellous interpretive illustrations. *Younger, middle.*

Lee, Dennis. Garbage delight. Ill. by Frank Newfeld. Macmillan, 1977. 64 pp. $10.95 hardcover [0-7715-9592-1].

Poet and artist, prize winners both, treat young readers to new amusements. *Middle.*

Lee, Dennis. Jelly Belly. Ill. by Juan Wijngaard. Macmillan, 1983. 64 pp. $9.95 hardcover [0-7715-9776-2].

A collection of poems at once nonsensical, thoughtful, and rollicking. Colourful realistic illustrations capture the magic and the gentle satire of this modern Mother Goose. *Younger, middle.*

Lee, Dennis. Lizzy's lion. Ill. by Marie-Louise Gay. Stoddart, 1984. 24 pp. $8.95 hardcover [0-7737-0078-1].
This rollicking story-poem about a little girl and her pet lion is enhanced by the saucy, coloured illustrations. *Younger.*

Little, Jean. Hey world, here I am! Ill. by Barbara Di Lella. Kids Can, 1986. 84 pp. $12.95 hardcover [0-921103-14-X]; $6.95 paper [0-919964-71-0].
Kate, the feisty character from *Look Through my Window*, offers a selection of her prose and verse poems about incidents in her life. *Middle, older.*

Molnar, Gwen. I said to Sam. Ill. by Carlos Freire. Scholastic-TAB, 1987. 46 pp. $4.95 paper [0-590-71367-1].
A read-aloud collection of nineteen verses about the adventures of the narrator, Sam, and their friends. *Middle.*

Musgrave, Susan. Gullband. Ill. by Rikki. Douglas & McIntyre, 1974. 50 pp. $4.95 paper [0-88894-162-5].
A poet stretches children's fantasy-quotient and delights them all the way. *Middle, older.*

Newman, Fran, ed. Round slice of moon and other poems for Canadian kids. Scholastic-TAB, 1980. 163 pp. $3.95 paper [0-590-71029-X].
A varied anthology of works by poets, 'famous, unknown, old, and young.' *Middle, older.*

Newman, Fran. Sunflakes and snowshine. Ill. by Claudette Boulanger. Scholastic-TAB, 1979. 47 pp. $3.50 paper [0-590-07622-1].
Starting with September two cunning poems and two coloured paintings capture children's activities for each month of the school year. *Middle.*

o huigin, sean. Blink: a strange book for children. Ill. by Barbara Di Lella. Black Moss, 1984. 24 pp. $5.95 paper [0-88753-118-0].
A free verse, illustrated poem that is intended to show what the world looks like through different eyes. *Middle, older.*

o huigin, sean. The Dinner party. Ill. by Maureen Paxton. Black Moss, 1984. 24 pp. $4.95 paper [0-88753-117-2].
Ghoulish illustrations and ghastly verbal images provide an appetizing menu for sturdy young stomachs. *Younger, middle.*

o huigin, sean. The Ghost horse of the Mounties. Ill. by Phil McLeod. Black Moss, 1983. 71 pp. $6.95 paper [0-88753-100-8].
An epic poem about a horse and its rider in the early days of the Northwest Mounted Police. *Older.*

o huigin, sean. Scary poems for rotten kids. Ill. by Anthony Le Baron. Black Moss, 1982. 38 pp. $4.95 paper [0-88753-087-7].
The slithery, slimy creatures in these poems will worm their way into the hearts of rotten kids with lively imaginations. *Middle.*

o huigin, sean. The Trouble with stitches. Ill. by Anthony Le Baron. Black Moss, 1981. 63 pp. $5.95 paper [0-88753-078-8].
A series of free form poems about childlike subjects that will appeal to children who like visually-appealing poems. *Middle, older.*

Pittman, Al. Down by Jim Long's stage: rhymes for children and young fish. Ill. by Pam Hall. Breakwater, 1981. 32 pp. $5.95 paper [0-919948-19-7].
A collection of short rhymes featuring the ways and dreams of various sea creatures from the Atlantic coast. *Younger.*

Poe, Edgar Allan. Annabel Lee. Ill. by Gilles Tibo. Tundra, 1987. 24 pp. $19.95 hardcover [0-88776-200-X].
Poe's poem of love between two children is illustrated with beautiful paintings that gently capture joy and sorrow. Also available in translation under the same title. *Younger, middle.*

Service, Robert W. The Collected poems of Robert Service. McGraw, 1971. 275 pp. $17.50 hardcover [0-7700-0041-X].
The spirit of the Canadian North comes alive in these humorous, exuberant, robust poems. *Older, young adult.*

Service, Robert W. The Cremation of Sam McGee. Ill. by Ted Harrison. Intro. by Pierre Burton. Kids Can, 1986. 32 pp. $14.95 hardcover [0-919964-92-3].
Brilliant shades and a simplified landscape add new dimensions to the classic Yukon tale of Sam McGee. *Younger to older.*

Simmie, Lois. An Armadillo is not a pillow. Ill. by Anne Simmie. Western Producer Prairie, 1986. 72 pp. $8.95 paper [0-88833-185-1].
Poems that recount day-to-day occurrences and observations are interspersed among the 'Look' poems, eleven poems about incredible (but real!) monsters. *Younger, middle.*

Simmie, Lois. Auntie's knitting a baby. Ill. by Anne Simmie. Western Producer Prairie, 1984. 70 pp. $14.95 hardcover [0-88833-160-6]; $8.95 paper [0-88833-123-1].
Held together by the narrator's keen observation of people, animals, and events around him, this is a rounded collection of poems representing a variety of moods. Humour, empathy, and wonder abound within the pages. *Younger, middle.*

Sneyd, Lola. The Asphalt octopus: a child's world in poetry. Ill. by Doug Sneyd. Simon & Pierre, 1982. 63 pp. $8.95 paper [0-88924-130-9].
Images of plants, insects, and ideas commonly found in the child's outdoor world are presented in rhyming verse. *Middle.*

Souster, Raymond. Flight of the roller-coaster: poems for younger readers. Selected by Richard Woollatt. Oberon, 1985. 89 pp. $11.95 paper [0-88750-580-5].
This collection of poems shows the poet's awareness of the everyday details of the world of the average Canadian. *Older.*

Stump, Sarain. There is my people sleeping. Gray's, 1974. 2nd ed. 158 pp. $3.95 paper [0-88862-056-3].
Line drawings illustrate poems about the meaning of Indian life. *Older.*

Swede, George. High wire spider. Ill. by VictoR GAD. Three Trees, 1986. 48 pp. $12.95 hardcover [0-88823-112-1]; $5.95 paper [0-88823-111-3].
More entertaining and penetrating poems to give readers something to think about. *Middle.*

Swede, George. Tick bird. Ill. by Katherine Helmer. Three Trees, 1983. 48 pp. $11.95 hardcover [0-88823-069-9]; $4.95 paper [0-88823-064-8].
Perceptive, provocative, and funny poems, including several haiku. *Middle, older.*

Swede, George. Time is flies. Ill. by Darcia Labrosse. Three Trees, 1984. 46 pp. $11.95 hardcover [0-88823-091-5]; $4.95 paper [0-88823-090-7].
Poems to make children think and laugh at the same time. A companion volume to *Tick bird*. *Middle, older.*

Wilson, Keith and Motheral, Elva, eds. The Poets' record: verses on Canadian history. Peguis, 1975. 118 pp. $7.50 hardcover [0-919566-41-3]; $3.25 paper [0-919566-42-1].
An excellent anthology of poems by historical figures like Thomas D'Arcy McGee, about the country's history up to modern times. *Older, young adult.*

Wynne-Jones, Tim. Mischief city. Ill by VictoR GAD. Groundwood, 1986. 36 pp. $12.95 hardcover [0-88899-049-9].
Poems that take place on a stage set speak with humour and truth about the frustrations of children and monsters. *Younger.*

PLAYS

Beissel, Henry. Inook and the sun. Macmillan, 1980. 80 pp. $6.95 paper [0-7715-9979-X].
A play for masks and marionettes re-creates Inuit life and legend. *Older.*

Betts, Jim. The Mystery of the Oak Island treasure. Playwrights, 1985. 105 pp. $5.95 paper [0-88754-420-7].
The tale of the search of Captain Kidd's fabulous treasure is full of excitement and spooky moments. 1983 Chalmers Children's Plays Award. *Middle.*

Bolt, Carol and Peterson, Len. Cyclone Jack, by Carol Bolt; Billy Bishop & the Red Baron, by Len Peterson. Ed. by Rolf Kalman. Simon & Pierre, 1975. 62 pp. $5.95 paper [0-88924-011-6].
Dramas about Tom Longboat, winner of the 1907 Boston Marathon, and Billy Bishop who shot down seventy-two German planes in the First World War. *Older.*

Campbell, John Gounod. Fox of a thousand faces. Playwrights, 1973. 49 pp. $3.50 paper [0-919834-73-6].
Excellent musical fantasy for children may be performed by adults or older children. *Middle, older.*

Campbell, Paddy. Chinook/Too many kings. Playwrights, 1977. 50 pp. $3.50 paper [0-88754-051-1].
Two plays for production 'in-the-round' allow for audience participation. Both are fantasies involving familiar characters. *Older.*

Deverell, Rex. You want me to be grown up, don't I? Playwrights, 1979. 36 pp. $3.50 paper [0-88754-168-2].
Five children discuss and demonstrate the worst thing an adult has done to them – for a real catharsis. *Older.*

Eight plays for young people: prairie performance II. Ed. by Joyce Dolittle. NeWest, 1984. 254 pp. $17.95 hardcover [0-920316-90-5]; $8.95 paper [0-920316-88-3].
Eight plays for young people by Prairie playwrights Jan Truss, W.O. Mitchell, Rex Deverell, and other playwrights. *Older, young adult.*

Foon, Dennis. Heracles. Talonbooks, 1978. 44 pp. $5.95 paper [0-88922-158-8].
A new reworking of an old Greek myth in which Heracles acquits his twelve labours only to sacrifice himself. *Older.*

Foon, Dennis. Raft baby. Talonbooks, 1978. 44 pp. $5.95 paper [0-88922-156-1].
A baby's starving parents set her afloat on a raft in the Peace River and she is saved downstream.

Fuerstenberg, Anna. Blind dates. Playwrights, 1983. 33 pp. $3.50 paper [0-88754-361-8].

Young adults talk about their 'fear of the future' and their day-to-day problems. *Young adult.*

Grieve, Walter. Animal parade: a children's musical. Waterloo Music, 1974. 12 pp. $1.85 paper. No ISBN.

A simple and simply-delightful musical play that children will enjoy as actors and audience. *Middle.*

Guay, Georgette. The Bling said hello/You'll never be the same: two plays for young people. Playwrights, 1979. 49 pp. $3.50 paper [0-88754-133-X].

Two science fiction plays using the same characters who face all-too-human dilemmas. *Older.*

Head, Sandra and **Surette, Roy.** Alice: a wonderland. Playwrights, 1983. 50 pp. $3.50 paper [0-88754-341-3].

Award-winning adaptation of *Alice in Wonderland* and *Through the looking glass*. Excellent dialogue and good pace. *Middle.*

Kalman, Rolf, ed. A Collection of Canadian plays, Volume IV. Simon & Pierre, 1975. 376 pp. $22.95 hardcover [0-88924-013-2].

Ten plays for children to enjoy by Eric Nicol, Carol Bolt, Leonard Peterson, and other Canadian playwrights. *Older.*

The Land called morning: three plays. Fifth, 1986. 112 pp. $14.95 hardcover [0-920079-26-1]; $5.95 paper [0-920079-24-5].

Three significant plays about young native people attacking the problems of growing up in a white society and dealing with their traditional values. *Older, young adult.*

McMaster, Beth. Let's hear it for Christmas/ Naciwonki cap: two children's plays. Ill. by Adriana Todeo. Simon & Pierre, 1986. 76 pp. $6.95 paper [0-88924-174-0].

Two one-act Christmas plays with audience participation. *Let's hear it for Christmas* is about Noise Control Officer Z.B. Snappish who tries to trick Santa Clauss into leaving all the Christmas toys at his house. *The Naciwonki Cap* is about Clarence Clackettt who wants to modernize Christmas. *Younger, middle.*

McMaster, Beth. The Haunted castle/Robena's rose-colored glasses. Ill. by David Sheridan. Simon & Pierre, 1986. 91 pp. $6.95 paper [0-88924-175-9].

Two one-act plays with audience participation. *The Haunted castle* tells of Gus the ghost who haunts the castle of King Krispen. *Robena's rose-colored glasses* is about the villainous Z.B. Quintee who wants to patent Robena's magical rose-colored glasses. *Younger, middle.*

McMaster, Beth. Put on the spot/When everybody cares: two children's plays. Simon & Pierre, 1977. 148 pp. $5.95 paper [0-88924-045-0].

In *Put on the spot* the animals in a zoo fight its closure. *When everybody cares* is about a robot in 1990 who fights prejudice successfully. *Older.*

Nicol, Eric. The Clam made a face: a play for children. Simon & Pierre, 1975. 36 pp. $5.95 paper [0-88770-693-2].

A play for children by a distinguished Canadian humorist. *Older.*

Novelli, Florence. Spindlerion and the princess/ Queen Cat of Furbit: two children's musicals. Music by Bernard A. Aaron. Playwrights, 1984. 76 pp. $4.95 paper [0-88754-351-0].

Two children's musicals about kings, queens, and princesses. In *Spindlerion and the princess*, Spindlerion hopes the princess will marry the robot he constructed. In *Queen Cat of Furbit*, Queen Cat hopes to marry Prince Gregov who is coming for a visit. *Middle.*

Reaney, James. Apple butter. Talonbooks, 1978. 31 pp. $5.95 paper [0-88922-152-9].

Reaney, James. Geography match. Talonbooks, 1978. 59 pp. $6.95 paper [0-88922-153-7].

Reaney, James. Ignoramus. Talonbooks, 1978. 49 pp. $6.95 paper [0-88922-155-3].

Reaney, James. Names and nicknames. Talonbooks, 1978. 37 pp. $5.95 paper [0-88922-154-5].

Four plays with Canadian themes, loosely constructed to allow for improvisation and audience participation. They are 'shamelessly patriotic and should be played recklessly and with all the stops pulled out.' *Older.*

Thomas, Colin. One thousand cranes. Simon & Pierre, 1987. 80 pp. $6.95 paper [0-88924-289-5].

Buddy's desire to join a peace march to promote a nuclear free world is juxtaposed with the deteriorating condition of Sadako, the young Japanese girl who dies of the effects of radioactivity nine years after the bombing of Japan. *Older.*

Truss, Jan. Oomeraghi oh and A Very small rebellion Playwrights, 1978. 45 pp. $3.50 paper [0-88754-06315].

Two plays, the first a fantasy and the second an historical drama of the Riel rebellion, for reading or performing by older children or adults. *Older.*

Watts, Irene N. A Blizzard leaves no footprints and three other participation plays for children. Playwrights, 1978. 39 pp. $3.50 paper [0-88754-096-1].

The four plays involve the audience in the action of dramatized Inuit legends, Japanese stories, and traditional tales, first produced by Edmonton's Citadel on Wheels/Wings Touring Company. *Middle.*

Watts, Irene N. A Chain of words. Talonbooks, 1978. 40 pp. $5.95 paper [0-88922-159-6].
These six short plays are based on familiar Japanese folk tales and borrow Kabuli production methods. *Older.*

FICTION

REALISTIC FICTION

see also
PUBLISHERS' SERIES
Kids Like Us
Series Canada
Series 2000

Alderson, Sue Ann. Comet's tale. Ill. by Georgia Pow Graham. Tree Frog, 1983. 126 pp. $5.95 paper [0-88967-047-1].
A zany family, a difficult aunt, and a growing dog make for a funny family story. *Middle.*

Alderson, Sue Ann. The Not impossible summer. Ill. by Christina Rother. Irwin, 1983. 116 pp. $8.95 paper [0-7720-1332-9].
Jenny spends a summer holiday in British Columbia where she makes friends and begins to understand the uncertainties of being an adolescent. *Older.*

Allen, Robert Thomas. The Violin. Ill. by George Pastic. McGraw, 1977. 79 pp. $10.95 paper [0-07-082620-X].
A quiet celebration of the music and friendship shared by a young boy and an old man. *Older.*

Batten, Jack. Tie-breaker. Irwin, 1984. 184 pp. $8.95 paper [0-7720-1448-5]. Avon, 1985. $3.50 paper [0-380-69881-1].
Responsibility and commitment loom large for sixteen-year-old Brad Fraser as he confronts the pressures of competitive tennis, drug dealing, and family relationships. *Older, young adult.*

Bellingham, Brenda. Two parents too many. Scholastic-TAB, 1985. 107 pp. $2.95 paper [0-590-71516-X].
Katy and Jenny, who already have a mother, a father, and a stepmother, try a variety of tricks to prevent their mother from remarrying. *Middle.*

Bilson, Geoffrey. Hockeybat Harris. Kids Can, 1984. 158 pp. $5.95 paper [0-919964-57-5].
A young English boy is sent off to live with a family in Canada during the bombings of World War II. *Middle.*

Blades, Ann. A Boy of Taché. Ill. by Ann Blades. Tundra, 1984. 23 pp. $11.95 hardcover [0-88776-023-6]; $5.95 paper [0-88776-034-1].
Charlie goes into the British Columbia wilderness with his Indian grandparents and

finds that only his skill can save his grandfather's life. Glowing varicoloured drawings. *Middle.*

Blakeslee, Mary. Edythe with a Y. Scholastic-TAB, 1987. 130 pp. $3.50 paper [0-590-71680-8].

After her new friends scoff at a magician, Edie tells a few white lies rather than admit that her father is one. *Older.*

Blakeslee, Mary. Halfbacks don't wear pearls. Scholastic-TAB, 1986. 140 pp. $3.50 paper [0-590-71682-4].

Jane and her friends set out to prove to their male classmates that there is equality between the sexes. *Older, young adult.*

Bradbury, Raymond. The War at Fort Maggie. Kids Can, 1982. 64 pp. $5.95 paper [0-919964-36-2].

Class 6P goes on a history field trip and students attempt to re-enact the famous siege of 1726 when privateers try to capture the fort from the British garrison; however, the unexpected occurs. *Middle.*

Bradford, Karleen. The Haunting of Cliff House. Scholastic-TAB, 1985. 105 pp. $2.95 paper [0-590-71517-8].

No sooner have Alison and her father arrived at the old house in Wales where they will spend the summer, than Alison begins to hear a voice call her name. *Older.*

Bradford, Karleen. I wish there were unicorns. Ill. by Greg Ruhl. Gage, 1983. 159 pp. $2.95 paper [0-7715-7005-8].

Against the backdrop and trauma of her parents' divorce and the family's move to an isolated farmhome, Rachel gradually – sometimes with anger, sometimes with fear, and finally with love – reaffirms her role and comes to terms with her dreams. *Middle.*

Brochmann, Elizabeth. Nobody asked me. Lorimer, 1984. 182 pp. $12.95 hardcover [0-88862-753-X]; $5.95 paper [0-88862-752-1].

Having led a solitary childhood, Rachel feels at sea when she is sent to live with relatives she barely knows. Developing relationships with her peers as well as with her aunt and uncle is a challenge. A coming-of-age story. *Older, young adult.*

Brochmann, Elizabeth. What's the matter girl? Fitzhenry & Whiteside, 1980. 121 pp. $11.95 hardcover [0-06-020677-2].

When Anna's beloved Uncle Arion returns from the war, his homecoming is not the joyful scene she has anticipated. *Older.*

Brown, Jamie. Superbike! Irwin, 1981. 180 pp. $11.95 hardcover [0-7720-1306-3].

Restoring and racing a Ducati 900 motorcycle helps Neil to rebuild foundering relationships with his step-father, mother, and girlfriend. *Young adult.*

Brown, Susan. Hey, Chicken Man. Scholastic-TAB, 1978. 165 pp. $2.95 paper [0-590-71627-1].

Twelve-year-old Tom overcomes his claustrophobia and saves his friend's life in this rite-of-passage story. Previously published under the title of *The Black tunnel. Middle.*

Burnford, Sheila. Bel Ria. McClelland & Stewart, 1984. 204 pp. $7.95 paper [0-7710-1786-3].

The author of *The Incredible journey* writes about a little circus dog's experiences in England during the Second World War. *Older, young adult.*

Butchart, Jaylene. Journey through a shadow. Seal, 1983. 63 pp. $2.50 paper [0-7704-1825-2].

Jamie, who has lived with his older brother and his brother's wife since the death of their parents in an accident, befriends a stray dog. *Older.*

Callaghan, Morley. Luke Baldwin's vow. Ill. by Michael Poulton. Scholastic-TAB, 1975. $2.95 paper. No ISBN.

Reissue of a famous novelist's story for children about a dog and a boy whose father's death begins a dialectical exploration of the young man's maturing process. *Older.*

Cameron, Silver Donald. The Baitchopper. Ill. by Alan Daniel. Lorimer, 1982. 167 pp. $12.95 hardcover [0-88862-599-5]; $5.95 paper [0-88862-598-7].

Thirteen-year-old Andrew becomes involved in the struggle to form a fisherman's union in Atlantic Canada. *Middle.*

Chetin, Helen. The Lady of the strawberries. Ill. by Anita Kunz. Irwin, 1978. 89 pp. $6.95 hardcover [0-88778-183-7].

Ten-year-old Jessica finds difficulties in accepting her parents' divorce and transfers her affections to 'The Lady of the Strawberries' when her mother leaves the family farm. *Older.*

Clark, Joan. Wild man of the woods. Viking Kestrel, 1985. 171 pp. $14.95 hardcover [0-670-80015-5]; $3.95 paper [0-14-031788-0].

Stephen's holiday in the Rockies becomes a real adventure when he meets a mysterious Indian mask carver and tries on the masks. *Older.*

Collura, Mary-Ellen Lang. Winners. Western Producer Prairie, 1984. 129 pp. $7.95 paper [0-88833-116-9].

When Jordy Threebears leaves his latest foster home to return to live on the reserve with his grandfather, he can no longer avoid issues that threaten him: his own Blackfoot heritage and the death of his mother. *Older, young adult.*

Connor, Ralph (pseud.). Glengarry school days. McClelland & Stewart, 1975. 340 pp. $6.95 paper [0-7710-9218-0].

Rural school days one hundred years ago had a warmth and humour we can still appreciate. *Older.*

Corriveau, Monique. A Perfect day for kites. Tr. by David Homel. Groundwood, 1981. 116 pp. $13.95 hardcover [0-88899-011-1]; $6.95 paper [0-88899-012-X].

A kite helps a young boy come to grips with the death of his mother and face his unhappy father. Translation of *Le garçon au cerf-volant. Older.*

Craig, John. Ain't lookin'. Scholastic-TAB, 1983. 247 pp. $2.95 paper [0-590-71181-4].

In the summer of 1939, white baseball player Joe Giffen wears a disguise of black shoe polish and plays first base with Chappie and His Colored All Stars. Based on true experiences, the story explains how an outstanding ball team survives in the face of prejudice. *Young adult.*

Craig, John. No word for good-bye. Irwin, 1979. 128 pp. $11.95 hardcover [0-88778-196-9].

Two boys, Ojibway and white, spend their fifteenth summer in the discovery of friendship. *Older.*

Craven, Margaret. I heard the owl call my name. Irwin, 1967. 138 pp. Educ.ed. $4.25 paper [0-7720-1321-7].

A dying priest learns to understand the Kwakiutl Indians in his British Columbia parish. *Older.*

Culleton, Beatrice. April Raintree. Pemmican, 1984. 187 pp. $9.95 trade paper [0-91943-03-2]; $4.95 paper [0-91943-32-6].

A powerful story about two Métis sisters who grow up in a harsh world. *Young adult.*

Cumming, Peter. A Horse called Farmer. Ill. by P. John Burden. Ragweed, 1984. 36 pp. $4.95 paper [0-920304-34-6].

After being sold and taken from the island home he loves, Farmer makes a miraculous journey over sandbars and ocean, and returns to his home. Based on an historical event. *Younger.*

Davies, Peter. Fly away Paul. PaperJacks, 1976. 213 pp. $2.75 paper [0-7701-0143-7].

A compelling story about a teenager who lives in a Home after his deserted mother suffers a breakdown. *Older, young adult.*

Doyle, Brian. Angel square. Groundwood, 1984. 128 pp. $6.95 paper [0-88899-034-0].

A personal story about a young boy who is growing up in Lower Town Ottawa just after World War II and realizes the absurdity of racism. *Older.*

Doyle, Brian. Hey, dad! Groundwood, 1978. 121 pp. $6.95 paper [0-88899-004-9].

Megan takes an unwanted holiday across Canada by car and grows toward a mature understanding of her family. *Older.*

Doyle, Brian. Up to Low. Groundwood, 1982. 116 pp. $6.95 paper [0-88899-017-0].

Young Tommy and Baby Bridget have had their share of hard times, but together they begin to understand the many facets of love and humanity. The style is subtle and blatant, hilarious and melancholy, written in counterpoint. *Older.*

Doyle, Brian. You can pick me up at Peggy's Cove. Groundwood, 1979. 120 pp. $6.95 paper [0-88899-001-4].

This sequel to *Hey,dad!* finds Ryan spending summer holidays at Peggy's Cove because his father has 'run away from home.' *Older.*

Duncan, Frances. Kap-Sung Ferris. Macmillan, 1977. 126 pp. $6.95 paper [0-7715-9606-5].

Two teen-aged girls suffer identity crises but overcome their problems through mutual help and friendship. *Older.*

Ellis, Sarah. The Baby project. Groundwood, 1986. 144 pp. $6.95 paper [0-88899-047-2].

Jessica finds that the arrival and death of a new baby brings joy and pain to the entire family. *Middle.*

Evans, Hubert. Son of the Salmon People. Harbour, 1981. 166 pp. $6.95 paper [0-920080-28-6].

Conflict and crisis culminate in this fast-moving story when a white promoter tries to turn a quiet Indian village into a tourist trap. *Older.*

Faulknor, Cliff. 'Johnny' Eagleclaw. Ill. by Richard A. Conroy. Lebel, 1982. 103 pp. $8.95 hardcover [0-920008-24-0].

Trying to adjust to a city school with white students is too much for Johnny, who proves that he can succeed on the rodeo circuit. *Middle.*

Forcade, Robert J. Watch for the breaking of day. Fitzhenry & Whiteside, 1986. 135 pp. $14.95 hardcover [0-88902-988-1].

In the summer of 1944, Rob refuses to accept the death of his father, Flying Officer William Judge, until his dog is also lost. *Older.*

Ford, Joan E. Skate like the wind. Ill. by Greg Ruhl. Gage, 1983. 127 pp. $2.95 paper [0-7715-7009-0].

Lindy experiences all the pressures, friendships, rivalries, and glories common to sports meets as she competes as a novice in the Canadian figure skating championship. *Middle.*

Fossey, S. Joan Danielson. The Indian summer of Arty Bigjim and Johnny Jack. Ill. by Harold M. Moore. Gullmasters, 1981. $8.95 paper [0-919517-00-5].

Arty and Johnny find trouble in Indian society and trouble in white society. After trying to run away, they face their difficulties, learning that each person must make his own way in life. *Older.*

Godfrey, Martyn. Here she is, Ms. Teeny Wonderful! Scholastic-TAB, 1984. 172 pp. $2.95 paper [0-590-71842-1].

Tough, bike-jumping Carol who dotes on her BMX wonders how she will survive the beauty and talent contest in which her mother has her entered. *Middle to young adult.*

Godfrey, Martyn. It isn't easy being Ms. Teeny Wonderful. Scholastic-TAB, 1987. 150 pp. $3.50 paper [0-590-71674-3].

Carol Weatherspoon's 'Ms. Teeny Wonderful' crown and her penchant for BMX racing and jumping involve her in the most trying of public relations schemes. *Middle to young adult.*

Godfrey, Martyn. Plan B is total panic. Lorimer, 1986. 101 pp. $12.95 hardcover [0-88862-851-X]; $6.95 paper [0-88862-850-1].

A pair of teens get more than they bargained for when they meet up with a grizzly bear. *Older.*

Grey Owl (pseud.). A Book of Grey Owl: pages from the writings of Wa-Sha-Quon-Asin. Ed. by E.E. Reynolds. Macmillan, 1976. 2nd ed. 272 pp. $7.95 paper [0-7715-9605-7].

Selections from all of the writings of Wa-Sha-Quon-Asin. *Young adult.*

Grey Owl (pseud.). The Men of the last frontier. Macmillan, 1976. 253 pp. $6.95 paper [0-7705-1393-X].

Written to arouse public interest in conservation. *Young adult.*

Grey Owl (pseud.). Sajo and the beaver people. Macmillan, 1977. 187 pp. $6.95 paper [0-7715-9816-5].

Two Ojibway children and two beaver kittens – orphans all – live exciting lives together in Northern Quebec. *Older, young adult.*

Grey Owl (pseud.). Tales of an empty cabin. Macmillan, 1975. 335 pp. $7.95 paper [0-7705-1299-2].

Short stories of the Canadian North. *Young adult.*

Gunnery, Sylvia. I'm Locker 145, who are you? Scholastic-TAB, 1984. 139 pp. $2.95 paper [0-590-71483-X].

Jodi, who is attending a new high school during her parents' trial separation, must decide whether she can trust someone who has been in a reform school. *Older.*

Gunnery, Sylvia. We're friends, aren't we? Scholastic-TAB, 1986. 166 pp. $3.50 paper [0-590-71619-0].

On the night of graduation, two of Elizabeth's greatest dreams are realized, only to be crushed by the death of her best friend. *Older, young adult.*

Halvorson, Marilyn. Cowboys don't cry. Irwin, 1984. 137 pp. $8.95 paper [0-7720-1445-0]. Dell, 1986. $3.25 paper [0-440-91303-9].

A poignant tale about a young boy who grows up with a father who is a former champion bull rider. *Older, young adult.*

Halvorson, Marilyn. Let it go. Irwin, 1985. 223 pp. $9.95 paper [0-7725-1523-9].

Lance's mother appears after an absence of almost ten years and he must come to grips with their relationship. *Older, young adult.*

Halvorson, Marilyn. Nobody said it would be easy. Irwin, 1987. 194 pp. $10.95 paper [0-7725-1652-9].

In this sequel to *Let it go*, Lance, Red, and Lance's cousin Kat survive a plane crash. *Older, young adult.*

Harris, Christie. Mystery at the edge of two worlds. Ill. by Lou Crockett. McClelland & Stewart, 1978. 175 pp. $14.95 hardcover [0-7710-3977-8].

Gangling Lark and her new summer friend Andy investigate the theft of valuable argillite Indian artifacts in this well-told story of suspense. *Older.*

Harris, Dorothy Joan. Don't call me Sugar Baby! Scholastic-TAB, 1983. 148 pp. $2.95 paper [0-590-71173-3].

Alison has trouble adjusting to her parents' separation and to being a diabetic teenager. *Older.*

Hiebert, Susan. Alphonse has an accident. Ill. by Eddy Cobiness. Peguis, 1974. 31 pp. $4.25 hardcover [0-919566-29-4].

A Cree Indian boy plays with matches and is taken four hundred miles to a Winnipeg hospital for burns. Sympathetically told. *Middle.*

Hood, Kit; Schuyler, Linda; and Jennings, Eve. Griff gets a hand and other stories. Ill. by Heather Collins. Lorimer, 1987. 112 pp. $12.95 hardcover [0-88862-870-6]; $4.95 paper [0-88862-869-2].

Friendship, loyalty, and family life are among the themes explored in three realistic stories set on Degrassi Street. *Middle.*

Hood, Kit; Schuyler, Linda; and Jennings, Eve. Griff makes a date and other stories. Lorimer, 1986. 109 pp. $12.95 hardcover [0-88862-997-4]; $4.95 paper [0-88862-996-6].

A collection of three stories focussed on the realistic tribulations experienced by the young people who inhabit Degrassi Street. Based on the movies produced by Playing With Time Inc. *Middle.*

Hood, Kit; Schuyler, Linda; and Jennings, Eve. Lisa makes the headlines and other stories. Lorimer, 1986. 112 pp. $12.95 hardcover [0-88862-994-X]; $4.95 paper [0-88862-993-1].

Lisa and her friend Casey decide to issue their own newspaper, the Degrassi Street Journal. Their story is one of three in this realistic depiction of day-to-day life in a Toronto community. *Middle.*

Houston, James. Black diamonds: a search for Arctic treasure. Ill. by James Houston. McClelland & Stewart, 1982. 170 pp. $14.95 hardcover [0-7710-4247-7]; $3.95 paper [0-7710-4248-5]. Penguin, 1983. $4.50 paper [0-14-031633-77].

Kayak and Matthew follow a trail to find gold and they make a rich and almost fatal discovery on remote Prince Charles Island. Sequel to *Frozen fire. Older.*

Houston, James. The Falcon bow: an Arctic legend. Ill. by James Houston. McClelland & Stewart, 1986. 96 pp. $14.95 hardcover [0-7710-4252-3].

Kungo, with the help of the magical falcon bow, must bring an end to the feuding and starvation of the Caribou Indians and the Inuit. *Middle.*

Houston, James Frozen fire. Penguin, 1979. 149 pp. $4.50 paper [0-14-031233-1].

Matthew's father goes missing so he and his Eskimo friend Kayak brave the Arctic winter in secret to search for him. *Older.*

Houston, James. Ice swords: an undersea adventure. Ill. by James Houston. McClelland & Stewart, 1985. 149 pp. $12.95 hardcover [0-7710-4255-8]; $3.95 paper [0-7710-4254-X].

Matt and his Inuit friend Kayak spend their Arctic summer helping scientists study the migration of whales. Their underwater explorations lead to sightings of the beautiful tusked narwhals and other fascinating – and sometimes life-threatening – sea creatures. *Middle, older.*

Houston, James. Long claws. Ill. by James Houston. McClelland & Stewart, 1981. 31 pp. $14.95 hardcover [0-7710-4256-6].

A young brother and sister journey to find a frozen caribou that will save their family from starvation in this Arctic adventure. *Middle.*

Houston, James. River runners: a tale of hardship and bravery. Penguin, 1981. 142 pp. $4.50 paper [0-14-031430-X].

A Naskapi boy Pashak and Scottish Andrew find challenges enough when they set up a fur trading outpost far inland from Fort Chimo. Another well-written modern adventure story by an award-winning author. *Older, young adult.*

Howarth, Mary. Could Dracula live in Woodford? Kids Can, 1983. 160 pp. $5.95 paper [0-919964-46-X].

Jenny, Beth, and their sheepdog friend Sam dare to explore the haunted McIver house and are frightened by 'something' worse than a ghost. *Middle.*

Hughes, Monica. Blaine's way. Irwin, 1986. 215 pp. $9.95 paper [0-7725-1564-6].

During Blaine's childhood years, the trains that rush past his father's fields promise escape from his southwestern Ontario homeland, the Great Depression, and troubled family relationships. *Young adult.*

Hughes, Monica. Hunter in the dark. Irwin, 1981. 131 pp. $12.95 hardcover [0-7720-1372-1]; Avon, 1984. 144 pp. $3.50 paper [0-380-67702-4].

On a solitary deer-hunting trip in the bush, leukemia victim Mike Rankin decides, not whether he will live or die, but how he will live and die. *Older, young adult.*

Hughes, Monica. Log jam. Irwin, 1987. 169 pp. $10.95 paper [0-7725-1654-5].

Fourteen-year-old Lenora is an unwilling participant in a camping expedition in the Alberta foothills with her mother, new step-father, and two new step-brothers, when she encounters seventeen-year-old Isaac Manyfeathers who has escaped from jail. *Young adult.*

Hughes, Monica. My name is Paula Popowich! Ill. by Leoung O' Young. Lorimer, 1983. 150 pp. $12.95 hardcover [0-88862-690-8]; $5.95 paper [0-88862-689-4].

Eleven-year-old Paula's move from Toronto to Edmonton brings her face to face with new friends, a new school, and a new family history. *Middle.*

Hughes, Monica. Treasure of the Long Sault. Ill. by Richard A. Conroy. Lebel, 1982. 89 pp. $8.95 hardcover [0-920008-25-9].

Before the channel for the new seaway is flooded, Neil is determined to locate the treasure that has been a district legend since the events of 1813 and the battle of Crysler's Farm. *Middle.*

Hunter, Bernice Thurman. As ever, Booky. Scholastic-TAB, 1985. 152 pp. $2.95 paper [0-590-71547-X].

Booky finishes school, gets a job, and meet L.M. Montgomery in this third title of the series which is set in the 1930s. *Older.*

Hunter, Bernice Thurman. Margaret in the middle. Scholastic-TAB, 1986. 149 pp. $3.50 paper [0-590-71681-6].

Margaret chooses to remain on the farm with her aunt and uncle but even that wise decision cannot spare her from the anguish of growing up. Sequel to *A Place for Margaret. Older.*

Hunter, Bernice Thurman. A Place for Margaret. Scholastic-TAB, 1984. 151 pp. $2.95 paper [0-590-71481-3].

In 1925 Margaret is sent to her uncle's farm near Shelburne to recuperate from tuberculosis. While she basks in the love of her aunt, uncle, and the horse Starr, she wonders how secure her place at home is. *Older.*

Hunter, Bernice Thurman. That scatterbrain Booky. Scholastic-TAB, 1981. 179 pp. $2.95 paper [0-590-71082-6].

Booky, a young girl growing up during the Depression, is introduced in this first volume of a trilogy that depicts family life of the 1930s.

Hunter, Bernice Thurman. With love from Booky. Scholastic-TAB, 1983. 160 pp. $2.95 paper [0-590-71220-9].

In the second part of a trilogy, Booky's life revolves around family relationships, her first love, and her first perm. *Older.*

Kaplan, Bess. The Empty chair. Western Producer Prairie, 1986. 160 pp. $8.95 paper [0-88833-205-X].

Rebecca learns much about herself as she tries to adjust to her mother's death. Originally published under the title of *Corner store. Older.*

Kleitsch, Christel and Stephens, Paul. Dancing feathers. Annick, 1985. 62 pp. $6.95 hardcover [0-920303-24-2]; $3.95 paper [0-920303-25-0].

Tafia, a young Ojibway girl from Spirit Bay, takes part in her first Pow-wow and gains an understanding of her heritage. Based on the CBC television series. *Middle.*

Kleitsch, Christel and Stephens, Paul. A Time to be brave. Ill. by Don Ense. Annick, 1985. 64 pp. $6.95 hardcover [0-920303-26-9]; $3.95 paper [0-920303-27-7].

Tafia overcomes her fear of trains when she realises that the train is her only hope of getting help for her father who has been injured in an accident. *Middle.*

Korman, Gordon. Beware the Fish! Ill. by Lea Daniel. Scholastic-TAB, 1980. 176 pp. $2.95 paper [0-590-71026-5].

Another humorous story about Bruno and Boots. This time the R.C.M.P. investigate their shenanigans. *Older.*

Korman, Gordon. Bugs Potter live at Nickaninny. Scholastic-TAB, 1983. 184 pp. $2.95 paper [0-590-71225-X].

Another in the series of mysteries focussing on Dave 'Bugs' Potter. Though confined to a family holiday in the wilderness, Bugs finds a way to ensure that his drums, highjinks, and hilarity surface and embroil the entire campsite. *Middle to young adult.*

Korman, Gordon. Don't Care High. Scholastic-TAB, 1985. 243 pp. $13.95 hardcover [0-590-33322-4]; $3.50 paper [0-590-40251-X].

Paul Abrams decides to do something about the apathy in his new high school. *Older, young adult.*

Korman, Gordon. Go jump in the pool. Ill. by Lea Daniel. Scholastic-TAB, 1979. 185 pp. $2.95 paper [0-590-71014-1].

Bruno and Boots return to terrorize Headmaster Sturgeon in this sequel to *This can't be happening at Macdonald Hall* when they attempt to raise $25,000 for a swimming pool. *Older.*

Korman, Gordon. I want to go home! Scholastic-TAB, 1981. 182 pp. $2.95 paper [0-590-33765-3].

Rudy Miller and Mike Webster detest summer camp and will mastermind any scheme that will play havoc with daily routines. *Middle to young adult.*

Korman, Gordon. No coins, please. Scholastic-TAB, 1984. 184 pp. $10.95 hardcover [0-590-71429-5].

Artie Geller concocts a series of money-making schemes during a cross-country camping trip. *Older.*

Korman, Gordon. Our man Weston. Scholastic-TAB, 1982. 230 pp. $2.95 paper [0-590-71123-7].

As soon as Tom discovers that his brother Sidney has brought two suitcases full of detective equipment rather than clothes to their summer jobs at Pine Grove Resort Hotel, he knows the next few weeks will be a series of madcap adventures. *Middle to young adult.*

Korman, Gordon. A Semester in the life of a garbage bag. Scholastic, 1987. 257 pp. $16.95 hardcover [0-590-40694-9].

In addition to choosing a deceased Canadian poet as the topic of their modern poetry assignment, Sean Delancey and Raymond Jardine also attempt to pass off Sean's grandfather as the poet, discredit the school's solar energy system, and win a trip to Greece. *Older, young adult.*

Korman, Gordon. Son of Interflux. Scholastic-TAB, 1986. 274 pp. $15.95 hardcover [0-590-40163-7].

Simon, son of the senior executive vice-president of Interflux, manipulates the student body and the student union bank account of Nassau County High School for the Visual, Literary, and Performing Arts to support a protest company called Antiflux. *Older, young adult.*

Korman, Gordon. This can't be happening at Macdonald Hall. Ill. by Lea Daniel. Scholastic-TAB, 1980. 124 pp. $2.95 paper [0-590-71046-X].

Room-mates with a penchant for practical jokes cause havoc at a southern Ontario boarding school when they are assigned to different dormitories. *Older.*

Korman, Gordon. The War with Mr. Wizzle. Scholastic-TAB, 1982. 224 pp. $2.95 paper [0-590-32643-0].

Bruno and Boots ensure that young Mr. Wizzle and his Magnetronic 515 computer have little chance to modernize Macdonald Hall. Hilarious antics abound as the two friends take on another challenge. *Middle to young adult.*

Korman, Gordon. Who is Bugs Potter? Ill. by Dino Kotopoulis. Scholastic-TAB, 1980. 179 pp. $2.95 paper [0-590-71036-2].

Keeping Dave 'Bugs' Potter, alias 'The Most', under control during the Canadian High School Musicians Concert in Toronto is almost more than bandmaster C. Fenton Darby can handle. Bugs's passion for drums, mystery, and a famous movie star result in an hilarious fast-paced adventure. *Middle to young adult.*

Kropp, Paul. Justin, Jay-Jay and the juvenile dinkent. Scholastic-TAB, 1986. 112 pp. $3.50 paper [0-590-71675-1].

Justin and Jay-Jay have a new babysitter named Fred whose good intentions are bound to get them all in trouble. *Middle, older.*

Langford, Cameron. The Winter of the fisher. Macmillan, 1985. 222 pp. $6.95 paper [0-7715-9891-2].

The realistic relationship between a fisher, a white trapper, and an Ojibway who empathizes with the animal's world. *Older, young adult.*

Leacock, Stephen. Sunshine sketches of a little town. McClelland & Stewart, 1958. 275 pp. $19.95 hardcover [0-7710-5040-2]; $3.95 paper [0-7710-9115-X].

Affectionate vignettes of a small Ontario town written by a master humorist. *Older, young adult.*

Lemna, Don. A Visit from Mr. Lucifer. Western Producer Prairie, 1984. 142 pp. $10.95 paper [0-88833-148-7].

In a collection of episodic stories set just after the Second World War, two boys discover the delights of their prairie farm home. *Young adult.*

Little, Jean. Different dragons. Viking Kestrel, 1986. 123 pp. $12.95 hardcover [0-670-80836-9].

Ben, who's afraid of a lot of things including dogs, is forced to spend some time with his Aunt Rose who surprises him with a special birthday present – a Labrador retriever. *Middle.*

Little, Jean. From Anna. Fitzhenry & Whiteside, 1977. 2nd ed. 201 pp. $3.50 paper [0-88902-373-5].

Everyone thinks Anna is awkward until a sympathetic teacher and new glasses prove otherwise. *Older.*

Little, Jean. Listen for the singing. Irwin, 1981. 215 pp. $6.95 paper [0-7720-1326-8].

This sequel to *From Anna* involves Anna and her German immigrant family in difficulties in wartime Canada. *Older.*

Little, Jean. Lost and found. Ill. by Leoung O'Young. Viking Kestrel, 1985. 82 pp. $12.95 hardcover [0-670-80835-0]; $3.95 paper [0-1403-1997-2].

Lucy moves to a new neighbourhood and is worried about making new friends until she gets a dog whose name is Trouble. *Middle.*

Little, Jean. Mama's going to buy you a mockingbird. Viking Kestrel, 1984. 213 pp. $12.95 hardcover [0-670-80346-4]; $3.95 paper [0-14-031737-6].

Though the death of his father has left an enormous void, Jeremy discovers that his father has given him several precious gifts which continue to give as Jeremy matures. *Older.*

Lunn, Janet. Double spell. Irwin, 1983. 134 pp. $5.95 paper [0-7720-1438-8].

Twins buy an antique doll that involves them in mystery and suspense. Also appeared in the U.S.A. as *Twin spell*. *Middle, older.*

Mackay, Claire. Exit Barney McGee. Ill. by David Simpson. Scholastic-TAB, 1979. 146 pp. $2.95 paper [0-590-71002-8].

When his mother remarries and has a baby, Barney feels unwanted and goes off to find his father. *Older.*

Mackay, Claire. The Minerva program. Lorimer, 1984. 178 pp. $12.95 hardcover [0-88862-717-3]; $5.95 paper [0-88862-716-5].

Minerva solves the computer mystery with the help of her brother 'Spiderman' and her other friends. *Middle, older.*

Mackay, Claire. Mini-bike hero. Ill. by Merle Smith. Scholastic-TAB, 1984 (rev.ed.). 105 pp. $2.95 paper [0-590-71413-9].

A contemporary novel that depicts Steve's obsession with mini-bikes and his ever-evolving relationship with his father. *Middle.*

Mackay, Claire. Mini-bike racer. Ill. by Merle Smith. Scholastic-TAB, 1978 (rev.ed.). 119 pp. $2.95 paper [0-590-71003-6].

Mini-bike racers Julie and Kim know that Steve wouldn't miss the race unless he had tangled with the missing convict. *Middle.*

Mackay, Claire. Mini-bike rescue. Scholastic-TAB, 1982. 138 pp. $2.95 paper [0-590-71100-8].

Julie quickly realizes that the dull summer that she had expected while working at Aunt Maureen's cabins may be the most dangerous summer of her life. *Middle.*

Mackenzie-Porter, Patricia. When an osprey sails. Ill. by Jenni Lunn. Nimbus, 1982. 160 pp. $9.95 paper [0-920852-26-2].

While spending three weeks with their father and his new wife on a sailboat in the waters of Nova Scotia, Jane and Mark unearth a smugglers ring and learn about their family. *Older.*

McNeil, Florence. Miss P and me. Irwin, 1982. 124 pp. $12.95 hardcover [0-7720-1374-8]. Scholastic-TAB, 1984. $2.95 paper [0-590-71050-8].

Jane's grade eight year in a Catholic school is filled with emotional conflict and humour. *Older.*

Major, Kevin. Dear Bruce Springsteen. Doubleday, 1987. 192 pp. $17.95 hardcover [0-385-29584-7].

Fourteen-year-old Terry Blanchard deals with his problems by confiding what he is experiencing and feeling in letters written to his idol Bruce Springsteen. *Older, young adult.*

Major, Kevin. Far from shore. Clarke, Irwin, 1980. 189 pp. $9.95 hardcover [0-7720-1312-8]; Dell, 1986. 224 pp. $3.95 paper [0-440-92585].

Stark realism pervades this story told from the viewpoints of several Newfoundlanders. *Young adult.*

Major, Kevin. Hold fast. Irwin, 1978. 170 pp. $6.95 paper [0-7720-1314-4]. Dell, 1986. $3.50 paper [0-440-93756-6].

Michael survives the break-up of his family life and works through it to find his own identity in this realistic novel of Newfoundland. *Older, young adult.*

Major, Kevin. Thirty-six exposures. Doubleday, 1984. 155 pp. $16.95 hardcover [0-385-29347-X].

Lorne's last weeks in high school are filled with unexpected turmoil in this sensitively-written novel. *Young adult.*

Manuel, Ella. That fine summer. Jesperson, 1983. 93 pp. $5.95 paper [0-920502-22-9].

A unique story, written in local dialect, that will introduce children to a Newfoundland coastal fishing village and people who may be poor in substance but are rich in spirit. *Middle.*

Markoosie. Harpoon of the hunter. McGill-Queen's, 1970. $9.95 hardcover [0-7735-0102-9]; $6.95 paper [0-7735-0232-7].

Canada's first Inuit novelist writes a starkly simple story of the struggle for survival in Canada's North. *Older.*

Marquis, Helen. The Longest day of the year. PaperJacks, 1974. 116 pp. $1.25 paper [0-7737-7056-9].

Three children are trapped in their prairie home by a blizzard the day before Christmas when their parents are away. *Middle.*

Martel, Suzanne. Peewee. Tr. by John Fleming. Scholastic-TAB, 1982. 128 pp. $2.95 paper [0-590-71094-X].

Yves, nicknamed Peewee by his team, has a passion for hockey and dreams of the day when he will join his heroes Belliveau and Richard on the ice. A fast-paced story filled with friendships, triumphs, and disappointments of young sports aficionados. Translation of *Pi-Oui. Middle.*

Millard, Nicky. The Green Angels. Scholastic-TAB, 1986. 137 pp. $2.95 paper [0-590-71620-4].

When a gang of young people from a government housing apartment attempt to turn a dump into a park, they find a skeleton, a treasure, and friendship. *Middle.*

Montero, Gloria. Billy Higgins rides the freights. Ill. by Olena Kassian. Lorimer, 1982. 119 pp. $12.95 hardcover [0-88862-578-2]; $5.95 paper [0-88862-579-0].

When thirteen-year-old Billy Higgins leaves school, he joins the countless unemployed in Vancouver's streets and climbs aboard the train travelling to Ottawa to protest the plight of the jobless. *Middle, older.*

Montero, Gloria. The Summer the whales sang. Lorimer, 1985. 165 pp. $12.95 hardcover [0-88862-904-4]; $5.95 paper [0-88862-903-6].

Vivi spends her thirteenth summer in Newfoundland where her mother is making a film about an old Basque whaling station. It is a time when Vivi confronts feelings about her own Basque heritage and about her family relationships. *Middle, older.*

Montgomery, Lucy M. Anne of Avonlea. McGraw, 1968. 367 pp. $11.95 hardcover [0-07-077695-4]; $2.45 paper [0-7700-0005-3].

Anne teaches school at Avonlea until she goes to college at the age of eighteen. Second in the Anne series. *Older, young adult.*

Montgomery, Lucy M. Anne of Green Gables. McGraw, 1942. 329 pp. $11.95 hardcover [0-7700-0006-1]; $2.45 paper [0-7700-0008-8].

The first of eight books on the blithe-spirited redhead of Prince Edward Island. *Older, young adult.*

Montgomery, Lucy M. Anne of Ingleside. McClelland & Stewart, 1939. 323 pp. $7.95 paper [0-7710-6154-4].

Anne's own children, Jem, Shirley, Walter and the twins, Nan and Di grow up together in lovely Prince Edward Island. Sixth in the Anne series. *Older, young adult.*

Montgomery, Lucy M. Anne of the Island. McGraw, 1968. 326 pp. $2.45 paper [0-7700-0011-8].

Anne graduates from college at Redmond, teaches at Valley Road, and promises to wait for Gilbert to finish medical school so they can marry. Third in the Anne series. *Older, young adult.*

Montgomery, Lucy M. Anne of Windy Poplars. McClelland & Stewart, 1973. 301 pp. $7.95 paper [0-7710-6175-7].

Anne teaches school in Summerside, P.E.I. for two years, and wins over the most difficult school board. Fourth in the Anne series. *Older, young adult.*

Montgomery, Lucy M. Anne's house of dreams. McClelland & Stewart, 1972. 291 pp. $7.95 paper [0-7710-6196-X].

Dr. Gilbert Blythe and his wife Anne begin life together at Four Winds Harbour. Fifth in the Anne series. *Older, young adult.*

Montgomery, Lucy M. Blue castle. McClelland & Stewart, 1926. 263 pp. $7.95 paper [0-7710-6217-6].

Set in Muskoka, Ontario. *Older, young adult.*

Montgomery, Lucy M. Chronicles of Avonlea. McGraw, 1980. 306 pp. $8.95 paper [0-07-092368-X].

Short stories. *Older, young adult.*

Montgomery, Lucy M. The Doctor's sweetheart and other stories. Comp. by Catherine McLay. McGraw, 1979. 190 pp. $13.95 hardcover [0-07-082790-7].

These fourteen previously-uncollected stories are among five hundred written by the author of *Anne of Green Gables* that appeared in popular magazines at the turn of the century. Lovers of Anne will respond to these stories of love. *Young adult.*

Montgomery, Lucy M. Emily climbs. McClelland & Stewart, 1974. 312 pp. $7.95 paper [0-7710-6259-1].

Emily goes to high school in Shrewsbury after she promises Aunt Elizabeth that she will write 'no word that was not strictly true.' Second in the Emily Starr trilogy. *Older, young adult.*

Montgomery, Lucy M. Emily of New Moon. McClelland & Stewart, 1925. 351 pp. $7.95 paper [0-7710-6238-9].

First of three Emily books – in which Emily prepares to be an author. *Older, young adult.*

Montgomery, Lucy M. Emily's quest. McClelland & Stewart, 1972. 262 pp. $7.95 paper [0-7710-6280-X].

Graduation from high school brings many changes into Emily's life, yet her love for Teddy Kent does not change and all ends happily in this third book in the Emily Starr trilogy. *Older, young adult.*

Montgomery, Lucy M. The Golden road. McGraw, 1944. 369 pp. $11.95 hardcover [0-7700-0077-0]; $8.95 paper [0-07-549205-9].

The Story Girl entertains her friends with her inventive, imaginative bent for telling an appropriate tale. *Older, young adult.*

Montgomery, Lucy M. Jane of Lantern Hill. McClelland & Stewart, 1977. 297 pp. $7.95 paper [0-7710-6301-6].

Jane spends joyful summers with her father in Prince Edward Island and dreary winters with her grandmother and mother in Toronto. *Older, young adult.*

Montgomery, Lucy M. Kilmeny of the orchard. McGraw, 1986. 256 pp. $8.95 paper [0-07-549203-2].

Kilmeny speaks through the music of her violin, then recovers her voice to save her true love. *Older, young adult.*

Montgomery, Lucy M. Magic for Marigold. McClelland & Stewart, 1977. 328 pp. $7.95 paper [0-7710-6322-9].

Marigold and her great-grandmother share the old woman's memories of the past on the last night of her life. *Older, young adult.*

Montgomery, Lucy M. Mistress Pat: a novel of Silver Bush. McClelland & Stewart, 1977. 338 pp. $7.95 paper [0-7710-6343-1].

This sequel to *Pat of Silver Bush* finds Jingle, now an architect, and Pat ready to be married. *Older, young adult.*

Montgomery, Lucy M. Pat of Silver Bush. McClelland & Stewart, 1974. 329 pp. $7.95 paper [0-7710-6364-4].

Pat Gardiner and Jingle Gordon grow up together in Prince Edward Island. *Older, young adult.*

Montgomery, Lucy M. Rainbow Valley. McClelland & Stewart, 1973. $7.95 paper [0-7710-6385-7].

About the children who played in Rainbow Valley and how they acquired a mother. Seventh in the Anne series. *Older, young adult.*

Montgomery, Lucy M. Rilla of Ingleside. McClelland & Stewart, 1973. 285 pp. $7.95 paper [0-7710-6406-3].

Rilla, youngest of the Ingleside children, grows up in the era of the First World War. Eighth in the Anne series. *Older, young adult.*

Montgomery, Lucy M. The Road to yesterday. McGraw, 1974. 251 pp. $11.95 hardcover [0-07-077721-7].

Posthumously published collection of fourteen stories about the characters who lived around the Blythe family home in Avonlea. *Older, young adult.*

Montgomery, Lucy M. The Story girl. McGraw, 1986. 365 pp. $8.95 paper [0-07-549204-0].

Felix and Beverley return to the Island and meet their cousin whose storytelling abilities have earned her the nickname The Story Girl. *Older, young adult.*

Montgomery, Lucy M. Tangled web. McClelland & Stewart, 1939. 324 pp. $7.95 paper [0-7710-6427-6].

Various adventures of the Penhallow clan including the affair of Aunt Becky's jug. *Older, young adult.*

Morgan, Allen. The Kids from B.A.D. Scholastic-TAB, 1984. 128 pp. $2.95 paper [0-590-71219-5].

Six entertaining cases from the files of the Barton Avenue Detectives. *Middle.*

Mowat, Farley. The Black joke. McClelland & Stewart, 1962. 177 pp. $6.95 paper [0-7710-6649-X].

Two plucky Newfoundland boys outsmart rum runners in this 1930s pirate story. *Older, young adult.*

Mowat, Farley. The Curse of the Viking grave. McClelland & Stewart, 1966. 243 pp. $7.95 paper [0-7710-6642-2].

Eskimo, Indian, and white friends find Viking relics in this sequel to *Lost in the barrens. Older, young adult.*

Mowat, Farley. The Dog who wouldn't be. Seal, 1980. $3.50 paper [0-7704-2128-8].

Hilarious adventures of Mutt, a dog who couldn't be convinced he wasn't a person. *Older.*

Mowat, Farley. Lost in the barrens. McClelland & Stewart, 1973. 244 pp. $7.95 paper [0-7710-6640-6].

A city boy and an Indian are forced to test their survival skills in the Canadian North. *Older, young adult.*

Mowat, Farley. Owls in the family. Ill. by Robert Frankenberg. McClelland & Stewart, 1973 (rev.ed.). 107 pp. $5.50 paper [0-7710-6647-3].

Misadventures of pet owls, Wol and Weeps, who shared the same family as Mutt, the dog who wouldn't be. *Middle.*

O'Hearn, Audrey. Me and Luke. Groundwood, 1987. 176 pp. $6.95 paper [0-88899-066-9].

A compassionate and convincing story about seventeen-year-old Matt who discovers he cannot abandon his newborn son, Luke. *Young adult.*

O'Keefe, Frank. Guppy love, or, the day the fish tank exploded. Kids Can, 1986. 138 pp. $5.95 paper [0-921103-04-2].

Falling in love with her grade five teacher leads Natalie into a series of misadventures, in a story told with humour and kindness. *Middle.*

Paperny, Myra. Take a giant step. Grolier, 1986. 173 pp. $13.95 hardcover [0-7172-2158-X]; $3.95 paper [0-7172-2157-1].

Buzz Bersh, a ten-year-old boy with great musical talent, comes to grips with his talent and his father's pressures, during the summer of 1941. *Middle, older.*

Pearson, Kit. The Daring game. Viking Kestrel, 1986. 225 pp. $12.95 hardcover [0-670-80751-6]; $4.95 paper [0-14-031932-8].
Eliza recounts the year spent at Vancouver's Ashdown Academy. Particularly memorable is her friendship with Helen, a defiant, mischievous girl who starts the daring game among her room-mates in the Yellow Dorm. *Middle, older.*

Pirot, Alison Lohans. Can you promise me spring? Scholastic-TAB, 1986. 178 pp. $3.50 paper [0-590-71616-6].
Lori has some growing up to do when her younger brother's illness is diagnosed as Hodgkin's disease. *Older, young adult.*

Pirot, Alison Lohans. Who cares about Karen? Scholastic-TAB, 1983. 149 pp. $2.95 paper [0-590-71148-2].
A high school music trip ends in disaster for Karen and her four companions when their car plunges over a rocky cliff. *Older, young adult.*

Plante, Raymond. My impossible uncle. Tr. by Rochelle Lisa Ash. Scholastic-TAB, 1987. 94 pp. $3.95 paper [0-590-716-99-9].
Julie tells the story of her impossible uncle Philibert who wants to break the world pole-sitting record to win the lady of his dreams. Translation of *Le record de Philibert Dupont. Middle, older.*

Poulsen, David A. The Cowboy Kid. Plains, 1987. 186 pp. $9.95 paper [0-920985-20-3].
Although Torontonian Clayton Findlay begins his six-month sojourn in southern Alberta as a most unwilling visitor, he amazes himself and others by his skill at his adopted rodeo lifestyle. *Middle.*

Razzell, Mary. Salmonberry wine. Groundwood, 1987. 192 pp. $6.95 paper [0-88899-062-6].
Sheila Brary's spirit is nearly crushed by the rigours of nursing school, the demands of intimidating instructors, the deceit of a senior surgeon, and the death of one of her patients. Sequel to *Snow apples. Young adult.*

Razzell, Mary. Snow apples. Groundwood, 1984. 160 pp. $7.95 paper [0-88899-032-4].
Lifelong goals for herself, intimacy with boys, and conflict with her domineering mother preoccupy Sheila in her sixteenth year. *Young adult.*

Reid, Malcolm. Salut, Gadou! Ill. by Rose Zgodzinski. Lorimer, 1982. 119 pp. $12.95 hardcover [0-88862-575-8]; $4.95 paper [0-88862-576-6].
A group of young people in Quebec City learn about the bitterness of fighting against power and authority. *Middle.*

Renaud, Bernadette. The Cat in the cathedral. Ill. by Josette Michaud. Tr. by Frances Morgan. Porcépic, 1983. 83 pp. $6.95 paper [0-88878-212-8].
A loving companionship quickly develops between the lonely organist and the independent, mischievous kitten. Translation of *Le chat de l'oratoire. Middle.*

Richardson, Gillian. One chance to win. Ill. by Em Lachance. Ragweed, 1986. 112 pp. $7.95 paper [0-920304-56-7].
To help pay for the film he needs to enter a photo contest, ten-year-old Wink gets a job at a nearby dog kennel. Unfortunately, all his prize-winning chances literally go up in smoke. *Middle.*

Richmond, Sandra. Wheels for walking. Groundwood, 1983. 158 pp. $7.95 paper [0-88899-021-7].
Emotional and physical strains confront eighteen-year-old Sally when an automobile accident leaves her a quadriplegic. *Older, young adult.*

Roberts, Charles G.D. Red Fox. Ill. by John Schoenherr. Scholastic-TAB, 1986. 187 pp. $3.50 paper [0-590-71604-2].
Roberts's only full-length animal biography tells 'the story of Red Fox's adventurous career in the Ringwaak wilds and of his final triumph over the enemies of his kind.' *Older.*

Roberts, Charles G.D. Seven bears. Ill. by Ken MacDougall. Scholastic-TAB, 1977. 124 pp. $2.95 paper [0-590-71018-4].
Selections from *Thirteen bears* that show Roberts at his best as an animal biographer. *Middle, older.*

Roberts, Ken. Crazy ideas. Groundwood, 1984. 96 pp. $5.95 paper [0-88899-028-6].
Innovation is the byword in Sceletown and Christine needs a 'crazy idea' in order to graduate from junior high school. *Middle.*

Roberts, Ken. Pop bottles. Groundwood, 1987. 87 pp. $5.95 paper [0-88899-059-6].
Will McCleary finds wealth in the yard of his family's newly-rented home: thousands of pop bottles, buried upside-down to make a glass sidewalk and patio! *Middle.*

Roy, Gabrielle. Cliptail. Ill. by François Olivier. Tr. by Alan Brown. McClelland & Stewart, 1980. 48 pp. $12.95 paper [0-7710-7843-9].
Mothering instincts are strong in Cliptail, an all-black cat with a stump of a tail, who knows all the likely hideaways for nests of kittens and ways to sustain them through long winter storms. *Younger, middle.*

Sadiq, Nazneen. Camels can make you homesick and other stories. Ill. by Mary Cserepy. Lorimer, 1985. 89 pp. $12.95 hardcover [0-88862-913-3]; $5.95 paper [0-88862-912-5].

A collection of short stories that explore the intertwining of Canadian and South Asian cultures. Among the young protagonists is Jaya who performs classical Indian dancing at a school assembly and Amit who treats his Bengali-born grandmother to dinner at McDonalds. *Middle.*

St. Pierre, Paul. Boss of the Namko Drive. Douglas & McIntyre, 1986. 115 pp. $8.95 paper [0-88894-494-2].

When his father gets hurt, fifteen-year-old Delore becomes the boss of a two hundred-mile cattle drive. Fine realistic writing. *Older, young adult.*

St. Pierre, Paul. Breaking Smith's quarter horse. Douglas & McIntyre, 1984. 164 pp. $7.95 paper [0-88894-431-4].

Epitomizes the realities of ranch life in British Columbia. Adapted from a television script. *Older, young adult.*

Seton, Ernest Thompson. Selected stories of Ernest Thompson Seton. Ed. by Patricia Morley. Univ. of Ottawa, 1978. 168 pp. $6.95 paper [0-7766-4339-8].

Five stories from *Wild animals I have known* and three with Canadian settings from his later writing. *Older, young adult.*

Seton, Ernest Thompson. Wild animals I have known. McClelland & Stewart, 1977. 304 pp. $5.95 paper [0-7710-9254-7].

Collection of true animal tales illustrated with the author's sympathetic pen-and-ink drawings. *Middle, older.*

Siamon, Sharon. Dirtbikes at hangman's clubhouse. Ill. by Greg Ruhl. Gage, 1984. 143 pp. $3.95 paper [0-7715-7013-9].

Wally and Serge's obsession with dirt bikes is turned to advantage when Wally's two sisters are kidnapped. *Older.*

Siamon, Sharon. Ski for your mountain. Ill. by Brenda Clark. Gage, 1983. 175 pp. $3.95 paper [0-7715-7007-4].

April's fear of heights is a dreadful handicap when she must go to live with her aunt, uncle, and cousin at their ski school on Snowbird Mountain. *Older.*

Smucker, Barbara. Amish adventure. Irwin, 1983. 158 pp. $8.95 paper [0-7720-1391-8]. Penguin, 1984. $3.95 paper [0-14-031702-3].

At first confused and shocked by their seemingly backward way of life, Ian comes to love and respect the Benders, an Amish family in southwestern Ontario. *Middle, older.*

Staunton, Ted. Maggie and me. Kids Can, 1986. 89 pp. $5.95 paper [0-921103-00-X].

Five humorous episodes from the lives of best friends Maggie and Cyril. *Middle.*

Stren, Patti. I was a 15-year-old blimp. Irwin, 1985. 185 pp. $12.95 hardcover [0-7725-1538-7]; Totem, 1985. 185 pp. $3.95 paper [0-00-223127-1].

In a desperate move to lose weight and gain popularity, Gabby Finkelstein resorts to a life-threatening lifestyle. *Older, young adult.*

Taylor, Cora. Julie. Western Prairie Producer, 1985. 101 pp. $7.95 paper [0-88833-172-X].

Psychic ability opens some doors for young Julie, but closes many more; Julie must learn how and when to use her amazing gift. *Older.*

Taylor, Lee. The Insect zoo and the wildcat hero. Scholastic-TAB, 1985. 124 pp. $2.95 paper [0-590-71518-6].

Maggie, an enthusiastic young entomologist, gives her baseball-playing brother an unexpected boost when her insect zoo is smashed in the stands. *Middle.*

Tennant, Veronica. On stage, please. Ill. by Rita Briansky. McClelland & Stewart, 1979 (rev.ed.). 176 pp. $7.95 paper [0-7710-8452-8].

Principal ballerina with the National Ballet of Canada writes an informative but entertaining story about ten-year-old Jennifer's pursuit of a career in dance. *Older.*

Truss, Jan. Jasmin. Groundwood, 1982. 196 pp. $7.95 paper [0-88899-014-6].

Responsibilities in a boisterous household, frustrations at school, and an overwhelming feeling of failure drive Jasmin into the wilderness. *Middle, older.*

Truss, Jan. Summer goes riding. Groundwood, 1987. 192 pp. $12.95 hardcover [0-88899-061-8].

Charlotte's single-minded ambition to own a horse is tempered with the loss of the family fortune, a tornado, and unexpected friendships. *Older.*

Waterton, Betty. The Dog who stopped the war. Adapted and ill. with stills from the movie. Groundwood, 1985. 90 pp. $4.95 paper [0-88899-040-5].

Over the Christmas holidays, two groups of children stage a mock war in the woods and fields around town. *Middle.*

Waterton, Betty. Quincy Rumpel. Groundwood, 1984. 94 pp. $5.95 paper [0-88899-036-7].

Waterton, Betty. Starring Quincy Rumpel. Groundwood, 1986. 115 pp. $5.95 paper [0-88899-048-0].

The Rumpels are a lively lot and none is more boisterous, impetuous, or caring than Quincy. With irrepressible thoughts of fame, eleven-year-old Quincy Rumpel considers the possibilities of helping her father advertise his latest project – the small round mini-trampolines called Rumpel Rebounders – on television. *Middle.*

Weir, Joan S. So, I'm different. Douglas & McIntyre, 1981. 107 pp. $13.95 hardcover [0-88894-320-2]; $6.95 paper [0-88894-334-2].

Nicky, the only Indian child in a well-to-do city school, discovers the value of being different. *Middle.*

Wieler, Diana J. Last chance summer. Western Producer Prairie, 1986. 114 pp. $7.95 paper [0-88833-203-3].

Having abandoned countless foster homes, Marl Silversides knows that the Jenner farm is his last hope of showing that he can fit in and follow the rules. *Older, young adult.*

Wilson, Budge. A House far from home. Scholastic-TAB, 1986. 130 pp. $3.50 paper [0-590-71679-4].

When their father's chronic cough causes a family separation, Lorinda and James are forced to spend six months living with a childless aunt and uncle and attending a new school in a city thousands of miles from home. *Middle.*

Wilson, Budge. Mr. John Bertrand Nijinsky and Charlie. Ill. by Terry Roscoe Boucher. Nimbus, 1986. 40 pp. $5.95 paper [0-920852-57-2].

Mr. John Bertrand Nijinsky was a crabby, lonely, old man until a skinny, scruffy, black cat named Charlie moved in with him. *Younger, middle.*

Wilson, Budge. The Worst Christmas present ever. Scholastic-TAB, 1984. 97 pp. $2.95 paper [0-590-71430-9].

Just when Lorinda and James's money-making schemes have earned them enough to buy their mother a beautiful red vase, they learn that she thinks it is hideous. *Middle.*

Wilson, Eric. Disneyland hostage. Totem, 1983. 119 pp. $2.95 paper [0-00-222637-5].

While visiting Disneyland, Liz and Aunt Melody are among a group taken hostage by terrorists. *Middle.*

Wilson, Eric. Ghost of Lunenburg Manor. Totem, 1982. 117 pp. $2.95 paper [0-00-222629-4].

Tom and Liz solve a mystery for Professor and Mrs. Zenick, a charming couple whose home is haunted and lives are threatened. *Middle.*

Wilson, Eric. The Lost treasure of Casa Loma. General, 1982. 103 pp. $2.95 paper [0-7736-7044-0].

Fake diamonds hidden in their new Toronto Blue Jays jackets nearly result in Liz and Tom Austen's deaths in this formula mystery. *Middle.*

Wilson, Eric. Murder on the Canadian. Irwin, 1976. 108 pp. $7.95 hardcover [0-370-11013-7].

A typical mystery story format that finds a junior detective involved in a killing on the Canadian National Railway's transcontinental train, the Canadian. *Middle.*

Wilson, Eric. Spirit in the rainforest. Collins, 1984. 143 pp. $13.95 hardcover [0-00-222856-4]. Totem, 1986. $3.50 paper [0-00-223049-6].

Liz and Tom try to unravel a counterfeit lottery ticket scam. *Middle.*

Wilson, Eric. Terror in Winnipeg. General, 1982. 103 pp. $2.95 paper [0-7736-7043-2].

When the daughter of a prominent industrialist is kidnapped by terrorists, Tom must outwit both the criminals and the police to save her life. *Middle.*

Wilson, Eric. The Unmasking of 'Ksan. Collins, 1986. 120 pp. $14.95 hardcover [0-00-223116-6].

The theft of the Raven clan mask leads Dawn, a Gitksan Indian, and her friend Graham deeper and deeper into mystery and danger. *Middle, older.*

Wilson, Eric. Vampires of Ottawa. Collins, 1984. 97 pp. $12.95 hardcover [0-00-222845-9]. Totem, 1985. $3.50 paper [0-00-222858-0].

Although some aspects of this book stretch credulity, Liz and Tom Austen fans will enjoy the mystery. *Middle.*

Wilson, Eric. Vancouver nightmare. Totem, 1978. 100 pp. $2.95 paper [0-00-222631-6].

Sequel to *Murder on the Canadian* features Tom helping to apprehend a drug ring. *Middle.*

Yee, Paul. Teach me to fly, Skyfighter! and other stories. Ill. by Paul Yee. Lorimer, 1983. 133 pp. $12.95 hardcover [0-88862-646-0]; $5.95 paper [0-88862-645-2].

A collection of five short stories featuring the interplay among children who live in Vancouver's Strathcona and Chinatown districts. *Middle.*

Young, Scott. A Boy at Leafs' camp. McClelland & Stewart, 1985. 256 pp. $3.95 paper [0-7710-9090-0].

A young boy unexpectedly tries out at the Leafs' hockey camp. *Middle, older.*

Young, Scott. Boy on defense. McClelland & Stewart, 1985. 246 pp. $3.95 paper [0-7710-9089-7].

In his dreams, seventeen-year-old Bill Spunska is a hockey hero. He realizes those dreams and signs a contract to join the Toronto Maple Leafs' training camp. *Middle, older.*

Young, Scott. Scrub on skates. McClelland & Stewart, 1985. 218 pp. $3.95 paper [0-7710-9088-9].

A school develops a hockey team and school spirit too. A hockey classic. *Middle, older.*

Zalan, Magda. In a big ugly house far from here. Ill. by Julius Varga. Porcépic, 1982. 87 pp. $6.95 paper [0-88878-206-3].

A collection of ten short stories about a young girl's childhood in Budapest during World War II. *Middle.*

HISTORICAL FICTION

see also
PUBLISHERS' SERIES
Northern Lights

Bellingham, Brenda. Storm Child. Lorimer, 1985. 124 pp. $12.95 hardcover [0-88862-794-7]; $5.95 paper [0-88862-793-9].

Isobel, a twelve-year-old girl whose father is a Scottish farmer and mother is a Peigan Indian, comes to grips with her personal identity. *Older.*

Bilson, Geoffrey. Death over Montreal. Kids Can, 1982. 109 pp. $5.95 paper [0-919964-45-1].

Jamie and his family emigrate to Canada from Scotland in the 1830s to escape the cholera epidemic and find disappointment and adventure in their new home. *Middle.*

Bilson, Geoffrey. Goodbye Sarah. Ill. by Ron Berg. Kids Can, 1982. 64 pp. $5.95 paper [0-919964-38-9].

Two young girls attempt to remain friends during the Winnipeg General Strike in 1919. *Middle.*

Bradford, Karleen. The Nine days queen. Scholastic-TAB, 1986. 200 pp. $3.50 paper [0-590-71617-4].

In 1554, sixteen-year-old Lady Jane Dudley is powerless against the political odds that make her queen and lead to her untimely death. *Older, young adult.*

Brandis, Marianne. The Quarter-pie window. Ill. by G. Brender à Brandis. Porcupine's Quill, 1985. 199 pp. $8.95 paper [0-88984-085-7].

In a sequel to *The Tinderbox*, Emma and her younger brother, John, go to the town of York to live and work in the care of their guardian, Mrs. McPhail. *Older, young adult.*

Brandis, Marianne. The Tinderbox. Ill. by G. Brender à Brandis. Porcupine's Quill, 1982. 155 pp. $8.95 paper [0-88984-064-4].

Emma holds together her family after a fire destroys the family home in this historical novel set in Southern Ontario in the 1830s. *Older, young adult.*

Clark, Joan. The Hand of Robin Squires. Ill. by William Taylor. Irwin, 1981. 145 pp. $6.95 paper [0-7720-1311-X]. Penguin, 1986. $3.95 paper [0-14-031905-0].

Pirates and buried treasure figure in an exciting adventure based on Nova Scotia's Oak Island mystery. *Older.*

Culleton, Beatrice. Spirit of the white bison. Ill. by Robert Kakaygeesick, Jr. Pemmican, 1985. 64 pp. $6.95 paper [0-919143-40-7].

The role of the bison changes when Europeans settle on the prairies and the importance of the bison diminishes. *Middle.*

Cutt, W. Towrie. Carry my bones northwest. Collins, 1973. 144 pp. $7.95 hardcover [0-00-184119-X].

Willie goes to live with his grandparents in the Orkney Islands after his father and Indian mother are killed in an Indian massacre at a Hudson's Bay post in 1794. *Older.*

Davidson, Marion and **Marsh, Audrey.** Smoke over Grand Pré. Breakwater, 1983. 208 pp. $5.95 paper [0-919519-25-3].

The adventures of Paul, an Acadian boy, and Swift Arrow, a young Indian, who spend the winter away from their families after being suspected of killing a soldier. Set in Nova Scotia during the period leading up to the eviction of the Acadians. *Older.*

Doerksen, Nan. Rats in the sloop. Ill. by Bill Johnson. Ragweed, 1986. 72 pp. $7.95 paper [0-920304-55-9].

In the summer of 1819, Johnny stows away on the sloop taking his sister Meg to their aunt and uncle in Fredericton. Recently orphaned, the children begin new lives in a new family. *Middle.*

Downie, Mary Alice and **Downie, John.** Honor bound. Oxford, 1980. 192 pp. $5.95 paper [0-19-540331-2].

A Loyalist family flees to Kingston at the close of the American War of Independence. *Older.*

Downie, Mary Alice and **Rawlyk, George A.** A Proper Acadian. Ill. by Ron Berg. Kids Can, 1980. 64 pp. $5.95 paper [0-919964-29-X].

During his father's illness Timothy is sent from Boston to live with Aunt Madeleine in Acadia. His fondness for a new culture and family keeps him in Acadia at a time of bitter conflict between the English and French in the 1750s. *Middle.*

Freeman, Bill. Danger on the tracks. Lorimer, 1987. 129 pp. $12.95 hardcover [0-88862-873-0]; $6.95 paper [0-88862-872-2].
Meg and Jamie Bains find jobs with the London Huron and Bruce Railway in 1870, but, before long, are on opposite sides of a fight between the railroad and stagecoach owners. *Older*.

Freeman, Bill. First spring on the Grand Banks. Lorimer, 1978. 171 pp. $12.95 hardcover [0-88862-221-X]; $5.95 paper [0-88862-220-1].
In this sequel to *The Last voyage of the Scotian* Meg and John Bains join their friend Canso in deep sea chases, shipwreck, and adventure on the Grand Banks of Newfoundland. *Older*.

Freeman, Bill. Harbour thieves. Lorimer, 1984. 138 pp. $12.95 hardcover [0-88862-747-5]; $5.95 paper [0-88862-746-7].
Meg and Jamie try to help support their family by selling newspapers in Toronto during the 1870s. *Older*.

Freeman, Bill. The Last voyage of the Scotian. Lorimer, 1976. 178 pp. $12.95 hardcover [0-88862-113-2]; $5.95 paper [0-88862-112-4].
This sequel to *Shantymen of Cache Lake* is an exciting adventure and 'a magnificent picture of conditions on the sailing ships of the 19th century.' *Older*.

Freeman, Bill. Shantymen of Cache Lake. Lorimer, 1975. 166 pp. $12.95 hardcover [0-0-88862-091-8]; $5.95 paper [0-88862-090-X].
Two young people whose father tried to organize a trade union among the lumber workers go to work at the Ottawa Valley lumber camp where he was murdered. *Older*.

Freeman, Bill. Trouble at Lachine Mill. Lorimer, 1983. 128 pp. $12.95 hardcover [0-88862-673-8]; $5.95 paper [0-88862-672-X].
A young girl and her brother become immersed in labour disputes when they are hired to work in a Montreal shirt factory in the 1870s. *Older*.

Fryer, Mary Beacock. Escape: adventures of a Loyalist family. Ill. by Stephen Clarke. Dundurn, 1982. 152 pp. $9.50 paper [0-919670-60-1].
The ten members of the Loyalist Seaman family escape to Canada when they are hounded as dissident Americans after the American Revolution in 1789. *Older*.

German, Tony. A Breed apart. McClelland & Stewart, 1985. 272 pp. $3.95 paper [0-7710-3266-8].
Duncan Cameron, born of Scot and Cree parents, returns to the wild northwest where he comes to grips with his own identity in this fast-paced novel set in the early 1800s. *Older, young adult*.

German, Tony. Tom Penny. McClelland & Stewart, 1983. 184 pp. $8.95 paper [0-7710-3265-X].
In an exciting story full of incredible adventures Tom Penny proves his worth as a hardy Upper Canadian pioneer when he is left an orphan in 1829. *Older, young adult*.

German, Tony. Tom Penny and the Grand Canal. McClelland & Stewart, 1982. 144 pp. $12.95 hardcover [0-7710-3260-9]; $8.95 paper [0-7710-3261-7].
Tom and his family become involved in a scheme to build a canal between Montreal and Georgian Bay in the 1830s. *Middle*.

Greenwood, Barbara. A Question of loyalty. Scholastic-TAB, 1984. 185 pp. $2.95 paper [0-590-71450-3].
Deborah hides a wounded rebel and his afraid of the consequences in this historical tale set in 1837. *Older, young adult*.

Hamilton, Mary. The Tin-lined trunk. Ill. by Ron Berg. Kids Can, 1980. 64 pp. $5.95 paper [0-919964-28-1].
Two London street children are sent to live and work in Canada during the British Child Emigration Movement in 1887. *Middle*.

Harris, Christie. Raven's cry. Ill. by Bill Reid. McClelland & Stewart, 1973. 193 pp. $7.95 paper [0-7710-4033-4].
A descendant of Haida chiefs decorates an inspired book about the tragic destruction of the Haida people by white fur traders. *Older*.

Hewitt, Marsha and **Mackay, Claire.** One proud summer. Women's, 1981. 159 pp. $6.95 paper [0-88961-048-7].
Following her father's death, thirteen-year-old Lucie joins the work force at Montreal Cottons and becomes embroiled in a bitter strike. *Older*.

Hudson, Jan. Sweetgrass. Tree Frog, 1984. 143 pp. $6.95 paper [0-88967-076-5].
A fifteen-year-old Blood Indian girl conquers disease, starvation, taboo, and loneliness in her struggle to achieve womanhood. *Older*.

Kogawa, Joy. Naomi's road. Ill. by Matt Gould. Oxford, 1986. 82 pp. $7.95 paper [0-19-540547-1].
Naomi is a child in kindergarten when the war forces a separation between her parents and her. In this story, based on a book for adults entitled *Obasan*, the internment of Japanese-Canadians is presented through Naomi's eyes. *Middle*.

Lottridge, Celia. The Juggler. Written from a film by Ariadne Ochrymovych. Still photography by Arne Glassbourg. North Winds, 1985. 38 pp. $11.95 hardcover [0-590-71519-4]; $4.95 paper [0-590-71520-8].

When he sneaks away to spend hours with young Barnaby the street musician and juggler, almost-blind André gains confidence and learns tricks his parents thought impossible. *Younger, middle.*

Lunn, Janet. Shadow in Hawthorn Bay. Lester & Orpen Dennys, 1986. 216 pp. $14.95 hardcover [0-88619-134-3]; $9.95 paper [0-88619-136-X].

Mary finds the land strange and frightening when she arrives in Upper Canada from Scotland in 1814. *Older, young adult.*

Martel, Suzanne. The King's daughter. Tr. by David Homel and Margaret Rose. Groundwood, 1982. 211 pp. $14.95 hardcover [0-88899-007-3]; $7.95 paper [0-88899-006-5].

Orphaned at age eight and subsequently raised in a convent school, Jeanne Chatel finds adventure, danger, and romance in New France where she journeys to live as a King's daughter – the bride of an unknown colonist. *Older, young adult.*

Reaney, James. The Boy with an R in his hand. Ill. by Leo Rampen. Porcupine's Quill, 1984 (rev.ed.). 102 pp. $7.95 paper [0-88984-059-8].

A reprinting of the 1965 edition, using the same plates, of 'a tale of the type-riot at William Lyon Mackenzie's printing office in 1826.' Excellent historical re-creation. *Older.*

Sass, Gregory. Redcoat. Ill. by Pat Foote-Jones. Porcupine's Quill, 1985. 95 pp. $7.95 paper [0-88984-083-0].

In a painful coming-of-age story, Shadrach Byfield flees his impoverished English home and finds himself caught in the War of 1812. *Young adult.*

Sharp, Edith Lambert. Nkwala. McClelland & Stewart, 1974. 125 pp. $7.95 paper [0-7710-8124-3].

A Salish Indian boy finds his totem and leads his people to a better hunting ground in this authentic and sympathetic story of Native life before the white incursion. *Middle, older.*

Smith, T.H. Cry to the night wind. Viking Kestrel, 1986. 160 pp. $12.95 hardcover [0-670-80750-8]; $4.95 paper [0-140-31931-X].

When David sails with his father to survey the western shores of Canada, he ventures from the ship and is captured by the coastal Indians. *Middle, older.*

Smucker, Barbara. Days of terror. Irwin, 1979. 156 pp. $8.95 hardcover [0-7720-1280-6]. Penguin, 1981. 152 pp. $4.50 paper [0-14-031306-0].

A Russian Mennonite family emigrates to a Western Canadian farm in the wake of the Revolution of 1917. *Older, young adult.*

Smucker, Barbara. Underground to Canada. Ill. by Tom McNeely. Irwin, 1977. 157 pp. $8.95 hardcover [0-7720-1111-7]. Penguin, 1978. 142 pp. $4.50 paper [0-14-031122-X].

Julilly and Liza escape the degradations of slavery via the Underground Railway from Mississippi to Canada before the American Civil War. *Older.*

Turner, D. Harold. To hang a rebel. Ill. by Merle Smith. Macmillan, 1977. 218 pp. $10.95 hardcover [0-7715-9368-6].

The Upper Canada Rebellion and William Lyon Mackenzie are convincingly re-created through the involvement of Doug Lachlan in the stirring events of 1837. *Older, young adult.*

Yee, Paul. The Curses of Third Uncle. Lorimer, 1986. 139 pp. $12.95 hardcover [0-88862-910-9]; $6.95 paper [0-88862-909-5].

British Columbia at the turn of the century is a dangerous place for a courageous fourteen-year-old Chinese girl determined to find her father who has mysteriously disappeared. *Older, young adult.*

FANTASY

Aubry, Claude. The Christmas wolf. Ill. by J.L. Shore. Tr. by Alice Kane. Irwin, 1983. 42 pp. $5.95 paper [0-7720-1439-6].

A starving wolf and a miracle on Christmas Eve restore our faith in humanity. Translation of *Le loup de Noël*. *Middle.*

Aubry, Claude. The King of the Thousand Islands. Ill. by Vesna Krstanovich. Tr. by Alice Kane. Irwin, 1983. 59 pp. $4.95 paper [0-7720-1441-8].

Out of boredom King Maha-Maha II does some very strange things. Translation of *Les îles du roi Maha Maha II*. *Middle.*

Bishop, Carroll Atwater. The Devil's diamond. Ill. by Anna Maria Gruda. Temenos, 1984. 36 pp. $12.95 hardcover [0-920189-00-8].

An eight-year-old princess goes on a valiant quest in an attempt to find help for her parents who have fallen under the spell of the Devil's diamond. *Middle.*

Blanchet, M. Wylie. A Whale named Henry. Ill. by Jacqueline McKay Mathews. Harbour, 1983. 46 pp. $8.95 paper [0-920080-33-2].

Humour and suspense are used to tell the story of Henry, a thirty-foot killer whale who impulsively swims into Sechelt Inlet. Illustrated with black and white line drawings and useful maps. *Middle.*

Bradford, Karleen. The Other Elizabeth. Ill. by Deborah Drew-Brook. Gage, 1982. 160 pp. $2.95 paper [0-7715-7004-X].

Strangely drawn to Cook's Tavern during her class visit to Upper Canada Village, Elizabeth slips back in time to 1813 and finds herself embroiled in the conflicts of the day. *Middle.*

Bradford, Karleen. The Stone in the meadow. Ill. by Greg Ruhl. Gage, 1984. 157 pp. $2.95 paper [0-7715-7014-7].
When visiting a family in Cornwall, Jennifer kindles inexplicable ties with Druid times. It all begins with the feeling of foreboding she has when she discovers the megalith in the meadow. *Middle.*

Clark, Joan. The Moons of Madeleine. Viking Kestrel, 1987. 221 pp. $12.95 hardcover [0-670-81284-6].
Madeleine must guard the Sacred Stones and meet First Woman before she can cross the boundary from childhood to womanhood. A companion to *Wild man of the woods. Older.*

Day, David. The Emperor's panda. Ill. by Eric Beddows. McClelland & Stewart, 1986. 112 pp. $14.95 hardcover [0-7710-2573-4].
Kung, a shepherd boy who lives during the time of China's ancient Celestial Empire, sets off on a heroic quest and meets many magical creatures. *Older.*

Dragland, Stan. Simon Jesse's journey. Groundwood, 1983. 120 pp. $6.95 paper [0-88899-025-1].
After Simon Jesse is drawn underground through the drain in his bathtub, he learns that his task is to lead the Horn People out of their dark captivity. *Middle.*

Duncan, Frances. The Toothpaste genie. Scholastic-TAB, 1981. 134 pp. $2.95 paper [0-590-71090-7].
Amanda finds an amazing purple genie in her new tube of toothpaste, a genie who is embarking on his first wish-granting mission. The results are at once hilarious and disastrous. *Middle.*

Gaetz, Dayle. Grandfather Heron finds a friend. Ill. by Anna Mah. Porcépic, 1986. 40 pp. $4.95 paper [0-88878-260-8].
Grandfather Heron and his new friend Grandmother Heron find a new way to catch fish when the water becomes too cold for their old legs. *Younger.*

Hall, Pamela. On the edge of the eastern ocean. Ill. by Pamela Hall. GLC, 1982. $12.95 hardcover [0-88874-055-7]; $7.95 paper [0-88774-056-5].
Separated from his family and Nation when they are attacked by a common enemy, the young puffin comes of age in unusual surroundings. His young wanderings and the tales he shares earn him special status when he returns home. *Middle.*

Harris, Christie. Sky man on the totem pole? McClelland & Stewart, 1975. 167 pp. $13.95 hardcover [0-7710-4027-X].
Fantasy combining West Coast Indians and space men who visit earth to find the secret of ecological balance. *Older.*

Hughes, Monica. Sandwriter. Methuen, 1986. 160 pp. $12.95 hardcover [0-458-80250-6]. Magnet, 1987. $3.95 paper [0-416-95520-7].
Although Antia has betrayed the kingdom of Roshan, Sandwriter still entrusts to her its secret and its future. *Older, young adult.*

Hughes, Monica. Space trap. Groundwood, 1984. 153 pp. $6.95 paper [0-88899-018-9].
Three children become captives of an alien civilization in this story that is set in the thirty-second century. *Older.*

Hutchins, Hazel J. Anastasia Morningstar and the crystal butterfly. Ill. by Barry Trower. Annick, 1984. 64 pp. $6.95 hardcover [0-920236-94-4]; $3.95 paper [0-920236-95-2].
When Sarah sees Anna turn Derek Henshaw into a frog, she is convinced that she has the ingredients for the best and most amazing science project. *Middle.*

Hutchins, Hazel J. The Three and many wishes of Jason Reid. Ill. by John Richmond. Annick, 1983. 63 pp. $6.95 hardcover [0-920236-60-X]; $3.95 paper [0-920236-61-8].
No eleven-year-old has considered more thoughtfully the use of wishes granted to him by the fairy world. *Middle.*

Johnston, Simon. A Song for Harmonica. Ill. by VictoR GAD. Three Trees, 1985. 40 pp. $11.95 hardcover [0-88823-107-5]; $4.95 paper [0-88823-105-9].
After helping Maestro Musico learn to write beautiful music, Harmonica earns her angel's wings. *Younger.*

Katz, Welwyn. False face. Groundwood, 1987. 160 pp. $12.95 hardcover [0-88899-063-4].
When Laney accidentally unearths an ancient miniature Indian mask in a nearby bog, she unwittingly releases forces that compel and threaten herself and others. *Older.*

Katz, Welwyn. The Prophecy of Tau Ridoo. Ill. by Michelle Desbarats. Tree Frog, 1982. 175 pp. $6.95 paper [0-88967-045-5].
When Jamie's toys mysteriously disappear one night after another, the Aubrey children realize that they too are part of the conflict between darkness and light. *Middle.*

Katz, Welwyn. Sun god, moon witch. Groundwood, 1986. 176 pp. $7.95 paper [0-88899-041-3].

Thorny spends the summer in a quiet English village and finds herself caught in a struggle between the powers of dark and the powers of light. *Older.*

Katz, Welwyn. Witchery Hill. Groundwood, 1984. 192 pp. $7.95 paper [0-88899-031-6].
Mike's summer holiday becomes a terrifying encounter with evil forces on the island of Guernsey. *Older.*

Kushner, Donn. A Book dragon. Macmillan, 1987. 224 pp. $16.95 hardcover [0-7715-9515-8].
A dragon shrinks to the size of an insect and, for five hundred years, guards a book in which a brother has painted his picture in the margins until a new challenge is presented to him by a ruthless developer. *Older.*

Kushner, Donn. Uncle Jacob's ghost story. Macmillan, 1984. 132 pp. $14.95 hardcover [0-7715-9806-8].
Lively and curious Uncle Jacob, who can find reason in most experience, is baffled by the sudden instances of make-believe and the frequent ghostly appearances he encounters in his home in the New World. A family tale that evokes both pride and uncertainty through the generations. *Middle.*

Kushner, Donn. The Violin maker's gift. Ill. by Doug Panton. Macmillan, 1980. 74 pp. $10.95 hardcover [0-7715-9735-5].
In a style reminiscent of the traditional tales, the author recounts the story of a violin maker who rescues an extraordinary bird and, in return, receives a rare gift. *Middle, older.*

Laurence, Margaret. Jason's quest. Ill. by Leslie Morrill. Seal, 1981. 211 pp. $2.95 paper [0-7704-1647-0].
A young mole accompanied by an owl and two cats seeks a cure for the wearying invisible sickness suffered by the inhabitants of Molanium. *Middle, older.*

Laurence, Margaret. The Olden days coat. Ill. by Muriel Wood. McClelland & Stewart, 1982 (rev.ed.). 35 pp. $13.95 hardcover [0-7710-4742-8].
Sal puts on the olden days coat she finds in her grandmother's trunk and suddenly she finds herself sixty years back in time. Sympathetic illustrations in full colour. *Middle.*

Lunn, Janet. The Root cellar. Lester & Orpen Dennys, 1981. 247 pp. $7.95 paper [0-919630-78-2]. Penguin, 1983. 250 pp. $3.95 paper [0-14-0316159].
Through the root cellar, Rose moves between present and past. The historical portions of this time travel fantasy are well-researched and have an exciting immediacy. *Older.*

McNeil, Florence. All kinds of magic. Groundwood, 1984. 155 pp. $6.95 paper [0-88899-035-9].
A summer holiday becomes an adventure when Gen meets an old lady who thinks that she's a ghost. *Older.*

Melling, O.R. The Druid's tune. Viking Kestrel, 1983. 235 pp. $17.95 hardcover [0-7226-5916-4]; $4.95 paper [0-14-031835-6].
Canadian teenagers, Rosemary and Jimmy, gain sensitivity and understanding as they travel through time to ancient Celtic Ireland. *Young adult.*

Melling, O.R. The Singing stone. Viking Kestrel, 1986. 206 pp. $16.95 hardcover [0-670-80817-2].
Having had the same dream again and again – the dream that rouses visions of mountain peaks, stormy skies, the woman with the long red hair, and the singing stone – Kay Warwick sets off for Ireland to unravel the mystery of the recurring symbols and her existence. *Older, young adult.*

Menotti, Gian Carlo. Amahl and the night visitors. Ill. by Michèle Lemieux. Morrow, 1986. 64 pp. $25.50 hardcover [0-688-05426-9].
A Christmas classic that has been illustrated with glowing watercolours by a Quebec artist. *Middle.*

Nichols, Ruth. The Marrow of the world. Ill. by Trina Schart Hyman. Gage, 1977. 168 pp. $4.75 paper [0-7715-1663-0].
Philip and Linda are drawn into a dramatic struggle for survival in the strange world under Georgian Bay waters. An award-winning quest fantasy. *Middle, older.*

Nichols, Ruth. A Walk out of the world. Harcourt Brace Jovanovich, 1969. 192 pp. $9.95 hardcover [0-7747-0110-2].
Judith and Tobit plunge through time into another world threatened by an evil sorcerer. *Middle, older.*

Nyberg, Morgan. Galahad Schwartz and the Cockroach Army. Groundwood, 1987. 96 pp. $6.95 paper [0-88899-037-5].
A zany story about Galahad who leaves his home in the jungle to settle with Grampa Schwartz in the corrupt city of Glitterville. *Middle.*

Pasnak, William. In the city of the king. Groundwood, 1984. 144 pp. $7.95 paper [0-88899-027-8].
Elena defies the evil powers that threaten the kingdom and saves the life of the king. *Older.*

Pearson, Kit. A Handful of time. Viking Kestrel, 1987. 186 pp. $14.95 hardcover [0-670-81532-2].

Sent alone to spend the summer with an aunt, uncle, and cousins whom she doesn't know, Patricia is quite happy to hide out in the guest cabin where she discovers an old watch that enables her to travel back in time. *Middle, older.*

Piper, Eileen. The Magician's trap. Ill. by Alan Daniel. Scholastic-TAB, 1976. 59 pp. $3.95 paper [0-590-71445-7].
A prince, under the spell of a wicked magician, is saved by a blind girl. Strikingly illustrated. *Middle.*

Plant, Maria R. Robin and the rainbow. Ill. by Veronika Martenova Charles. Three Trees, 1985. 56 pp. $12.95 hardcover [0-88823-095-8]; $4.95 paper [0-88823-096-6].
Robin jumps on a magical merry-go-round in the schoolyard and re-unites her family. *Middle.*

Richler, Mordecai. Jacob Two-Two and the dinosaur. Ill. by Norman Eyolfson. McClelland & Stewart, 1987. 85 pp. $14.95 hardcover [0-394-88704-2].
When everyone realizes that Jacob's pet lizard, Dippy, is really a dinosaur, Jacob and Dippy must run away. Sequel to *Jacob Two-Two meets the Hooded Fang. Middle.*

Richler, Mordecai. Jacob Two-Two meets the Hooded Fang. Ill. by Fritz Wegner. McClelland & Stewart, 1975. 84 pp. $12.95 hardcover [0-7710-7282-4]. Seal, 1981. $2.95 paper [0-7704-2109-1].
Fantastical adventures of a boy too young, too little, too misunderstood. *Middle, older.*

Smucker, Barbara. White mist. Irwin, 1985. 159 pp. $9.95 paper [0-7725-1542-5]. Penguin, 1986. $4.95 paper [0-14-032144-6].
A time-slip fantasy in which May Appleby comes to terms with her Indian heritage. *Middle, older.*

Sullivan, Nick. The Seventh princess. Scholastic-TAB, 1983. 107 pp. $2.95 paper [0-590-71282-9].
Jennifer is transported in a horse-drawn carriage to the kingdom of Eladeria where, with the help of an enchanted dwarf and the magical Paladian school, she confronts the evil sorceress Swenhill. *Middle.*

Taylor, Barbara. The Man who stole dreams. Ill. by Judie Shore. Women's, 1983. 45 pp. $5.95 paper [0-88961-082-7].
Sara and Tony help the people recover their lost dreams. *Middle.*

Troendle, Yves. Raven's children. Ill. by Raymond Verdaguer. Oolichan, 1979. 211 pp. $12.95 hardcover [0-88982-019-8]; $8.95 paper [0-88982-020-1].
Using the traditional tales of the Tsimshian Indians, the author has created an epic about two Indian children. Includes the Raven stories. *Older.*

Walsh, Ann. Your time, my time. Porcépic, 1984. 156 pp. $16.95 hardcover [0-88878-220-9]; $6.95 paper [0-88878-219-5].
The gold ring she finds in the Barkerville cemetery becomes Elizabeth's escape to an earlier time and place where she is well-loved although not always fully understood. *Older, young adult.*

SCIENCE FICTION

Baltensperger, Peter. Guardians of time. Three Trees, 1984. 109 pp. $12.95 hardcover [0-88823-084-2]; $4.95 paper [0-88823-082-6].
In the year 2263, Finnegan Turpin is banished from the computerized Earth because he thinks and dreams. *Older.*

Godfrey, Martyn. Alien war games. Scholastic-TAB, 1984. 142 pp. $2.95 paper [0-590-71224-1].
A futuristic story that explores the clash between a highly-developed imperialistic human culture and the resourceful Diljug. *Older.*

Godfrey, Martyn. The Vandarian incident. Scholastic-TAB, 1981. 106 pp. $3.50 paper [0-590-71080-X].
When their academy is destroyed by a Vandarian warship, two space cadets must survive on a hostile planet to rescue the galaxy leaders who are en route to a peace conference. *Older.*

Hill, Douglas. The Huntsman. Macmillan, 1982. 144 pp. $15.95 hardcover [0-689-5024-0]. Piccolo, 1984. 144 pp. $3.95 paper [0-330-26956-9].
Finn Ferral, who has an exceptional knowledge of the wilderness, sets off on a quest to rescue his foster father and his sister. *Older.*

Hill, Douglas. Warriors of the wasteland. Macmillan, 1983. 144 pp. $13.95 hardcover [0-689-50222-2]. Piccolo, 1984. 128 pp. $3.95 paper [0-330-28452-5].
Finn Ferral and his Bloodkin companion, Baer, continue their search for Jena, Finn's sister, who was captured by aliens. Sequel to *The Huntsman. Older.*

Hughes, Monica. Beckoning lights. Ill. by Richard A. Conroy. LeBel, 1982. 79 pp. $8.95 hardcover [0-920008-23-2].
During a wilderness trip in the Canadian Rockies, telepathic twins Jack and Julia uncover the mystery of the strange lights and Julia undertakes a mission for the aliens. *Middle, older.*

Hughes, Monica. Crisis on Conshelf Ten. Collins, 1975. 192 pp. $9.95 hardcover [0-241-89211-2]. Magnet, 1985. 144 pp. $3.95 paper [0-416-89990-0].

The first child born on the moon, Kepler Masterman, journeys to Earth with his father, the moon's governor, but cannot adjust to Earth's gravity and lives in an undersea lab with friends. *Older, young adult.*

Hughes, Monica. Devil on my back. Atheneum, 1985. 170 pp. $14.95 hardcover [0-689-31095-1]. Magnet, 1985. 176 pp. $3.95 paper [0-458-80240-9].

Lord Tomi makes many enlightening discoveries about the world and its inhabitants when he suddenly finds himself outside Arc One, the computer-controlled society. *Young adult.*

Hughes, Monica. The Dream catcher. Methuen, 1986. 171 pp. $14.95 hardcover [0-458-80720-6]; $3.95 paper [0-416-95520-7].

In a sequel to *Devil on my back,* Ruth and a few companions venture from their psychic society of Arc Three and attempt to make contact with the inhabitants of Arc One. *Young adult.*

Hughes, Monica. Earthdark. Magnet, 1981. 128 pp. $3.95 paper [0-416-21070-8].

In this sequel to *Crisis on Conshelf Ten* Kepler Masterman returns to the moon and rebels against its rigid lifestyle by leaving the base for a forbidden ride on the lunar surface with dire results. *Older, young adult.*

Hughes, Monica. The Guardian of Isis. Collins, 1981. 140 pp. $14.95 hardcover [0-241-10597-8]. Magnet, 1982. $3.95 paper [0-416-24570-6].

In the year 2136 A.D., the settlement of Isis has returned to a primitive state. Jody N'Komo searches for the Guardian to learn the secrets of the past. A sequel to *Keeper of the Isis light. Older, Young Adult.*

Hughes, Monica. The Isis peddlar. Collins, 1982. 121 pp. $14.95 hardcover [0-241-10834-9]. Magnet, 1981. 128 pp. $3.95 paper [0-416-44650-7].

In the final book in the Isis trilogy, scoundrel Mike O'Flynn nearly destroys the community with greed and violence. *Older, young adult.*

Hughes, Monica. Keeper of the Isis light. Collins, 1980. 136 pp. $12.95 hardcover [0-241-10405-X]. Magnet, 1981. 144 pp. $3.95 paper [0-416-21030-9].

After living together on the planet of Isis for sixteen years, Olwen learns that the Guardian has irrevocably altered her appearance to ensure her survival. *Older, young adult.*

Hughes, Monica. Ring-rise, ring-set. Julia Macrae, 1982. 130 pp. $19.83 hardcover [0-86203-069-2]. Magnet, 1983. 129 pp. $3.95 paper [0-416-22930-1].

Liza deliberately leaves the City on the Hill, where scientists are searching for a solution to the impending Ice Age that appears to threaten Earth, and embarks on a cross-cultural struggle for survival. *Young adult.*

Hughes, Monica. The Tomorrow city. Collins, 1978. 137 pp. $15.95 hardcover [0-241-89887-0]. Magnet, 1982. 137 pp. $3.95 paper [0-416-22420-2].

Caro and David attempt to free the city from the control of C-Three, a computer that has become too powerful. *Young adult.*

Martel, Suzanne. The City under ground. Tr. by Norah Smaridge. Groundwood, 1982. 157 pp. $6.95 paper [0-88899-019-7].

A novel that explores the tenuous link of the enclosed highly-regulated city of here and now with the natural world of 'beforetime.' Translation of *Surreal 3000. Middle.*

Martel, Suzanne. Robot alert. Tr. by Patricia Sillers. Kids Can, 1985. 189 pp. $9.95 hardcover [0-919964-82-6].

The robots that belong to Adam and Eve are much more than the toys they seem. They are ambassadors from an alien world, positioned on earth to avert an intergalactic war. Love, friendship, and obedience are all themes in this science fiction novel. Translation of *Nos amis robots. Middle, older.*

Matas, Carol. The Fusion factor. Fifth, 1986. 117 pp. $3.95 paper [0-920079-25-3].

The nightmare of a kidnapping, time travel to a bleak future, developing friendships, and the loving support that can emanate from family come together in this contemporary novel. *Middle.*

SHORT STORY COLLECTIONS

Cummings, Tom. Gopher Hills. Western Producer Prairie, 1983. 110 pp. $9.95 paper [0-88833-109-9].

The author uses people and incidents from his own past to create the town of Gopher Hills, a prairie town in the year of 1914. *Older, young adult.*

Sawicki, Leo. Anytime stories. Ill. by Michael Robinson. Penumbra, 1986. $7.95 paper [0-920806-78-3].

Short short stories, reminiscent of traditional Indian tales, each followed by a list of questions and a project. *Middle.*

Shivers in your nightshirt: eerie stories to read in bed. Ill. by Kathy Kaulbach. Children's Writers' Workshop, 1986. 106 pp. $5.95 paper [0-9692342-1-X].

Tingling but not terrifying stories of uncanny situations created by members of the Childrens' Writers' Workshop, Halifax. *Middle.*

Whitaker, Muriel, ed. Great Canadian animal stories. Ill. by Vlasta Van Kampen. Hurtig, 1982. 232 pp. $9.95 paper [0-88830-231-2].

Seton and Roberts initiated a new literary genre, the animal biography. Included here are sixteen stories representative of Canada's best, beautifully illustrated. *Older.*

Whitaker, Muriel, ed. The Princess, the hockey player, magic and ghosts: Canadian stories for children. Ill. by Vlasta Van Kampen. Hurtig, 1980. 158 pp. $5.95 hardcover [0-88830-194-4].

Many well-loved authors are represented in this collection of fourteen short stories ranging from fantasy to adventure and realism. *Older.*

Whitaker, Muriel, ed. Stories from the Canadian North. Ill. by Vlasta Van Kampen. Hurtig, 1980. 191 pp. $12.95 hardcover [0-88830-188-X].

This collection of stories by renowned authors celebrates the Canadian North. *Older.*

GEOGRAPHY AND TRAVEL

DESCRIPTION AND TRAVEL

see also
PUBLISHERS' SERIES
The Canada Series
Canadian Rainbow Series – Cities
Canadian Rainbow Series – Provinces

Bruemmer, Fred. Children of the North. Ill. by Fred Bruemmer. Optimum, 1979. 159 pp. $16.95 hardcover [0-88890-095-3].

Through observations and photographs gathered during travels in the Canadian North, the author-photographer presents a view of northern children: their birth, growth, and aspirations. *Older, young adult.*

Clery, Val. Canada in colour. Ill. by Bill Brooks. Hounslow, 1972. 77 pp. $17.95 hardcover [0-88882-000-3]; $9.95 paper [0-88882-008-9].

Photographs of Canada, the vast and beautiful country, linked by a brief text. *All ages.*

Clery, Val, ed. Seasons of Canada. Ill. by Bill Brooks. Hounslow, 1979. 96 pp. $17.95 hardcover [0-88882-041-0].

Short introductions to a visual feast of the seasons across Canada. *All ages.*

Dommasch, Hans. Prairie giants. Western Producer Prairie, 1986. 127 pp. $29.95 hardcover [0-88833-196-7].

A photographic survey of the prairie grain elevator. *Young adult.*

Evans, Millie and **Mullen, Eric.** Nova Scotia's Oak Island: the world's greatest treasure hunt. Four East, 1984. 64 pp. $6.95 paper [0-920427-01-4].

A summary of the treasure hunt that has lasted two hundred years on Oak Island, site of the 'Money Pit.' *Older.*

Haegert, Dorothy. Children of the first people. Arsenal Pulp, 1983. 128 pp. $18.95 paper [0-88978-145-1].
Black and white photographs of native Indian children are interspersed with the recollections of ten West Coast elders. A perceptive juxtaposition of old and new ways. *Older, young adult.*

Harrison, Ted. Children of the Yukon. Ill. by Ted Harrison. Tundra, 1984. 24 pp. $11.95 hardcover [0-88776-092-9].
Captivating captioned paintings of Yukon scenes that reveal the unique lives of northern children. *Middle.*

Hattori, Gene. Saskatchewan: the colour of a province. Western Producer Prairie, 1987. 62 pp. $12.95 hardcover [0-88833-227-0]; $9.95 paper [0-88833-228-9].
A slim volume of forty photographs that capture the personality and perspective of Saskatchewan, past and present. *All ages.*

Lim, John. Merchants of the mysterious East. Ill. by John Lim. Tundra, 1981. 32 pp. $6.95 hardcover [0-88776-130-5].
Storytellers, frog vendors, spice grinders, and kite shops all emerge through the personalized text and striking illustrations of Singapore. *Younger, middle.*

Macdonald, R.H. Four seasons west. Western Producer Prairie, 1975. 116 pp. $33.00 hardcover [0-919306-55-1].
'A photographic odyssey of the three Prairie Provinces.' *All ages.*

MacLennan, Hugh. Seven rivers of Canada. Macmillan, 1978. 170 pp. $5.95 paper [0-7705-1562-2].
Historical, geographical, and personal descriptions of seven great Canadian rivers. *Older, young adult.*

Russell, Andy. The Rockies. Hurtig, 1975. 160 pp. $24.95 hardcover [0-88830-094-8].
Vibrant colour photographs and a lyrical text celebrate the natural beauty of the Rockies. *Older.*

Steltzer, Ulli. Building an igloo. Ill. by Ulli Steltzer. Douglas & McIntyre, 1981. 32 pp. $10.95 hardcover [0-88894-325-3].

A brief text supported by black and white photographs describe the steps involved in constructing an igloo. *Younger, middle.*

Tanobe, Miyuki. Québec je t'aime/I love you. Ill. by Miyuki Tanobe. Tundra, 1984. 48 pp. $9.95 hardcover [0-88776-072-4]; $2.95 paper [0-88776-156-9].
'A Japanese artist's hymn to Quebec in painting and descriptive prose.' Bilingual text complements twenty-two beautiful full-colour paintings. *Middle.*

MAPS

Atlas of Canada. Reader's Digest, 1981. 220 pp. $29.95 hardcover [0-88850-096-3].
This atlas is divided in four parts: thematic pages, facts about Canada, maps of Canada, and the Gazetteer Index to the maps. *Middle to young adult.*

Harris, R. Cole, ed. Historical atlas of Canada. Volume 1. From the beginning to 1800. Univ. of Toronto, 1987. 204 pp. $95.00 hardcover [0-8020-2495-5].

Kemball, Walter G. Canadian Oxford intermediate atlas. Oxford, 1984. 93 pp. $9.50 paper [0-19-540459-9].
Thematic, historical, topographical, and political maps of Canada and the world. *Older, young adult.*

Kemball, Walter G., ed. The New Canadian Oxford atlas. Illustrated. Oxford, 1985 (rev.ed.). 183 pp. $11.95 paper [0-19-540486-6].
Handsome maps of Canada and the world. Contains statistics and thematic and topographical maps of continents and regions. *Middle to young adult.*

Kerr, D.G.G. Historical atlas of Canada. Nelson, 1975. 3rd rev.ed. 100 pp. $22.95 hardcover [0-17-600409-2]; $13.70 paper [0-17-600408-4].

Matthews, Geoffrey and **Morrow, Robert, Jr.** Canada and the world: an atlas resource. Prentice, 1985. 201 pp. $29.95 hardcover [0-13-113846-4] (trade ed.); $19.95 hardcover [0-13-113986-X] (school ed.).
Current, accurate, and detailed information on a wide range of topics (exploration, climate, industry, transportation, and others). Also provides coverage of the world. Full-colour maps. *Middle to young adult.*

BIOGRAPHY

see also
PUBLISHERS' SERIES
Canadian Pathfinder Series
The Canadians
Canadians All Series
Picture Life Series
Profiles in Canadian Literature

Armstrong, Audrey L. The Blacksmith of Fallbrook: the story of Walter Cameron – blacksmith, woodcarver, raconteur. Musson, 1979. 96 pp. $6.95 paper [0-7737-1050-2].

An octogenarian blacksmith recalls village life as it centred on his blacksmith shop. Oral history for older and mature readers. *Older, young adult.*

Barker, George. Forty years a chief. Ill. by Judith Anne Rempel. Peguis, 1979. 102 pp. $10.00 hardcover [0-919566-68-5].

An exemplary native chief won the franchise for his people, helped to get registered traplines in Manitoba, and helped to organize the Manitoba Indian Brotherhood. *Older.*

Barkhouse, Joyce. A Name for himself: a biography of Thomas Head Raddall. Irwin, 1986. 87 pp. $5.95 paper [0-7725-1566-2].

The life of one of Canada's distinguished but little known authors is presented in an interesting, readable style. Interspersed with photographs and excerpts from Raddall's diary. *Older.*

Blakely, Phyllis Ruth. Nova Scotia's two remarkable giants. Lancelot, 1970. 48 pp. $2.00 paper [0-88999-002-6].

An amusing and informative account of Anna Swan and Angus McAskill who toured the world in circuses. *Older.*

Brooks, Martha. A Hill for looking. Ill. by Beverly Dancho. Prints by Dr. A.L. Paine. Queenston, 1982. 195 pp. $14.95 hardcover [0-919866-78-6]; $7.95 paper [0-919866-79-4].

In this heart-warming story, the author tells about her life as a ten-year-old who lived at a sanatorium in rural Manitoba where her father was a doctor and her mother was a nurse. *Middle, older.*

Campbell, Maria. Halfbreed. Goodread Biographies, 1983. 157 pp. $4.95 paper [0-88780-116-1].

A half-white half-Indian girl lives in poverty and degradation and overcomes them to tell her story. *Older, young adult.*

Carr, Emily. The Book of Small. Irwin, 1986. . 168 pp. $4.95 paper [0-7725-1613-8].

One of Canada's foremost painters writes about her childhood in Victoria, British Columbia. *Older.*

Caswell, Maryanne. Pioneer girl. McGraw, 1979. 124 pp. $9.95 paper [0-07-082969-1].

The lively letters of a fourteen-year-old to her grandmother evoke pioneer experience in Saskatchewan in 1885. *Older.*

Collins, Robert. Butter down the well: reflections of a Canadian childhood. Western Producer Prairie, 1980. 149 pp. $7.95 paper [0-88833-130-4].

Collins recounts rib-tickling, heart-warming, and candid memories of his childhood on a homestead in southern Saskatchewan during the years of the Depression and Second World War. *Older, young adult.*

Dempsey, Hugh A. The Gentle persuader: a biography of James Gladstone, Indian senator. Western Producer Prairie, 1986. 225 pp. $14.95 paper [0-88833-208-4].

A sensitive biography of the first treaty Indian to be appointed to the Senate of Canada, written by his son-in-law. *Young adult.*

Endicott, Marion. Emily Carr: the story of an artist. Women's, 1981. 64 pp. $9.95 paper [0-88961-070-3].

Carr's childhood, education, experiences as an art teacher and landlady, and later years as a recognized artist are briefly discussed. Her feelings of isolation and loneliness are adeptly expressed. *Middle.*

Fardy, B.D. Jerry Potts: Paladin of the plains. Sunfire, 1984. 144 pp. $5.95 paper [0-919531-18-0].

During the last half of the nineteenth century, Metis Jerry Potts served as scout, guide, and interpreter to Canadian Indians, settlers, and Mounted police. *Young adult.*

Ford, Karen; MacLean, Janet and **Wansbrough, Michael B.** Great Canadian lives: portraits in heroism to 1867. Nelson, 1985. 280 pp. V.1. $24.95 hardcover [0-17-602027-6].

An attractive approach to Canadian history with single page entries on explorers and other historical figures. *Younger, middle.*

Forrest, Diane. The Adventurers: ordinary people with special callings. Ill. by Phil Clark. Wood Lake, 1983. 127 pp. $7.95 paper [0-919599-10-9].

Brief biographical sketches of ten ordinary men and women whose Christian beliefs led to a life of adventure and service to humanity. *Middle, older.*

French, Alice. My name is Masak. Peguis, 1976. 110 pp. $5.00 paper [0-919566-56-1].

An Eskimo girl growing up in the north before World War II is influenced by the Inuit and white societies which divide her loyalties. *Older, young adult.*

Gaitskell, Susan. Emily. Ill. by Kellie Jobson. Three Trees, 1986. 24 pp. $12.95 hardcover [0-88823-118-0]; $5.95 paper [0-88823-120-2].

A fictionalized biography of Emily Carr as a child. *Younger.*

Grey Owl (pseud.). Pilgrims of the wild. Penguin, 1982. 282 pp. $3.95 paper [0-14-005628-9].

A wilderness autobiography by the Englishman who would be an Indian. *Young adult.*

Gross, George. Donald Jackson, king of the blades. Queen City, 1977. 156 pp. $10.00 hardcover [0-9690508-1-X].

The hard work and sacrifice required to become a champion are seen in the life of this dynamic figure skater. *Older.*

Hacker, Carlotta. The Indomitable lady doctors. Goodread Biographies, 1984. 259 pp. $5.95 paper [0-88780-129-3].

A lively account of Canada's pioneer medical women. *Young adult.*

Hancock, Lyn and **Dowler, Marion.** Tell me, grandmother. Ill. by Douglas Tait. McClelland & Stewart, 1985. 147 pp. $9.95 paper [0-7710-3809-7].

Young Dennis Dowler loved hearing the stories that his grandmother, Jane Howse Livingston, told about her life as early Alberta pioneer and wife of trader Sam Livingston. *Middle, older.*

Hanson, Christilot. Canadian entry. Irwin, 1966. 140 pp. $3.25 paper [0-7720-0519-2].

An inspiring autobiography of Canada's Olympic dressage champion. *Older.*

Heaps, Leo. A Boy called Nam: the true story of how one little boy came to Canada. Macmillan, 1984. 95 pp. $14.95 hardcover [0-7715-9799-1].

An account of a ten-year-old Vietnamese boy's journey from Vietnam to Macao to Canada. *Older.*

Henderson, Gordon. Sandy Mackenzie, why look so glum? Ill. by Pik. Deneau, 1979. 30 pp. $6.95 paper [0-88879-042-2].

Lear-like whimsical verses and matching humorous drawings sketch memorable profiles of our prime ministers from John A. to Joe Who. *Older.*

Hill, Kay. Joe Howe: the man who was Nova Scotia. McClelland & Stewart, 1980. 221 pp. $12.95 hardcover [0-7710-4096-2].

A fearless young newspaper editor became a champion of the ordinary people and represented them in the legislature throughout a stormy and distinguished career. *Older, young adult.*

Johnston, Jean. Wilderness women: Canada's forgotten history. Irwin, 1973. 241 pp. $5.95 paper [0-88778-127-6].

About eight little-known women who followed the men who settled Canada and contributed to their country's development. *Young adult.*

Kurelek, William. Lumberjack. Ill. by William Kurelek. Tundra, 1974. 41 pp. $17.95 hardcover [0-88776-052-X]; $5.95 paper [0-88776-082-1].

A strong, healthy eighteen-year-old spends the summer in Northern Ontario's logging camps; then his older self recalls it vividly in words and pictures. *Older.*

Kurelek, William. A Prairie boy's summer. Ill. by William Kurelek. Tundra, 1984. 48 pp. $14.95 hardcover [0-88776-058-9]; $7.95 paper [0-88776-116-X].

A companion volume to *A Prairie boy's winter* that evokes the Thirties on the prairies. *Middle.*

Kurelek, William. A Prairie boy's winter. Ill. by William Kurekek. Tundra, 1984. 40 pp. $14.95 hardcover [0-88776-022-8]; $7.95 paper [0-88776-102-X].

A realist painter recalls his Western chidhood in evocative captions and paintings that capture the artist's view of himself as a young boy. *Middle.*

Lim, John. At grandmother's house. Ill. by John Lim. Tundra, 1984. 32 pp. $9.95 hardcover [0-88776-089-9]; $2.95 paper [0-88776-157-7].

Stylized, delicate drawings and vivid reminiscences of childhood in Singapore and especially at grandmother's house. *Older.*

Lim, Sing. West coast Chinese boy. Ill. by Sing Lim. Tundra, 1979. 64 pp. $6.95 hardcover [0-88776-121-6].

Vancouver's Chinatown in the 1920s provided the ideal environment for children to grow unhampered. Appropriate monotypes, humorous sketches, nostalgic vignettes. *Older, young adult.*

MacEwan, Grant. Marie Anne: the frontier adventures of Marie Anne Lagimodière. Western Producer Prairie, 1984. 246 pp. $13.95 paper [0-88833-138-X].

A fictionalized biography of Marie Anne Lagimodière, the first white woman to settle in the Northwest and the grandmother of Louis Riel. *Older, young adult.*

McKenzie, Ruth. Laura Secord: the lady and the legend. McClelland & Stewart, 1971. 136 pp. $9.95 paper [0-7710-5800-4].

The well-known legend about Laura Secord and a cow is shown to be false, but her place as a heroine is upheld. *Middle.*

Maynard, Fredelle Bruser. Raisins and almonds. Penguin, 1985. 201 pp. $6.95 paper [0-14-008078-3].

A heart-warming story about growing up in a Jewish family on the Canadian prairies through the hungry Thirties. *Young adult.*

Melady, John. Cross of Valour. Scholastic-TAB, 1985. 149 pp. $2.95 paper [0-590-71510-0].

Fourteen Canadians have been awarded the Cross of Valour for acts of the most conspicuous courage in circumstances of extreme peril. The events leading to these awards are retold here. *Older, young adult.*

Montgomery, Lucy M. The Alpine path: the story of my career. Fitzhenry & Whiteside, 1984. 96 pp. $9.95 hardcover [0-88902-019-1].

Anne of Green Gables's author writes a light-hearted but sincere account of her early years. *Young adult.*

Ondaatje, Christopher. The Prime ministers of Canada: Macdonald to Mulroney. Pagurian, 1985. 206 pp. $19.95 hardcover [0-88932-117-5]; $9.95 paper [0-88932-125-6].

Life and times of the Prime Ministers from the first to the present day. *Older.*

Pitseolak, Peter. Peter Pitseolak's escape from death. Ill. by Peter Pitseolak. Tr. by Dorothy Eber. McClelland & Stewart, 1977. 47 pp. $9.95 paper [0-7710-3030-4].

Realistic drawings and direct narrative detail a brush with death on an ice pan drifting away from the Cape Dorset shore into the Hudson Straits. *Older.*

Redsky, James. Great leader of the Ojibway: Mis-Quona-Queb. McClelland & Stewart, 1972. 127 pp. $8.95 paper [0-7710-7421-2].

Biography of a great chief based on the oral tradition of his people. *Older.*

Robinson, Helen Caister. Joseph Brant: a man for his people. Academic, 1971. 178 pp. $8.95 hardcover [0-7747-0052-1].

Famous Indian leader, war chief of the Iroquois, and a captain in the British army during the American Revolution. *Older, young adult.*

Robinson, Helen Caister. Mistress Molly, the brown lady: a portrait of Molly Brant. Dundurn, 1980. 159 pp. $16.50 hardcover [0-919670-47-4].

Based on research and documentation, this fictionalized biography tells the story of the Head of the Society of the Six Nations Matrons. *Older, young adult.*

Savage, Candace. Our Nell: a scrapbook biography of Nellie L. McClung. Western Producer Prairie, 1979. 253 pp. $12.95 paper [0-88833-033-2].

'A scrapbook biography of Nellie L. McClung, perhaps the most celebrated and controversial woman in Canadian public life': politician, author and feminist reformer, 1873-1951. *Older, young adult.*

Scrivener, Leslie. Terry Fox: his story. McClelland & Stewart, 1981. 176 pp. $14.95 hardcover [0-7710-8017-4]; $6.95 paper [0-7710-8018-2].

A biography of cancer-victim Terry Fox who ran two-thirds of the way across Canada to raise money for cancer research. *Young adult.*

Takashima, Shizuye. A Child in prison camp. Ill. by Shizuye Takashima. Tundra, 1971. 75 pp. $14.95 hardcover [0-688-30113-4]; $5.95 paper [0-88776-074-0].

With sensitivity and no rancour the artist recalls her childhood in a World War II prison camp in the Canadian Rockies. *Middle, older.*

Tetso, John. Trapping is my life. Irwin, 1970. 116 pp. $4.95 paper [0-88778-153-5].

A Slavey Indian trapper reflects on his life along the traplines near Fort Simpson on the Mackenzie river. *Older.*

Trueman, Stuart. The Ordeal of John Gyles. McClelland & Stewart, 1966. 155 pp. $7.95 paper [0-7710-8604-0].
Captured by Maliseet Indians, a boy lived nine years as their slave. *Young adult.*

Vineberg, Ethel. Grandmother came from Dworitz. Ill. by Rita Briansky. Tundra, 1987. 64 pp. $3.95 paper [0-88776-195-X].
An illuminating story, confidentially told and sympathetically illustrated, about a Canadian grandmother's life in the Jewish pale of Russia in the late nineteenth century. *Middle, older.*

Woodcock, George. 100 great Canadians. Hurtig, 1980. 160 pp. $18.95 hardcover [0-88830-193-6]; $12.95 paper [0-88830-184-7].
Brief biographies of Canadian historians, politicians, artists, scientists, clergymen, and others who have contributed to the growth of this country. *Older.*

HISTORY

ARCHAEOLOGY
see also
PUBLISHERS' SERIES
Canadian Prehistory Series

McGhee, Robert. The Burial at L'Anse-Amour. National Museum of Man, 1976. 24 pp. $1.95 paper [0-660-00019-9].
A strangely moving reconstruction of possible events that might have led to this burial site on the Labrador coast of the Strait of Belle Isle, excavated in 1974. *Older.*

NATIVE PEOPLES
see also
PUBLISHERS' SERIES
How They Lived in Canada
Native People of Canada Series
Native Peoples Series

Anderson, Daniel and Anderson, Alda M. The Métis people of Canada: a history. Alberta Federation of Métis Settlement Associations, 1978. 128 pp. $6.90 paper [0-7715-8330-3].
A considered, straightforward history of the Métis people from the days of the fur trade through the Pemmican wars to the movement for Métis rights. *Older.*

Ashwell, Reg. Coast Salish: their art, culture and legends. Hancock, 1981. 88 pp. $4.95 paper [0-88839-009-2].
Chapters on tribal origins, food, crafts, and religion with pertinent photographs of the West Coast Salish people. *Older.*

Ashwell, Reg. Indian tribes of the Northwest. Ill. by J.M. Thornton. Hancock, 1981. 89 pp. $4.95 paper [0-919654-53-3].
Brief text and outstanding photographs serve as an introduction for children to the various Native tribes. *Older.*

Brasser, Ted J. 'Bo'jou, Nejee!': profiles of Canadian Indian art. National Museum of Man, 1976. 204 pp. $16.95 paper [0-660-00008-3].
A catalogue of an exhibition of early Canadian Indian artifacts, appropriately illustrated with exquisite photographs. *Older, young adult.*

Common, Dianne L. Little Loon and the Sun Dance. Ill. by Carol A. Kemp. Pemmican, 1982. 23 pp. $3.25 paper [0-919143-30-X].
Little Loon, an Assiniboine Indian, attends a ceremony at which his baby sister receives her name and later watches the young warrriors prepare for the Sun Dance. *Middle.*

Common, Dianne L. Little Wild Onion of the Lillooet. Ill. by Carol A. Kemp. Pemmican, 1982. 28 pp. $3.25 paper [0-919143-29-6].
As Kelora and her family return to their winter house in the Fraser Canyon, the reader learns how the Lillooet build a winter house, prepare food, and fish for salmon. Two legends are also woven into the story. *Middle.*

Common, Dianne L. Marie of the Metis. Ill. by Greg Pruden. Pemmican, 1982. 22 pp. $3.25 paper [0-919143-31-8].
Marie learns the story of the Metis, assists her mother after the buffalo hunt, and meets Louis Riel. *Middle.*

Dempsey, Hugh A. Indian tribes of Alberta. Glenbow-Alberta Institute, 1978. 88 pp. $4.95 paper [0-919224-00-8].

Students, particularly in Alberta, will find this a concise and objective illustrated review of the history of ten Indian tribes native to that province. No index. *Older, young adult.*

Dewdney, Selwyn. They shared to survive. Ill. by Franklin Arbuckle. Macmillan, 1975. 220 pp. $8.95 hardcover [0-7705-1320-4].

How Native peoples of Canada lived in harmony with nature. Graphic line drawings. *Older.*

George, Dan. My heart soars. Ill. by Helmut Hirnschall. Hancock, 1981. 95 pp. $14.95 hardcover [0-919654-15-0].

A famous representative of his people expresses Indian beliefs with simplicity and dignity. Sympathetically illustrated. *Older.*

Halpin, Marjorie M. Totem poles: an illustrated guide. Univ. of British Columbia, 1981. 58 pp. $8.95 paper [0-7748-0141-7].

A guide 'designed to help people see and appreciate totem poles and other massive wood carvings which are unique to the Indian peoples of the Pacific Northwest Coast.' *Older, young adult.*

Hawkins, Elizabeth M. Indian weaving, knitting, basketry of the Northwest. Hancock, 1978. 32 pp. $3.50 paper [0-88839-006-8].

Excellent photographs with descriptions of traditional and modern arts include masks, totems, jewellery, weaving, and knitting. *All ages.*

Jenness, Diamond. The Indians of Canada. Univ. of Toronto, 1977. 7th ed. 432 pp. $10.00 paper [0-8020-6326-8].

First published in 1932 this is the definitive work on Canada's Native peoples by a pioneer in anthropology. *Older.*

Jenness, Eileen. The Indian tribes of Canada. McGraw, 1966. 123 pp. $9.95 paper [0-7700-6010-2].

A comprehensive discussion of the societal responses to their environment made by the Native peoples of Canada. Detailed line drawings enhance the narrative. *Older.*

Johnston, Basil. Ojibway ceremonies. McClelland & Stewart, 1982. 188 pp. $18.95 hardcover [0-7710-4446-1].

In a narrative based on fact, the author describes ceremonies intrinsic to Ojibway culture, such as the Naming Ceremony, the Vision Quest, and the Ritual of the Dead. *Older, young adult.*

Jordan, Wendy Adler. By the light of the Qulliq: Eskimo life in the Canadian Arctic. Smithsonian Institution, 1979. 43 pp. $13.00 paper [0-86528-000-2].

This introduction to the Inuit way of life is splendidly illustrated with photographs of soapstone and ivory carvings and pencil drawings. *Younger, middle.*

Kaiper, Dan and **Kaiper, Nan.** Tlingit: their art, culture and legends. Hancock, 1981. 95 pp. $4.95 paper [0-88839-010-6].

An introduction to the social life and legends of the Northern Pacific Coast Tlingit people. *Older.*

Kidd, Kenneth E. Canadians of long ago. Academic, 1951. $4.74 paper [0-7747-1208-2].

Outline history of Indian life before European immigration. Distinctive line drawings. *Middle.*

Lussier, Antoine S. and **Sealey, D. Bruce.** The Métis, Canada's forgotten people. Pemmican, 1983. 200 pp. $9.95 paper [0-919213-39-1].

A comprehensive, straightforward history of the Métis in Canada, including a careful documentation of the Riel Rebellion in 1885. *Older, young adult.*

MacDonald, George F. Ninstints: Haida world heritage site. Univ. of British Columbia, 1983. 60 pp. $8.95 paper [0-7748-0163-8].

Although the Kunghit Haida of Ninstints did not survive the onslaught of Western civilization, archaeologists are now working to preserve a record of this nineteenth century Haida village. *Older.*

Marsh, Winifred Petchey. People of the Willow: the Padlimiut tribe of the Caribou Eskimo. Anglican Book Centre, 1983. $11.95 hardcover [0-919891-01-2].

Delicate watercolour sketches make an intimate detailed record of Inuit life about forty years ago. *Older.*

Pachano, Jane. Changing times: Baby William/ Les temps changent: Bébé William. Ill. by J. Eitzen and J. Rabbitt Ozores. James Bay Cree Cultural Education Centre, 1985. 18 pp. $7.50 paper [0-920791-00-X].

A comparison of the birth and care of Cree babies today and in the past, illustrated with drawings. Valuable, although some pages of text imprinted on the illustrations are difficult to read. *Younger.*

Pachano, Jane. Changing times: Bobby and Mary at home/Les temps changent: Bobby et Mary chez eux. Ill. by T. Eitzen. Tr. by Jacqueline Gravelle. James Bay Cree Cultural Education Centre, 1985. 27 pp. $9.00 paper [0-920791-04-2].

The contemporary lifestyle of two Cree children is compared to that led by their grandparents when they were children. Illustrated with photographs and line drawings. *Younger.*

Pachano, Jane. Changing times: clothing/Les temps changent: le vêtement. Tr. by Renée Cartier. James Bay Cree Cultural Education Centre, 1985. 18 pp. $11.00 paper [0-920791-02-6].
A comparison of Cree clothing practises today and in the times of our grandparents. Illustrated with contrasting photographs, coloured for present day, sepia for the past. *Younger.*

Pachano, Jane. Changing times: transportation/Les temps changent: moyens de transport. James Bay Cree Cultural Education Centre, 1985. 20 pp. $11.00 paper [0-920791-14-X].
A comparison of past and present means of transportation among the Cree Indians of James Bay. *Younger.*

Pachano, Jane. Cree customs: Walking-Out Ceremony/Coutumes Cries: la cérémonie des premiers pas. Ill. by J. Pachano and R. Pachano. James Bay Cree Cultural Education Centre, 1984. 20 pp. $11.50 paper [0-920791-06-9].
Cree children participate in the Walking-Out Ceremony that symbolizes the first day of a Cree child's life as a hunter or a woman. *Younger.*

Purich, Donald. Our land: native rights in Canada. Lorimer, 1986. 252 pp. $14.95 hardcover [0-88862-975-3]; $7.95 paper [0-88862-974-5].
A thoughtful consideration of the past, present, and future of the native land claims. *Young adult.*

Shilling, Arthur. The Ojibway dream. Ill. by Arthur Shilling. Tundra, 1986. 48 pp. $29.95 hardcover [0-88776-173-9].
Through prose, poetry, and brilliantly-coloured paintings, the artist presents his concept of the Indian spirit. *Older.*

Steltzer, Ulli. A Haida potlatch. Douglas & McIntyre, 1984. 81 pp. $16.95 hardcover [0-88894-438-1].
In 1981, Steltzer recorded in photographs a potlatch held in Masset, B.C. Subsequent interviews added to the text. *Older.*

Stewart, Hilary. Indian fishing: early methods on the Northwest coast. Douglas & McIntyre, 1977. 188 pp. $16.95 paper [0-88894-332-6].
Fishing is placed within the whole context of Indian culture through pictures, drawings, and a readable text. *Older.*

Such, Peter. Vanished peoples: the Archaic, Dorset and Beothuk peoples of Newfoundland. NC Press, 1978. 94 pp. $16.95 hardcover [0-919600-84-0]; $8.95 paper [0-919600-83-2].
A readable account of the extinct Beothuks, early inhabitants of Newfoundland. Many maps, drawings, and photographs are included. *Older.*

Updike, Lee R. Our people: Indians of the Plains. Western Producer Prairie, 1974. 12 pp. $3.95 paper [0-88833-039-1].
Plains Indian life before European immigration depicted in twelve captioned drawings. *Middle.*

Whitehead, Ruth Holmes. Elitekey: Micmac material culture from 1600 A.D. to the present. Nova Scotia Museum, 1980. 84 pp. $5.95 paper [0-919680-13-5].
Beginning with an explanation of Micmac art as it existed before and after contact with the Europeans, this concise volume goes on to describe developments to the present day. Illustrated with photographs. *Older.*

Whitehead, Ruth Holmes and **McGee, Harold.** The Micmac: how their ancestors lived five hundred years ago. Ill. by Kathy Kaulbach. Nimbus, 1983. 60 pp. $9.95 hardcover [0-920852-23-8]; $5.95 paper [0-920852-21-1].
An account of the habits and traditions of the Micmac Indians of the Maritime provinces, as they lived five hundred years ago. *Middle, older.*

Williams, Sophia and **Williams, Saul.** Weagamow notebook. Natural Heritage, 1978. 45 pp. $3.50 paper [0-920474-02-0].
The diary and drawings of two Ojibway children who record their trip to the family's trapline winter camp capture a way of life fast disappearing. *Middle.*

CANADIAN HISTORY

see also
PUBLISHERS' SERIES
Canadian Pathfinder Series
Canadiana Scrapbook Series
The Canadians
Century of Canada Series
Focus on Canadian History Series
Grolier Album Series
Growth of a Nation Series
We Built Canada

Anderson, Allen and **Tomlinson, Betty.** Greetings from Canada: an album of unique Canadian postcards from the Edwardian era 1900-1916. Macmillan, 1978. 88 pp. $10.95 hardcover [0-7705-1736-6].
Elaborates school days, the Klondike, and winter sports among other subjects. *Middle, older.*

Anderson, Frank W. and **Turnbull, Elsie G.** Tragedies of the Crowsnest Pass. Heritage, 1983. 96 pp. $5.95 paper [0-919214-58-4].
Coal mine disasters, rock slides, and fires have plagued the Crowsnest Pass mining region of southern Alberta and British Columbia. *Older.*

Benn, Carl. The Battle of York. Mika, 1984. 62 pp. $6.00 paper [0-919303-86-2].
A straightforward account of the American attack on the Town of York (Toronto) in April 1813. Illustrated with archival photographs and maps. *Older.*

Brown, Cassie and **Horwood, Harold.** Death on the ice. Doubleday, 1978. 270 pp. $5.95 paper [0-385-05037-2].
Re-creates the great Newfoundland sealing disaster of 1914 when 254 sealers died, the victims of greed, carelessness, and misunderstanding. *Young adult.*

Cashman, Tony. A Picture history of Alberta. Illustrated. Hurtig, 1979. 215 pp. $15.95 hardcover [0-88830-157-X].
Some four hundred photographs from the archives of the Glenbow-Alberta Institute arranged into twenty-six topics with lengthy captions recall Alberta's early days. *Older.*

Chafe, J.W. Extraordinary tales from Manitoba's history. Manitoba Historical Society, 1973. 180 pp. $5.50 hardcover [0-7710-1951-3].
Strange vignettes, a sidelight on the history of a province. *Older, young adult.*

Collard, Eileen. Clothing in English Canada circa 1867 to 1907. The author, 1975. 72 pp. $20.00 paper [0-9690552-C-X].
Profusely illustrated with patterns and photographs, this outline of the clothing worn by adults gives an invaluable record of the period. *Older.*

The Corrective Collective. Never done: three centuries of women's work in Canada. Women's, 1974. 150 pp. $7.95 school ed. [0-88961-010-X]; teacher's guide $2.95 paper [0-88961-051-7].
Beautifully-designed book on the lives of our unsung pioneer heroines. *Older, young adult.*

Douglas, W.A.B. Gunfire on the lakes; the naval war of 1812-1814 on the Great Lakes and Lake Champlain/Cannonnades sur les lacs; la guerre navale de 1812-1814 sur les Grands Lacs et le lac Champlain. National Museums, 1977. 33 pp. $3.25 paper [0-660-00102-0].
Bilingual account. *Older, young adult.*

Einarsson, Magnus. Everyman's heritage: an album of Canadian folk life. National Museum of Man, 1978. 201 pp. $12.95 hardcover [0-660-00101-2]; $10.95 paper [0-660-00124-1].
A fascinating family album of the people who settled Canada; a photographic essay with brief connecting bilingual text; a multicultural celebration. *Older.*

Guillet, Edwin C. The Story of Canadian roads. Univ. of Toronto, 1966. 246 pp. $30.00 hardcover [0-8020-1414-3].
Emphasizes the importance of roads in Canadian social and economic development, from portage trail to Trans Canada Highway. *Young adult.*

A Harvest yet to reap; a history of Prairie women. Illustrated. Women's, 1976. 240 pp. $20.00 hardcover [0-88961-030-4]; $8.95 paper [0-88961-029-0].
This is a heart-rending chronicle of the hardships endured by women who settled the Prairies; it documents the 'courage, creativity, hope, good humour and even occasional joy' in the lives of our incredible foremothers. *Older, young adult.*

Hull, Raymond; Soules, Gordon; and **Soules, Christine.** Vancouver's past. Soules, 1974. 96 pp. $11.95 hardcover [0-919574-02-5].
Brief overview of the city's history and development. *Older.*

Jefferys, C.W. and **McLean, T.W.** The Picture gallery of Canadian history. Vol. 1 – Discovery to 1783; vol. 2 – 1763 to 1830; Vol. 3 – 1830-1900. McGraw, 1942. Vol.1 $4.95 paper [0-07-077702-0]; Vol.2 $12.50 paper [0-07-0777 703-9]; Vol.3 $12.50 paper [0-07-077704-7].
Illustrations of historical events, maps, portraits, artifacts make an important pictorial record of Canada's development. *Middle, older.*

Jones, Mary Fallis. The Confederation generation. Royal Ontario Museum, 1978. 128 pp. $12.50 hardcover [0-88854-212-7]; $5.95 paper [0-88854-220-8]; school ed. $5.25 paper [0-88854-215-1].
A social and material history of the 1860s through the 1880s as seen through the eyes of 'respectable' and 'prosperous' English-speaking urban central Canadians. *Older.*

Kelly, William and **Kelly, Nora.** The Horses of the Royal Canadian Mounted Police: a pictorial history. Doubleday, 1984. 288 pp. $29.95 hardcover [0-385-19544-3].
An explanation of the active and ceremonial roles of horses in the work of the R.C.M.P., illustrated with photographs. *Older.*

MacLean, Harrison John. The Fate of the Griffon. Griffin, 1974. 118 pp. $8.95 hardcover [0-88760-069-7].
La Salle's ship, built in 1679 above Niagara Falls, was proved a naval carcass in 1955 after it was found off the Bruce Peninsula near Tobermory, Ontario. *Young adult.*

Metson, Graham and **MacMechan, Archibald.** The Halifax Explosion: December 6, 1917. McGraw, 1978. 173 pp. $14.95 paper [0-07-082798-2].
MacMechan's complete text of the Halifax Disaster, and documents and pictures bring the Explosion to vivid reality. *Older, young adult.*

Mika, Nick and **Mika, Helma.** United Empire Loyalists, pioneers of Upper Canada. Mika, 1978. 256 pp. $40.00 hardcover [0-919303-09-9].

This comprehensive and well-researched treatment of the United Empire Loyalists is an important contribution to Canada's early social history. *Young adult.*

Moore, Christopher. The Loyalists: revolution, exile, settlement. Macmillan, 1984. 218 pp. $27.95 hardcover [0-7715-9781-9].
In this account of the Loyalist immigration to Canada, the author presents the personalities behind the movement. *Young adult.*

Morgan, Murray. One man's gold rush. Douglas & McIntyre, 1973. 213 pp. $16.95 paper [0-88894-019-X].
Fascinating pictorial documentary of the Klondike gold rush. *Older.*

Neatby, Leslie H. Link between the oceans. Academic, 1960. 139 pp. $5.95 hardcover [0-7747-0057-2].
The search for Sir John Franklin's lost expedition for the discovery of the Northwest Passage. *Older.*

Patton, Janice. The Exodus of the Japanese. McClelland & Stewart, 1974. 47 pp. $5.95 paper [0-7710-1379-5].
Poignant description of the expulsion of Japanese-Canadians from British Columbia. *Older.*

Pierce, Patricia. Canada, the missing years: the lost images of our heritage, 1895-1924. Stoddart, 1985. 160 pp. $24.95 hardcover [0-7737-2052-9].
Captioned photographs of Canada and its people during the years of early nationhood. *Middle to young adult.*

Schmidt, René. Canadian disasters. Scholastic-TAB, 1986. 124 pp. $2.95 paper [0-590-71525-9].
Twenty-eight tragic events in Canada's history are documented in vignettes with photographs. *Middle.*

Schuyler, George. Saint John: scenes from a popular history. Nimbus, 1984. 80 pp. $12.95 paper [0-919380-44-1].
Five episodes in the history of the city of Saint John, New Brunswick are outlined and illustrated with photographs. *Older.*

Stanton, James B., ed. Ho for the Klondike. Hancock, 1974. 62 pp. $2.95 paper [0-919654-11-8].
A collection of photographs, chronologically arranged, plus a brief text document the Klondike gold rush. *Older.*

Toye, William. Cartier discovers the St. Lawrence. Ill. by Laszlo Gal. Oxford, 1979. 32 pp. $5.95 paper [0-19-540348-7].
Based on material from the author's *The St. Lawrence*, handsomely illustrated. *Middle.*

Wilson, Bruce. As she began: an illustrated introduction to Loyalist Ontario. Dundurn, 1981. 125 pp. $14.95 paper [0-919670-54-7].
A look at the social aspects of Loyalist migration from the United States to Canada during the period from 1775 to 1791. Illustrated with archival photographs and sketches. *Older, young adult.*

PIONEER LIFE

Armstrong, Audrey L. Harness in the parlour: a book of early Canadian fact & folklore. Musson, 1974. 90 pp. $6.95 paper [0-7737-1005-1].
Informal history of the customs, beliefs, and attitudes of Canada's early pioneers. *Older.*

Armstrong, Audrey L. Sulphur and molasses: home remedies and other echoes of the Canadian past. Ill. by Merle Smith. Musson, 1977. 96 pp. $5.95 paper [0-7737-1013-2].
Rural remedies of the pioneers make a useful addition to our folklore. *Older.*

Jameson, Anna B. Winter studies and summer rambles in Canada. McClelland & Stewart, 1965. 172 pp. $5.95 paper [0-7710-9146-X].
A gentlewoman's view of York and the countryside of Upper Canada, originally published in 1838. *Older.*

Kurelek, William and **Engelhart, Margaret S.** They sought a new world: the story of European immigrants to North America. Ill. by William Kurelek. Tundra, 1985. 48 pp. $14.95 hardcover [0-88776-172-0].
Paintings and commentary realistically depict the dreams and hardships, work and leisure, and family and community that were part of the European immigrant's experience in his new country. *Middle to young adult.*

Milnes, Herbert. Settlers' traditions. Ill. by Herbert Milnes. Boston Mills, 1980. 96 pp. $7.95 paper [0-919822-87-4].
This description of the household and agricultural practises of settlers in Upper Cnaada is illustrated with exceptionally-fine pencil drawings of tools and procedures. *Older, young adult.*

Moodie, Susanna. Roughing it in the bush. McClelland & Stewart, 1962. $4.95 paper [0-7710-9131-1].
By a recent immigrant to Upper Canada who describes pioneer life as she experienced it in the backwoods in the mid-nineteenth century. *Young adult.*

Ryder, Huia G. Antique furniture by New Brunswick craftsmen. McGraw, 1986. 180 pp. $10.95 paper [0-07-092979-3].
Pioneer artifacts show how the colonists furnished their homes. *Older.*

Symons, R.D. Grandfather Symons' homestead book. Ill. by R.D. Symons. Western Producer Prairie, 1981. 80 pp. $9.95 paper [0-88833-082-0].
An intimate view of homesteading on the Canadian prairies. Text and illustration depict the family's seasonal activity from wood cutting and shinny on the slough in winter to threshing the harvest in the fall. *Younger, middle.*

REFERENCE

Akrigg, G.P.V. and Akrigg, Helen B. British Columbia place names. Sono Nis, 1986. 346 pp. $29.95 hardcover [0-919203-96-5]; $16.50 paper [0-919203-49-3].

Avis, Walter S. and others. Concise dictionary of Canadianisms. Gage, 1973. 294 pp. $9.95 paper [0-7715-1968-0].

Avis, Walter S. and others. Gage intermediate dictionary. Ill. by Lewis Parker. Gage, 1980 (rev.ed.). $24.95 hardcover [0-7715-9523-9]; Educ.ed. $18.95 hardcover [0-7715-1982-6].

Banfield, A.F. The Mammals of Canada. Univ. of Toronto, 1974. 438 pp. $30.00 hardcover [0-8020-2137-9].

Bourinot, John George. Bourinot's rules of order. Ed. by Geoffrey H. Stanford. McClelland & Stewart, 1977. 3rd rev.ed. 112 pp. $7.96 paper [0-7710-8335-1].

Bowers, Neal. Index to Canadian children's records. Lunenburg County District Teacher's Centre, 1984. 48 pp. $6.00 paper. No ISBN.

Brown, Thomas. The Place names of the province of Nova Scotia. Canadiana, 1969. 2nd ed. 200 pp. $35.00 hardcover [0-88812-143-1].

Canada. Department of Fisheries and Oceans. Freshwater fishes of Canada. Canadian Government, 1985. 960 pp. $24.95 paper [0-660-10239-0].

Canada. Statistics Canada. The Canada handbook. Statistics Canada, 1986. 376 pp. $15.00 paper [0-660-12083-6].

Canadian almanac & directory 1987. Copp Clark Pitman, 1987. $84.95 hardcover [0-7730-4096-X].

The Canadian dictionary for children. Collier Macmillan, 1979. 724 pp. $18.95 hardcover [0-02-991210-5].

The Canadian encyclopedia. Hurtig, 1985. 3 vols. v.1 [0-88830-271-1]; v.2 [0-88830-270-3]; v.3 [0-88830-272-X].

Canadian students' dictionary. Houghton Mifflin, 1983. 1184 pp. $14.95 hardcover [0-395-34994-X].

The Canadian world almanac and book of facts 1987. Global, 1986. 618 pp. $15.95 hardcover [0-7715-3988-6]; $7.96 paper [0-7715-3989-4].

CANSCAIP membership directory 1987. CANSCAIP (Box 280, Station L, Toronto, Ontario. M6E 4Z2), 1987. $12.00 paper. Free with membership.

A valuable reference book for school and public libraries containing the address, phone number, biographical and bibliographical information for 190 Canadian authors, illustrators, and performers.

Carter, Floreen Ellen. Place names of Ontario. Phelps, 1984. $195.00 hardcover [0-920298-39-7].

Connections two: writers and the land. Manitoba School Library Audio Visual Association, 1983. 124 pp. $10.00 paper [0-920082-009].

Corbeil, Jean-Claude. The Stoddart visual dictionary. 1986. 760 pp. $29.95 hardcover [0-7737-2093-6].

Dictionary of Canadian biography. Volume I. 1000-1700. Brown, George W. and Trudel, Marcel, eds. Univ. of Toronto, 1966. 755 pp. $65.00 hardcover [0-8020-3142-0].

Dictionary of Canadian biography. Volume II. 1701-1740. Hayne, David and Vachon, André, eds. Univ. of Toronto, 1969. 759 pp. $65.00 hardcover [0-8020-3240-0].

Dictionary of Canadian biography. Volume III. 1741-1770. Halpenny, Francess G. general ed. Univ. of Toronto, 1974. 782 pp. $65.00 hardcover [0-8020-3314-8].

Dictionary of Canadian biography. Volume IV. 1771-1800. Halpenny, Francess G. general ed. Univ. of Toronto, 1979. 913 pp. $65.00 hardcover [0-8020-3351-2].

Dictionary of Canadian biography. Volume V. 1801-1820. Halpenny, Francess G. general ed. Univ. of Toronto, 1983. 1044 pp. $65.00 hardcover [0-8020-3398-9].

Dictionary of Canadian biography. Volume VI. 1821-1835. Halpenny, Francess G. general ed. Univ. of Toronto, 1987. 1200 pp. $65.00 hardcover [0-8020-3436-5].

Dictionary of Canadian biography. Volume VIII. 1851-1860. Halpenny, Francess G. general ed. Univ. of Toronto, 1985. 1129 pp. $65.00 hardcover [0-8020-3422-5].

Dictionary of Canadian biography. Volume IX. 1861-1870. Halpenny, Francess G. general ed. Univ. of Toronto, 1976. 967 pp. $65.00 hardcover [0-8020-3319-9].

Dictionary of Canadian biography. Volume X. 1871-1880. La Terreur, Marc, ed. Univ. of Toronto, 1972. 823 pp. $65.00 hardcover [0-8020-3287-7].

Dictionary of Canadian biography. Volume XI. 1881-1890. Halpenny, Francess G. general ed. Univ. of Toronto, 1982. 1092 pp. $65.00 hardcover [0-8020-3367-9].

Dictionary of Canadian biography. Index. Volume I-IV. 1000-1800. Univ. of Toronto, 1981. $40.00 hardcover [0-8020-3326-1].

Dictionary of literary biographies. Vol. 53 Canadian writers since 1960: First series. Ed. by W.H. New. Gale Research Company, 1986. 445 pp. $88.00 hardcover.

Hamilton, Robert M. and Shields, Dorothy. The Dictionary of Canadian quotations and phrases. McClelland & Stewart, 1982. 1063 pp. $35.00 hardcover [0-7710-3846-1].

Holmgren, Patricia and Holgmren, Eric. Over 2000 place names of Alberta. Western Producer Prairie, 1977. 3rd ed. 210 pp. $11.95 paper [0-919306-75-6].

Introducing ... Canadian children's authors and illustrators. Canadian Children's Book Centre, 229 College Street, 5th floor, Toronto, Ontario. M5T 1R4. $30.00 for complete set, $1.00 each, minimum order of 10.

A set of biographical sheets in a folder of fifty-three Canadian authors and illustrators. Portraits and bibliographies included.

Kallman, Helmut; Potvin, Gilles; and Winters, Kenneth, eds. Encyclopedia of music in Canada. Univ. of Toronto, 1981. 1076 pp. $85.00 hardcover [0-8020-5509-5].

Kobayashi, Terry and Bird, Michael. A Compendium of Canadian folk artists. Boston Mills, 1985. 241 pp. $14.95 paper [0-919783-32-5].

McDonough, Irma, ed. Profiles. 2nd ed. Canadian Library Association, 1975. 159 pp. $5.00 paper [0-88802-109-7].

McDonough, Irma, ed. Profiles 2: authors and illustrators, children's literature in Canada. Canadian Library Association, 1982. 170 pp. $12.00 paper [0-88802-163-1].

Interviews with authors and illustrators of Canadian children's books. Portraits and bibliographies included.

McQuarrie, Jane and Dubois, Diane. Canadian picture books/Livres d'images canadiens. Reference, 1986. 217 pp. $24.00 hardcover [0-919981-12-7]; $18.00 paper [0-919981-09-7].

Meet the author: poster kits. Canadian Children's Book Centre, 229 College Street, 5th floor, Toronto, Ontario. M5T 1R4. $15.00 each kit or 2 for $20.00.

The kits include poster-photographs and bio-bibliographies on Canadian authors and illustrators. Kit No.1 and Kit No.2 are out of print. Kit No.3 includes Mary Alice Downie, Bill

Freeman, Kay Hill, Janet Lunn, Kevin Major, Douglas Tait. Kit No.4 includes Ron Berg, Brian Doyle, Frances Duncan, Gordon Korman, Robert Munsch, Gordon Penrose. Kit No.5 includes Alan Daniel, Tony German, Margaret Laurence, Claire Mackay, Suzanne Martel, Mark Thurman.

Mellen, Peter. The Group of Seven. McClelland & Stewart, 1983 (rev.ed.). 231 pp. $59.95 hardcover [0-7710-5820-9].

Ripley, Gordon and **Mercer, Anne,** eds. Who's who in Canadian literature 1985-86. Reference, 1985. 399 pp. $32.00 hardcover [0-919981-06-2].

Robinson, Sinclair and **Smith, Donald.** Practical handbook of Quebec and Acadian French/Manuel pratique du français québécois et acadien. Anansi, 1984. 302 pp. $14.95 paper [0-88784-137-6].

Russell, E.T. What's in a name: the story behind Saskatchewan place names. Western Producer Prairie, 1980 (rev.ed.). 350 pp. $12.95 paper [0-88833-053-7].

Snow, Kathleen M.; Dabbs, Rickey; and **Gorosh, Esther.** Subject index to Canadian poetry in English for children and young people. Canadian Library Association, 1986. 2nd ed. 307 pp. $25.00 paper [0-88802-202-6].

Toye, William, ed. The Oxford companion to Canadian literature. Oxford, 1983. 843 pp. $45.00 hardcover [0-19-540283-9]; $24.95 paper [0-19-540479-3].

Treasures: Canadian children's book illustration. Canadian Children's Book Centre, 1986. 63 pp. $15.00 paper. No ISBN.

Weber, Ken, ed. Puffin Canadian beginner's dictionary. Penguin, 1984. 240 pp. $7.95 paper [0-14-031698-1].

MAGAZINES FOR YOUNG PEOPLE

The following titles would enhance collections serving children and young adults. Contact the Canadian Periodical Publishers' Association for a checklist of their member periodicals. Reviews of Canadian magazines are found in *Emergency Librarian* in their 'Magazines for Young People' column that appears in each issue.

The Beaver: exploring Canada's history. Published by Hudson's Bay Company, Hudson's Bay House, 77 Main Street, Winnipeg, Manitoba. R3C 2R1. Bi-monthly. $18.00 for one year in Canada and the United States. Other countries $24.00 for one year.

'The interests of *The Beaver* cover the territory with which the company has been or is now associated' – exploration, mining, native people, geology, animals.

Buzz. Published by the Grey Bruce Arts Council, Box 184, Owen Sound, Ontario. N4K 5P3. Three issues per year. $5.00 for one year or $2.00 for single copies.

A children's literary arts magazine which features short stories, poems, articles, art work, puzzles, games, and contests by Canadian writers and artists for six to twelve year olds.

76 MAGAZINES FOR YOUNG PEOPLE

Canada and the world. Published by Maclean Hunter. 777 Bay Street, Toronto, Ontario. M5W 1A7. 9 issues per year, September to May. $12.50 for one year, payment with order. Lower rate for bulk subscriptions.

Short analytical articles with an historical perspective on current social and political issues.

Canadian geographic. Published by the Royal Canadian Geographical Society, 488 Wilbrod St., Ottawa, Ontario. K1N 6M8. Bi-monthly. $19.00 for one year. Outside Canada $25.00. $3.25 for single copies.

Outstanding coverage of Canadian geography, resources, and people.

Chickadee. Published by The Young Naturalist Foundation. Chickadee, 56 The Esplanade, Suite 304, Toronto, Ontario. M5E 1A7. Ten issues per year. $17.00 for 10 issues. $30.00 for 20 issues. Overseas $22.00 for 10 issues. $40.00 for 20 issues.

A younger version of *Owl* magazine suitable for children under eight. As well as many colourful illustrations, there are stories, puzzles, and games to spark interest in nature. Indexed in *Children's magazine guide*.

Children's book news. Published by the Canadian Children's Book Centre, 229 College Street, 5th floor, Toronto, Ontario. M5T 1R4. 4 issues per year. Free. People wishing to receive a copy should write to the Centre. Available in bulk. Subscription for four issues: 50 copies $20.00; 100 copies $25.00; 500 copies $60.00.

A sixteen-page publication on the children's book industry in Canada, including information about authors and illustrators, Canadian bookstores, as well as a children's page with fascinating activities. A must for school and public libraries.

Cycle Canada. Published by Brave Beaver Pressworks, 411 Richmond Street East, Toronto, Ontario. M5A 3S5. 12 issues per year. $19.95 for one year; $34.95 for two years; $49.95 for three years. Outside Canada add $6.00 per year.

For the motorcycle enthusiast.

Flabbergast. Published by Youth Science Foundation, Suite 904, 151 Slater Street, Ottawa, Ontario. K1P 5H3. 11 issues per year. $14.00 for 11 issues; $26.00 for 22 issues. $20.00 for one year in the United States; $25.00 a year international.

A science magazine with hands-on science activities, puzzles, games, short story contests, and informative feature articles. For children between the ages of seven and fourteen years.

Flare. Published by Maclean Hunter, 777 Bay Street, Toronto, Ontario. M5W 1A7. 12 issues per year. $16.00 for one year.

This magazine features fashions and fads for teen-aged girls. Excellent topical articles.

Graffiti. Published by Quebec Rock Group, C.P. 70, Succ. Longueil, Québec. J4K 4Y3. 12 issues per year. $28.00 for one year.

This magazine which is the English language version of *Québec Rock*, gives a lively picture of contemporary pop culture. Feature articles on various rock artists and groups.

MVP: Canada's sports magazine. Published by MVP Magazine, 3 Church Street, Suite 304, Toronto, Ontario. M5E 1B2. 8 issues per year. $14.95 for one year. Other countries add $6.00.

A magazine that covers only Canadian sports. Concentrates on in-depth profiles of players and coaches. Articles illustrated with photographs and drawings.

Nature Canada. Published by the Canadian Nature Federation, 75 Albert Street, Ottawa, Canada. K1P 6G1. Quarterly. Available with annual membership in Canadian Nature Federation: Individuals $25.00; Family $30.00; Sustaining $50.00; Life $600.00. Subscriptions are available to schools and libraries at $20.00 per year.

Glossy paper, coloured photographs, well-known writers make Canada's national nature magazine a joy to read.

North/Nord. Published by Department of Indian and Northern Affairs. Quarterly. Free by writing to the Managing Editor, Communications Branch. Indian and Northern Affairs Canada, Ottawa. K1A 0H4.

Excellent source of topical information on all aspects of life in the Canadian North.

Outdoor Canada. Published by Outdoor Canada Publishing, 801 York Mills Road, Suite 301, Don Mills, Ontario. M3B 1X7. 8 times per year. $14.00 for one year. Outside Canada add $5.00 per year.

Informative and well-written articles on all aspects of outdoor wilderness recreation.

Owl. Published by The Young Naturalist Foundation, Owl, 56 The Esplanade, Suite 304, Toronto, Ontario. M5E 1A7. Ten issues per year. $17.00 for 10 issues. $30.00 for 20 issues. Overseas $22.00 for 10 issues; $40.00 for 20 issues.

A well-conceived, well-produced magazine intended for children ages seven to thirteen. Special feature articles as well as regular columns, stories, games, and puzzles. Indexed in *Children's magazine guide*.

Rock express. Published by Rock Express Communications Inc., 37 Madison Avenue, Toronto, Ontario. M5R 2S3. 12 issues per year. $15.50 for one year.

A rock magazine devoted to newsbriefs on Canadian and international rock artists. Feature articles on various rock artists, groups, and promoters. Critical reviews of new records, videos, concerts, books, and films.

Ski Canada. Published by Maclean Hunter, 777 Bay Street, 7th floor, Toronto, Ontario. M5W 1A7. 6 issues per year. $9.00 for one year.

Designed for the amateur skier, contains general skiing news, profiles of skiers, and tips to help the reader ski better.

TG: Teen generation. Published by Teen Generation Inc., 202 Cleveland St., Toronto, Ontario. M4S 2W6. 6 issues per year. $10.00 for one year. $14.00 for two years. Special bulk rates available to schools.

A magazine for young adults including career information, news, views, music, and fashion reviews.

Youth science news. Published by the Youth Science Foundation, 151 Slater Street, Suite 904, Ottawa, Ontario. K1P 5H3. Six issues per year. $6.00 for one year.

A publication for high school students that keeps readers abreast of current scientific issues and career trends as reported by high school students from across Canada.

PUBLISHERS' SERIES

THE CANADA SERIES

11 volumes. McGraw. $12.95 each, hardcover. Profusely-illustrated geographies of all the provinces covering industry, government, historical highlights, personalities, environment in a clear concise text. *Older, young adult.*

Hocking, Anthony; Alberta. [0-07-082687-0]

Hocking, Anthony; British Columbia. [0-07-082690-0]

Hocking, Anthony; Canada. [0-07-082693-5]

Hocking, Anthony; Manitoba. [0-07-082688-9]

Hocking, Anthony; New Brunswick. [0-07-082686-2]

Hocking, Anthony; Newfoundland. [0-07-082684-6]

Hocking, Anthony; Nova Scotia. [0-07-082685-4]

Hocking, Anthony; Ontario. [0-07-082683-8]

Hocking, Anthony; Prince Edward Island. [0-07-082691-9]

Hocking, Anthony; Quebec. [0-07-082691-9]

Hocking, Anthony; The Yukon and Northwest Territories. [0-07-082694-3]

CANADIAN ARTISTS SERIES

10 volumes. The National Gallery. Prices vary. Well-illustrated, well-written monographs that young people can enjoy. *Older, young adult.*

Dorais, Lucie. J.W. Morrice. $8.95 paper [0-88884-525-1], #8.

Finley, Gerald. George Heriot. $3.95 paper [0-88884-369-0], #5.

Gagnon, François. Paul-Emile Borduas. $3.95 paper [0-88884-217-6], #3.

Harper, J. Russell. William G.R. Hind. $3.25 paper [0-88884-273-2], #2.

Ostiguy, Jean-René. Charles Huot. $8.95 paper [0-88884-370-4], #7.

Reid, Dennis. Bertram Brooker. $2.95 paper [0-88884-372-0], #1.

Reid, Dennis. Edwin H. Holgate. $5.95 paper [0-88884-314-3], #4.

Stacey, Robert. C.W. Jeffreys. $8.95 paper [0-88884-529-4], #10.

Varley, Christopher. Frederick H. Varley. $5.95 paper [0-88884-371-2], #6.

Zemans, Joyce. Jock MacDonald. $8.95 paper [0-88884-527-8], #9.

CANADIAN PATHFINDER SERIES

Illustrated biographies of Canadian historical figures intended for grade 5 and 6. Boxed items highlight aspects of the time. *Middle.*

Moore, Christopher. Samuel de Champlain. [0-71721947-X].

Moore, Christopher. William Cornelius Van Horne. [0-7172-2161-X].

Schemenauer, Elma. John A. Macdonald. [0-7172-1948-8].

Willoughby, Brenda. Pauline Johnson. [0-7172-1949-6].

Zola, Meguido and Town, Florida. Alexander Graham Bell. [0-71721950-X].

CANADIAN PREHISTORY SERIES

6 volumes. Van Nostrand. Prices vary.

Significant archeological findings documented by leading scholars reveal the life of our native peoples before Jacques Cartier landed in Canada. Colour plates, photographs, diagrams, maps. *Older, young adult.*

MacDonald, G.F. and Inglis, R.I. The Dig. $7.50 paper [0-660-00007-5].

McGhee, Robert. Canadian Arctic prehistory. $12.95 paper [0-660-02477-2].

Tuck, James A. Newfoundland and Labrador prehistory. $5.50 paper [0-660-02475-6].

Wright, J.V. Ontario prehistory. $5.50 paper [0-660-02473-X].

Wright, J.V. Québec prehistory. $8.50 paper [0-660-02478-0].

Wright, J.V. Six chapters of Canada's prehistory. $5.50 paper [0-660-02474-8].

CANADIAN RAINBOW SERIES – CITIES

16 volumes. GLC Silver Burnett. $5.21 hardcover, $3.56 paper.

With colour photographs, illustrations, and diagrams, this collection covers the geography, history, people, government, and future of Canadian cities. *Younger, middle.*

Schemenauer, Elma. Hello Calgary. Hardcover [0-88874-251-7]; paper [0-88874-235-5].

Schemenauer, Elma. Hello Charlottetown. Hardcover [0-88874-252-5]; paper [0-88874-236-3].

Schemenauer, Elma. Hello Edmonton. Hardcover [0-88874-253-3]; paper [0-88874-237-1].

Schemenauer, Elma. Hello Fredericton. Hardcover [0-88874-254-1]; paper [0-88874-238-X].

Schemenauer, Elma. Hello Halifax. Hardcover [0-88874-254-1]; paper [0-88874-238-X].

Schemenauer, Elma. Hello Montreal. Hardcover [0-88874-256-8]; paper [0-88874-240-1].

Schemenauer, Elma. Hello Ottawa. Hardcover [0-88874-257-6]; paper [0-88874-241-X].

Schemenauer, Elma. Hello Quebec City. Hardcover [0-88874-258-4]; paper [0-88874-242-8].

Schemenauer, Elma. Hello Regina. Hardcover [0-88874-259-2]; paper [0-88874-243-6].

Schemenauer, Elma. Hello St. John's. Hardcover [0-88874-259-2]; paper [0-88874-243-6].

Schemenauer, Elma. Hello Toronto. Hardcover [0-88874-261-4]; paper [0-88874-245-2].

Schemenauer, Elma. Hello Vancouver. Hardcover [0-88874-262-2]; paper [0-88874-246-0].

Schemenauer, Elma. Hello Victoria. Hardcover [0-88874-263-0]; paper [0-88874-247-9].

Schemenauer, Elma. Hello Whitehorse. Hardcover [0-88874-264-9]; paper [0-88874-248-7].

Schemenauer, Elma. Hello Winnipeg. Hardcover [0-88874-265-7]; paper [0-88874-249-5].

Schemenauer, Elma. Hello Yellowknife. Hardcover [0-88874-266-5]; paper [0-88874250-9].

CANADIAN RAINBOW SERIES – PROVINCES

12 volumes. GLC Silver Burnett. $5.06 hardcover, $3.38 paper.

Illustrated in full colour, this collection covers geography, cities, industry, points of interest, people, and history. *Younger, middle.*

Learning about ... Alberta. Hardcover [0-88874-116-2]; paper [0-88874-166-9].

Learning about ... British Columbia. Hardcover [0-88874-115-4]; paper [0-88874-165-0].

Learning about ... Canada. Hardcover [0-88874-113-8]; paper [0-88874-163-4].

Learning about ... The Canadian North. Hardcover [0-88874-114-6]; paper [0-88874-164-2].

Learning about ... Manitoba. Hardcover [0-88874-118-9]; paper [0-88874-168-5].

Learning about ... New Brunswick. Hardcover [0-88874-121-9]; paper [0-88874-171-5].

Learning about ... Newfoundland. Hardcover [0-88874-124-3]; paper [0-88874174-X].

Learning about ... Nova Scotia. Hardcover [0-88874-122-7]; paper [0-88874-172-3].

Learning about ... Ontario. Hardcover [0-88874-119-7]; paper [0-88874-169-3].

Learning about ... Prince Edward Island. Hardcover [0-88874-123-5]; paper [0-88874-173-1].

Learning about ... Quebec. Hardcover [0-88874-120-0]; paper [0-88874-170-7].

Learning about ... Saskatchewan. Hardcover [0-88874-117-0]; paper [0-88874-167-7].

CANADIANA SCRAPBOOK SERIES

15 volumes. Prentice. Order will be processed for ten copies or multiples of ten copies, or an individual title only. A package of ten books is $85.00, individual titles $8.50, paper.

Large folio format displays to advantage the numerous photographs and accompanying text that bring significant historical periods of our history into focus. *All ages.*

Bondy, Robert Joseph. Canada: windows on the world. [0-13-113951-7].

Bondy, Robert Joseph and **Mattys, William Charles.** The Confident years: Canada in the 1920's. [0-13-167551-6].

Bondy, Robert Joseph and **Mattys, William Charles.** Years of promise: Canada 1945-1963. [0-13-971846-X].

Brown, Graham Leslie and **Fairbairn, Douglas Hall.** Pioneer settlement in Canada 1763-1895. [0-13-676320-0].

Dicks, Stewart Kinloch. Les Canadiens: the French in Canada 1600-1867. [0-13-530568-3].

Dicks, Stewart Kinloch. A Nation launched: Macdonald's dominion 1867-1896. [0-13-609354-X].

Dicks, Stewart Kinloch and **Santor, Donald Murray.** The Great Klondike gold rush 1896-1904. [0-13-363952-5].

Fairbairn, Douglas Hall and **Brown, Graham Leslie.** A Nation beckons: Canada 1896-1914. [0-13-609271-3].

Mennil, Paul Delmar. The Depression years: Canada in the 1930's. [0-13-199018-7].

Osborne, Kenneth. Canadians at work: labour, unions and industry. [0-13-114141-4].

Santor, Donald Murray. Canada's native people. [0-13-112904-X].

Santor, Donald Murray. Canadians at war 1914-1918. [0-13-113456-6].

Santor, Donald Murray. Canadians at war 1939-1945. [0-13-113514-7].

Santor, Donald Murray. Discovery and exploration: a Canadian adventure. [0-13-215970-8].

Telford, W.P. Canadian – American relations. [0-13-114109-0].

THE CANADIANS

Fitzhenry & Whiteside. $4.95 each, paper.

Short (about sixty pages each) succinct biographies of Canadian personalities, intended for students. Photos and drawings add to the readers' enjoyment. *Older, young adult.*

Barnett, Donald. Poundmaker. [0-88902-221-6].

Bassett, John M. Henry Larsen. [0-88902-230-5].

Bassett, John M. Laura Secord. [0-88902-202-X].

Bassett, John M. Samuel Cunard. [0-88902-206-2].

Bassett, John M. Timothy Eaton. [0-88902-210-0].

Bassett, John M. and **Petrie, A. Roy.** William Hamilton Merritt. [0-88902-200-3].

Benham, Mary Lile. Nellie McClung. [0-88902-219-4].

Careless, J.M.S. George Brown. [0-88902-667-X].

Collins, Paul. Hart Massey. [0-88902-241-0].

Cosentino, Frank. Ned Hanlan. [0-88902-248-8].

Damania, Laura. Egerton Ryerson. [0-88902-212-7].

Gardner, Alison. James Douglas. [0-88902-222-4].

Gillen, Mollie. Lucy Maud Montgomery. [0-88902-244-5].

Granatstein, J.L. Mackenzie King. [0-88902-228-3].

Green, Lorne. Sandford Fleming. [0-88902-671-8].

Hall, D.J. Clifford Sifton. [0-88902-223-2].

James, Donna. Emily Murphy. [0-88902-500-2].

McDougall, Bruce. Charles Mair. [0-88902-240-2].

McDougall, Bruce. John Wilson. [0-88902-672-6].

McNaught, Kenneth. J.S. Woodsworth. [0-88902-663-7].

Mayles, Stephen. William Van Horne. [0-88902-216-X].

Murphy, Larry. Thomas Keefer. [0-88902-227-5].

Neering, Rosemary. Emily Carr. [0-88902-207-0].

Neering, Rosemary. Louis Riel. [0-88902-214-3].

Petrie, A. Roy. Alexander Graham Bell. [0-88902-209-7].

Petrie, A. Roy. Sam McLaughlin. [0-88902-205-4].

Redekop, Magdalene. Ernest Thompson Seton. [0-88902-661-0].

Saunders, Robert. R.B. Bennett. [0-88902-653-X].

Sealey, D. Bruce. Jerry Potts. [0-88902-678-5].

Shaw, Margaret M. Frederick Banting. [0-88902-229-1].

Sheffe, Norman. Casimir Gzowski. [0-88902-211-9].

Sheffe, Norman. Goldwin Smith. [0-88902-224-0].

Sturgis, James. Adam Beck. [0-88902-246-1].

Waite, Peter. John A. Macdonald. [0-88902-231-3].

Wilson, Mary C. Marion Hilliard. [0-88902-215-1].

CANADIANS ALL: PORTRAITS OF OUR PEOPLE

6 volumes published. Methuen. $6.50 each, paper. Well and not so well known Canadians whose lives will inspire young people. *Older, young adult.*

Angus, Terry and White, Shirley. Canadians all: portraits of our people. [0-458-91270-0].

Angus, Terry and White, Shirley. Canadians all 2: portraits of our people. [0-458-93860-2].

Kahn, Charles and Kahn, Maureen. Canadians all 3: portraits of our people. [0-458-94250-2].

Cowan, Doris and Weber, Ken. Canadians all 4: portraits of our people. [0-458-96909-X].

Angus, Terry; Cowan, Doris; Grant, Janet. and Sass, Greg. Canadians all 5: portraits of our people. [0-458-99060-4].

Angus, Terry. Canadians all 6: portraits of our people. [0-458-80030-9].

CENTURY OF CANADA SERIES

8 volumes. Grolier. $12.95 each, hardcover.

An analysis of the social, political, and economic history of Canada from Confederation to the present. Illustrations, maps, and an index. *Older.*

Bennett, Paul W. Years of promise: 1896-1911. [0-7172-1854-6].

Bliss, Michael. Years of change: 1967-1985. [0-7172-1857-0].

Bothwell, Robert. Years of victory: 1939-1949. [0-7172-1862-7].

English, John. Years of growth: 1948-1967. [0-7172-1856-2].

Horn, Michael. Years of despair: 1929-1939. [0-7172-1861-9].

Morton, Desmond. Years of conflict: 1911-1921. [0-7172-1844-9].

Skeoch, Alan. Years of hope: 1921-1929. [0-7172-1860-0].

Waite, P.B. Years of struggle: 1867-1879. [0-7172-1852-X].

FOCUS ON CANADIAN HISTORY SERIES

17 volumes published. Grolier. $10.95 each, hardcover.

This series covers specific incidents or topics in Canadian history. Selected biographies of leading figures of the times are included. Photographs, illustrations, and an index. *Older.*

Bercuson, David Jay and Palmer, Howard. Settling the Canadian West. [0-7172-1865-1].

Bliss, Michael. Confederation: a new nationality. [0-7172-1809-0].

Flanagan, Thomas and Rocan, Claude. Rebellion in the Northwest: Louis Riel and the Métis people. [0-7172-1885-6].

Gough, Barry. Gold Rush! [0-7172-1845-7].

Macleod, R.C. The Mounties. [0-7172-1864-3].

Monet, Jacques SJ. Union of the Canadas: 1840-1867. [0-7172-1867-8].

Moody, Barry. The Acadians. [0-7172-1810-4].

Morton, Desmond. New France and war. [0-7172-1853-8].

Morton, Desmond. Sieges of Quebec. [0-7172-1886-4].

Patterson, E. Palmer. Indian peoples of Canada. [0-7172-1819-8].

Ray, Janet. Towards women's rights. [0-7172-1811-2].

Skeoch, Alan. United Empire Loyalists and the American Revolution. [0-7172-1821-X].

Turner, Wesley. Life in Upper Canada. [0-7172-1802-3].

Wilson, Desmond. Labour in Canada. [0-7172-1820-1].

Wilson, Keith. Fur trade in Canada. [0-7172-1870-4].

Wilson, Keith. Railways in Canada: the iron link. [0-7172-1817-1].

Wilson, Keith. Red River Settlement. [0-7172-1841-4].

GROLIER ALBUM SERIES

Grolier. $9.95 each, paper.

A companion to 'Focus on Canadian history.' Photographs, illustrations, and archival materials add to topics being discussed. *Older.*

Morton, Desmond. Album of the Great War. [0-7172-1609-8].

Skeoch, Eric. Album of New France. [0-7172-1889-9].

Wilson, Keith. The Fur trade in Canada. [0-7172-1824-4].

Wilson, Keith. Album of Western settlement. [0-7172-1880-0].

GROWTH OF A NATION SERIES

21 volumes. Fitzhenry & Whiteside. $4.95 each, paper.

Intended for school use, these brief illustrated social histories illuminate specific periods in Canadian life. *Middle.*

Cochrane, Jean. The School. [0-88902-192-9].

Garrod, Stan. Confederation. [0-88902-188-0].

Garrod, Stan. Journeys of exploration. [0-88902-191-0].

Garrod, Stan. The North. [0-88902-184-8].

Garrod, Stan. Voyages of discovery. [0-88902-190-2].

Garrod, Stan and Neering, Rosemary. In the pioneer home. [0-88902-187-2].

Garrod, Stan and Neering, Rosemary. Building a new life. [0-88902-183-X].

Garrod, Stan and Neering, Rosemary. Life in Acadia. [0-88902-180-5].

Garrod, Stan and Neering, Rosemary. Life in New France. [0-88902-181-3].

Garrod, Stan and Neering, Rosemary. Life of the Loyalist. [0-88902-182-1].

Matresky, Jim and Larkin, Bill. World War I. [0-88902-518-5].

Neering, Rosemary. Building of the railway. [0-88902-177-5].

Neering, Rosemary. The Depression. [0-88902-188-9].

Neering, Rosemary. Energy. [0-88902-195-3].

Neering, Rosemary. Fur trade. [0-88902-179-1].

Neering, Rosemary. Gold Rush. [0-88902-175-9].

Neering, Rosemary. Government. [0-88902-192-5].

Neering, Rosemary. North West Mounted Police. [0-88902-176-7].

Neering, Rosemary. Settlement of the West. [0-88902-178-3].

Ryan, Judith. The Mine. [0-88902-186-4].

Schultz, Mike. The Store. [0-88902-193-7].

Trump, Christopher. Canada in space. [0-88902-638-6].

HOW THEY LIVED IN CANADA

7 volumes. Douglas & McIntyre. $6.95 each, paper. These well-illustrated, simply-written social histories of our native peoples' life before the white man came will inform any reader. *Middle, older.*

Campbell, Maria. People of the buffalo: how the Plains Indians lived. [0-88894-329-6].

Campbell, Maria. Riel's people: how the Métis lived. [0-88894-393-8].

McConkey, Lois. Sea and cedar: how the North West Coast Indians lived. [0-88894-371-7].

Marshall, Ingeborg. The Red ochre people: how Newfoundland's Beothuck Indians lived. [0-88894-367-9].

Ridington, Jillian. People of the long house: how the Iroquoian tribes lived. [0-88894-357-1].

Ridington, Robin and **Ridington, Jillian.** People of the trail: how the northern forest Indians lived. $10.95 hardcover [0-88894-221-4]; $6.95 paper [0-88894-412-8].

Siska, Heather Smith. People of the ice: how the Inuit lived. [0-88894-404-7].

IN YOUR COMMUNITY

3 volumes. Dent. $3.25 each, paper.
How the community is served by its social service workers. *Younger.*

Dobson, Murray. Dobson, Vera and **Peters, James.** The Letter carrier. [0-460-92925-9].

Peters, James and **Dobson, Murray.** The Policeman. [0-460-94139-9].

Peters, James. Peters, Julie and **Dobson, Murray.** The Firefighter. [0-460-91669-6].

KIDS LIKE US

12 volumes. Methuen. Prices below.
These multicultural readers by Beverley Allinson and Barbara O'Kelly feature four youngsters of different ethnic backgrounds – Chinese, Chilean, Trinidadian, and Jamaican – who are friendly neighbours in Toronto. *Middle, older.*

$9.95 per set, paper (use ISBN 0-458-92130); $3.95 each title.
Click. [0-458-92150-5].
Flashback. [0-458-92110-6].
Trips. [0-458-92170-X].
Wallpaper. [0-458-92130-0].

$9.95 per set, paper (use ISBN 0-458-92850); $3.95 each title.
Groaning ups. [0-458-92490-3].
Short stop. [0-458-92510-1].
Small talk. [0-458-92500-4].
Turkey pops. [0-458-92480-6].

$9.95 per set, paper (use ISBN 0-458-93460); $3.95 each title.
The Hardcastle legacy. [0-458-93140].
The Phantom sailors. [0-458-93150-0].
The Secret formula. [0-458-93120].
The Westwoods monster. [0-458-93130].

KIDS OF CANADA SERIES

9 volumes. Lorimer. $3.95 each, paper.
Meant for beginning readers, these short simple stories deal with everyday problems faced by ordinary kids. Realistic full-colour illustrations. *Younger.*

Allison, Rosemary. The Pillow. [0-88862-944-3].

Atwood, Margaret and **Barkhouse, Joyce.** Anna's pet. [0-88862-941-9].

Dewdney, Selwyn. The Hungry time. [0-88862-948-6].

Dickson, Barry. Afraid of the dark. [0-88862-943-5].

Kidd, Bruce. Hockey showdown. [0-88862-946-X].

Kidd, Bruce. Who's a soccer player. [0-88862-253-8].

Laurence, Margaret. Six darn cows. [0-88862-942-7].

O'Young, Leoung. Mike and the bike. [0-88862-947-8].

We make Canada shine: poems by children. $3.95 paper [0-88862-288-0]; $9.95 hardcover [0-88862-289-9].

KON-SKELOWH / WE ARE THE PEOPLE SERIES

Theytus. $4.50 each, paper.
A series of four stories based on Indian legends and culture originating from the Okanagan Valley in British Columbia. Illustrated by Ken Edwards with black and white drawings. *Middle.*

How food was given. [0-919441-07-6].
How names were given. [0-919441-11-4].
How turtles set the animals free. [0-919441-14-9].

Amstrong, Jeannette. Neeka and Chemai. [0-919441-13-0].

NATIVE PEOPLE OF CANADA SERIES

4 volumes. D.C. Heath. $4.43 each, paper.
Colourful illustrations and simply-written text give an excellent introduction to the lives of native people. *Middle.*

Cass, James. Ekahotan, the corn grower: Indians of the eastern woodlands. [0-669-95039-4].

Cass, James. Mistatin, the buffalo hunter: Indians of the plains. [0-669-95036-X].

Cass, James. Ochechak, the caribou hunter: Indians of the Subarctic. [0-669-95037-8].

Cass, James. Oyai, the salmon fisherman and woodworker: Indians of the north Pacific coast. [0-669-95038-6].

NATIVE PEOPLES SERIES

Grolier. $9.95 each, hardcover.

These well-illustrated books explore the lives and customs of native people in Canada past and present. *Middle, older.*

Goller, Claudine. Algonkian hunters of the Eastern Woodlands. [0-7172-1846-5].

Kirkness, Verna. Indians of the Plains. [0-7172-1855-4].

Patterson, Palmer and Patterson, Nancy-Lou. Iroquoians of the Eastern Woodlands. [0-7172-1859-7].

NATURAL HISTORY NOTEBOOK SERIES

5 volumes. National Museum of Natural Sciences. $2.95 each, paper.

Illustrated by Charles Douglas these one page 'fillers' include a line drawing and a succinct description of animals, birds, reptiles, amphibians, and insects found in Canada. *Middle.*

Natural History Notebook No.1 [0-660-00092-X].
Natural History Notebook No.2 [0-660-00094-6].
Natural History Notebook No.3 [0-660-10341-9].
Natural History Notebook No.4 [0-660-10321-4].
Natural History Notebook No.5 [0-660-10750-3].

NATURE'S CHILDREN SERIES

Grolier. $11.95 each, hardcover.

Easy-to-read books with full-page, coloured photographs of familiar animals. A series that will delight animal lovers. *Middle.*

Dingwall, Laima. Bison. [0-7172-1925-9].

Dingwall, Laima. Deer. [0-7172-1896-1].

Dingwall, Laima. Muskrats. [0-7172-1921-6].

Dingwall, Laima. Opossum. [0-7172-1926-7].

Dingwall, Laima. Porcupines. [0-7172-1902-X].

Dingwall, Laima. Raccoons. [0-7172-1898-8].

Dingwall, Laima. River otter. [0-7172-1980-9].

Dingwall, Laima. Skunks. [0-7172-1942-9].

Dingwall, Laima. Walrus. [0-7172-1938-0].

Dingwall, Laima. Woodchucks. [0-7172-1905-4].

Greenland, Caroline. Ants. [0-7172-1914-3].

Greenland, Caroline. Black bears. [0-7172-1911-9].

Greenland, Caroline. Coyote. [0-7172-1924-0].

Greenland, Caroline. Grizzly bears. [0-7172-1920-8].

Greenland, Caroline. Polar bears. [0-7172-1944-5].

Grier, Katherine. Downy woodpecker. [0-7172-1922-4].

Grier, Katherine. Cougars. [0-7172-1928-3].

Grier, Katherine. Hummingbirds. [0-7172-1608-X].

Harbury, Martin. Wild horses. [0-7172-1936-4].

Horner, Susan. Mice. [0-7172-1903-8].

Ivy, Bill. Bighorn sheep. [0-7172-1907-0].

Ivy, Bill. Frogs. [0-7172-1916-X].

Ivy, Bill. Gulls. [0-7172-1623-3].

Ivy, Bill. Mallard ducks. [0-7172-1901-1].

Ivy, Bill. Monarch butterfly. [0-7172-1923-2].

Ivy, Bill. Spiders. [0-7172-1607-1].

Ivy, Bill. Weasels. [0-7172-1913-5].

Kelsey, Elin. Bees. [0-7172-1900-3].

Kelsey, Elin. Beavers. [0-7172-1894-5].

Kelsey, Elin. Owls. [0-7172-1899-6].

Lottridge, Celia and Horner, Susan. Prairie dogs. [0-7172-1939-9].

Martin, Pamela. Elk. [0-7172-1940-2].

Peck, George K. Squirrels. [0-7172-1912-7].

Ross, Judy. Canada goose. [0-7172-1919-4].

Ross, Judy. Caribou. [0-7172-1935-6].

Ross, Judy. Loons. [0-7172-1915-1].

Ross, Judy. Moose. [0-7172-1918-6].

Ross, Judy. Wolves. [0-7172-1941-0].

Savage, Candace. Pelicans. [0-7172-1938-5].

Schemenauer, Elma. Pronghorns. [0-71721933-X].

Schemenauer, Elma. Salmon. [0-7172-1917-8].

Shawver, Mark. Sea lions. [0-7172-1934-8].

Shawver, Mark. Whales. [0-7172-1897-X].

Switzer, Merebeth. Chipmunks. [0-7172-1893-7].

Switzer, Merebeth. Hawks. [0-7172-1937-2].

Switzer, Merebeth. Lynx. [0-7172-1909-7].

Switzer, Merebeth. Muskox. [0-7172-1932-1].

Switzer, Merebeth. Rabbits. [0-7172-1895-3].

Switzer, Merebeth. Red fox. [0-7172-1904-6].

Switzer, Merebeth. Seals. [0-7172-1910-0].

Switzer, Merebeth. Snakes. [0-7172-1929-1].

Switzer, Merebeth. Turtles. [0-7172-1946-1].

Taylor, David. Sharks. [0-7172-1621-7].

Theberge, John B. and Theberge, Mary T. Grouse. [0-7172-1931-3].

Zola, Melanie. Alligators. [0-7172-1906-2]. Index/Guide. [0-7172-2167-9].

NORTHERN LIGHTS

6 volumes. Irwin. $6.95 each, hardcover.
Personal adventures woven around a fragment of Canadian life will involve beginning readers in memorable experiences. *Younger, middle.*

Downie, Mary Alice. The Last ship. Ill. by Lissa Calvert. [0-88778-201-9].

Hamilton, Mary. The Sky caribou. Ill. by Debi Perna. [0-887778-203-5].

McSweeney, Susanne. The Yellow flag. Ill. by Brenda Clark. [0-88778-204-3].

Rawlyk, George. Streets of gold. Ill. by Leoung O'Young. [0-88778-202-7].

Swainson, Donald and Swainson, Eleanor. The Buffalo hunt. Ill. by Mark Smith. [0-88778-206-X].

Tanaka, Shelley. Michi's New Year. Ill. by Ron Berg. [0-88778-205-1].

PICTURE LIFE SERIES

Grolier. Prices vary, hardcover.
High interest, low reading level books about the lives of some well-known people. *Middle, older.*

Bonic, Thomas. Pope John Paul II. $9.95 [0-7172-1866-X].

Coady, Mary Frances. Steve Podborski. $8.95 [0-7172-1833-3].

Zola, Meguido. Gretzky! Gretzky! Gretzky! $8.95 [0-7172-1826-1].

Zola, Meguido. Karen Kain. $8.95 [0-7172-1834-1].

Zola, Meguido and Zola, Melanie. Terry Fox. $9.95 [0-7172-1881-3].

Zola, Melanie and Zola, Meguido. Sharon, Lois & Bram. $8.95 [0-7172-1849-X].

PROFILES IN CANADIAN LITERATURE

Dundurn. 6 volumes. $16.50 each, paper.
A series of essays on Canadian authors. Each essay acquaints the reader with the writer's work, followed by a chronology of the author's life and comments by and about the author. Alice Munro, Gabrielle Roy, Anne Hébert, Roch Carrier, Timothy Findley are some of the authors found in these books. Edited by Jeffrey M. Heath. *Young adults.*

Profiles in Canadian literature. V.1. [0-919670-46-6].
Profiles in Canadian literature. V.2. [0-919670-50-4].
Profiles in Canadian literature. V.3. [0-919670-58-X].
Profiles in Canadian literature. V.4. [0-919670-59-8].
Profiles in Canadian literature. V.5. [1-55002-001-3].
Profiles in Canadian literature. V.6. [1-55002-002-1].

SERIES CANADA

Collier Macmillan. $4.95 each, paper.
High interest fiction. *Older, young adult.*

Bell, Bill. Metal head. [0-02-947430-2].
Godfrey, Martyn. The Beast. [0-02-947160-5].
Godfrey, Martyn. Fire! Fire! [0-947300-4].
Godfrey, Martyn. Get lost. [0-947440-X].
Godfrey, Martyn. Ice hawk. [0-947310-1].
Godfrey, Martyn. Rebel yell. [0-02-947410-8].
Godfrey, Martyn. Spin out. [0-02-947170-2].
Godfrey, Martyn. Wild night. [0-02-947420-5].
Ibbitson, John. The Wimp. [0-02-947280-6].
Kropp, Paul. Amy's wish. [0-02-947140-1].
Kropp, Paul. Baby, Baby. [0-02-997640-5].
Kropp, Paul. Burn out. [0-02-991290-3].
Kropp, Paul. Dead on. [0-02-990190-4].
Kropp, Paul. Dirt bike. [0-02-990200-2].
Kropp, Paul. Dope deal. [0-02-991270-9].
Kropp, Paul. Fair play. [0-02-990210-X].
Kropp, Paul. Gang war. [0-02-997620-0].
Kropp, Paul. Hot cars. [0-02-991260-1].
Kropp, Paul. Micro man. [0-02-947150-8].
Kropp, Paul. No way. [0-02-990180-4].
Kropp, Paul. Runaway. [0-02-991280-6].
Kropp, Paul. Snow ghost. [0-02-997610-3].
Kropp, Paul. Take off. [0-02-947290-3].
Kropp, Paul. Wild one. [0-02-997620-8].

SERIES 2000

High interest fiction. *Older, young adult.*
Collier Macmillan. $4.95 each, paper.

Godfrey, Martyn. The Last war. [0-02-947380-2].

Godfrey, Martyn. More than weird. [0-02-953499-2].

Ibbitson, John. The Wimp and easy money. [0-02-953502-6].

Ibbitson, John. The Wimp and the jock. [0-02-947390-X].

Kropp, Paul. Jo's search. [0-02-947370-5].

Kropp, Paul. Death ride. [0-02-947360-8].

Kropp, Paul. Not only me. [0-02-953500].

Kropp, Paul. Under cover. [0-02-953501-8].

SPECIAL DAYS SERIES

Grolier. $11.95 each, hardcover.
Information about special days celebrated in Canada. Illustrated. *Middle*.

Zola, Meguido. Hallowe'en. [0-7172-1890-2].

Zola, Meguido. Thanksgiving. [0-7172-1891-0].

Zola, Meguido and Dereume, Angela. Remembrance Day. [0-7172-1847-6].

WE BUILT CANADA

11 volumes published, more projected. Irwin. $6.95 each, paper.
Short, illustrated social histories on Canadian pioneers for students. *Middle, older*.

Angel, Barbara and Angel, Michael. Letitia Hargrave and life in the fur trade. [0-7725-5295-9].

Davies, Colin. Louis Riel and the new nation. [0-7725-5293-2].

Gregor, Alexander D. Vilhajalmur Stefansson and the Arctic. [0-7725-5287-8].

King, Dennis. The Grey Nuns and the Red River settlement. [0-7725-5294-0].

Klippenstein, Lawrence. David Klassen and the Mennonites. [0-7725-5296-7].

Osborne, K.W. R.B. Russell and the labor movement. [0-7725-5288-6].

Sealey, D. Bruce. Cuthbert Grant and the Métis. [0-7725-5285-1].

Sealey, D. Bruce. The Mounties and law enforcement. [0-7725-5292-4].

Wilson, Keith. Donald Smith and the Canadian Pacific Railway. [0-7725-5289-4].

Wilson, Keith. George Simpson and the Hudson's Bay Company. [0-7725-5286-X].

Wright, Helen K. Nellie McClung and women's rights. [0-7725-5290-8].

ZAP SERIES

9 volumes. Fitzhenry & Whiteside. $3.95 each, paper.
'A compelling conglomeration of fact, story, poetry, history, legend and folklore, games, and interviews with a sprinkling of things to do.' *Middle, older*.

Zap eating. [0-88902-205-X].

Zap fire. [0-88902-251-8].

Zap flying. [0-88902-257-7].

Zap hockey. [0-88902-256-9].

Zap magic. [0-88902-252-6].

Zap monsters. [0-88902-081-2].

Zap music. [0-88902-253-4].

Zap underground. [0-88902-255-7].

Zap water. [0-88902-254-2].

ZOO BOOK SERIES

12 volumes. Heath. $2.94 each, paper.
Sixteen-page booklets written by Judy Ross and designed to appeal to animal lovers and zoo visitors include well-chosen colour photos and enough pertinent facts to satisfy young students. *Younger to older*.

Amanda, the gorilla. [0-669-95006-8].

Brum, the Siberian tiger. [0-669-00822-2].

Castor, the beaver. [0-669-95003-3].

Dassen, the penguin. [0-669-00845-1].

Falstaff, the hippopotamus. [0-669-0084806].

Khan, the camel. [0-669-00847-8].

Lobo, the timber wolf. [0-669-00823-0].

Mias, the orangutan. [0-669-00846-X].

Snowflake, the polar bear. [0-669-00820-6].

Tequila, the African elephant. [0-669-00821-4].

Tonto, the South African fur seal. [0-669-95005-X].

Turk, the moose. [0-669-95004-1].

AWARD BOOKS

AMELIA FRANCES HOWARD-GIBBON AWARD

This award for the best illustrated children's book of the year has been presented since 1971 by the Canadian Associaton of Children's Librarians. A committee of CACL members chooses the winning book and the award is presented at the annual CLA conference in June of the year following the award year. The illustrator must be a Canadian citizen, and the book must be published in Canada. The prize is a sterling gilt medal suitably engraved.

1971 *The Wind has wings:* poems from Canada, compiled by Mary Alice Downie and Barbara Robertson. Ill. by Elizabeth Cleaver. Oxford, 1968.

1972 *A Child in prison camp*, by Shizuye Takashima. Ill. by Shizuye Takashima. Tundra, 1971.

1973 *Au-delà du soleil/Beyond the sun*, by Jacques de Roussan. Ill. by Jacques de Roussan. Tundra, 1972.

1974 *A Prairie boy's winter*, by William Kurelek. Ill. by William Kurelek. Tundra, 1973.

1975 *The Sleighs of my childhood/Les traîneaux de mon enfance*, by Carlo Italiano. Ill. by Carlo Italiano. Tundra, 1974.

1976 *A Prairie boy's summer*, by William Kurelek. Ill. by William Kurelek. Tundra, 1975.
Runner up: *The Witch of the North*, by Mary Alice Downie. Ill. by Elizabeth Cleaver. Oberon, 1975.

1977 *Down by Jim Long's stage*, by Al Pittman. Ill. by Pam Hall. Breakwater, 1976.
Runner up: *Québec je t'aime/I love you*, by Miyuki Tanobe. Ill. by Miyuki Tanobe. Tundra, 1976.

1978 *The Loon's necklace*, by William Toye. Ill. by Elizabeth Cleaver. Oxford, 1977.
Runner up: *Garbage delight*, by Dennis Lee. Ill. by Frank Newfeld. Macmillan, 1977.

1979 *A Salmon for Simon*, by Betty Waterton. Ill. by Ann Blades. Douglas & McIntyre, 1978.
Runner up: *Great Canadian animal stories*, edited by Muriel Whitaker. Ill. by Vlasta Van Kampen. Hurtig, 1978.

1980 *The Twelve dancing princesses*, by Janet Lunn. Ill. by Laszlo Gal. Methuen, 1979.
Runners up: *Great Canadian adventure stories*, edited by Muriel Whitaker. Ill. by Vlasta Van Kampen. Hurtig, 1979; and *The Olden days coat*, by Margaret Laurence. Ill. by Muriel Wood. McClelland & Stewart, 1979.

1981 *The Trouble with princesses*, by Christie Harris. Ill. by Douglas Tait. McClelland & Stewart, 1980.
Runners up: *The Buffalo hunt*, by Donald Swainson and Eleanor Swainson. Ill. by James Tughan. PMA Books, 1980; and *Michi's New Year*, by Shelley Tanaka. Ill. by Ron Berg. PMA Books, 1980.

1982 Ytek and the Arctic orchid: an Inuit legend, by Garnet Hewitt. Ill. by Heather Woodall. Douglas & McIntyre, 1981.
Runners up: *The Mare's egg*, by Carole Spray. Ill. by Kim LaFave. Camden House, 1981; and *Merchants of the mysterious East*, by John Lim. Ill. by John Lim. Tundra, 1981.

AWARD BOOKS 87

1983 *Chester's barn*, by Lindee Climo. Ill. by Lindee Climo. Tundra, 1982.
Runner up: *A Northern alphabet*, by Ted Harrison. Ill. by Ted Harrison. Tundra, 1982.

1984 *Zoom at sea*, by Tim Wynne-Jones. Ill. by Ken Nutt. Groundwood, 1983.
Runner up: *The Little mermaid*, retold by Margaret Crawford Maloney. Ill. by Laszlo Gal. Methuen, 1983.

1985 *Chin Chiang and the dragon's dance*, by Ian Wallace. Ill. by Ian Wallace. Groundwood, 1984.
Runners up: *The Owl and the pussycat*, by Edward Lear. Ill. by Ron Berg. North Winds, 1984; and *The Hockey sweater*, by Roch Carrier. Ill. by Sheldon Cohen. Tundra, 1984.

1986 *Zoom away*, by Tim Wynne-Jones. Ill. by Ken Nutt. Groundwood, 1985.
Runners up: *By the sea: an alphabet book*, by Ann Blades. Ill. by Ann Blades. Kids Can, 1985; and *The Sorcerer's apprentice*, by Robin Muller. Ill. by Robin Muller. Kids Can, 1985.

1987 *Moonbeam on a cat's ear*, by Marie-Louise Gay. Ill. by Marie-Louise Gay. Stoddart, 1986.
Runner up: *Have you seen birds?*, by Joanne Oppenheim. Ill. by Barbara Reid. North Winds, 1986.

CANADA COUNCIL CHILDREN'S LITERATURE PRIZES

This award was established in 1975 and included two annual prizes of $5000 in recognition of outstanding contributions to Canadian literature for children in the English and French languages. Since 1980, four annual prizes of $5000 are given each year, one each to an English-language writer, a French-language writer, an illustrator of an English-language book, and an illustrator of a French-language book. A panel of judges is appointed by The Canada Council and the prizes are presented each year in a different city across the country. All books for children written or illustrated by Canadian citizens are eligible, whether published in Canada or abroad. The award is announced the year following the year of publication.

1975 *Shantymen of Cache Lake*, by Bill Freeman. Lorimer, 1975.

1976 *The Wooden people*, by Myra Paperny. Little Brown, 1976.

1977 *Listen for the singing*, by Jean Little. Clarke, Irwin, 1977.

1978 Text: *Hold fast*, by Kevin Major. Clarke, Irwin, 1978. Illustration: *A Salmon for Simon*, by Betty Waterton. Ill. by Ann Blades. Douglas & McIntyre, 1978.

1979 Text: *Days of terror*, by Barbara Smucker. Clarke, Irwin, 1979. Illustration: *The Twelve dancing princesses*, by Janet Lunn. Ill. by Laszlo Gal. Methuen, 1979.

1980 Text: *The Trouble with princesses*, by Christie Harris. McClelland & Stewart, 1980. Illustration: *Petrouchka*, by Elizabeth Cleaver. Ill. by Elizabeth Cleaver. Macmillan, 1980.

1981 Text: *The Guardian of Isis*, by Monica Hughes. Hamish Hamilton, 1981. Illustration: *Ytek and the Arctic orchid: an Inuit legend*, by Garnet Hewitt. Ill. by Heather Woodall. Douglas & McIntyre, 1981.

1982 Text: *Hunter in the dark*, by Monica Hughes. Clarke, Irwin, 1982. Illustration: *ABC/123: the Canadian alphabet and counting book*, by Vlasta Van Kampen. Ill. by Vlasta Van Kampen. Hurtig, 1982.

1983 Text: *The Ghost horse of the Mounties*, by sean o huigin. Black Moss, 1983. Illustration: *The Little mermaid* by Margaret Crawford Maloney. Ill. by Laszlo Gal. Methuen, 1983.

1984 Text: *Sweetgrass*, by Jan Hudson. Tree Frog, 1984. Illustration: *Lizzy's lion*, by Dennis Lee. Ill. by Marie-Louise Gay. Stoddart, 1984.

1985 Text: *Julie*, by Cora Taylor. Western Producer Prairie, 1985. Illustration: *Murdo's story*, by Murdo Scribe. Ill. by Terry Gallagher. Pemmican, 1985.

1986 Text: *Shadow in Hawthorn Bay*, by Janet Lunn. Lester & Orpen Dennys, 1986. Illustration: *Have you seen birds?*, by Joanne Oppenheim. Ill. by Barbara Reid. North Winds, 1986.

1987 Text:

Illustration:

CANADIAN LIBRARY ASSOCIATION BOOK-OF-THE-YEAR FOR CHILDREN AWARD

This is the longest-standing Canadian award given annually for the best children's book, chosen by a committee of members of the Canadian Association of Children's Librarians, a section of the Canadian Library Association. The award is presented at the annual CLA conference in June of the year following the award year. To merit consideration a book must have been published in Canada, written by a Canadian citizen, or written on a Canadian subject. Regulations governing the award have been changed a number of times; therefore two awards are listed for 1966. The prize is a sterling gilt medal suitably engraved.

1947 *Starbuck Valley winter*, by Roderick Haig-Brown. Morrow, 1943.

1948 No award.

1949 *Kristli's trees*, by Mabel Dunham. McClelland & Stewart, 1948.

1950 *Franklin of the Arctic*, by Richard S. Lambert. McClelland & Stewart, 1949.

1951 No award.

1952 *The Sun horse*, by Catherine Anthony Clark. Macmillan, 1951.

1953 No award.

1954 No award.

1955 No award.

1956 *Train for Tiger Lily*, by Louise Riley. Macmillan, 1954.

1957 *Glooskap's country and other Indian tales*, by Cyrus Macmillan. Oxford, 1955.

1958 *Lost in the barrens*, by Farley Mowat. Little, Brown, 1956.

1959 *The Dangerous cove: a story of early days in Newfoundland*, by John F. Hayes. Copp, Clark, 1957.

1960 *The Golden phoenix and other French-Canadian fairy tales*, by Marius Barbeau. Retold by Michael Hornyansky. Oxford, 1958.

1961 *The St. Lawrence*, by William Toye. Oxford, 1959.

1962 No award.

1963 *The Incredible journey: a tale of three animals*, by Sheila Burnford. Little, Brown, 1961.

1964 *The Whale people*, by Roderick Haig-Brown. Collins, 1962.

1965 *Tales of Nanabozho*, by Dorothy M. Reid. Oxford, 1963.

1966 *The Double knights: more tales from round the world*, by James McNeill. Oxford, 1964.

1966 *Tikta'liktak: an Eskimo legend*, by James Houston. Longmans, 1965.

1967 *Raven's cry*, by Christie Harris. McClelland & Stewart, 1966.

1968 *The White archer: an Eskimo legend*, by James Houston. Longmans, 1967.

1969 *And to-morrow the stars: the story of John Cabot*, by Kay Hill. Dodd, Mead, 1968.

1970 *Sally go round the sun: 300 songs, rhymes and games of Canadian children*, by Edith Fowke. McClelland & Stewart, 1969.

1971 *Cartier discovers the St. Lawrence*, by William Toye. Oxford, 1970.

1972 *Mary of Mile 18*, by Ann Blades. Tundra, 1971.

1973 *The Marrow of the world*, by Ruth Nichols. Macmillan, 1972.

1974 *The Miraculous hind*, by Elizabeth Cleaver. Holt, 1973.

1975 *Alligator pie*, by Dennis Lee. Macmillan, 1974.
Runner up: *Slave of the Haida*, by Doris Andersen. Macmillan, 1974.

1976 *Jacob Two-Two meets the Hooded Fang*, by Mordecai Richler. Little, Brown, 1975.
Runner up: *A Prairie boy's summer*, by William Kurelek. Tundra, 1975.

1977 *Mouse Woman and the vanished princesses*, by Christie Harris. McClelland & Stewart, 1976.
Runner up: *Simon and the golden sword*, by Frank Newfeld. Oxford, 1976.

1978 *Garbage delight*, by Dennis Lee. Macmillan, 1977.
Runner up: *Underground to Canada*, by Barbara Smucker. Clarke, Irwin, 1977.

1979 *Hold fast*, by Kevin Major. Clarke, Irwin, 1978.
Runner up: *A Salmon for Simon*, by Betty Waterton. Douglas & McIntyre, 1978.

1980 *River runners: a tale of hardship and bravery*, by James Houston. McClelland & Stewart, 1979.
Runners up: *The Olden days coat*, by Margaret Laurence. McClelland & Stewart, 1979; and *Days of terror*, by Barbara Smucker. Clarke, Irwin, 1979.

1981 *The Violin maker's gift*, by Donn Kushner. Macmillan, 1980.
Runner up: *The Trouble with princesses*, by Christie Harris. McClelland and Stewart, 1980.

1982 *The Root cellar*, by Janet Lunn. Lester & Orpen Dennys, 1981.
Runners up: *Long claws*, by James Houston. McClelland & Stewart, 1981; and *Ytek and the Arctic orchid: an Inuit legend*, by Garnet Hewitt. Douglas & McIntyre, 1981.

1983 *Up to Low*, by Brian Doyle. Groundwood, 1982.
Runner up: *Jasmin*, by Jan Truss. Groundwood, 1982.

1984 *Sweetgrass*, by Jan Hudson. Tree Frog, 1984.
Runner up: *Jelly Belly*, by Dennis Lee. Macmillan, 1983.

1985 *Mama's going to buy you a mockingbird*, by Jean Little. Viking Kestrel, 1984.
Runners up: *Cowboys don't cry*, by Marilyn Halvorson. Irwin, 1984; and *Witchery Hill*, by Welwyn Katz. Groundwood, 1984.

1986 *Julie*, by Cora Taylor. Western Producer Prairie, 1985.
Runner up: *Wild man of the woods*, by Joan Clark. Viking Kestrel, 1985.

1987 *Shadow in Hawthorn Bay*, by Janet Lunn. Lester & Orpen Dennys, 1986.
Runners up: *The Emperor's panda*, by David Day. McClelland and Stewart, 1986; and *Sun god, moon witch*, by Welwyn Katz. Groundwood, 1986.

ELIZABETH MRAZIK-CLEAVER CANADIAN PICTURE BOOK AWARD

The annual award, in the amount of $1,000, is administered by the Canadian Section of the International Board on Books for Young People. Established in 1986, the award will be given for the best illustrated picture book published in Canada (English or French) during the previous calendar year.

1986 *By the sea: an alphabet book*, by Ann Blades. Ill. by Ann Blades. Kids Can, 1985.

1987 *Have you seen birds?* by Joanne Oppenheim. Ill. by Barbara Reid. Scholastic-TAB, 1986.

NATIONAL CHAPTER IODE BOOK AWARD

In 1985, the National Chapter of the Canadian IODE established an annual award carrying a cash value of $3000 for the best English language book written for children thirteen and under, and containing at least three hundred words of text. The book must be written by a Canadian citizen and must be published in Canada. The winner is chosen by a five member panel of judges, which include the National President, the National Education Secretary, a third IODE member appointed annually by the National Education Committee, and two non-members who are recognized specialists in the field of children's literature. The award may be divided between two people.

1985 *Winners*, by Mary-Ellen Lang Collura. Western Producer Prairie, 1984.

1986 *The Quarter-pie window*, by Marianne Brandis. Porcupine's Quill, 1985.

1987 *Shadow in Hawthorn Bay*, by Janet Lunn. Lester & Orpen Dennys, 1986.

MAX AND GRETA EBEL MEMORIAL AWARD FOR CHILDREN'S WRITING

This award carrying a cash value of $100 is given to a children's book that contributes to a greater understanding among people of different backgrounds, cultures, and/or generations. The winning title must be written by a Canadian citizen. The award is administered by the Canadian Society of Children's Authors, Illustrators, and Performers (CANSCAIP). The award is judged by a panel of persons knowledgeable about Canadian children's books.

1986 *Winners*, by Mary-Ellen Lang Collura. Western Producer Prairie, 1984.

1987

RUTH SCHWARTZ CHILDREN'S BOOK AWARD

This award of $2000 was established in 1975 in memory of Toronto bookseller, Ruth Schwartz. The prize is awarded annually to the writer or creative source of an outstanding work of Canadian children's literature. The award is sponsored by the Canadian Booksellers Association and the Ontario Arts Council. The award is presented by the Canadian Booksellers Association, usually at their annual convention, or by any other group appointed by the Ontario Arts Council. The winning book must be published in Canada during the previous year and the author must be a Canadian citizen. The award may be divided between two people.

1976 Mordecai Richler. *Jacob Two-Two meets the Hooded Fang*. McClelland & Stewart, 1975.

1977 Robert Thomas Allen. *The Violin*. McGraw-Hill Ryerson, 1976.

1978 Dennis Lee. *Garbage delight*. Macmillan, 1977.

1979 Kevin Major. *Hold fast*. Clarke, Irwin, 1978.

1980 Barbara Smucker. *Days of terror*. Clarke, Irwin, 1979.

1981 Suzanne Martel. *The King's daughter*. Groundwood, 1980.

1982 Marsha Hewitt and Claire Mackay. *One proud summer*. Women's, 1981.

1983 Jan Truss. *Jasmin*. Groundwood, 1982.

1984 Tim Wynne-Jones. *Zoom at sea*. Groundwood, 1983.

1985 Jean Little. *Mama's going to buy you a mockingbird*. Viking Kestrel, 1984.

1986 Robert Munsch. *Thomas' snowsuit*. Annick, 1985.

1987 Barbara Reid. *Have you seen birds?* by Joanne Oppenheim. Ill. by Barbara Reid. North Winds, 1986.

TORONTO IODE AWARD

Since 1974, the Municipal Chapter of Toronto Independent Order of the Daughters of the Empire in cooperation with the Toronto Public Library Board has presented an award to encourage the publication of books for children between the ages of six and twelve years. The award carries a prize of $1000 and is given annually to either an author or illustrator of a children's book written or illustrated by a Canadian citizen residing in Toronto or surrounding area and published in the preceding twelve months. The selection is made by a panel consisting of Toronto Public Library staff and representatives of the Municipal Chapter of the Toronto IODE.

1974 William Kurelek. *A Prairie boy's winter*. Tundra, 1973.

1975 Dennis Lee. *Alligator pie*. Macmillan, 1974.

1976 Aviva Layton. *How the kookaburra got his laugh*. McClelland & Stewart, 1976.

1977 William Toye. *The Loon's necklace*. Oxford, 1977.

1978 Laszlo Gal for his illustrations in *My name is not Odessa Yarker*, by Marian Engel. Kids Can, 1977; *Why the man in the moon is happy*, by Ronald Melzack. McClelland & Stewart, 1977; *The Shirt of the happy man*, by Mariella Bertelli. Kids Can, 1977.

1979 Janet Lunn. *The Twelve dancing princesses*. Methuen, 1978.

1980 Olena Kassian for her illustrations in *Afraid of the dark*, by Barry Dickson. Lorimer, 1980; and *The Hungry time*, by Selwyn Dewdney. Lorimer, 1980.

1981 Bernice Thurman Hunter. *That scatterbrain Booky*. Scholastic-TAB, 1981.

1982 Kathy Stinson. *Red is best*. Annick, 1982.

1983 Tim Wynne-Jones. *Zoom at sea*. Groundwood, 1983.

1984 Ian Wallace. *Chin Chiang and the dragon's dance*. Groundwood, 1984.

1985 Robin Muller. *The Sorcerer's apprentice*. Kids Can, 1985.

1986 Barbara Reid for her illustrations in *Have you seen birds?* by Joanne Oppenheim. North Winds, 1986.

1987

VICKY METCALF AWARD

The $2000 award presented annually is donated by Mrs. Vicky Metcalf and administered by the Canadian Authors' Association. The award is given to any Canadian writer (citizen or landed immigrant) who has produced a body of work (more than three books) with appeal for children ages seven to seventeen. Submissions are judged by a panel of experts, and the recipient of the award is announced each June at the Canadian Authors' Association Annual Conference.

1963 Kerry Wood

1964 John F. Hayes

1965 Roderick Haig-Brown

1966 Fred Swayze

1967 John Patrick Gillese

1968 Lorraine McLaughlin

1969 Audry McKim

1970 Farley Mowat

1971 Kay Hill

1972 William Toye

1973 Christie Harris

1974 Jean Little

1975 Lyn Harrington

1976 Suzanne Martel

1977 James Houston

1978 Lyn Cook

1979 Cliff Faulknor

1980 John Craig
1981 Monica Hughes
1982 Janet Lunn
1983 Claire Mackay
1984 Bill Freeman
1985 Edith Fowke
1986 Dennis Lee
1987 Robert Munsch

VICKY METCALF SHORT STORY AWARD

Presented annually by the Canadian Authors' Association to the Canadian writer (citizen or landed immigrant) of the best children's short story published in Canada in the previous year. The selection is made by an independent panel of judges, and the award carries a prize of $1000. The prize is given at the annual awards dinner of the Canadian Authors' Association.

1979 Marina McDougall. 'The Kingdom of riddles' in *Ready or not*. Ed. by Jack Booth. (Language Patterns Impressions Reading Series) Holt, Rinehart and Winston, 1978.

1980 Estelle Salata. 'Blind date' in *Time enough*. Ed. by Jack Booth. (Language Patterns Impressions Reading Series) Holt, Rinehart and Winston, 1979.

1981 James Houston. 'Long claws' in *The Winter fun book*. Ed. by Laima Dingwall and Annabel Slaight. Greey de Pencier, 1980.

1982 Barbara Greenwood. 'A Major resolution' in *Contexts*. (An intermediate level anthology) Nelson Canada, 1981.

1983 Monica Hughes. 'The Iron barred door' in *Anthology 2*. Nelson Canada. 1982.

1984 P. Colleen Archer. 'The Dog who wanted to die'. *JAM Magazine*, Volume 4, Number 1 (September/October), 1983.

1985 Martyn Godfrey. Here she is, Ms. Teeny-Wonderful! *Crackers Magazine*, Number 12 (Spring), 1984.

1986 Diana J. Wieler. 'The Boy who walked backwards.' Western Producer Prairie, 1985.

1987 Isabel Reimer. 'The Viking dagger.' in *Of the Jigsaw*. Peguis, 1986.

YOUNG ADULT CANADIAN BOOK AWARD

This prize has been established by the Saskatchewan Library Association as an annual award for the best English-language Canadian book for young adults. The winning book must be a work of creative literature (novel, play, or poetry) for young adults, written by a Canadian citizen or landed immigrant, and published in Canada. The winning book is selected by a seven-person committee representing Saskatchewan librarians, educators, authors, and individuals working with young adults.

1981 *Far from shore*, by Kevin Major. Clarke, Irwin, 1980.

1982 *Superbike!*, by Jamie Brown. Clarke, Irwin, 1981.

1983 *Hunter in the dark*, by Monica Hughes. Clarke, Irwin, 1982.

1984 *The Druid's tune*, by O.R. Melling. Viking Kestrel, 1983.

1985 *Winners*, by Mary-Ellen Lang Collura. Western Producer Prairie, 1984.

1986 *The Quarter-pie window*, by Marianne Brandis. Porcupine's Quill. 1985.

1987 *Shadow in Hawthorn Bay*, by Janet Lunn. Lester & Orpen Dennys, 1986.

PROFESSIONAL MEDIA

PROFESSIONAL TOOLS

Amey, L.J. The Canadian school housed-public library. Illustrated with photographs and charts. Dalhousie University Libraries and School of Library Service, 1979. 488 pp. $16.50 paper [0-7703-0159-2]. (Occasional paper number 24)

This large volume brings together all essential information on the school-housed public library, stressing the Canadian experience.

Animal world in Canadian books for children and young people/Le monde animal dans les livres de jeunesse canadiens. Prepared by Irene E. Aubrey. National Library of Canada, 1983. 24 pp. Free [0-662-52331-8].

An alphabetically-annotated list of some of the best Canadian animal stories published in English and French for children and young people. All annotations are in English and in French.

Aubrey, Irene E. Notable Canadian children's books, 1975-1979/Un choix de livres canadiens pour la jeunesse 1975-1979. National Library of Canada, 1985. 103 pp. $8.95 paper [0-660-53040-6]; $10.75 other countries.

Critical evaluations of some of the outstanding books produced in Canada for children and young people from 1975 to 1979. The reviews are written in English and French. Two indexes give access to books by author, illustrator, translator, subject, and literary awards.

Aubrey, Irene E. Pictures to share: illustration in Canadian children's books/Images pour tous: illustration de livres canadiens pour enfants. National Library of Canada, 1987. 59 pp. $4.95 paper [0-660-53763-X]; $5.95 other countries.

Divided into three parts (from the nineteenth century to 1959, from 1960 to 1979, and from 1980 to 1985), this revised edition gives a representative selection of the books illustrated by Canadian illustrators. Brief annotations are included with each entry. An alphabetical index by author and title is included.

Austrom, Liz, ed. Young relationships: a booktalk guide to novels for Grades 6 through 9. B.C. Teacher-Librarians' Assoc., 1983. Dist. by Bill Scott, Box 985, Hope, B.C., V0X 1L0. 151 pp. $7.50 paper. No ISBN.

A collection of booktalks for grades six to nine including American, British, and Canadian titles. Written by teacher-librarians in British Columbia, each entry includes booktalk information, plot summary, theme(s) and related titles, a list of read-aloud passages, and the Fry readability level. A subject index, as well as a title index, is included.

Blostein, Fay. Invitations, celebrations: a handbook of ideas and techniques for book talks to junior and senior high school students. Ontario Library Association, 1980. $8.95 paper [0-88969-013-8].

A wealth of creative and exciting ideas to motivate young people to read.

Butler, Marian, ed. Canadian books in print: author and title index. Univ. of Toronto, 1987. 1040 pp. $70.00 hardcover [0-8020-4634-7]. Quarterly service (microfiche and hardcover) $110.00.

This invaluable index to Canadian publications is further enhanced by three updates per year on microfiche.

Butler, Marian, ed. Canadian books in print: subject index. Univ. of Toronto, 1987. 642 pp. $55.00 hardcover [0-8020-4635-5].

This subject access to Canadian books lists 26,000 titles in 700 subject categories.

Canadian books for younger children. The Canadian Book Information Centre, annual. Free. (self-addressed stamped business envelope).

Canadian books for older children. The Canadian Book Information Centre, annual. Free. (self-addressed stamped business envelope).

Arranged by subjects, these two flyers list Canadian children's books published by members of the Canadian Book Information Centre. Each entry includes ordering information and a brief description. Not selected.

Canadian films for children and young adults. Prepared by the Canadian Association of Children's Librarians. Canadian Library Association, 1987. 33 pp. $10.00 paper [0-88802-219-0].

A comprehensive and annotated list of Canadian films to help librarians in planning and conducting film programmes and in selecting films for their 16 mm film collections.

Canadian translations/Traductions canadiennes 1986. National Library of Canada, 1987. 496 pp. $36.25 loose leaf [0-660-53802-4]; other countries $43.50.

A compilation of translations published in Canada and catalogued by the National Library during 1986. The list is divided in two parts: subject and author-title.

Cariou, Mavis; Cox, Sandra J.; and Bregman, Alvan. Canadian selection: books and periodicals for libraries. Univ. of Toronto, 1986. 2nd ed. 501 pp. $65.00 hardcover [0-8020-4630-4].

This annotated guide lists some 5400 books and 250 periodicals for small- and medium-sized libraries. No children's books are listed but it is valuable as a reference resource for librarians working in public libraries.

Children's choices of Canadian books. Citizens' Committee on Children, Box 6133, Station J, Ottawa, Ontario. K2A 1T2. 1979 v.1 $3.50 paper [0-9690205-0-3], ed. by Margaret Cauhey. 1981 v.2 $5.00 paper [0-9690205-1-1], ed. by Margaret Cauhey. 1984 v.3 $7.00 paper [0-9690205-2-X], ed. by Margaret Cauhey. 1985 v.4/4 issues $15.00 looseleaf [0-9690205-3-8], ed. by Jane Charlton.

Read by children, the books are divided in six groups from the books enjoyed by 90 per cent or more of the readers in group 1 to the ones not enjoyed by the readers in group 6. For each story, the type of story, the setting, the time, a brief annotation, and the reactions of the children are given.

CSLA policy statement: a recommended curriculum for education for school librarianship. Canadian Library Association, 1982. 11 pp. $2.00 paper [0-88802-174-7].

Dick, Judith. Not in our schools?!!! School book censorship in Canada: a discussion guide. Canadian Library Association, 1982. 97 pp. $15.00 paper [0-88802-162-3].

'Intended as a readable, informative general guide for parents, teachers, administrators and others who are becoming increasingly concerned about the choice of school books in Canada,' this guide provides a national focus on book censorship.

Driscoll, Dianne; Shields, Patricia; and Austrom, Liz. Fuel for change: cooperative program planning and teaching. British Columbia Teacher-Librarians' Association (2235 Burrard, Vancouver, B.C. V6J 3H9), 1986. 186 pp. No ISBN.

A collection of co-operatively developed units that offer a range of grade levels, subject areas, teaching strategies, and student products.

England, Claire, ed. Guide to basic reference materials for Canadian libraries. Univ. of Toronto, 1984. 309 pp. $25.00 paper [0-8020-6581-3].

Divided into four sections (General reference, Humanities, Social Sciences, and Science and Technology), entries are annotated to indicate their scope and special features.

England, Claire and Fasick, Adele M. Childview: evaluating and reviewing materials for children. Libraries Unlimited, 1987. 200 pp. $23.50 hardcover [0-87287-519-9].

A guide for teachers and librarians involved in reviewing and evaluating both print and non-print materials for children from the toddler to pre-teen. The authors analyse different types and formats of books through picture books, fiction, poetry, traditional materials, biography and history, information books, dictionaries and encyclopedias, and non-print materials.

Gagnon, André and Gagnon, Ann, eds. Meeting the challenge: library service to young adults. Canadian Library Association, 1985. 158 pp. $15.00 paper [0-88802-193-3].

A collection of fifteen articles on how and why to provide library service to young adults, contributed by Canadian librarians who are in the vanguard of service to young adults in school and public libraries.

Greater Vancouver Library Federation. Read to me: libraries, books and your baby. Greater Victoria Library Federation, 110-6545 Bonsor Avenue, Burnaby, B.C. V5H 1H3. Colour videotape, 15 minutes. 1 copy $50.00, 2 or more $30.00 each. Available VHS, Beta or 3/4" Umatic formats.

This videotape aimed at parents of young children emphasizes the importance of reading to babies in the development of language skills and imagination. Excellent for parent groups.

Halpenny, Francess G. Canadian collections in public libraries. Book and Periodical Development Council, 1985. 280 pp. $50.00 spiral bound [0-9692164-0-8].

Findings of the research project commissioned by the Department of Communications to acquire data 'about the nature of collections of Canadian print materials in public libraries.'

Haycock, Ken and **Haycock, Carol-Ann**, eds. Kids and libraries: selections from *Emergency Librarian*. Dyad Services, 1984. 229 pp. $25.00 paper [0-920175-00-7].

A selection of sixty-one articles and editorials published in *Emergency Librarian* from 1973 to 1983 'that reflects the issues and concerns of teachers and librarians working with young people in school and public libraries.'

Hébert, Françoise. Report on photocopying in Canadian libraries. Canadian Library Association, 1987. $55.00 paper [0-88802-233-6].

Levetzow, Joanna von. How to start and maintain a toy library. Canadian Association of Toy Libraries (300 Montrose Avenue, Toronto, Ontario. M6G 3G9), 1986. 3rd ed. 38 pp. $6.00 paper [0-919051-01-4].

A basic guide to help organizations establish a toy library in their community.

Library service to children: CACL pamphlet series. Ed. by Ann Gagnon for the Canadian Association of Children's Librarians. Canadian Library Association, 1987. 10 pamphlets $5.00 each, 5 of any title $20.00. #1 Guidelines for children's services, by Ann Gagnon. #2 Budgeting for children's services, by Callie Israel. #3 Collection development, by Lynne Bernard. #4 Time for tots: library Service to toddlers, by Virginia Van Vliet. #5 Preschool storytimes, by Ken Roberts. #6 Programming for school-aged children, by Melody Wood. #7 Multicultural programming, by Rita Cox, with Ann Gagnon. #8 Audio-visual media for children in the public library, by Linda Pearse. #9 Computers in the library, by Pamela Maki-Carolli and Lynne McKechnie. #10 Community outreach and publicity, by Kathleen Petrie.

The pamphlets provide an overview of theory and practice in children's librarianship. A useful tool for small- and medium-sized libraries. The pamphlets are three-hole punched for collection in a binder.

Kogan, Marilyn H. and **Whalen, George.** Handbook for school library organization. McGraw, 1980. 224 pp. $23.50 hardcover [0-07-077833-7].

This complete guide combines detailed, thorough cataloguing procedures with up-to-date information on computerization, commercial cataloguing, and networking.

Lorimer, Rowland M. The Nation in the schools. OISE, 1984. 113 pp. $15.50 paper [0-7744-0271-7].

Lorimer documents the lack of Canadian content and orientation in schools.

Meet the author: sound filmstrips or video format. Canadian Children's Book Centre, 229 College Street, 5th floor, Toronto, Ontario. M5T 1R4. Filmstrip $54.95; Video format (VHS or Beta) $73.00.

An introduction to Canadian authors for children and young people based on conversations with authors and readings from their works. Now available are Elizabeth Cleaver, Brian Doyle, James Houston, Monica Hughes, Gordon Korman, Dennis Lee, Jean Little, Farley Mowat, Claire Mackay, Robert Munsch, Barbara Smucker, Kathy Stinson, Patti Stren, Eric Wilson, Janet Lunn, Bernice Thurman Hunter.

Mystery and adventure in Canadian books for children and young people/Romans policiers et histoires d'aventures canadiens pour la jeunesse. List prepared by Irene E. Aubrey. National Library of Canada, 1983. 18 pp. Free [0-662-52484-5].

An annotated booklist of English and French children's mystery and adventure books. The list is arranged alphabetically by author and includes a title index. Annotations are in French and in English.

Our choice/your choice catalogue. Canadian Children's Book Centre, 229 College Street, 5th floor, Toronto, Ontario. M5T 1R4. Annual.

The books included in the catalogue are selected by a committee of independent children's book specialists. Each entry is annotated and listed according to subject, reading level, and interest level. An excellent buying tool for people involved in the selection of Canadian children's books.

Ryder, Dorothy E. Canadian reference sources. Canadian Library Association, 1981. 2nd ed. 311 pp. $20.00 hardcover [0-88802-156-9].

Invaluable guide to Canadian reference books for library collection building.

Sports and games in Canadian children's books/Livres canadiens sur les sports et jeux pour la jeunesse. Prepared by Irene E. Aubrey. National Library of Canada, 1982. 12 pp. Free [0-662-51763-6].

An annotated booklist of French and English children's books on sports and games including fiction and non-fiction titles. The list is arranged alphabetically by author and includes a title and subject index. Annotations are in French and in English.

Thorne, Eunice A. and Matheson, Edward, eds. The Book trade in Canada/L'industrie du livre au Canada. Ampersand, 1986. Annual $27.50 paper [920262-20-1].

Includes pertinent information on publishers and distributors, sales agents and wholesalers, industry-related organizations, booksellers, and literary awards and prizes.

Weihs, Jean; Lewis, Shirley; and Macdonald, Janet. Non book materials: the organization of integrated collections. Canadian Library Association, 1979. 134 pp. 2nd ed. $12.00 paper [0-88802-130-5].

Comprehensive manual for all aspects of a media centre's collection. Interprets AACR2 and is companion volume to that code.

Where books come from. Canadian Children's Book Centre, 229 College Street, 5th floor, Toronto, Ontario. M5T 1R4. $15.00 for each kit.

An educational kit which describes all the processes involved in the production of books in Canada. The package includes a full-colour poster by Clive Dobson, a set of ten showcards which describe each production process, a teacher's guide, , and a sample of a colour key.

LITERARY HISTORY & CRITICISM

Amtmann, Bernard. A Bibliography of Canadian children's books and books for young people 1841-1867/Livres de l'enfance et livres de la jeunesse au Canada 1841-1867. Bernard Amtmann, 1977. VII, 124 pp. $25.00 paper. No ISBN.

Amtmann, Bernard. Early Canadian children's books 1763-1840:a bibliographical investigation into the nature of early Canadian children's books and books for young people/Livres de l'enfance et livres de la jeunesse au Canada 1763-1840: Etude bibliographique. Bernard Amtmann, n.d. No ISBN.

Bibliographic investigations of works 'suitable for and available to juvenile readers, even if not always intended for them' published and printed in Canada up to 1867. Sources and locations are cited.

Demers, Patricia and Moyles, Gordon, eds. From instruction to delight: an anthology of children's literature to 1850. Oxford, 1982. 310 pp. $11.50 paper [0-19-540384-3].

Excerpts and complete works from children's literature written (or translated) in English up to 1850. Explanations and illustrations.

Egoff, Sheila, ed. One ocean touching: papers from the first Pacific Rim Conference on children's literature. Scarecrow, 1979. 260 pp. $17.50 hardcover [0-8108-1199-5].

Papers include contributions by Claude Aubry, Suzanne Martel, Ivan Southall, and Leon Garfield.

Egoff, Sheila, ed. The Republic of childhood: a critical guide to Canadian children's literature in English. Oxford, 1975. 2nd ed. $7.95 paper [0-19-540233-2].

An historical survey of Canadian children's books published after 1950, dealing with legends, fantasy, folk and fairy tales, historical fiction, animal stories, history, biography, and five other categories.

Egoff, Sheila. Thursday's child: trends and patterns in contemporary children's literature. American Library Association, 1981. 323 pp. $22.00 hardcover [0-8389-0327-4].

Critical analysis of the wide range of imaginative literature for children issued since the 1960s. British, American, and Canadian books are discussed.

Egoff, Sheila; Stubbs, Gordon, T.; and Ashley, L.F., eds. Only connect: readings on children's literature. Oxford, 1980. 471 pp. $12.50 paper [0-19-540309-6].

A well-chosen collection of essays on children's literature. Includes two by Sheila Egoff.

Landsberg, Michele. Michele Landsberg's guide to children's books: with a treasury of more than 350 great children's books. Penguin, 1985. 272 pp. $12.95 paper [0-14-007136-9].

A discussion of Landsberg's favourite books from picture books to young adult novels followed by an extensively annotated list arranged alphabetically by title under suitable age groupings.

Saltman, Judith. Modern Canadian children's books. Oxford, 1987. 128 pp. $8.95 paper [0-19-540572-2].

A survey of Canadian children's books published from 1975 to 1985 that provides an overview of significant titles in the major genres of picture books, fiction, the oral tradition, and poetry. A list of the titles mentioned is included at the end of each chapter.

Saltman, Judith, ed. The Riverside anthology of children's literature. 6th ed. Houghton Mifflin, 1985. 1373 pp. $44.95 hardcover [0-395-35773-X].

The author presents an overview of children's literature from classical to contemporary writing. Canadian authors and poets are included.

Toronto Public Libraries. The Osborne collection of early children's books, 1566-1910: a catalogue. Ed. by Judith St.John. Toronto Public Libraries, 1966. Vol.1 $25.00 [0-919486-25-8]; Vol.2 $30.00 [0-919486-54-1].

Two comprehensive annotated catalogues of early children's books housed in Boys and Girls House, originally donated by Edgar G. Osborne and enlarged by donations and acquisitions.

STORYTELLING

Andersen, Lorrie; Aubrey, Irene E. and McDiarmid, Louise. Storytellers' rendezvous: Canadian stories to tell to children. Ill. by BoKim Louie. Canadian Library Association, 1979. 110 pp. $15.00 paper [0-88802-132-1].

Especially chosen for storytellers by storytellers these Canadian stories, folk tales, legends, and poems offer excellent fare for story hours. Telling time and age suitability are included.

Appleseed: the newsletter of The Storytellers School of Toronto. The Storytellers School of Toronto, 1986-. Free with membership.

Published twice a year, this newsletter includes announcements of upcoming public events, notices of useful books and resources, informational articles, as well as news about the school.

Aubrey, Irene E.; McDiarmid, Louise; and Andersen, Lorrie. Storytellers' encore: more Canadian stories to tell to children. Canadian Library Association, 1984. 61 pp. $18.00 paper [0-88802-179-8].

As in *Storytellers' rendezvous* these Canadian stories, folk tales, legends, and poems are ideal for storytelling. Many selections have been collected orally. Telling time and age suitability are included.

Barton, Bob. Tell me another: storytelling and reading aloud at home, at school and in the community. Pembroke, 1986. 158 pp. $9.95 paper [0-921217-02-1].

A guide to help storytellers select stories and tell them aloud both with or without a book.

Kane, Alice. Songs and sayings of an Ulster childhood. Ed. by Edith Fowke. McClelland & Stewart, 1983. 254 pp. $16.95 hardcover [0-7710-3210-2].

A lifetime collection of rhymes, with comments on historical and personal significance.

MacNeil, Joe Neil. Tales until dawn: the world of a Cape Breton Gaelic story-teller. Tr. by John W. Shaw. McGill-Queen's, 1987. 460 pp. $50.00 hardcover [0-7735-0559-8]; $15.95 paper [0-7735-0560-1].

A collection of riddles, games, sayings, and folktales from Cape Breton told by Joe Neil MacNeil who talks about his life in the community and the tradition of folklore in the area.

PERIODICALS

Books for young people. Published in the months of February, April, June, August, October, and December as a supplement to *Quill and quire*. 56 The Esplanade, Suite 213, Toronto, Ontario. M5E 1A7. (0033-6491). $18.00 per year, or included in *Quill & quire* subscription.

Books in Canada. Canadian Review of Books Ltd., 366 Adelaide Street East, Suite 432, Toronto, Ontario. M5A 3X9. Nine issues per year. $14.95. Elsewhere $17.95 (0045-2564).

Canadian periodical index. Info Globe, 444 Front Street West, Toronto, Ontario. M5V 2S9. Monthly and cumulated annually. $200.00 for libraries serving a population less than 30,000. All other subscribers $595.00. (0008-4714).

CM: a reviewing journal of Canadian materials for young people. Canadian Library Association, 602-200 Elgin Street, Ottawa, Ontario. K1P 1L5. Six issues per year. $30.00. $6.00 single issue. (0821-1450).

Canadian children's literature/Littérature canadienne pour la jeunesse. A journal of criticism & review/une revue de critiques et de comptes rendus. Canadian Children's Literature Association, University of Guelph, Department of English, Guelph, Ontario. N1G 2W1. Quarterly. $16.00 per year; $5.00 single issue. (0319-0080).

Children's book news. Published by the Canadian Children's Book Centre, 229 College Street, 5th floor, Toronto, Ontario. M5T 1R4. Four issues per year. Individual copy free. Bulk rates available.

Emergency librarian. Dyad Services, P.O. Box 46258, Station G, Vancouver, British Columbia, V6R 4G6. Bimonthly, except July and August. $40 per year.

Free! The Newsletter of free materials and services. Dyad Services, P.O. Box 1563, Buffalo, NY 14240. Five issues per year. $15.00 per year prepaid. $18.00 if billed. (0708-4625).

Government of Canada publications/ Publications du gouvernement du Canada. Canadian Government Publishing Centre, Supply and Services Canada, Ottawa, Ontario. K1A 0S9. Quarterly plus yearly index. $21 per year. Other countries $25.20.

Mask 'n melody: drama and music for Canadian schools (K-8). InnovEd Resources, 210-3501 – 8th St. E., Saskatoon, Saskatchewan. S7H 0W5. Three issues per year. $22.00. $8.50 single issue.

Each issue contains three to five plays and six to ten songs with Canadian themes.

Quill & quire. 56 The Esplanade, Toronto, Ontario, M5E 1A7. Monthly with supplements. $40.00 per year. (0033-6491)

School libraries in Canada: the journal of the Canadian School Library Association. Canadian Library Association, 602-200 Elgin Street, Ottawa, Ontario. K2P 1L5. Four issues per year (October, January, March, and May). Available to CSLA members. $35.00 per year in Canada, $35.00 (U.S.) elswhere. (0227-3780)

LIVRES CANADIENS POUR LA JEUNESSE

LIVRES CARTONNES

Anastasiu, Stéphane. Chez moi. Ill. par Stéphane Anastasiu. Ovale, 1984. 8 volets. $2.95 cartonné, fermeture Velcro [2-89186-039-X]. (Plimage)
Un livre-accordéon présentant l'intérieur d'une maison d'un côté et, de l'autre, un lexique illustré d'objets choisis. *Tout-petits.*

Assathiany, Sylvie et Pelletier, Louise. Dors petit-ours. Ill. par Philippe Béha. Ovale, 1982. 14 p. $3.95 cartonné [2-89186-023-3]. (Bébé-livre)
Les parents de petit-ours trouve une solution au problème de petit-ours qui ne veut pas dormir dans son lit parce qu'il a peur de la nuit. *Tout-petits.*

Assathiany, Sylvie et Pelletier, Louise. Grand-maman. Ill. par Philippe Béha. Ovale, 1983. 14 p. $3.95 cartonné [2-89186-029-2]. (Bébé-livre)
Les visites de grand-maman à chaque mercredi sont très spéciales pour petit-ours. *Tout-petits.*

Assathiany, Sylvie et Pelletier, Louise. J'aime Claire. Ill. par Philippe Béha. Ovale, 1982. 14 p. $3.95 cartonné [2-89186-020-9]. (Bébé-livre)
Un petit garçon oublie vite l'absence de ses parents lorsqu'il se fait garder par Claire. *Tout-petits.*

Assathiany, Sylvie et Pelletier, Louise. Mes cheveux. Ill. par Philippe Béha. Ovale, 1982. 14 p. $3.95 cartonné [2-89186-022-5]. (Bébé-livre)
Dominique décide finalement de se faire couper les cheveux mais juste un petit peu. *Tout-petits.*

Assathiany, Sylvie et Pelletier, Louise. Mon bébé-soeur. Ill. par Philippe Béha. Ovale, 1983. 14 p. $3.95 cartonné [2-89186-032-2]. (Bébé-livre)
Même s'il doit partager, petit-ours est bien content d'avoir une petite soeur parce que c'est lui le plus grand. *Tout-petits.*

Assathiany, Sylvie et Pelletier, Louise. Où est ma tétine? Ill. par Philippe Béha. Ovale, 1983. 14 p. $3.95 cartonné [2-89186-031-4]. (Bébé-livre)
Petit ours se rend compte qu'il n'a plus besoin de sa tétine pour s'endormir. *Tout-petits.*

Assathiany, Sylvie et Pelletier, Louise. Pipi dans le pot. Ill. par Philippe Béha. Ovale, 1982. 14 p. $3.95 cartonné [2-89186-021-7]. (Bébé-livre)
Catherine n'a plus besoin de couche puisqu'elle fait maintenant pipi dans son pot. *Tout-petits.*

Assathiany, Sylvie et Pelletier, Louise. Quand ça va mal. Ovale, 1983. 14 p. $4.95 cartonné [2-89186-030-6]. (Bébé-livre)
Tout va mal aujourd'hui et le petit s'exprime. *Tout-petits.*

Automne. Ill. par Sylvie Talbot. Ovale, 1981. 14 p. $3.95 cartonné [2-89186-010-1]. (Bébé-livre)
Textes et illustrations décrivent activités et caractéristiques de l'automne. *Tout-petits.*

Béha, Philippe. L'arbre. Ill. par Philippe Béha. Ovale, 1984. 8 volets $2.95 cartonné, fermeture Velcro [2-89186-035-7]. (Plimage)
Un livre-accordéon présentant un arbre d'un côté et, de l'autre, un lexique illustré d'objets et d'animaux choisis. *Tout-petits.*

Côté, Marie-Josée. Ma rue. Ill. par Marie-Josée Côté. Ovale, 1984. 8 volets $2.95 cartonné, fermeture Velcro [2-89186-036-5]. (Plimage)
Un livre-accordéon illustrant une rue d'un côté et, de l'autre, un lexique illustré d'êtres et d'objets. *Tout-petits.*

Eté. Ill. par Sylvie Talbot. Ovale, 1981. 14 p. $3.95 cartonné [2-89186-009-8]. (Bébé-livre)
Courtes phrases qui riment et des illustrations décrivent activités et caractéristiques de l'été. *Tout-petits.*

Gay, Marie-Louise. Blanc comme neige. Ill. par Marie-Louise Gay. Ovale, 1984. 14 p. $3.95 cartonné [2-89186-044-6]. (Bébé-livre)
Sept couleurs sont introduites dans des scènes amusantes. *Tout-petits.*

Gay, Marie-Louise. Un léopard dans mon placard. Ill. par Marie-Louise Gay. Ovale, 1984. 14 p. $3.95 cartonné [2-89186-046-2]. (Bébé-livre)
Une initiation aux prépositions dans des scènes amusantes. *Tout-petits.*

Gay, Marie-Louise. Petit et grand. Ill. par Marie-Louise Gay. Ovale, 1984. 14 p. $3.95 cartonné [2-89186-045-4]. (Bébé-livre)
Différents concepts sont introduits à chaque page dans des activités que les jeunes reconnaîtront. *Tout-petits.*

Gay, Marie-Louise. Rond comme ton visage. Ill. par Marie-Louise Gay. Ovale, 1984. 14 p. $3.95 cartonné [2-89186-043-8]. (Bébé-livre)
Une initiation aux différentes formes géométriques dans des situations familières aux tout-petits. *Tout-petits.*

Hiver. Ill. par Sylvie Talbot. Ovale, 1981. 14 p. $3.95 cartonné [2-89186-011-X]. (Bébé-livre)
Texte et illustrations décrivent activités et caractéristiques de l'été. *Tout-petits.*

Levert, Mireille. Le train. Ill. par Mireille Levert. Ovale, 1984. 8 volets $2.95 cartonné, fermeture Velcro [2-89186-038-1]. (Plimage)
Un livre-accordéon présentant l'intérieur d'un train passager d'un côté et, de l'autre, un lexique illustré d'êtres et d'objets choisis. *Tout-petits.*

Printemps. Ill. par Sylvie Talbot. Ovale, 1981. 14 p. $3.95 cartonné [2-89186-008-X]. (Bébé-livre)
Texte court sous forme de rimes et illustrations simples décrivent les activités et les caractéristiques du printemps. *Tout-petits.*

Sylvestre, Daniel. Voyaginaires. Ill. par Daniel Sylvestre. Ovale, 1984. $6.95 cartonné [2-89186-037-3]. (Imagimots)
Sept pages d'illustrations divisées en deux permettront aux jeunes de composer d'étranges véhicules. *Tout-petits.*

ALBUMS

Alderson, Sue Ann. Anne-Marie Maginol tu me rends folle. Ill. par Fiona Garrick. Tr. par Claire Sabourin. Tree Frog, 1981. 49 p. $4.95 collé [0-88967-043-9]; $8.95 relié [0-88967-044-7].
Les impertinences d'une petite fille exaspèrent la maman; les récriminations de la mère affectent la petite fille. Amusante réconciliation. Traduction de *Bonnie McSmithers (you're driving me dithers)*. *Tout-petits*.

Anfousse, Ginette. La cachette. Ill. par Ginette Anfousse. La Courte échelle, 1976. 20 p. $5.95 broché [2-89021-015-4].
N'ayant personne avec qui jouer, une petite fille possédant un tamanoir invite le lecteur à jouer avec elle à la cache-cache. *Tout-petits*.

Anfousse, Ginette. La chicane. Ill. par Ginette Anfousse. La Courte échelle, 1978. 24 p. $5.95 broché [2-89021-017-0].
Une chicane est survenue entre Jiji et Cloclo Tremblay. *Tout-petits*.

Anfousse, Ginette. L'école. Ill. par Ginette Anfousse. La Courte échelle, 1983. 22 p. $5.95 broché [2-89021-041-3].
Jiji relate les aventures de sa première journée d'école à son bébé-tamanoir-mangeur-de-fourmis-pour-vrai. *Tout-petits*.

Anfousse, Ginette. La fête. Ill. par Ginette Anfousse. La Courte échelle, 1983. 22 p. $5.95 broché [2-89021-042-1].
Le chat rose que Jiji reçoit pour célébrer son cinquième anniversaire de naissance est merveilleux, beau, et gentil, mais il ne pourra jamais remplacer son bébé-tamanoir-mangeur-de-fourmis-pour-vrai. *Tout-petits*.

Anfousse, Ginette. L'hiver ou le bonhomme sept heures. Ill. par Ginette Anfousse. La Courte échelle, 1980. 22 p. $5.95 broché [2-89021-024-3].
Histoire qui traduit bien la peur du bonhomme sept heures. *Tout-petits*.

Anfousse, Ginette. Je boude. Ill. par Ginette Anfousse. La Courte échelle, 1986. 22p. $5.95 broché [2-89021-061-8].
Jiji est de mauvaise humeur et boude dans son coin parce qu'elle a été punie par ses parents après avoir été insupportable toute la journée. *Tout-petits*.

Anfousse, Ginette. Mon ami Pichou. Ill.par Ginette Anfousse. La Courte échelle, 1976. 20 p. $5.95 broché [2-89021-014-6].
A l'arrivée de l'automne, Pichou, un tamanoir, est de mauvaise humeur. *Tout-petits*.

Anfousse, Ginette. La petite soeur. Ill. par Ginette Anfousse. La Courte échelle, 1986. 22 p. $5.95 broché [2-89021-060-X].
Jiji qui n'a que Pichou regarde avec un oeil d'envie le bébé-soeur de Cloclo Tremblay. *Tout-petits*.

Anfousse, Ginette. Le savon. Ill. par Ginette Anfousse. La Courte échelle, 1980. 22 p. $5.95 broché [2-89021-023-5].
Jiji doit reprendre son bain après s'être salie de chocolat et de boue. *Tout-petits*.

Asselin, Claude. Un beau soleil. Ill. par Claude Asselin. Héritage, 1980. 16 p. $3.95 broché [0-7773-2537-3].
Un texte clair, en gros caractères, des images aux lignes simples racontent le plaisir d'une journée dans la vie du soleil. *Tout-petits*.

Asselin, Claude. Un petit nuage. Ill. par Claude Asselin. Héritage, 1977. 28 p. $4.95 broché [0-7773-2513-6].
L'histoire d'un petit nuage esseulé. *Tout-petits*.

Aubin, Michel. Mon petit frère Bertrand. Ill. par Hélène Desputeaux. Boréal Jeunesse, 1986. 24 p. $6.95 collé [2-89052-172-9]. (Madeleine)
Histoire amusante qui raconte les situations quotidiennes d'une petite fille et de son petit frère. *Tout-petits, débutants.*

Bénard, Christian. En été. Ill. par Christian Bénard. Du Raton Laveur, 1984. 12 p. $3.95 broché [2-920660-00-4]. (Images de chez nous)
Dans cet album sans texte, des tableaux en double page décrivent des scènes familières aux jeunes. Les nombreux détails susciteront leur intérêt. *Tout-petits.*

Bourgeois, Paulette. Benjamin et la nuit. Ill. par Brenda Clark. Tr. par Christiane Duchesne. Scholastic-TAB, 1986. 32 p. $4.95 collé [0-590-71738-3].
La tortue Benjamin qui a peur des endroits sombres, réalise que plusieurs animaux ont aussi peur de quelque chose et décide finalement d'entrer dans sa carapace. Traduction de *Franklin in the dark. Tout-petits.*

Bourgeois, Paulette. Les petites bottes de la grande Sarah. Ill. par Brenda Clark. Tr. par Lucie Duchesne. Scholastic-TAB, 1987. 32 p. $5.95 collé [0-590-71821-5].
Les pieds de Sarah ont grandi et c'est avec difficulté qu'elle se résigne à ne plus porter ses bottes jaunes et brillantes. Traduction de *Big Sarah's little boots. Tout-petits.*

Bussières, Simone. Les fables des trois commères. Ill. par Laurent Bédard. Les Presses Laurentiennes, 1962. 32 p. $1.75 collé [2-89015-009-7].
Trois contes amusants et humoristiques: l'aventure de monsieur et madame Bobby (l'histoire de deux chiens), Ratapon le chat et Tigris le rat, et l'histoire du petit canard qui voulait se faire paon. *Débutants.*

Cailloux, André. Le Noël de Zéphirin. Ill. par Danielle Poisson. Paulines, 1985. 23 p. $5.95 broché [2-89039-072-1]. (Prisme)
Un conte de Noël avec comme personnage principal Zéphirin, un jeune sapin. *Tout-petits, débutants.*

Carrier, Roch. Le chandail de hockey. Ill. par Sheldon Cohen. Toundra, 1984. 24 p. $14.95 relié [0-88776-171-2]; $5.95 broché [0-88776-176-3].
Un jeune joueur de hockey dont le héros est Maurice Richard reçoit par la poste un chandail de hockey des Maple Leaf de Toronto au lieu de celui des Canadiens de Montréal que sa mère avait commandé dans le catalogue Eaton. *Débutants, moyens.*

Cloutier, Cécile. La giraffe. Ill. par Mireille Levert. Pierre Tisseyre, 1984. 16 p. $3.95 broché [2-89051-113-8]. (Coeur de pomme)
Son long cou attire à la giraffe beaucoup de moqueries des autres animaux de la forêt. *Tout-petits.*

Constantineau, Céline. Olivier le forgeron. Ill par Dominique Laquerre. Québec/Amérique, 1985. 24 p. $7.95 broché [2-89037-238-3].
Le coq-girouette fabriqué par Olivier le forgeron se retrouve miraculeusement perché sur le clocher de l'église. *Débutants, moyens.*

Coulombe, Pauline. Mon ami parmi les oiseaux. Ill. par Huguette Dunnigan. Paulines, 1979. 15 p. $2.75 broché [2-89039-018-7]. (Contes du pays)
Un récit lent et tendre qui raconte l'amitié entre un vieillard et un petit garçon. *Débutants.*

Duchesne, Christiane. Ah, ces oiseaux! Ill. par Barbara Reid. Scholastic-TAB, 1986. 32 p. $4.95 broché [0-590-71612-3].
Un chat promet aux oiseaux de son entourage de ne pas les attaquer même s'il a une envie folle de les manger. *Tout-petits.*

Duchesne, Christiane. L'enfant de la maison folle. Ill. par Christiane Duchesne. La maison folle, 1980. 32 p. $5.95 broché [2-920113-00-3].
La maison folle réapparaît chaque matin et dévoile d'étonnants animaux qui travaillent à la rendre attrayante pour la visite d'un enfant. *Tout-petits.*

Duchesne, Christiane. Lazaros Olibrius. Ill. par Christiane Duchesne. Héritage, 1975. 13 p. $3.95 broché [0-7773-2511-X].
L'entente cordiale réalisée par le rire. *Tout-petits.*

Duchesne, Christiane. Quel beau petit! Ill. par Barbara Reid. Scholastic-TAB, 1986. 31 p. $4.95 broché [0-590-71669-7].
Les progrès du petit veau dernier-né de madame Foin, mère très affectueuse envers son petit, sont suivis avec intérêt par les animaux de la ferme et par le fermier. *Tout-petits.*

Duchesne, Christiane. Le serpent vert. Ill. par Christiane Duchesne. Héritage, 1978. 16 p. $3.95 broché [0-7773-2514-4].
L'histoire d'un serpent et d'un oeuf racontée en quelques mots et magnifiquement illustrée. *Tout-petits.*

Duchesne, Christiane. Le triste dragon. Ill. par Christiane Duchesne. Héritage, 1975. 13 p. $3.95 broché [0-7773-2512-8].
Cette fantaisie est pleine de joie de vivre. *Tout-petits.*

Evans, Denise. Le petit fabriquant de jouets. Ill. par June Lawrason. Tr. par Françoise Marois. Scholastic-TAB, 1986. 32 p. $4.95 broché [0-590-71684-0].

Le rêve de Jonathan de devenir fabriquant de jouet se réalise lorsqu'un étranger l'invite à venir travailler pour lui dans son usine. Traduction de *The Toymaker. Tout-petits.*

Fernandes, Eugenie. Quelle journée. Ill. par Eugenie Fernandes. Tr. par Lucie Duchesne. Scholastic-TAB, 1987. 28 p. $5.95 collé [0-590-71627-4].

Après une journée difficile, une petite fille réalise que sa maman l'aime toujours. Traduction de *A Difficult day. Tout-petits.*

Gagnon, Cécile. Alfred dans le métro. Ill. par Louise Blanchard. Héritage, 1983. 16 p. $3.95 broché [0-7773-2558-6].

Dans le métro de Montréal, trois enfants chassent un lapin qui s'est échappé d'une boîte. *Tout-petits.*

Gagnon, Cécile. Bonjour l'arbre. Ill. par Darcia Labrosse. Du Raton Laveur, 1985. 21 p. $5.95 broché [2-920660-05-0].

L'iceberg sur lequel jouait Léon, petit ours polaire, s'éloigne du rivage et conduit ce dernier vers les pays chauds où il rencontre son premier arbre. *Tout-petits.*

Gagnon, Cécile. Histoire d'Adèle Viau et de Fabien Petit. Ill. par Darcia Labrosse. Pierre Tisseyre, 1982. 24 p. $7.95 broché [2-89051-065-4].

Afin de réaliser son rêve d'habiter un appartement au quarante-deuxième étage, Adèle Viau devient laveuse de vitres des gratte-ciel et rencontre un homme pas plus grand qu'elle sur les lieux de son travail. *Tout-petits.*

Gagnon, Cécile. J'ai chaud. Ill. par Darcia Labrosse. Du Raton Laveur, 1986. 24 p. $5.95 broché [2-920660-06-3].

Raton laveur devient coiffeur et débarasse Léon de sa trop lourde fourrure lorsque ce dernier se plaint de la chaleur. Ceci fait le bonheur des oiseaux qui se construisent des nids avec le poil blanc de Léon. *Tout-petits.*

Gagnon, Cécile. J'ai faim. Ill. par Darcia Labrosse. Du Raton Laveur, 1986. 24 p. $5.95 broché [2-920660-07-1].

Afin d'apaiser sa faim, Léon mange toutes sortes de bonnes choses et se retrouve avec un mal de coeur à la fin de la journée. *Tout-petits.*

Gagnon, Cécile. Le pierrot de Monsieur Autrefois. Ill. par Josée La Perrière. Mondia, 1981. 32 p. $7.35 broché [2-89114-107-5].

Chez un antiquaire, un pierrot joue la comédie avec les marionnettes d'Anne-Marie, une petite fille qui l'a découvert dans la vitrine. *Débutants.*

Gagnon, Cécile. Plumeneige. Ill. by Suzanne Duranceau. Héritage, 1980. 16 p. $3.95 broché [0-7773-2534-9].

Un bonhomme de neige prend vie et s'anime. *Tout-petits.*

Gagnon, Cécile. Le roi de Novilande. Ill. par Darcia Labrosse. Pierre Tisseyre, 1981. 24 p. $7.95 broché [2-89051-055-7]. (Le marchand de Sable)

Barnabé, le vagabond ramasseur de vieilleries, rêvait qu'il était roi. *Débutants.*

Garrett, Jennifer. La reine qui avait volé le ciel. Ill. par Linda Hendry. Tr. par Françoise Marois. Scholastic-TAB, 1986. 32 p. $4.95 collé [0-590-71614-X].

Jeune Tabatha trouve un moyen pour forcer la reine Queue-de-Rat à renoncer à sa robe à la texture et aux couleurs du ciel et sauve ainsi les habitants de Bamble de la famine. Traduction de *The Queen who stole the sky. Tout-petits, débutants.*

Gauthier, Bertrand. Le chouchou. Ill. par Daniel Sylvestre. La Courte échelle, 1987. 24 p. $6.95 broché [2-89021-068-9].

Un malentendu au sujet d'un crayon rouge ébranle l'amitié entre Zunik et Ariane. *Tout-petits.*

Gauthier, Bertrand. Maman. Ill. par Daniel Sylvestre. La Courte échelle, 1987. 24 p. $6.95 broché [2-89021-069-3].

La mère de Zunik qui n'est que mentionnée dans les deux premiers livres de la série, est finalement introduite. *Tout-petits.*

Gauthier, Bertrand. Zunik. Ill. par Daniel Sylvestre. La Courte échelle, 1984. 24 p. $5.95 broché [2-89021-046-4].

Vivant seul avec son père, Zunik, un jeune de la maternelle, nous raconte quelques épisodes de sa vie scolaire et familiale. *Tout-petits.*

Gauthier, Bertrand. Zunik dans le championnat. Ill. par Daniel Sylvestre. La Courte échelle, 1986. 24 p. $5.95 broché [2-89021-058-8].

C'est la partie finale de hockey et Zunik qui joue comme gardien de buts, aimerait bien que son équipe gagne pour recevoir un trophée. *Tout-petits.*

Gay, Marie-Louise. La soeur de Robert. Ill. par Marie-Louise Gay. La Courte échelle, 1983. 24 p. $5.95 broché [2-89021-038-3].

Un frère et une soeur qui se jouent de mauvais tours continuellement, s'allient pour jouer un tour à leur mère. *Tout-petits.*

Gay, Marie-Louise. Voyage au claire de lune. Ill. par Marie-Louise Gay. Héritage, 1986. 32 p. $9.95 relié [2-7625-2571-3].

Toby et Rose décrochent la lune et partent en voyage accompagnés d'un chat blanc et d'une souris vêtue d'un pyjama. Traduction de *Moonbeam on a cat's ear*. *Tout-petits*.

Gay, Marie-Louise. De zéro à minuit. Ill. par Marie-Louise Gay. La Courte échelle, 1981. 22 p. $5.95 broché [2-89021-025-1].

Les chiffres 0 à 9 deviennent des personnages farfelus présentés dans des situations humoristiques. *Tout-petits*.

Gilman, Phoebe. L'arbre aux ballons. Ill. par Phoebe Gilman. Tr. par Christiane Duchesne. Scholastic-TAB, 1985. 32 p. $4.95 broché [0-590-71258-6].

Avec l'aide du magicien, la princesse Héloïse parvient à alerter son père et ce dernier punit l'archiduc qui avait ordonné la destruction de tous les ballons pendant l'absence du roi. Traduction de *The Balloon tree*. *Tout-petits*.

Green, John F. Un dragon dans la garde-robe. Ill. par Linda Hendry. Tr. par Lucie Duchesne. Scholastic-TAB, 1987. 32 p. $4.95 broché [0-590-71711-1].

Une surprise attend ceux qui ne veulent pas croire qu'il y a un dragon dans la garde-robe de Jonathan. Traduction de *There's a dragon in my closet*. *Tout-petits*.

Hall, Pam. Sur les îles des pierres dansantes. Ill. par Pam Hall. Tr. par Michelle Tisseyre. Pierre Tisseyre, 1982. 48 p. $8.95 relié [2-89051-0070].

Un petit macareux qui vient de passer plusieurs jours à la dérive, est accueilli par les guetteurs de l'île disparue de Funk. *Débutants, moyens*.

Harber, Frances. Le roi a des oreilles d'âne. Ill. par Maryann Kovalski. Tr. par Christiane Duchesne. Scholastic-TAB, 1986. 28 p. $4.95 broché [0-590-71528-3].

Le tailleur royal trouve un moyen de camoufler les deux oreilles d'âne qui ont poussées sur la tête du vain roi Kyungmoon Wang et sauve ainsi sa vie. Traduction de *My king has donkey's ears*. *Tout-petits, débutants*.

Harris, Dorothy Joan. Théo et les quatre saisons. Ill. par Vlasta Van Kampen. Tr. par Cécile Gagnon. Scholastic-TAB, 1986. 32 p. $4.95 broché [0-590-71678-6].

Théo tortue réalise qu'il n'aurait pas eu besoin de partir à la recherche des saisons parce qu'elles sont aussi venues à son étang. Traduction de *Four seasons for Toby*. *Tout-petits*.

Hazbry, Nancy. Au revoir cauchemars! Ill. par Roy Condy. Tr. par Danielle Thaler. Scholastic-TAB, 1983. 32 p. $4.95 broché [0-590-71223-3].

Des idées sont suggérées pour aider les jeunes à affronter les monstres effrayants rencontrés dans les mauvais rêves. Traduction de *How to get rid of bad dreams*. *Tout-petits*.

Houde, Pierre. La ballade de Monsieur Bedon. Ill. par Pierre Houde. Du Raton Laveur, 1985. 21 p. $5.95 broché [2-920660-04-7].

Après plusieurs tentatives, Monsieur Bedon trouve finalement un moyen pour entendre la musique de la terre. Il monte à califourchon sur des grosses notes échappées d'un tuba géant et part en ballade autour de la terre. *Tout-petits, débutants*.

Julandré. Une puce dans l'espace. Ill. par Francine Loranger. Héritage, 1976. 32 p. $3.95 broché [0-7773-2502-0].

Grâce à son ingéniosité, Pucette sera la première puce à marcher sur la lune. *Tout-petits*.

Kovalski, Maryann. Martha et Edouard. Ill. par Maryann Kovalski. Tr. par Christiane Duchesne. Scholastic-TAB, 1986. 32 p. $5.95 collé [0-590-71366-3].

Plusieurs années de séparation n'altèrent pas l'amitié entre les deux chiens Martha et Edouard. Après les retrouvailles, ils vivent aussi heureux qu'auparavant. Traduction de *Brenda and Edward*. *Tout-petits*.

Labrosse, Darcia. Où est le chat? Ill. par Darcia Labrosse. Pierre Tisseyre, 1981. 23 p. $3.95 broché [2-89051-0595-5]. (Coeur de Pomme)

Livre-jeu qui propose la recherche du 'cha' dans les phrases et les illustrations. *Tout-petits*.

Labrosse, Darcia. Où est le ver? Ill. par Darcia Labrosse. Pierre Tisseyre, 1984. 19 p. $3.95 broché [2-89051-112-X]. (Coeur de pomme)

Comme dans l'album précédent, le tout-petit doit rechercher le 'ver' dans les diverses situations illustrées. *Tout-petits*.

Larose, Céline. Macail. Ill par Pierre Larose. Leméac, 1982. 26 p. $6.95 broché [2-7609-9843-6].

Macail l'épouvantail laisse un oiseau faire son nid dans son chapeau de paille. *Tout-petits*.

Larose, Céline. Petit soulier. Ill. par Pierre Larose. Leméac, 1979. 42 p. $9.95 relié [2-7609-9830-4].

Un soulier perdu est à la recherche de son compagnon. *Tout-petits*.

Larose, Céline. Une tomate inquiète. Ill. par Pierre Larose. Leméac, 1979. 28 p. $9.95 relié [2-7609-9829-0].

Une tomate s'interroge sur son identité. Ouvrage imprimé en gros caractères avec illustrations simples. *Tout-petits*.

Ledoux, Lucie. La 8e merveille. Ill. par Lucie Ledoux. Lidec, 1979. 22 p. $6.75 relié [2-7608-1502-1].

Quand une petite fille ferme les yeux, elle voyage très loin et 'sans un sou en poche.' *Débutants*.

Ledoux, Lucie. Le voyage à la recherche du temps. Ill. par Philippe Béha. Mondia, 1981. 48 p. $8.50 broché [2-89114-029-X].

Trois enfants partis à la recherche du temps reviennent sur terre sans l'avoir trouvé. *Débutants*.

Lessard, Marie. En hiver. Ill. par Marie Lessard. Du Raton Laveur, 1984. 12 p. $3.95 broché [2-920660-01-2]. (Images de chez nous)

Dans cet album sans texte, des tableaux en double page décrivent des scènes familières aux jeunes. Les nombreux détails susciteront leur intérêt. *Tout-petits*.

L'Heureux, Christine. Les déguisements d'Amélie. Ill. par Mireille Levert. La Courte échelle, 1986. 23 p. $5.95 broché [2-89021-059-6].

Amélie aime se déguiser et elle ne manque aucune occasion pour montrer les différentes facettes de sa personnalité. *Tout-petits*.

L'Heureux, Christine. Les vacances d'Amélie. Ill. par Suzanne Langlois. La Courte échelle, 1982. 22 p. $5.95 broché [2-89021-033-2].

Au lendemain de Noël, Amélie s'invente une vieille amie avec qui elle va passer des moments très agréables. Publié auparavant sous le titre *Les vacances de Noël*. *Tout-petits*.

Major, Henriette. Si l'herbe poussait sur les toits. Ill. par Suzanne Langlois. Leméac, 1985. 23 p. $8.95 broché [2-7609-9836-3]. (Littérature de jeunesse)

Grâce aux super-graines de Monsieur Chlorophylle, la ville de Bétonville est transformée en un coin de verdure. *Débutants*.

Marcotte, Danielle. Les nuits d'Arthur. Ill. par Philippe Béha. Ovale, 1986. 28 p. $5.95 broché [2-89186-070-5].

Arthur le cochon a peur de l'ombre de la nuit jusqu'à ce qu'elle lui enseigne une formule magique qui le transporte dans un monde rempli de couleurs. *Tout-petits*.

Mia/Klaus. Claire-de-la-lune et Barbarou. Paulines, 1985. $15.95 relié [2-89039-063-2]. (Album jeunesse)

Conte qui aborde le thème de la mort. Quand Barbarou meurt, l'ange le guide vers l'autre vie de liberté et d'amour. Illustré avec des photographies. *Débutants*.

Morgan, Allen. Le bonhomme d'Hélène. Ill. par Brenda Clark. Tr. par Christiane Duchesne. Scholastic-TAB, 1986. 31 p. $5.95 collé [0-590-71751-0].

A l'arrivée du printemps, Hélène trouve une solution pour ne pas s'ennuyer de son bonhomme de neige durant l'été. Traduction de *Sadie and the snowman*. *Tout-petits*.

Morgan, Allen. Le camion. Ill. par Michael Martchenko. Tr. par Raymonde Longval-Ducreux. La Courte échelle, 1986. 31 p. $5.95 broché [2-89021-056-1].

Après une nuit bien mouvementée, Mathieu retrouve sa camionnette dans les poches de son manteau. Traduction de *Matthew and the midnight tow truck*. *Tout-petits*.

Munsch, Robert. Le bébé. Ill. par Michael Martchenko. Tr. par Raymonde Longval-Ducreux. La Courte échelle, 1983. 24 p. $5.95 broché [2-89021-043-X].

Robin trouve un bébé dans un trou et part à la recherche de quelqu'un qui peut s'en charger. Traduction de *Murmel, Murmel, Murmel*. *Tout-petits*.

Munsch, Robert. Le dodo. Ill. par Michael Martchenko. La Courte échelle, 1986. 24 p. $5.95 broché [2-89021-055-3].

Simon finit par s'endormir même si le reste de la famille se querelle à grands cris en bas. Traduction de *Mortimer*. *Tout-petits*.

Munsch, Robert. L'habit de neige. Ill. par Michael Martchenko. La Courte échelle, 1987. 24 p. $6.95 broché [2-89021-070-7].

Un jeune garçon refuse de mettre son habit de neige malgré l'insistance de sa mère, de son professeur et du directeur d'école. Traduction de *Thomas' snowsuit*. *Tout-petits*.

Munsch, Robert. Le métro en folie. Ill. par Michael Martchenko. Tr. par Catherine Navreau. Gallimard, 1982. 32 p. $3.95 collé [2-07-039079-9]. (Folio benjamin)

Trop, c'est trop! Un jour, Oliver se retrouve avec une station de métro dans son salon. Traduction de *Jonathan cleaned up – then he heard a sound*. *Tout-petits, débutants*.

Munsch, Robert. Papa, réveille-toi. Ill. par Michael Martchenko. La Courte échelle, 1987. 24 p. $6.95 broché [2-89021-071-5].

Le père de David se promène dans des endroits impensables durant son sommeil. Traduction de *David's father*. *Tout-petits*.

Munsch, Robert. La princesse à la robe de papier. Ill. par Michael Martchenko. Tr. par Françoise Marois. Scholastic-TAB, 1981. 29 p. $3.95 broché [0-590-71127-X].

Enlevé par le dragon, le prince Roland ne manifeste aucune reconnaissance lorsque la princesse Elizabeth réussit par ruse à le libérer. Son arrogance enrage tellement Elizabeth qu'elle décide de ne pas l'épouser. Traduction de *The Paperbag princess*. *Tout-petits*.

Paré, Roger. L'alphabet. Ill. par Roger Paré. La Courte échelle, 1985. 24 p. $19.95 [2-89021-050-2].
Un livre-jeu avec casse-tête pour apprendre à lire en s'amusant. *Tout-petits.*

Paré, Roger. Plaisirs de chat. Ill. par Roger Paré. La Courte échelle, 1983. 24 p. $5.95 broché [2-89021-044-8].
Deux chats passent leur temps à se faire plaisir l'un et l'autre. *Tout-petits.*

Pomminville, Louise. L'Abécédaire de Pitatou. Ill. par Louise Pomminville. Leméac, 1979. 54 p. $9.95 relié [2-7609-9831-2].
Présentation agréable, cependant l'auteur a choisi de ne représenter dans l'illustration que quelques mots de chaque liste. *Tout-petits.*

Pomminville, Louise et Deprez, Marie Rose. Pitatou et la neige. Ill. par Louise Pomminville. Leméac, 1978. 28 p. 7.95 relié [0-7761-9827-0].
Les merveilleux oiseaux de la forêt de Nulle-Part transmettent encore une fois leur message d'amour et d'amitié. *Tout-petits.*

Poulin, Stéphane. Ah! belle cité/A Beautiful city ABC. Ill. par Stéphane Poulin. Toundra, 1985. 36 p. $14.95 relié [0-88776-175-5].
Un abécédaire bilingue sur Montréal capturant la diversité de cette grande ville. *Tout-petits.*

Poulin, Stéphane. Album de famille. Ill. par Stéphane Poulin. Michel Quintin, 1986. 24 p. $6.50 broché [2-920438-12-3]. (Pellicule)
Pellicule, photographe animalier de réputation internationale, présente des portraits d'une trentaine de familles animales. *Tout-petits, débutants.*

Poulin, Stéphane. As-tu vu Joséphine? Ill. par Stéphane Poulin. Toundra, 1986. 24 p. $12.95 relié [0-88776-188-7].
Dans les rues de Montréal, Daniel suit la chatte Joséphine qui va de place en place pour finalement se rendre à la fête aux chats. *Tout-petits.*

Poulin, Stéphane. Peux-tu attraper Joséphine? Ill. par Stéphane Poulin. Toundra, 1987. 24 p. $12.95 relié [0-88776-199-2].
La chatte de Daniel décide d'accompagner ce dernier à l'école et crée une commotion que l'on n'oubliera pas de si tôt. *Tout-petits.*

Poupart, Jean-Marie. Nuits magiques. Ill. par Suzanne Duranceau. La Courte échelle, 1982. 21 p. $4.95 broché [2-89021-032-4].
Dans son rêve, les amis de Marie-Luce sont transformés en des animaux bizarres avec qui elle s'amuse toute la nuit. *Tout-petits, débutants.*

Reid, Barbara. Un, deux, trois, voilà la mère l'oie. Ill. par Barbara Reid. Adaptée par Ormonde De Kay. Scholastic-TAB, 1987. 40 p. $5.95 collé [0-590-71883-3].
Des illustrations détaillées et délicates en plasticine viennent décorer ces contes de la mère l'oie. *Tout-petits.*

Richards, Nancy Wilcox. Antoine, le grognon. Ill. par Werner Zimmerman. Tr. par Martine Connat. Scholastic-TAB, 1987. 24 p. $4.95 collé [0-590-71716-2].
Après avoir essayé les différentes suggestions de sa femme, le fermier Grognon ne se plaint plus jamais de la chaleur et d'être fatigué. *Tout-petits.*

Roy, Gabrielle. Courte-Queue. Ill. par François Olivier. Internationales Alain Stanké, 1979. 48 p. $8.95 broché [2-7604-0053-0].
La chatte Courte-Queue réussit à sauver ses petits en les escamotant. *Débutants.*

Roy, Gabrielle. Ma vache Bossie. Ill. par Louise Pomminville. Leméac, 1976. 46 p. $8.95 relié [0-7761-9823-8].
Une petite fille reçoit comme cadeau de fête une vache que l'on nomme Bossie. *Débutants.*

Scalabrini, Rita. La famille Citrouillard aux poissons des chenaux. Ill. par Rita Scalabrini. Leméac, 1979. 38 p. $9.95 relié [2-7609-9828-2].
Un album relatant un événement annuel à Trois-Rivières. *Tout-petits, débutants.*

Soulières, Robert. Le bal des chenilles. Ill. par Michèle Lemieux. Pierre Tisseyre, 1979. 22 p. $3.95 broché [2-89051-016-6].
Une chenille, seule pour le bal, fait passer une annonce et trouve ainsi un papillon pour l'accompagner. Illustrations en noir et blanc. *Tout-petits.*

Soulières, Robert. Une bien mauvaise grippe. Ill. par Michèle Lemieux. Pierre Tisseyre, 1980. 21 p. $3.95 broché [2-89051-016-6].
Gertrude l'autruche consulte tour à tour le vautour, le lion, la giraffe, le perroquet, la chouette et le pingouin pour soigner la grippe de son ami le serpent Félix. Illustrations en noir et blanc. *Tout-petits.*

Soulières, Robert. L'homme aux oiseaux. Ill. par Micheline Pelletier. Québec/Amérique, 1981. 32 p. $12.95 relié [2-89037-098-4].
Le juge décide qu'il faudrait réviser la loi interdisant à l'homme aux oiseaux de jouer de la flûte pour plus de trois oiseaux à la fois lorsqu'il entend ce dernier jouer un air mélodieux pour faire plaisir à ces derniers. *Tout-petits, débutants.*

Soulières, Robert. Seul au monde. Ill. par Philippe Béha. Québec/Amérique, 1982. 32 p. $7.95 broché [2-89037-122-0]. (Jeunesse)

Différent des autres physiquement, un homme erre de ville en ville jusqu'au jour où il rencontre quelqu'un qui lui ressemble et, tous les deux, ils finissent par se faire accepter par la société. *Débutants.*

Soulières, Robert. Tony et Vladimir. Ill. par Philippe Béha. Pierre Tisseyre, 1984. 31 p. $7.95 broché [2-89051-103-0].

Grâce à un imprésario astucieux, Tony devient un chanteur de renommée internationale. Une fois le succès obtenu cependant, il réalise qu'il n'est plus maître de lui-même et décide de retourner à sa vie simple d'auparavant. *Tout-petits, débutants.*

Staunton, Ted. Opération herbe à puces. Ill. par Tina Holdcroft. Tr. par Lucie Duchesne. Scholastic-TAB, 1987. 29 p. $5.95 collé [0-590-71854-7].

Un garçon est terrorisé par une bande d'élèves jusqu'au jour où un moyen génial est trouvé pour les éloigner. Traduction de *Taking care of Crumley. Tout-petits.*

Stinson, Kathy. Le livre tout nu. Ill. par Heather Collins. Tr. par David Homel. Annick, 1987. 32 p. $4.95 broché [0-920303-96-X].

Les parties du corps humain sont illustrées dans différentes situations qui susciteront les jeunes à la discussion. Traduction de *The Bare naked book. Tout-petits.*

Stinson, Kathy. Le rouge c'est bien mieux. Ill. par Robin Baird Lewis. Adaptée par Paule Daveluy. Annick, 1986. 25 p. $5.95 broché [0-920303-71-4].

Sophie n'aime que le rouge et rien ne peut lui faire changer d'idée. Traduction de *Red is Best. Tout-petits.*

Thurman, Mark. L'anniversaire de Douglas. Ill. par Mark Thurman. Tr. par Duguay Prieur Enr. Héritage, 1986. 24 p. $4.95 broché [2-7625-2575-6]. (Douglas l'éléphant)

Douglas est désappointé de ne pas avoir reçu le planeur télécommandé qu'il désirait pour son anniversaire. Traduction de *The Birthday party. Tout-petits.*

Thurman, Mark. La bicyclette neuve. Ill. par Mark Thurman. Tr. par Duguay Prieur Enr. Héritage, 1986. 24 p. $4.95 broché [2-7625-2572-1]. (Douglas l'éléphant)

Douglas réalise que c'est beaucoup plus intéressant de partager ses jouets avec ses amis. Traduction de *The Elephant's new bicycle. Tout-petits.*

Thurman, Mark. De vieux amis, de nouveaux amis. Ill. par Mark Thurman. Tr. par Duguay Prieur Enr. Héritage, 1986. 24 p. $4.95 broché [2-7625-2574-4]. (Douglas l'éléphant)

Douglas réalise qu'Albert est toujours son ami même si ce dernier semble être plus intéressé à Eléonore. Traduction de *Old friends, new friends. Tout-petits.*

Thurman, Mark. Le mensonge. Ill. par Mark Thurman. Tr. par Raymonde Longval-Ducreux. La Courte échelle, 1982. 22 p. $4.95 broché [2-89021-030-8].

Regrettant d'avoir raconté une blague à ses amis, Didier décide de leur avouer son mensonge au risque de perdre leur amitié. Traduction de *The Lie that grew and grew. Tout-petits.*

Thurman, Mark. Un rhume d'éléphant. Ill. par Mark Thurman. Tr. par Barbara Creary et Bertrand Gauthier. La Courte échelle, 1981. 23 p. $4.95 broché [2-89021-029-6].

Après avoir essayé quelques méthodes suggérées par ses amis pour guérir son rhume, Didier décide que la meilleure façon est de rester au lit et de se reposer. Traduction de *The Elephant's cold. Tout-petits.*

Tibo. La nuit du grand coucou. Ill. par Tibo. La Courte échelle, 1984. 24 p. $4.95 broché [2-89021-048-0].

Quand tout et tous sont endormis, les animaux de la ville, de la ferme et du cirque enfilent leurs costumes des soirs de fête et se réunissent pour célébrer la fête du grand coucou. *Tout-petits.*

Vanhee-Nelson, Louise. Archibaldo le dragon. Ill. par Philippe Béha. Paulines & Médiaspaul, 1983. 27 p. $5.95 broché [2-89039-897-8].

Même s'il ne peut plus cracher des feux d'artifices hauts et forts pour les enfants comme il le faisait avant son opération, Archibaldo réalise que les gens du village ont toujours besoin de lui. *Tout-petits.*

Vigneault, Gilles. Les quatre saisons de Piquot. Ill. par Hugh John Barrett. Nouvelles éditions de l'Arc, 1979. 36 p. et disque. $14.95 broché [2-89016-000-9].

Un petit chef-d'oeuvre littéraire déclamé sur disque. *Débutants.*

Wynne-Jones, Tim. Le matou marin. Ill. par Ken Nutt. Tr. par Françoise Marois. Scholastic-TAB, 1984. 32 p. $4.95 collé [0-590-71207-0].

Le chat Bébert adore l'eau et son rêve de faire un tour en mer se réalise finalement lorsqu'il se rend chez Maria, une amie mystérieuse de son oncle Roy. Traduction de *Zoom at sea. Tout-petits, débutants.*

BANDES DESSINEES

Benoît, François et **Simard, Rémy.** Fraude électrique. Ill. par Rémy Simard. Ovale, 1984. 40 p. $8.95 [2-89186-040-3]. (Les aventures de Ray Gliss)
Des criminels sont déjoués par le jeune héros, Ray Gliss, et ses adjuvants. *Moyens, grands, aînés.*

Gaboury, Serge. Le mangeur d'étoiles. Ill. par Serge Gaboury. Ovale, 1982. 32 p. $7.95 relié [2-89186-015-2]. (Les aventures de Célestin)
Une histoire de science-fiction dans laquelle le cosmonaute Célestin et son ami Moustic doivent faire face à des ennemis.

Goldstyn, Jacques. Les aventures des petits débrouillards. Ill. par Jacques Goldstyn. La Presse, 1986. 63 p. $10.95 relié [2-89043-194-0].
Aventures extraites du *Je me petit-débrouille*, le magazine mensuel du Club des petits débrouillards. *Moyens.*

Munson, Harold. Koli. Orion, 1979. 23 p. $1.95 collé [2-89124-004-9].
Personnifie la vie d'un manchot. Illustrations en noir et blanc. *Débutants.*

Prouche. Woodozz et le robot sculpteur. Coeur de pomme, 1985. 32 p. $4.95 broché [2-920564-01-3].
Dans la galaxie Bozz-Trozz vivent des habitants à la recherche de connaissances et de pommes. Electrozz et Bozz sont envoyés en mission sur la terre. *Moyens.*

Viau, Normand. Humphrey Beauregard dans Eliess Nut l'incorrigible. Ill. par Perron. Ovale, 1984. 46 p. $8.95 relié [2-89186-142-X].
Le fils d'un grand patron de la pègre réussit à mettre tout le monde dans le pétrin lorsqu'il décide de devenir policier. *Moyens, grands, aînés.*

LEGENDES

Barbeau, Marius. Il était une fois. Ill. par Claude Poirier. Héritage, 1976. 127 p. $5.95 collé [0-7773-4403-3]. (Pour lire avec toi)
Légendes canadiennes recueillies autrefois par Marius Barbeau. *Moyens.*

Beaugrand, Honoré. La chasse-galerie. Fides, 1979. 112 p. $3.50 collé [2-7621-0806-3]. (Bibliothèque québécoise)
Recueil de légendes de traditions et de mythes de la fin du dix-neuvième siècle par des écrivains qui ont tâché d'écouter les histoires du peuple. Paru d'abord en 1900. *Aînés.*

Bussières, Johanne. Les feux follets. Ill. par Josée Dombrowski. Ovale, 1981. 32 p. $9.95 relié [2-89186-007-1]. (Légendes du Québec)
A Saint-François de l'île d'Orléans, des rumeurs circulent à l'effet que les bois sont devenus le royaume de milliers de diables. *Débutants.*

Chénard, Madeleine. La chasse-galerie. Ill. par France Lebon. Ovale, 1980. 29 p. $9.95 relié [2-89186-003-9]. (Légendes du Québec)
Cette légende raconte l'aventure de Joseph Rivard et de ses compagnons bûcherons qui voyagent en chasse-galerie pour célébrer la fête de Noël dans leur village. *Débutants.*

Choquette, Robert. Le sorcier d'Anticosti et autres légendes canadiennes. Ill. par Michèle Théorêt. Fides, 1975. 123 p. $8.50 collé [0-7621-0560-9]. (Goéland)
Seize récits qui appartiennent à la tradition orale du Québec. *Moyens, grands.*

Cleaver, Nancy. Le brave petit Tamia. Ill. par Laszlo Gal. Tr. par Françoise Marois. Scholastic-TAB, 1981. 31 p. $2.95 broché [0-590-71120-2].
Légende amérindienne qui raconte comment le petit écureuil fut griffé par l'ours en voulant secourir des hommes. Traduction de *How the chipmunk got its stripes*. *Débutants, moyens.*

Dupont, Jean-Claude. Contes de bûcherons. Quinze, 1976, 1979. 215 p. $12.95 collé [0-8856-5090-5].
Un conteur de 'mentries' raconte à la façon des gens de la Beauce quelques bonnes histoires du répertoire québécois. *Aînés.*

Finnigan, Joan. Regarde, il y a des géants partout!. Ill. par Richard Pelham. Adaptée par Jacques de Roussan. Toundra, 1983. 40 p. $19.95 relié [0-88776-154-2].
La légende canadienne de Jos Montferrand, le géant de la vallée de l'Outaouais, est racontée avec verve et humour. Traduction de *Look! The land is growing giants*. *Débutants.*

Gallant, Melvin. Ti-Jean: Contes acadiens. Ill. par Bernard Leblanc. Acadie, 1973. 165 p. $4.95 collé [2-7600-0099-0].
Ti-Jean surmonte tous les obstacles et survit aux mauvais sorts. *Grands.*

Houle, Denise. Contes québécois. Ill. par Datherien Sapon. Ville-Marie, 1981. 32 p. $8.95 relié [2-89194-026-1]
Adaptation de *La chasse-galerie* ou *Le tapis magique de Québec* d'après Honoré Beaugrand ainsi que *Le vaisseau-fantôme* ou *La légende du rocher percé* d'après Louis Fréchette. *Moyens.*

Landry, Louis. Glausgab, créateur du monde: La véritable histoire du Grand Manitou algonquin. Ill. par Yseult Ferron. Paulines, 1981. 100 p. $4.95 collé [2-89039-837-4]. (Jeunesse-pop)
Dans ce premier volume, Glausgab acquiert ses pouvoirs surnaturels de son père, le Grand Aigle. Il mate des monstres. Il crée l'homme. *Grands.*

Landry, Louis. Glausgab, le protecteur: La véritable histoire du Grand Manitou algonquin. Ill. par Yseult Ferron. Paulines, 1981. 108 p. $4.95 collé [2-89039-838-2]. (Jeunesse-pop)

Dans ce second volume, Glausgab protège son peuple contre les Otnéyarés et sa famille contre Pitché, l'ensorceleuse. Il comble les voeux de ses admirateurs. *Grands.*

Laquerre, Dominique. Oscar, le cheval à la queue tressée. Ill. par Dominique Laquerre. Québec/Amérique, 1980. 32 p. $9.95 relié [2-89037-026-7].

Des petits lutins viennent la nuit jouer de drôles de tours au cheval du cultivateur. *Débutants.*

Lebailly, Andrée. Les contes du Chalin aux îles Saint-Pierre et Miquelon. Leméac, 1984. 150 p. $19.95 collé [2-7609-9852-5]. (Jours de Fête)

Neuf contes inspirés de l'histoire et du peuple de Saint-Pierre et Miquelon. *Moyens, grands.*

Lemieux, Germain. Contes de mon pays. Héritage, 1980. 158 p. $5.95 collé [0-7773-3010-5]. (Katimavik)

Des contes amusants extraits de la collection 'Les Vieux m'ont conté' présentés par le Centre franco-ontarien de folklore. *Moyens, grands.*

Marcotte, Danielle. Par la bave de mon crapaud. Ill. par Philippe Béha. Ovale, 1984. 25 p. $9.95 relié [2-89186-049-7]. (Légendes du Québec)

Flo est accusée par son père d'avoir volé la cassette de bois contenant des pièces d'or. Avec l'aide de son amie Moustique et du fils de la sorcière, elle réussit à trouver les instruments qui permettront à la sorcière Mi de démasquer le coupable. *Débutants.*

Maxine. L'ogre de Niagara. Ill. par Michèle Devlin. Adapt. de Henriette Major. Héritage, 1981. 123 p. $3.95 collé [0-7773-4422-X]. (Petits classiques)

Metayer, Maurice. Contes de mon igloo. Ill. par Agnes Nanogak. Flammarion, 1973. 128 p. $4.00 collé [2-253-02775-8]. (Castor-poche)

Traduction de récits drôles ou tragiques qui donnent un intéressant aperçu de la culture des esquimaux du Canada. *Grands, aînés.*

Muller, Robin. Mollie Whuppie et l'ogre de la forêt. Ill. par Robin Muller. Tr. par Christiane Duchesne. Scholastic-TAB, 1983. 44 p. $4.95 collé [0-590-71171-7].

Après avoir été abandonnée dans la forêt avec ses deux soeurs aînées, Mollie Whuppie réussit à déjouer le géant et sauve ainsi ses soeurs du danger qui les menaçait. Traduction de *Mollie Whuppie and the giant. Débutants, moyens.*

Muller, Robin. La princesse Souillon. Ill. par Robin Muller. Tr. par Françoise Marois. Scholastic-TAB, 1984. 38 p. $5.95 collé [0-590-71412-0].

La princesse Souillon délivre sa soeur du terrible sort que les sorcières ont jeté sur elle. Traduction de *Tatterhood. Débutants, moyens.*

Muller, Robin. La vieille dame et le chaudron magique. Ill. par Robin Muller. Tr. par Lucie Duchesne. Scholastic-TAB, 1987. 30 p. $5.95 collé [0-590-71818-5].

La vieille dame rencontre finalement le joueur de tours que tous craignent au village et, à sa grande surprise, ils deviennent de très bons amis. Traduction de *The lucky old woman. Débutants, moyens.*

Noël, Michel. Les Mista Amisk de Piekouagami: Les castors géants du Lac Saint-Jean. Ill. par Joanne Ouellet. Leméac, 1984. 47 p. $9.95 broché [2-7609-9851-7].

Les castors géants réussissent à déjouer le géant Windigo qui avait l'intention de tuer tous les castors de la région. *Moyens.*

Piette, Robert. Le cheval du nord. Ill. par Gaétan Laroche. Ovale, 1980. 32 p. $9.95 relié [2-89186-000-4]. (Légendes du Québec)

Album qui raconte avec humour les exploits d'Alexis Lapointe, dit le trotteur, qui était reconnu pour ses courses extrêmement rapides. *Débutants.*

Piette, Robert. La grange aux lutins. Ill. par Josée Dombrowski. Ovale, 1980. 28 p. $9.95 relié [2-89186-001-2]. (Légendes du Québec)

Deux lutins espiègles emmêlent la queue et la crinière de la jument du père Dumas et lui font faire de folles randonnées jusqu'au jour où grand-père Dumas trouve un moyen de chasser les lutins. *Débutants.*

Piette, Robert. Jos Montferrand, le géant de l'Outaouais. Ill. par Yvon Bouchard. Ovale, 1981. 32 p. $9.95 relié [2-89186-006-3]. (Légendes du Québec)

L'homme fort s'illustra comme défenseur des droits des canadiens-français dans les chantiers de l'Outaouais. *Débutants.*

Piette, Robert. Le Noël de Savarin. Ill. par Josée Dombrowski. Ovale, 1980. 32 p. $9.95 relié [2-89186-001-2]. (Légendes du Québec)

Au village de St.Georges de Beauce, Savarin, un riche avare, reçoit la visite d'un quêteux qu'il refuse d'abriter à la veille de Noël. *Débutants.*

Piette, Robert. La sirène de Percé. Ill. par Sylvie Talbot. Ovale, 1981. 32 p. $9.95 relié [2-89186-004-7]. (Légendes du Québec)

Un jeune pêcheur gaspésien veut garder une sirène qu'il vient de trouver dans ses filets. *Débutants.*

Piette, Suzanne. Le chien d'or. Ill. par France Lebon. Ovale, 1981. 32 p. $9.95 relié [2-89186-00505]. (Légendes du Québec)
Les aventures d'un marchand de Québec au XVIIIe siècle alors qu'un concurrent déloyal veut s'approprier la mystérieuse plaque du chien d'or. *Débutants.*

Soulières, Robert. Le baiser maléfique. Ill. par Stéphane Jorisch. Ovale, 1985. 24 p. $9.95 relié [2-89186-016-6]. (Légendes du Québec)
Le bel inconnu qui se présente à la fête donnée par Rose Latulippe pour souligner le Mardi-Gras, n'est autre que le diable en personne. *Débutants.*

Tonnerova, Maria. Contes de Bohème. Ill. par Pierre Decelles. Héritage, 1981. 118 p. $5.95 collé [0-7773-4421-1]. (Petits classiques)
Adaptation des plus beaux contes de Bohème mettant en vedette Jean, un fils de paysan qui sait montrer qu'il est plus fin que les riches et les puissants. *Moyens.*

Villeneuve, Jocelyne. Nanna Bijou: Le géant endormi. Ill. par Luc Robert. Prise de Parole, 1981. 46 p. $6.95 relié [0-920814-34-4].
Nana Bijou révèle au chef Shinuvauk le secret d'un passage souterrain où sont cachées des réserves de métal précieux. Lorsque le secret est dévoilé à l'homme blanc, une tempête de fin du monde éclate. *Moyens.*

Villeneuve, Jocelyne. La Princesse à la mante verte. Ill. par Luc Robert. Prise de Parole, 1983. 95 p. $7.95 relié [0-920814-54-9]. (Contes et légendes)
Forcée de conduire la tribu des Sioux au camp des Ojibwés, la princesse à la mante verte qui avait été enlevée par la tribu des Sioux, entraîne ces derniers à leur perte dans les remous de la rivière Kaminstiqua. *Moyens.*

Warnant-Côté, Marie-Andrée. Les tours de Maître Lapin. Ill. par Michèle Parsons. Héritage, 1976. 126 p. $5.95 collé [0-7773-4402-5]. (Pour lire avec toi)
Légendes indiennes introduisant Maître Lapin, personnage inventé autrefois par les indiens, qui est un incorrigible joueur de tours. *Moyens.*

Wilson, Serge. Ti-Jean et le gros roi. Ill. par Claude Poirier. Héritage, 1977. 126 p. $5.95 collé [0-7773-4409-2]. (Pour lire avec toi)
Très bonne version de contes du Centre franco-ontarien de folklore. Le lecteur ne peut que s'amuser de la malice de Ti-Jean profitant de la naïveté du roi. *Débutants, moyens.*

RELIGION

Grisé, Yolande. Le monde des dieux. Hurtubise, 1985. 334 p. collé [2-89045-639-0].
Une initiation aux vieux mythes de l'humanité, la mythologie gréco-romaine par les textes. *Aînés.*

Major, Henriette. La bible en papier. Ill. par Claude Lafortune. Fides, 1979. $10.95 relié [2-7621-0796-2].
Ce livre inculquera aux jeunes le goût de la recherche et leur montrera qu'on peut obtenir des résultats valables et utiles avec des moyens modestes. *Moyens.*

Major, Henriette. L'évangile en papier. Ill. par Claude Lafortune. Fides, 1977. 94 p. $9.95 relié [2-7621-0654-0].
Ce livre nous présente les personnages de la Bible. *Moyens.*

SCIENCES SOCIALES

Blakely, Cindy et **Drinkwater, Suzanne.** Prudence! Le guide de sécurité pour les enfants. Tr. par Marie-Claude Vianna. Ill. par Barbara Klumder. Trécarré/Sommerville House, 1986. 30 p. $11.95 [2-89249-183-5].

Ouvrage réalisé par parents-secours afin d'alerter les parents et protéger les enfants des dangers possibles quand les jeunes sont seuls à l'extérieur du foyer. Traduction de *The Look out book!: a child's guide to street safety*. *Débutants, moyens.*

Brisebois, Raymond. Le système métrique apprivoisé. Ill. par Eric Thomas et André Thomas. Lidec, 1974. 61 p. $1.90 collé [0-7608-6181-9].

A l'aide de dessins amusants et de graphiques comparatifs, l'auteur introduit le système métrique. *Moyens, grands.*

Doucet, Paul. Vie de nos ancêtres en Acadie: Coutumes, croyances et religion populaire Acadie, 1979. 32 p. $7.50 broché [2-7600-0036-2].

Doucet, Paul. Vie de nos ancêtres en Acadie: Le vêtement. Acadie, 1979. 40 p. $8.50 broché [2-7600-0037-0].

Ouvrages à l'intention des élèves, avec des questions dans les marges. Illustré. *Moyens, grands.*

Le Blanc, Monique. Parle-moi de la ceinture fléchée! Fides, 1977. 107 p. $4.50 broché [2-7621-0661-3]. (Comment faire)

Seul ouvrage sur ce sujet à s'adresser directement aux jeunes. Ce livre d'initiation au fléché traite de tous les aspects du sujet. *Moyens, grands.*

Martel, Suzanne. Tout sur Noël. Ill. par Josée Guberec. Fides, 1977. 179 p. $7.95 collé [2-7621-0649-4]. (Comment faire)

Jeux, cantiques, décorations, recettes, bricolages, contes, historique ... vraiment tout sur Noël! *Moyens, grands.*

Montpetit, Raymond. Le temps des fêtes au Québec. Homme, 1978. 285 p. $8.00 collé [0-7759-0662-0].

A l'aide de textes et de documents iconographiques d'époque du début de la colonie au 19e siècle, cet ouvrage documentaire trace un portrait des Québécois en fête. *Aînés.*

Pachano, Jane et **Ozores, J. Rabbit.** Images des Cris de la Baie James. Ill. par J. Eitzen; R. Menarick et M. Orr. Le Centre culturel et éducatif Cri de la Baie James, 1983. 56 p. $10.95 collé. Pas de ISBN.

Illustre la vie et les coutumes des Cris de la Baie James. *Débutants.*

SCIENCES PURES

voir
COLLECTIONS
Le monde animal
Le monde merveilleux des animaux

Beaudin, Louise et Quintin, Michel. Guide des mammifères terrestres du Québec, de l'Ontario et des Maritimes. Nomade, 1983. 301 p. $19.50 relié [2-920438-00-X].
Guide des mammifères terrestres illustré de photographies en couleurs, à l'information codée et classifiée par thèmes. *Grands, aînés.*

Clarke, Arthur H. Les mollusques d'eau douce du Canada. Tr. par Aurèle La Rocque. Musée national des sciences naturelles, 1980. 416 p. $39.95 relié [0-660-00023-7].
Manuel d'identification qui illustre 179 espèces. Illustrations en noir et blanc et planches en couleurs. *Grands, aînés.*

David, Normand et Paquette, Gaétan. Comment nourrir les oiseaux autour de chez-soi? Québec-Science, 1982. 70 p. $6.95 collé [2-920073-25-7].
Guide indispensable pour ceux qui s'intéressent aux oiseaux. *Moyens, grands.*

Douglas, Charles. Carnets d'histoire naturelle. Musées nationaux du Canada. Série no 1, 1977. 108 p. $2.50 broché [0-660-00093-8]; Série no 2, 1978. 144 p. $2.50 broché [0-660-00095-5]; Série no 3, 1980. 114 p. $2.50 broché ; Série no 4, 1981. $2.50 broché [0-660-90263-X].

Expériences scientifiques du Centre des sciences de l'Ontario. Ill. par Tina Holdcroft. Tr. par Francine de Lorimier. Héritage, 1987. 86 p. $9.95 collé [2-7625-4649-4].
Soixante-cinq expériences amusantes et instructives. Chaque expérience utilise des articles que les jeunes pourront trouver à la maison. *Débutants, moyens.*

Guide du botaniste amateur. Edition revue et adaptée de *Le botaniste amateur en campagne* du R.P. Louis-Marie, o.c.s.o. Agriculture Québec, 1976. 110 p. $4.95 collé [0-7754-2432-3].
Ouvrage illustré pour ceux qui veulent s'initier au monde végétal. Présenté sous forme de calendrier, facilitant la découverte des plantes propres aux mois mentionnés (Avril à Octobre). *Grands, aînés.*

Huot, Guy. L'observation des oiseaux. Marcel Broquet, 1981. 184 p. $12.95 collé [2-89000-041-9]. (Jeunes naturalistes)
Comment identifier les oiseaux, les observer et établir une liste cumulative d'observations. Contient également un calendrier des immigrations. *Moyens, grands.*

Kassian, Olena. Plouf le dauphin passe à l'action. Ill. par Olena Kassian. Tr. par Christiane Duchesne. Scholastic-TAB, 1984. 24 p. $2.25 broché [0-590-71461-9].
Plus petit que les autres dauphins, Plouf est le seul qui peut entrer dans la caverne pour secourir un bébé dauphin incapable de trouver la sortie. *Tout-petits.*

Kassian, Olena. Zou la loutre trouve une maison. Ill. par Olena Kassian. Tr. par Christiane Duchesne. Scholastic-TAB, 1984. 24 p. $2.25 broché [0-91987-92-1].
Zou la loutre part à la recherche d'un nouvel endroit pour vivre lorsque sa famille ne peut trouver assez de nourriture pour se rassasier dans la rivière. *Tout-petits.*

Lacoursière, Estelle. L'arbrier québécois. Ill. par Pierre Leduc. Québec Science Editeur, 1982. 99 p. $8.95 collé [2-920073-17-6].
Un album présentant une cinquantaine d'arbres et d'arbustes trouvés au Québec. *Moyens, grands.*

Lacoursière, Estelle. L'herbier québécois. Ill. par Pierre Leduc. Québec Science Editeur, 1982. 69 p. $13.95 collé [2-920073-22-2].
Un album présentant une soixantaine de mauvaises herbes choisies parmi les plus courantes au Québec. *Moyens, grands.*

Lacoursière, E. et Therrien, J. L'étang apprivoisé. Ill. par C. Tremblay. Marcel Broquet, 1984. 104 p. $14.95 collé [2-89000-134-2]. (Jeunes naturalistes)

Les auteurs décrivent un écosystème de chez nous. *Moyens, grands.*

Laforge, M. La forêt derrière les arbres. Ill. par A. Lauzon. Marcel Broquet, 1985. 238 p. $16.95 collé [2-89000-140-7]. (Jeunes naturalistes)

Une initiation à la faune et la flore de nos forêts. *Moyens, grands.*

Lahaie, Pierre et Laganière, Benoît. Les baleines viennent-elles dans le golfe Saint-Laurent? Sont-elles de gros poissons? Ill. par Suzanne Verret et Henri Larouche. Entreprises culturelles, 1986. 34 p. $6.00 broché [2-7614-0217-0].

Composée dans le cadre d'un projet éducatif, cette brochure tente d'initier les élèves visitant l'Aquarium du Québec aux baleines du golfe Saint-Laurent. *Moyens, grands.*

Lamoureux, Gisèle. Plantes sauvages printanières. Editeur officiel du Québec, 1975. 247 p. $8.95 collé [0-7754-2352-1].

Un manuel d'identification et d'utilisation. Photographies en couleurs. *Moyens, grands, aînés.*

Lane, Peter. Les oiseaux d'hiver au Québec. Héritage, 1980. 110 p. $4.95 collé [0-0773-5385-7].

Les habitudes, les besoins des espèces d'oiseaux qui doivent affronter les rigueurs du froid de l'hiver québécois. Illustrations en noir et blanc. *Grands, aînés.*

Melançon, Claude. Les poissons de nos eaux. Jour, 1973. 456 p. $11.00 collé [0-7760-1103-7].

On retrouve dans cet ouvrage illustré presque toutes les espèces de poissons d'eau douce du Québec. *Grands, aînés.*

Plantes sauvages des villes, des champs et en bordure des chemins. Québec/Science, 1983. 208 p. $12.95 collé [2-920174-07-X].

Pour apprendre à reconnaître les plantes, le moment de leur floraison, leur habitat et leur folklore, leurs utilisations médicinales et culinaires, et leur intérêt agricole. Y sont suggérées des méthodes d'éradication des 'mauvaises herbes' sans l'emploi d'herbicides chimiques. *Aînés.*

Plantes sauvages du bord de la mer. Fleurbec, 1985. 286 p. $15.95 collé [2-920174-08-8].

Guide d'identification pour apprendre à connaître les fleurs, les plantes, les algues et arbustes du bord de la mer. *Grands, aînés.*

Porsild, A.E. Plantes sauvages des montagnes Rocheuses. Ill. par Dagny Tande Lid. Musée national des sciences naturelles, 1974. 454 p. $6.95 collé [0-660-00069-5].

Permet d'identifier près de 400 espèces de plantes alpines et sub-alpines que l'on trouve partout dans les Rocheuses. Illustrations en couleurs. *Grands, aînés.*

Prescott, Jacques et Richard, Pierre. Mammifères du Québec et de l'est du Canada. France-Amérique, 1982. Tome 1 $12.95 collé [2-89001-123-2]; tome 2 $12.95 collé [2-89001-124-0].

Documentaires servant à identifier les différents mammifères. *Moyens, grands.*

Prévost, Bernard. Les papillons du Québec. Homme, 1976. $6.00 broché [0-7759-0500-3].

Cent une photos, quelques clefs d'identification, un index et une claire description des moeurs et de l'aspect des papillons du Québec. *Grands, aînés.*

Les principaux insectes défoliateurs des arbres du Québec. Québec, Ministère de l'Energie et des Ressources, 1979. 188 p. $7.95 collé [2-551-03428-0].

Un guide d'identification des insectes qui se nourrissent du feuillage des essences forestières. Limité aux espèces les plus importantes ou communément rencontrées. Photographies en couleurs. Pas de texte. *Moyens.*

Professeur Scientifix. Le petit débrouillard. Ill. par Jacques Goldstyn. Québec-Science, 1981. 123 p. $12.95 relié [2-920073-18-4]. (Des petits débrouillards)

Soixante-six expériences faciles à réaliser à la maison et sans danger, seul ou avec un coup de main des parents. *Moyens, grands.*

Professeur Scientifix. 66 nouvelles expériences pour les petits débrouillards. Ill. par Jacques Goldstyn. Québec-Science, 1983. 137 p. $12.95 relié [2-920073-29-X]. (Des petits débrouillards)

Soixante-six expériences faciles à réaliser à la maison et sans danger, seul ou avec un coup de main des parents. *Moyens, grands.*

Professeur Scientifix et Laracque, Bernard. Encore des expériences. Ill. par Jacques Goldstyn. Québec-Science, 1985. 119 p. $12.95 relié [2-920073-35-4]. (Des petits débrouillards)

Troisième livre d'expériences pour les enfants curieux qui veulent savoir comment fabriquer une boussole, pourquoi certains objets flottent sur l'eau, ou si l'eau chaude peut geler avant l'eau froide et bien d'autres expériences. *Moyens, grands.*

Provencher, Paul. Mes observations sur les insectes. Homme, 1977. $5.00 collé [0-77559-0537-2]. (Sport)

L'auteur y étudie l'anatomie et la physiologie générale et présente en détail quatorze espèces d'insectes et deux espèces d'arachnides que le lecteur pourra observer dans la nature québécoise. *Grands, aînés.*

Provencher, Paul. Mes observations sur les mammifèeres. Homme, 1976. 158 p. $6.95 collé [0-7750-0503-8]. (Sport)

Une étude illustrée des mammifères du Québec. *Grands, aînés.*

Provencher, Paul. Mes observations sur les poissons. Homme, 1976. 124 p. $5.00 collé [2-7759-0499-6]. (Sport)

Une étude illustrée des poissons du Québec par un spécialiste de la vie en plein air. *Grands, aînés.*

Québec. Ministère de l'Agriculture des Pêcheries et de l'Alimentation. Guide du botaniste amateur. Ed. Officiel du Québec, 1982. 110 p. $4.95 collé [EOQ12923-9].

Un guide pour identifier les plantes et connaître le cycle de floraisons des fleurs du Québec. *Grands, aînés.*

Québec. Ministère des Terres et Forêts. Petite flore forestière du Québec. Editeur officiel du Québec/Editions France-Amérique, 1974. 216 p. $5.95 collé [0-7754-1792-0].

Manuel pratique servant à l'identification des espèces les plus courantes et de leurs principales caractéristiques. *Moyens, grands, aînés.*

Simard, Claire. Nature amie; sciences de la nature. Tome 1. Ill. par Jean-Denis Fleury. Paulines. 42 p. $9.75 collé [0-88840-529-4]. (Documentation Video-Presse)

En compagnie de Mimi et petit Jo, l'enfant de quatre à sept ans apprend à explorer le monde qui l'entoure. *Tout-petits, débutants.*

Suzuki, David et Hehner, Barbara. Les insectes. Ill. par Robert Tuckerman. Tr. par Marie-Claude Desorcy. Etudes vivantes, 1986. 96 p. $9.95 collé [2-7607-0302-9].

Projets et expériences scientifiques complètent cette introduction au monde fascinant des insectes. Traduction de *Looking at insects.* *Moyens.*

Suzuki, David et Hehner, Barbara. Les plantes. Tr. par Marie-Claude Désorcy. Etudes Vivantes, 1986. 96 p. $9.95 collé [0-7607-0301-0].

Projets et expériences scientifiques complètent cette introduction au monde des végétaux. Traduction de *Looking at plants. Moyens.*

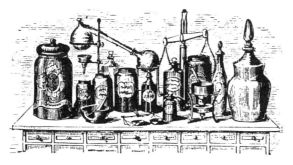

TECHNIQUES (SCIENCES APPLIQUEES)

Beauchamp-Richards, Huguette et Richards, Robert. Jardinez avec le professeur Scientifix: Des expériences pour toutes les saisons. Ill. par Jacques Goldstyn. Québec-Science, 1982. 149 p. $14.95 relié [2-920073-24-9]. (Des petits débrouillards)

Les rudiments de jardinage sont expliqués par le professeur Scientifix. Des projets faciles à réaliser sont décrits. *Moyens, grands.*

Beauchamp-Richards, Huguette. Les petits marmitons. Ill. par Jacques Goldstyn. Québec-Science, 1986. 96 p. $9.95 collé (Des petits débrouillards)

L'adjointe du professeur Scientifix montre à préparer des mets succulents et nutritifs. *Moyens, grands.*

Beaulieu, Jacques. Les voyages fantastiques de Globulo. Ill. par Jacques Goldstyn. Québec-Science, 1982. 104 p. $12.95 relié [2-920073-23-0]. (Des petits débrouillards)

Une explication du système sanguin, du système nerveux, de la bouche et des microbes. Jeux et expériences viennent compléter l'information. *Moyens, grands.*

Climo, Lindee. La grange de Chester. Ill. par Lindee Climo. Tr. par Jacques de Roussan. Soleil Diffusion, 1982. 32 p. $13.95 relié [2-88058-011-0].

Un récit détaillé des occupations quotidiennes de Chester, un agriculteur de l'île-du-Prince-Edouard. Illustrations simples et réalistes des animaux de la ferme. Une excellente introduction aux animaux de la ferme. Traduction de *Chester's barn*. *Tout-petits, débutants.*

Gendron, Lionel. La merveilleuse histoire de la naissance. Homme, 1969. 93 p. $6.85 collé [0-7759-0171-7].

Le livre le plus complet sur ce sujet. *Moyens, grands.*

Harel, Louise et Doucet-Leduc, Hélène. Qu'est-ce qui mijote. La Presse, 1976. 139 p. $6.95 collé [0-7777-0128-6].

Un livre de cuisine qui s'adresse aux jeunes et aux débutants de tous les âges. *Moyens, grands, aînés.*

Martel, Suzanne. Goûte à tout. Ill. par Cécile Gagnon. Fides, 1977. 80 p. $7.95 collé [2-7621-0666-4].

Conçu pour les 'cuisiniers paresseux, les gens pressés, les nouveaux mariés, les enfants cordons-bleus, les étudiants, les célibataires.' Mise en page des recettes n'est pas toujours claire. *Grands, aînés.*

Mazalto, Michèle et Mazalto, Maurice. Adèle Mystère et Clément Secret. Guy Saint-Jean, 1984. 48 p. $7.95 collé [2-920340-13-1]. (Information sexuelle)

Information pertinente sur les questions sexuelles que se posent les adolescents. *Grands.*

Mazalto, Michèle et Mazalto, Maurice. Jean-Claude et Béatrice. Guy Saint-Jean, 1983. 31 p. $6.95 collé [2-920340-12-3]. (Information sexuelle)

Deux enfants posent des questions à leurs parents sur l'origine des bébés, l'anatomie et la vie sexuelle. *Débutants, moyens.*

Richards, Robert. L'animalerie des petits débrouillards. Ill. par Jacques Goldstyn. Québec-Science, 1986. 96 p. $8.95 collé [2-920073-40-0]. (Des petits débrouillards)

Les jeunes apprennent comment choisir un animal de compagnie et comment le dresser et lui donner les soins appropriés. *Moyens, grands.*

Robert, Jocelyne et Jacob, Jo-Anne. Ma sexualité. Ill. par Tibo. L'Homme, 1986. 3 vols. 80 p. $7.95 chac. [2-7619-0581-4] (0-6 ans); [2-7619-0582-2] (6 à 9 ans); [2-7619-0583-0] (9 à 12 ans).

Ouvrages agréables et utiles qui renseignent clairement les enfants d'aujourd'hui par des auteurs sexologues qui connaissent leur public-lecteur. *Tout-petits à grands.*

Suzuki, David et Hehner, Barbara. Les sens. Ill. par Peter Grau. Tr. par Marie-Claude Désorcy. Etudes vivantes, 1987. 96 p. $9.95 collé [2-7607-0313-4].

Projets excitants et expériences scientifiques complètent ce guide à la découverte des sens et de leur fonctionnement. Traduction de *Looking at senses*. *Moyens.*

LES ARTS

ARTS DECORATIFS, MINEURS ET GRAPHIQUES

Corriveau, Bernadette. Le chas de l'aiguille. Ill. par Louise Méthé. Fides, 1978. 120 p. $4.50 collé [2-7621-0679-6]. (Comment faire)
Introduit à la couture et stimule grâce à toutes sortes d'idées. Volume attrayant et très agréable à consulter. *Moyens, grands.*

Gilliland, Jillian et Downie, Mary Alice. Artisan de la nature. Tr. par Martine Connat. Scholastic-TAB, 1984. 65 p. $2.95 collé [0-590-71222-5].
Activités simples à réaliser utilisant des objets de la nature tels des pissenlits, des glands, des joncs de marais. Les étapes de réalisation sont illustrées et indiquées clairement. Traduction de *Stones and cones. Débutants.*

Kurelek, William. Noëls nordiques: Les rêves de Noël d'un garçon des Prairies. Ill. par William Kurelek. Fides, 1980. 46 p. $5.75 relié [2-7621-1006-8].
Noëls de cowboys, de cheminots, de fermiers, d'Inuits et de pauvres gens. Magnifiques illustrations de ce peintre canadien. Traduction de *Northern nativity. Moyens.*

Mérinat, Eric. Les marionnettes de papier. Ill. par Eric Merinat. Etincelle, 1975. 96 p. $4.95 broché [0-88515-064-3].
Ouvrage illustré qui amusera les enfants. *Moyens, grands.*

Méthé, Louise. Techniques d'impression. Fides, 1977. 120 p. $4.50 collé [0-7621-0648-6]. (Comment faire)
Pour apprendre les techniques de base de l'impression: empreintes avec les doigts, les tissus, les pommes de terre et les fruits, etc. *Moyens, grands.*

Vachon, Hélène. Livres à fabriquer soi-même. Ill. par Tibo. Documentor, 1985. 94 p. $8.95 spirale [2-89123-106-6].
Les étapes pour fabriquer un livre sont expliquées clairement, de la couverture à l'emboîtage et à la reliure. *Moyens, grands.*

MUSIQUE

Butler, Edith. L'Acadie sans frontières. Leméac, 1977. 129 p. $6.95 collé [0-7761-4660-2]. (Mon pays mes chansons)
Répertoire de chansons traditionnelles et de chansons modernes de l'Acadie. *Aînés.*

Cailloux, André. Virginie chante ... les instruments de musique. Ill.par François Ladouceur. Héritage/Radio-Canada, 1980. 20 p. $2.95 broché [0-7773-4320-7].
Virginie, un gentil batracien ventriloque, propose aux petits une agréable leçon de solfège. D'après une émission télévisée. *Tout-petits.*

Cailloux, André. Virginie chante ... la locomotion. Ill. par François Ladouceur. Héritage/Radio-Canada, 1981. 20 p. $2.95 broché [0-7773-4322-3].
Chanson pour les tout-petits qui raconte les moyens de locomotion qui conduisent Virginie et ses amis à la fête de Benjamin. *Tout-petits.*

Michaud, Josette. La perdriole. Ill. par Josette Michaud. Leméac, 1982. 28 p. $6.95 broché [2-7609-9842-8].
Une chanson folklorique joliment illustrée. Un animal différent est introduit avec chaque couplet. La notation musicale occupe la page du centre. *Tout-petits.*

Passe-Partout. Chansons et comptines. Editeur Officiel de Québec, 1984. 2 vols. $5.99 chac. rel. spirale [vol.1 EOQ 15793-3; vol.2 EOQ 22459-2].
Chansons et comptines tirées de l'émission de télévision et illustrées en couleurs. *Tout-petits.*

La poulette grise. Ill. par Louise Méthé. Leméac, 1973. 16 p. $5.95 relié [2-7609-9847-9]. (Littérature de jeunesse)

Le texte d'une comptine bien connue qui va ravir les petits. *Tout-petits.*

Rancourt, Roger. Ensemble, si on chantait. C.P. 267, Beauceville, Québec, G0M 1A0, 1986. 192 p. $7.95 rel. spirale [2-8929-4001-X].

Ce carnet contient les mots de quatre cent chansons pour permettre aux jeunes de chanter ensemble. *Débutants, moyens, grands, aînés.*

Roy, Raoul. Le chant de l'alouette. Presses de l'université Laval/Radio-Canada, 1969. 104 p. $3.00 collé [2-7637-6436-3].

Cinquante chansons folkloriques du Canada français. *Grands.*

LOISIRS: SPECTACLES, JEUX, SPORTS

Cibles; esprit et techniques des scouts et guides. Novalis, 1979. 382 p. $8.00 collé [2-89088-001-X].

Une mise à jour de l'édition de 1954 qui met à la portée de tous des moyens et des techniques pour la vie de plein air. *Grands, aînés.*

Meeker, Howie. L'ABC du hockey. Homme, 1973. 168 p. $5.00 collé [0-77590401-5]. (Sport)

Ce volume décrit les techniques de base du hockey afin d'aider les jeunes à jouer plus efficacement. *Moyens, grands, aînés.*

Robinson, Larry et McFarlane, Brian. Larry Robinson le jeu défensif. Ill. par Chuck Nicholls. Tr. par Louis de Lorimier. Homme, 1981. $6.95 collé [2-7619-0195-9].

Les rudiments des techniques défensives et offensives sont enseignés par l'auteur, défenseur des Canadiens de Montréal. *Grands, aînés.*

LANGUAGE ET LITTERATURE

ANTHOLOGIES

Grisé, Yolande. Des mots pour se connaître. Fides, 1982. 213 p. $9.95 relié [2-7621-1144-7].

Recueil de textes pour les adolescents par des auteurs franco-ontariens. *Grands, aînés.*

Grisé, Yolande. Parli, parlo, parlons. Fides, 1982. 143 p. $6.95 relié [2-7621-1142-0].

Poèmes, comptines, chansons, contes et récits par des auteurs de l'Ontario. *Débutants, moyens.*

Grisé, Yolande. Pour se faire un nom. Fides, 1982. 313 p. $12.95 relié [2-7621-1145-5].

Anthologie des grands auteurs, recueil de proses et de poèmes depuis la venue des Français en Ontario. *Aînés.*

Grisé, Yolande. Les yeux en fête. Fides, 1982. 197 p. $8.95 relié [2-7621-1143-9].

Pièces poétiques et histoires par des auteurs franco-ontariens. *Moyens.*

POESIE

Bussières, Simone. C'est ta fête. Ill. par Renée Leblanc. Laurentiennes, 1981. 62 p. $4.95 collé [2-89015-026-7]. (Le poète et l'enfant)

Comptines et fantaisies sur une myriade de thèmes familiers aux jeunes enfants. *Tout-petits, débutants.*

Bussières, Simone. Dans mon petit violon. Ill. par Denis Robitaille. Laurentiennes, 1985. 62 p. $4.95 collé [2-89015-045-3].

Comptines et poèmes fantaisistes pour les jeunes enfants. *Tout-petits, débutants.*

Cailloux, André. Ecoute, mon ami. Ill. par Renée Grégoire. Paulines, 1984. 30 p. $5.95 broché [2-89039-969-9]. (Prisme)
L'auteur présente un assortiment de poèmes traitant les thèmes des saisons et des animaux. Disponible en disque avec la voix de l'auteur. *Débutants, moyens.*

Cailloux, Grand-père. Je te laisse une caresse. Ill. par Gilles Tibo. La Courte échelle, 1976. 24 p. $5.95 broché [2-89021-001-4].
Poésies et comptines écrites et illustrées avec humour. Tirées du disque *Chansons et comptines de grand-père Cailloux. Débutants.*

Cailloux, Grand-père. Mon grand-père a un jardin. Ill. par Philippe Béha. La Courte échelle, 1979. $5.95 broché [2-89021-013-8].
Des comptines charmantes sur des thèmes que les enfants aimeront: animaux, fruits, amitié. Les illustrations chaleureuses donnent le goût de lire et relire le texte. Cassette et disque disponibles. *Tout-petits.*

Comptines traditionnelles du Canada français. Ill. par Michèle Leclerc, Louise Méthé et Yolande Chatillon. Leméac, 1974, 1982. 32 p. $8.95 broché [2-7609-9846-0].
Des comptines populaires du répertoire traditionnel. *Tout-petits.*

Crapauds et autres animaux. Ill. par différents illustrateurs. La Courte échelle, 1981. 24 p. $6.95 broché. [2-89021-028-6].
Un bestiaire par différents auteurs et illustrateurs du Québec. *Débutants.*

Germain, Georges-Hébert. Croque-notes. Ill. par différents illustrateurs. La Courte échelle, 1984. 22 p. $5.95 broché [2-89021-047-2].
Pour initier les jeunes à la musique, neuf instruments de musique sont présentés aux jeunes. Illustrations fantaisistes et originales accompagnent un texte poétique. *Tout-petits, débutants.*

Leclerc, Félix. Adagio. Ill. par Marcellin Dufour. Fides, 1976. 156 p. $8.50 collé [2-7621-0018-4]. (Goéland)

Leclerc, Félix. Allegro. Ill. par Albert Rousseau. Fides, 1976. 156 p. $8.50 collé [2-7621-0617-6]. (Goéland)

Leclerc, Félix. Andante. Ill. par Nicole Benoît. Fides, 1975. 133 p. $8.50 collé [2-7621-0561-7]. (Goéland)
Trois recueils de contes, de fables et de poèmes qui célèbrent la nature et la vie canadienne. *Grands, aînés.*

Leclerc, Félix. Dialogues d'hommes et de bêtes. Fides, 1979. 235 p. $4.50 collé [2-7621-0804-7]. (Bibliothèque québécoise)
Aventures féériques de visions d'étoiles filantes et de musique d'oiseaux. Anthologie de fables. *Aînés.*

Pasquet, Jacques. Des animaux pour rire. Ill. par Jean-Christian Knaff. Ville-Marie, 1982. 24 p. $8.95 relié [2-89194-060-1].
Poèmes simples et farfelus ayant pour sujet les animaux. Illustrés en noir et blanc. *Débutants.*

Plante, Raymond. Clins d'oeil & pieds de nez. Ill. par Johanne Pépin. La Courte échelle, 1982. 24 p. $4.95 broché [2-89021-035-9].
Texte de chansons humoristiques et fantaisistes composées pour l'émission *'La boîte à lettres'* produite par Radio-Canada. La notation musicale n'est pas fournie. *Moyens.*

Poe, Edgar Allan. Annabel Lee. Ill. par Gilles Tibo. Tr. par Stéphane Mallarmé. Toundra, 1987. 24 p. $19.95 relié [0-88776-203-4].
Artiste québécois Tibo a situé ce poème par Edgar Allan Poe de l'amour d'un jeune pêcheur pour une belle et mystérieuse fille venant d'un autre monde dans la Gaspésie des années 1930. *Débutants, moyens.*

La vache et d'autres animaux. Ill. par différents illustrateurs. La Courte échelle, 1982. 22 p. $5.95 broché [2-89021-031-6].
Un recueil de poèmes magnifiquement illustrés ayant pour sujet les animaux. *Débutants, moyens.*

Vigneault, Gilles. Le grand cerf-volant; poèmes, contes et chansons. Nouvelles éditions de l'Arc, 1986. 233 p. $9.95 collé [2-02-009389-8]. (Virgule)
Contes, poèmes, chansons à texte. Réédition du répertoire du chansonnier, écrivain, conteur et poète. *Aînés.*

THEATRE

Cailloux, André. François et l'oiseau du Brésil, suivi de Tombé des étoiles. Leméac, 1977. 151 p. $8.95 collé [0-7761-9906]. (Théâtre pour enfants)
Deux pièces de théâtre. Dans *François et l'oiseau du Brésil*, un oiseau venu du Brésil apporte beaucoup d'imprévus à la forge du père Evarist. *Tombé des étoiles* se déroule au laboratoire de monsieur Plume, astronome farfelu. *Moyens.*

Camirand, François; Lauvaux, Yves; Noël, Michel O.; et Rioux, Monique. L'Umiak. VLB éditeur, 1984. 96 p. $9.95 collé [2-89005-202-8].
Récit légendaire traitant de la culture Inuit. *Grands, aînés.*

Dubé, Jasmine. Bouches décousues. Leméac, 1985. 159 p. $9.95 collé [2-7609-9914-9]. (Théâtre pour enfants)

Sylvie et Julien racontent les aggressions sexuelles auxquelles ils sont soumis de la part des adultes. *Moyens, grands.*

Lebeau, Suzanne. Les petits pouvoirs. Leméac, 1983. 164 p. $9.95 collé [2-7609-9911-4]. (Théâtre pour enfants)

Pièce de théâtre qui décrit les relations d'un jeune garçon avec ses parents. *Moyens, grands.*

Lebeau, Suzanne. Ti-Jean voudrait ben s'marier mais ... Leméac, 1985. 129 p. $8.95 collé [2-7609-9913-0]. (Théâtre pour enfants)

Pièce de théâtre qui encourage la participation des enfants. Vers 1800, dans le village de La Prairie, Ti-Jean et Madelon s'aiment mais le père de la fille impose à Ti-Jean trois épreuves. *Moyens, grands.*

Lepage, Roland. Icare. Ill. par Jacques Léveillé. Leméac, 1979. 125 p. $8.95 collé [2-7609-9908-4]. (Théâtre pour enfants).

Fantaisie mythologique pour enfants. *Moyens, grands.*

Mignault, Guy. Bonjour, Monsieur de La Fontaine. Leméac, 1982. 149 p. $9.95 collé [2-7609-9910-6]. (Théâtre pour enfants)

Une adaptation théâtrale de quelques unes des fables de La Fontaine. Une pièce de théâtre que les jeunes pourront monter en entier ou quelques scènes seulement. *Moyens, grands.*

Morency, Pierre. Marlot dans les merveilles. Leméac, 1975. 114 p. $8.95 collé [0-7761-9905-6]. (Théâtre pour enfants)

Une pièce de théâtre dont l'intrique captivante et fascinante intéressera les élèves des écoles élémentaires. *Débutants, moyens.*

Morin, Paule-Nicole. Théâtre mot magique; marionnettes, jeux scéniques, ombres chinoises. Guérin, 1981, 1983. 2 vols. $11.65 chac. collé [v.1 2-7601-0301-3; v.2 2-7601-0908-9].

Pièces qui peuvent être facilement montées par des enfants avec l'aide d'adultes. *Débutants, moyens.*

Noël, Michel; Boulard, Roselyne; et Ouellet, Joanne. La malédiction de Tchékapesh. VLB éditeur, 1986. 114 p. $9.95 collé [2-89005-228-1].

Grand-mère Outarde, Lièvre, Renard Usé, Souris Trotteuse et Castor à Queue tentent de délivrer le soleil qui a été emprisonné par Tchékapesh. *Moyens, grands.*

Renaud, Bernadette. Une boîte magique très embêtante. Leméac, 1981. 125 p. $7.95 collé [2-7609-9909-2]. (Théâtre pour enfants)

Après avoir écrit au Père Noël, Mari-Jo reçoit une boîte magique qui lui permet de réaliser tous ses désirs. *Moyens.*

Sabourin, Marcel. Pleurer pour rire. VLB éditeur, 1984. 115 p. $9.95 collé [2-89005-195-1].

Faut-il pleurer? Faut-il en rire? Cette pièce apporte une réponse originale à ce dilemme en préconisant de laisser libre cours à ses sentiments. *Moyens, aînés.*

Saint-Pierre, Christiane. 12 saynètes de Noël. Louis Riel, 1986. 40 p. $12.00 broché [0-920859-08-9].

Saynètes faciles à interpréter pour les jeunes de la première à la sixième année. *Débutants, moyens.*

ROMANS

Ainsley, Luc. Kadel. Fides, 1986. 155 p. $10.00 collé [2-7621-1318-0].
Un jeune historien doit affronter les maîtres impitoyables de la forêt interdite de Cournaden en vue de découvrir un site historique. *Grands, aînés.*

Allen, Robert Thomas. Le violon. Photographies de George Pastic. Tr. par Claire Martin. Pierre Tisseyre, Cercle du livre de France, 1976. 79 p. $9.95 collé [0-7753-0092-6].
Née du film *Le violon*, c'est une histoire d'amour entre un enfant, un vieillard et un violon. *Débutants.*

Andersen, Doris. Esclave des Haïdas. Tr. par Laurent Brault. Flammarion, 1983. 319 p. $4.95 collé [2-08-161780-3]. (Castor-poche)
Au cours d'un raid mené par des membres de la tribu des Haïdas, le fils du chef de la tribu des Salish se fait enlever. Traduction de *Slave of the Haida. Grands, aînés.*

Anfousse, Ginette. Les catastrophes de Rosalie. Ill. par Marisol Sarrazin. La Courte échelle, 1987. 95 p. $5.95 collé [2-89021-065-0]. (Roman-jeunesse)
Rosalie a exactement neuf ans, sept mois, trois jours ... et sept mères. Adoptée par ses tantes, elle grandit avec ses amis et ses idées bien à elle. *Moyens, grands.*

Anfousse, Ginette. Fabien 1: Un loup pour Rose. Ill. par Ginette Anfousse. Leméac, 1982. 40 p. $8.95 broché [2-7609-9844-4].
Fabien promet de partir à la recherche d'un loup qui conviendra à Rose, un raton laveur albinos, pour finalement découvrir que Rose est un être unique. *Moyens.*

Anfousse, Ginette. Fabien 2: Une nuit au pays des malices. Ill. par Ginette Anfousse. Leméac, 1982. 40 p. $8.95 broché [2-7609-9845-2].
Avec son miroir, Fabien envoie un message à la planète Vénus et reçoit la visite de quatre de ses habitants. *Moyens.*

Aubert de Gaspé, Phillipe. Les anciens canadiens. Fides, 1970. 360 p. $5.95 collé [2-7021-0201-4].
Deux amis, l'un écossais, l'autre français, deviennent ennemis par la guerre de la conquête [1760]. *Grands, aînés.*

Aubry, Claude. Agouhanna. Ill. par Marc Senécal. Fides, 1981. 110 p. $4.95 collé [2-7621-1099-8]. (Quatre vents)
A six ans, Agouhanna le petit Iroquois doit subir sa première épreuve, mais il ne manifeste aucune joie à recevoir ses premières flèches bien rangées dans un petit carquois de cuir. *Moyens.*

Benoît, Jean. Le tournoi. Paulines, 1976. 157 p. $5.95 relié [0-88840-576-6]. (Jeunesse-pop)
Voici la suite de *Une ... Deux ... Trois prises. T'es mort.* Les deux romans peuvent être lus séparément avec intérêt. Roman sportif très vivant. *Moyens.*

Benoît, Jean. Une ... Deux ... Trois prises. T'es mort. Paulines, 1976. 149 p. $5.95 relié. [0-88840-575-8]. (Jeunesse-pop)
Une équipe de baseball, le Pee-Wee du Saint-Mathias, grâce à un nouvel instructeur dynamique et compétent, réussit à se classer pour le tournoi du parc Lafontaine. *Moyens.*

Bilson, Geoffrey. Adieu, Sarah! Traduit par Françoise Marois. Kids Can, 1981. 64 p. $3.95 collé [0-919964-48-6].

Deux jeunes filles tentent de préserver leur amitié durant la grève de Winnipeg en 1919. Traduction de *Goodbye Sarah*. *Débutants, moyens.*

Bilson, Geoffrey. Mort sur Montréal. Tr. par Danielle Thaler. Kids Can, 1982. 119 p. $3.95 collé [0-919964-50-8].
En 1830, une famille écossaise immigre au Canada pour échapper à l'épidémie de choléra. Aventures et désappointements viendront bouleverser leurs vies. Traduction de *Death over Montreal*. *Débutants, moyens.*

Boucher, Claudette. Jamais plus les chevaux. Fides, 1981. 236 p. $8.95 collé [2-7621-1102-1]. (Intermondes)
L'arrivée du vieux cheval Jolicoeur soulève des réactions différentes chez Françoise et Caroline Gingras. *Aînés.*

Brouillet, Chrystine. Le complot. La Courte échelle, 1985. $5.95 collé [2-89021-052-9]. (Roman-jeunesse)
Avec l'aide de Sophie Tremblay, Jean-François organise un complot pour forcer son beau-père à abandonner son projet de construction d'une usine qui mettrait en danger l'environnement. *Moyens, grands.*

Cailloux, André. Les aventures de Frizelis. Ill. par Francine Nault. Héritage, 1980. 127 p. $5.95 collé [0-7773-4418-1]. (Pour lire avec toi)
Une série de contes amusants mettant en vedette Frizelis, le petit lutin tout habillé de vert et portant un chapeau à trois cornes avec grelots. *Débutants, moyens.*

Callaghan, Morley. La promesse de Luke Baldwin. Tr. par Michelle Tisseyre. Pierre Tisseyre, 1980. 207 p. 7.95 collé [2-89051-031-X]. (Deux solitudes, jeunesse)
Orphelin, le jeune Luke est adopté par son oncle, un homme pratique. Le garçon y fait l'apprentissage de la vraie vie. Traduction de *Luke Baldwin's vow*. *Grands.*

Cantin, Roger et Patenaude, Danyèle. La guerre des tuques. Québec/Amérique, 1984. 168 p. $4.95 collé [2-89037-220-0]. (Jeunesse-Romans)
Durant les vacances de Noël, une guerre de boules de neige est organisée entre deux armées d'enfants. Lorsque l'adversité grandit entre les deux groupes, la mort d'un chien va ramener la paix. *Moyens.*

Carbet, Marie-Madeleine. Contes de Tantana. Ill. par Jacques Léveillé. Leméac, 1980. 187 p. $9.95 collé [2-7609-9833-9].
Dans une langue imagée, l'auteur raconte les expériences d'enfants antillais et québécois.

Carrier, Roch. Les enfants du bonhomme dans la lune. Stanké, 1983. $5.95 collé [2-7604-0210-X]. (Québec 10/10)
Contes touchants et amusants. *Aînés.*

Carrier, Roch. La fleur et autres personnages. Paulines, 1985. 98 p. $4.95 collé [2-89039-042-X]. (Lectures-VIP)
Nouvelles qui transposent dans un cadre actuel des souvenirs de l'auteur. *Aînés.*

Carrier, Roch. Ne faites pas mal à l'avenir. Paulines, 1984. 109 p. $4.95 collé [2-89039-960-5]. (Lectures-VIP)
Nouvelles qui font réfléchir à la vie et aux relations humaines. Texte tiré de la revue Vidéo-Presse. *Aînés.*

Carrier, Roch. Les voyageurs de l'arc-en-ciel. Ill. par François Olivier. Stanké, 1980. 40 p. $9.95 collé [2-7604-0096-4].
Un garçon et une fille partent à la conquête de l'or déposé par Dieu au bout de l'arc-en-ciel. *Moyens.*

Chabot, Cécile. Et le cheval vert. Fides, 1980. 144 p. $8.50 collé [2-7621-1008-4]. (Goéland)
Trois petites filles vivent à la campagne à l'ombre d'un merveilleux et tendre quotidien. Elles grandissent et c'est la fin des rires et des jeux. Contes qui permettront de cavaler sur les plages de l'enfance. *Grands.*

Champagne, Carole. Tobi et le gardien du lac. Ill. par Daniel Sylvestre. Héritage, 1984. 127 p. $5.95 collé [2-7625-4448-3]. (Pour lire avec toi)
Malgré l'interdiction de son grand-père, Tobi s'approche du lac et est entraîné dans une aventure où il rencontrera les créatures qui habitent les eaux du lac et où il réussira à vaincre un monstre marin. *Débutants.*

Chetin, Helen. La dame épouvantail. Ill. par Nicole Lévesque. Tr. par Louis-Bertrand Raymond. Fides, 1981. 126 p. $4.95 collé [2-7621-1100-5]. (Quatre Vents)
Après le divorce de ses parents, Jessica, seule à la ferme, parle à la dame épouvantail du champ de framboises. Traduction de *The Lady of the strawberries*. *Grands.*

Choquette, Adrienne. Je m'appelle Pax: Histoire d'un chien heureux qui médite sur son bonheur. Presses Laurentiennes, 1974. 56 p. $4.00 collé [2-89015-008-9].
Histoire d'un chien boxer choyé de tous et très heureux de son sort. Abondamment illustrée de photographies. *Moyens.*

Clark, Joan. La main de Robin Squires: Le mystère de l'île aux Chênes. Tr. par Claude Aubry. Pierre Tisseyre, 1984. 179 p. $9.95 collé [2-89051-158-8]. (Deux solitudes, jeunesse)

Désirant caché son trésor volé dans une voûte souterraine d'Oak Island, Edouard s'accommode les services du père de Robin qui développe un système ingénieux pour protéger le trésor contre ceux qui tenteraient de s'en accaparer. Lorsque ce dernier meurt, Robin qui s'y connaît en mécanique, doit accompagner son oncle lors de son deuxième voyage. Traduction de *The Hand of Robin Squires*. *Grands*.

Clermont, Marie-Andrée. Alerte au lac des loups. Ill. par André Bergeron. Fides, 1980. 138 p. $8.50 collé [2-7621-1000-9]. (Goéland)
Au coeur des Laurentides, une dizaine d'adolescents campent insouciants jusqu'à ce qu'ils flairent le mystère. *Grands, aînés*.

Clermont, Marie-Andrée. Les aventures de la canicule. Fides, 1982. 181 p. $6.95 collé [2-7621-1173-0]. (Mille-îles)
Quatre cinéastes amateurs tentent de retrouver Manubuis, un domaine enchanteur, et résolvent le mystère qui entoure les lieux depuis de nombreuses années. *Grands*.

Clermont, Marie-Andrée et Morgan, Frances. Jour blanc. Pierre Tisseyre, 1986. 183 p. $10.95 collé [2-89051-316-5]. (Conquêtes)
Quatre étudiants se retrouvent sur une île de glace dans l'océan Arctique et aident l'équipe scientifique à retrouver l'ABIPAN-3, l'arme la plus destructive construite dans l'histoire de l'humanité. *Grands, aînés*.

Corriveau, Monique. Les compagnons du soleil. Fides, 1976. 3 vols. $9.95 chacun, collé [0-7755-0592-7] [0-7755-0593-5] [0-7755-0594-3]; $24.95 pour les 3 vol. [2-7621-0985-X].
Une trilogie passionnante de science-fiction où deux mondes s'affrontent. *Grands, aînés*.

Corriveau, Monique. Le garçon au cerf-volant. Ill. par Louise Méthé. Fides, 1974. 137 p. $6.95 collé [2-7621-0515-3]. (Goéland)
Un livre de qualité rempli d'aventures, plein de beauté et de poésie. Le roman de l'amitié entre un père et son fils. *Moyens*.

Corriveau, Monique. Max. Fides, 1985. 140 p. $4.95 collé [2-7621-1262-3].
Max Ricard est accusé de vol avec tentative de meurtre. Le jeune chercheur en physique nucléaire tente de retrouver le vrai coupable. Dans la même série: *Max au rallye, Max contre Macbeth, Max en planeur*. *Aînés*.

Corriveau, Monique. Patrick et Sophie en fusée. Héritage, 1979. 265 p. $5.95 collé [0-7773-3005-4]. (Katimavik)
Durant leurs vacances, les jumeaux Vincent et Sophie montent à bord d'une fusée et voyagent à travers le temps. Sophie en profite pour écrire un livre racontant l'extraordinaire aventure qu'ils vivent dans une tribu Micmac. *Moyens*.

Corriveau, Monique. La petite fille du printemps. Ill. par Louise Pomminville. Fides, 1978, 1984. 122 p. $7.95 collé [2-7621-1218-4]. (Mille-îles)
Cette histoire d'orpheline malheureuse sera populaire auprès de nombreux lecteurs. *Moyens*.

Corriveau, Monique. Les saisons de la mer. Ill. par Louise Méthé. Fides, 1975, 1985. 154 p. $7.95 collé [2-7621-1233-8]. (Mille-îles)
Histoire de Marie-Lou et de son frère David vivant dans le décor d'une petite île au large de Terre-Neuve. *Grands*.

Corriveau, Monique. Le secret de Vanille. Ill. par Colette Crespo. Fides, 1962, 1985. 117 p. $8.50 collé [2-7621-1094-7]. (Mille-îles)
Un captivant roman mystère. Une histoire riche de couleurs locales et de vie enfantine. *Moyens*.

Corriveau, Monique. Le Wapiti. Ill. par Mélinda Wilson. Fides, 1978. 177 p. $8.50 collé [2-7621-0685-0]. (Goéland)
Après avoir été accusé injustement de meurtre, un jeune garçon se sauve de Québec et est capturé par des Iroquois. *Grands, aînés*.

Côté, Denis. Les géants de Blizzard. Ill. par Serge Chapleau. La Courte échelle, 1985. 90 p. $5.95 collé [2-89021-053-7]. (Roman-jeunesse)
Des jeux galactiques mettent en péril la planète. Braal, Chrysalide et Elée s'envolent vers Blizzard avertir le monde du danger qui les guette. *Grands*.

Côté, Denis. Hockeyeurs cybernétiques. Paulines, 1983. 115 p. $5.95 collé [2-89039-908-7]. (Jeunesse-pop)
Un roman de science-fiction dans lequel une série de trois rencontres est organisée entre les meilleurs hockeyeurs du monde et une équipe de robots programmés pour jouer au hockey. *Grands*.

Côté, Denis. La pénombre jaune. Paulines, 1986. 125 p. $5.95 collé [2-89039-068-3]. (Jeunesse-pop)
En rencontrant Bob Moraine, un homme inquiet, Francine et René sont entraînés dans une aventure insolite où ils doivent affronter Monsieur Ling, un adversaire cruel et sans scrupule. *Aînés*.

Côté, Denis; Pelletier, Francine; Sernine, Daniel; et Warnant-Côté, Marie-Andrée. Planéria: Anthologie de science-fiction. Pierre Tisseyre, 1985. 191 p. $9.95 collé [22-89051-297-5]. (Conquêtes)
Un recueil contenant quatre nouvelles de science-fiction. *Grands, aînés*.

Coulombe-Côté, Pauline. Contes de ma ville. Ill. par Fernande Lefebvre. Héritage, 1981. 124 p. $5.95 collé [0-7773-4423-8]. (Pour lire avec toi)

Des contes qui se passent dans une grande cité où habitent des enfants et des animaux qui y ont des aventures parfois tristes, parfois amusantes. *Moyens.*

Cutler, Ebbitt. La vieille sauvage. Ill. par Bruce Johnson. Tr. par Maryse Côté. Fides, 1980. 74 p. $2.75 collé [2-7621-1026-2]. (Intermondes) Souvenirs d'enfance qui tracent le portrait de madame Dey, une Iroquoise rencontrée au cours de vacances dans les Laurentides. Traduction de *The Last noble savage. Aînés.*

Cyr, Céline. Les prisonniers de Monsieur Alphonse. Ill. par Caroline Mérola. Québec/Amérique, 1986. 116 p. $4.95 collé [2-89037-316-9]. (Jeunesse-Romans) Au cours d'une excursion, cinq enfants du Lac-Beauport surpris par un orage trouvent refuge dans une vieille grange habitée par un étrange personnage. *Moyens.*

Daveluy, Paule. Et la vie par devant. Paulines, 1984. 107 p. $4.95 collé [2-89039-953-2]. (Lectures-VIP)
Texte tiré de la revue Vidéo-Presse. *Aînés.*

Daveluy, Paule. La maison des vacances: Une année du tonnerre 1. Ill. par Lise Thérien. Fides, 1981. 137 p. $8.50 collé [0-7621-0662-1] (Goéland).
Un condensé retravaillé de *L'été enchanté* et *Drôle d'automne,* mis au présent par l'auteur. *Grands, aînés.*

Daveluy, Paule. Pas encore seize ans.... Paulines, 1982. 125 p. $4.95 collé [2-89039-072-2]. (Lectures-VIP)
Texte tiré de la revue Vidéo-Presse. *Aînés.*

Daveluy, Paule. Rosanne et la vie: Une année du tonnerre 2. Ill. par Lise Thérien. Fides, 1981. 137 p. $8.50 collé [2-7621-0663-X] (Goéland).
Après maintes péripéties, Rosanne Fontaine épouse David Saint-Germain, son patron au poste de radio où elle travaille. Un condensé revu et remanié par l'auteur de *Cet hiver-là* et *Cher printemps. Grands, aînés.*

Décary, Marie. Amour, réglisse et chocolat. La Courte échelle, 1985. 94 p. $5.95 collé [2-89021-051-0].
Rose Néon adore le chocolat. Sa phobie est l'amour. Son père en lui proposant le mariage l'invite à une aventure abracadabrante d'amitié et d'amour. *Grands.*

Deschênes, Josseline. L'autobus à Margo. Ill. par Suzanne Duranceau. Héritage, 1981. 126 p. $5.95 collé [0-7773-4425-4]. (Pour lire avec toi)

Un vieil autobus scolaire à la retraite reprend vie et devient magique. *Moyens.*

Deschênes, Josseline. Le cheval de plume. Ill. par Claire Langlois. Héritage, 1983. 120 p. $5.95 collé [0-7773-4434-3]. (Pour lire avec toi)
Martin et Zoé lors d'une randonnée dans les bois, découvre le cheval blanc que les gens du village croient dangereux. *Moyens.*

Desjardins, Denis. Des bleus et des bosses. Québec/Amérique, 1983. 174 p. $4.95 collé [2-89037-185-9]. (Jeunesse)
En tentant de récupérer l'invention du professeur Aiguille volée par l'espion V. Polydore, les jeunes Albin, Berri, Myrian et le chien Popsikeul récoltent plus que leur part de bleus et de bosses. *Grands.*

Deslongchamps, Roxanne. Les Ozerov – v.1 L'héritier. Ill. par Paule Girard. Fides, 1978. 273 p. $3.50 collé [2-7621-0686-9].
Karel Tchernytchev découvre qu'il est petit-fils du roi Alexandre IX et, par conséquent, héritier du trône. *Grands, aînés.*

Desrosiers, Sylvie. La patte dans le sac. Idée de Pierre Huet. Ill par Daniel Sylvestre. La Courte échelle, 1987. 93 p. $5.95 collé [2-89021-063-4]. (Roman-jeunesse)
Un gros chien laid et son propriétaire sont arrêtés par un douanier pour possession de drogue. Tout le monde du village se trouve mêlé à l'affaire. *Moyens, grands.*

Doyle, Brian. En montant à Low. Tr. par Claude Aubry en collaboration avec Danielle Aubry. Pierre Tisseyre, 1986. 98 p. $9.95 collé [2-89051-303-3]. (Deux solitudes, jeunesse)
Durant ses vacances à Low, Tommy se lie d'amitié avec Bridget dont le père se meurt d'un cancer. Traduction de *Up to Low. Grands, aînés.*

Doyle, Brian. Je t'attends à Peggy's Cove. Tr. par Claude Aubry. Pierre Tisseyre, 1982. 119 p. $9.95 collé [2-89051-067-0]. (Deux solitudes, jeunesse)
Envoyé passer l'été avec sa tante à Peggy's Cove après le départ inexpliqué de son père, Ryan essaie de trouver un moyen de ramener ce dernier. Traduction de *You can pick me up at Peggy's Cove. Grands, aînés.*

Dufour, Josée. Le testament de Madame Legendre. Fides, 1987. 112 p. $4.50 collé. (Les enquêtes de Gloria)
Après la mort inattendue d'une vieille voisine, une lettre troublante met Gloria sur la piste d'une mystérieuse affaire. *Grands.*

Dufour, Josée. Vol à retardement. Fides, 1987. 112 p. $4.50 collé [2-7621-1304-0]. (Les enquêtes de Gloria)

A douze ans, Gloria enquête une fraude informatique. *Grands.*

Duncan, Frances. Amanda et le génie. Ill. par Michèle Devlin. Tr. par Marie-Andrée Clermont. Heritage, 1984. 125 p. $5.95 collé [0-7773-4433-5]. (Pigeon vole)

L'apprenti génie qui sort du tube de dentifrice à chaque fois qu' Amanda le presse, ne peut exécuter qu'un seul voeu par jour. Traduction de *The Toothpaste genie. Moyens, grands.*

Freeman, Bill. Le dernier voyage du Scotian. Tr. par Maryse Côté. Pierre Tisseyre, 1982. 210 p. $8.95 collé [2-89051-06406]. (Deux solitudes, jeunesse)

Cette suite au roman *Les hommes du chantier* fait ressortir les difficultés que devaient subir les hommes qui affrontaient la mer vers 1873. *Grands, aînés.*

Freeman, Bill. Les hommes du chantier. Ill. de photos. Tr. par Sylvie de Lorimier avec la collaboration de Robert Guy Scully. Héritage, 1980. 190 p. $7.95 collé [0-7773-3862-9].

Récit des aventures de deux jeunes travailleurs dans un camp de bûcherons de la vallée de l'Outaouais vers les années 1870. Traduction de *Shantymen of Cache Lake. Grands, aînés.*

Freeman, Bill. Premier printemps sur le grand Banc de Terre-Neuve. Tr. par Maryse Côté. Pierre Tisseyre, 1983. 224 p. $9.95 collé [2-89051-095-6]. (Deux solitudes, jeunesse)

Accompagné de sa femme et de John et Meg Bains, Canso s'empare du Newfoundlander que le marchand Hunter veut s'accaparer et s'enfuit à Tower Rock où un vieil ami de son père accepte de les aider. Traduction de *First spring on the Grand Banks. Grands, aînés.*

Gagnon, Cécile. Alfred dans le métro. Ill. par Cécile Gagnon. Héritage, 1980. 122 p. $5.95 collé [0-7773-4419-X]. (Pour lire avec toi)

Les aventures de trois enfants à la poursuite d'un lapin blanc dans le métro de la ville de Montréal. *Débutants.*

Gagnon, Cécile. L'ascenseur d'Adrien. Ill. par Philippe Germain. Héritage, 1986. 54 p. $4.95 collé [2-7625-4010-0]. (Libellule)

Avec l'aide d'Ange-Aimée et Gilbert, deux employés sans emploi depuis l'automatisation du vieil hôtel trouve un moyen de recycler l'ascenseur. *Débutants.*

Gagnon, Cécile. L'épouvantail et le champignon. Ill. par Cécile Gagnon. Héritage, 1978. 126 p. $5.95 collé [0-7733-4411-4]. (Pour lire avec toi)

Un recueil de contes dans lequel les enfants retrouveront les mêmes personnages que dans le livre *Plumeneige. Débutants, moyens.*

Gagnon, Cécile. La maison Miousse ou les bienfaits d'une tempête. Amitié, 1983. 53 p. $5.95 [2-700-202430]. (Ma première amitié)

Les familles d'Omer et d'Onil Miousse habitent la même maison et se chamaillent du matin au soir. *Débutants, moyens.*

Gagnon, Cécile. Opération marmotte. Ill. par Cécile Gagnon. Héritage, 1984. 125 p. $5.95 collé [2-7625-4447-5]. (Pour lire avec toi)

Quatre jeunes explorent une station en construction du métro de Montréal et y découvrent un médaillon qui va permettre aux archéologues d'identifier avec certitude des objects trouvés dans le tunnel souterrain. *Débutants, moyens.*

Gagnon, Cécile. Plumeneige. Ill. par Cécile Gagnon. Héritage, 1976. 126 p. $5.95 collé [0-7733-4405-X]. (Pour lire avec toi)

Une série de charmantes histoires se déroulant au village de Plumetis ayant pour thèmes principaux l'hiver et la neige. *Débutants, moyens.*

Gagnon, Gilles. Un fantôme à bicyclette. Héritage, 1986. 58 p. $6.00 collé [2-7625-4010-0]. (Libellule)

Jasmine possède une bicyclette qui semble entraîner les enfants dans une curieuse aventure de fantômes. *Débutants, moyens.*

Gagnon, Madeleine. Les samedis fantastiques. Paulines, 1986. 115 p. $4.95 collé [2-89039-102-7]. (Lectures-VIP)

Tous les samedis, Hélène et les amis de la bande vivent des aventures extraordinaires. *Grands.*

Gagnon, Maurice. Simon. Héritage, 1975, 1979. 222 p. $5.95 collé [0-7773-3006-7]. (Katimavik)

Le portrait intime d'un hockeyeur qui joue dans une équipe professionnelle. *Moyens.*

Gaudreault-Labrecque, Madeleine. Gueule-de-loup. HMH Jeunesse, 1985. 164 p. $7.95 collé [2-89045-642-0]. (Les aventures de Michel Labre)

Michel Labre et son compagnon sont soupçonnés et emprisonnés pour un crime qui a eu lieu dans les caves du séminaire de Québec. Leur amie, Geneviève Marion, se charge de l'enquête et prouve leur innocence. *Grands.*

Gauthier, Bertrand. Ani Croche. Ill. par Gérard Frischeteau. La Courte échelle, 1985. 86 p. $5.95 collé [2-89021-054]. (Roman-jeunesse)

D'une façon humoristique, Ani Croche raconte les péripéties de sa vie quotidienne. *Grands.*

Gauthier, Bertrand. Le journal intime d'Ani Croche. Ill. par Gérard Frischeteau. La Courte échelle, 1987. 94 p. $5.95 collé [2-89021-062-6]. (Roman-jeunesse)

Ani Croche dédie son journal intime à sa poupée Olivia et y confie les événements de sa vie quotidienne à l'école et avec son père et sa mère et leurs amis respectifs. *Grands.*

German, Tony. Tom Penny. Tr. par Claude Aubry. Fides, 1981. 253 p. $5.95 collé [2-7621-1038-6]. (Mille-îles)
Un adolescent et sa mère quittent l'Angleterre pour s'installer dans une contrée sauvage et lointaine, le Canada. Traduction de *Tom Penny. Aînés.*

German, Tony. Tom Penny et les géants de l'Outaouais. Tr. par Claude Aubry. Fides, 1982. 209 p. $5.95 collé [2-7621-1161-7]. (Mille-îles)
Au début des années 1830, Tom et son oncle Matthew se joignent à une équipe de bûcherons et de draveurs dans les chantiers de la Gatineau. Traduction de *River race. Aînés.*

Grandbois-Paquin, Gabrielle. La petite fille aux yeux rouges. Ill. par André Bergeron. Fides, 1978. 169 p. $8.50 collé [0-7755-0672-9]. (Goéland)
La petite Bernadette Rousseau a perdu sa mère et ce drame influencera toute sa jeunesse. Cette histoire de la mère d'Alain Grandbois nous plonge dans l'atmosphère du début du siècle. *Grands, aînés.*

Grosbois, Paul de. Les initiés de la Pointe-aux-cageux. Hurtubise HMH, 1986. 120 p. $6.95 collé [2-89045-796-6].
Six adolescents réussissent à retrouver une somme d'argent volée il y a plusieurs années et aident Jos Montferrand à capturer des voleurs de bois. *Moyens, grands.*

Grosbois, Paul de. Métro caverne. Paulines, 1986. 79 p. $5.95 collé [2-89039-103-5]. (Jeunesse-pop)
Au retour d'une journée à l'île Sainte-Hélène, Benoît et Gabrielle vivent une inquiétante aventure dans le métro. *Grands.*

Guèvremont, Germaine. En pleine terre. Ill. par André Bergeron. Fides, 1976. 140 p. $8.50 collé [0-7621-0598-6]. (Goéland)
Réédition du premier ouvrage de l'auteur paru en 1942. Un recueil de quatorze tableaux paysans et de quatre contes de la région soreloise transmettant l'héritage des ancêtres et leur parlure savoureuse. *Aînés.*

Guèvremont, Germaine. Le Survenant. Fides, 1982. 224 p. $4.50 collé [2-7621-0821-7]. (Bibliothèque québécoise)
Le drame de l'extinction de la dynastie paysanne des Beauchemin. *Aînés.*

Halvorson, Marilyn. En toute liberté. Tr. par Marie-Andrée Clermont. Fides, 1986. 288 p. $9.95 collé [2-7621-1345-8]. (Mille-îles)

L'arrivée inattendue de la mère de Lance qui a délaissé son fils dix ans auparavant, ébranle ce dernier et met en péril son avenir. Traduction de *Let it go. Grands, aînés.*

Hémon, Louis. Maria Chapdelaine. Fides, 1970. 216 p. $3.95 collé [2-7621-0824-1]. (Bibliothèque québécoise)
Un tableau de la vie des colons du Lac Saint-Jean. *Aînés.*

Hewitt, Marsha et Mackay, Claire. Un été inoubliable. Tr. par Francine Pominville. Remue-ménage, 1983. 186 p. $9.95 collé [2-89091-046-6].
Les événements de la grève à la Montréal Cottons sont relatés par Lucie Laplante qui, à 13 ans, a du quitter l'école pour travailler à l'usine. Traduction de *One proud summer. Grands, aînés.*

Houston, James. Akavak. Tr. par Anne-Marie Chapouton. Flammarion, 1980. 152 p. $3.50 collé [2-08-161701-3]. (Castor poche)
Pour son premier grand voyage à travers les glaces, un jeune esquimau affronte avec son grand-père des dangers de plus en plus terribles. Traduction de *Akavak. Moyens, grands.*

Houston, James. L'archer blanc. Tr. par Maryse Côté. Héritage, 1978. 93 p. $5.95 collé [0-7773-4103-4].
Cette légende nous parle de vengeance, nous introduit aux traditions des esquimaux et nous transmet subtilement bien des valeurs humaines. Traduction de *The White archer. Grands.*

Houston, James. Les casse-cou de la rivière Koksoak. Tr. par Claude Aubry. Fides, 1984. 167 p. $9.95 collé [2-7621-1234-6]. (Mille-îles)
Une solide amitié se développe entre Andrew Stewart, un jeune écossais, et Pashah, un jeune Naskapi, durant le voyage périlleux qu'ils doivent entreprendre pour établir un poste de traite de fourrure à Ghost Lake. Traduction de *River Runners. Grands, aînés.*

Houston, James. Matt et Kayak: Une aventure du Grand Nord. Tr. par Léo Lack et Robert Fouques Duparc. Stock, 1980. 189 p. $16.00 collé [2-234-00924-3]. (Mon bel oranger)
Accompagné de son ami esquimau Kaya, Matt, sans prévenir personne, part à la recherche de son père porté disparu à la suite d'une tempête. Traduction de *Frozen Fire: a tale of courage. Grands, aînés.*

Houston, James. Le passage des loups. Tr. par Anne-Marie Chapouton. Flammarion, 1980. 128 p. $3.50 collé [2-08-161716-1]. (Castor-Poche)
Punik, un jeune esquimau, part à la recherche des caribous pour sauver sa famille qui se meurt lentement de faim. Traduction de *Wolf run: a Caribou Eskimo tale. Moyens, grands.*

Houston, James. Tikta'liktak. Ill. par James Houston. Tr. par Maryse Côté. Héritage, 1978. 104 p. $5.95 collé [0-7773-3015-6]; Flammarion, 1982. 104 p. $3.95 collé [2-08-161759-5].
Un jeune Inuit affamé, flottant à la dérive depuis trois jours, atteint enfin une île déserte. Traduction de *Tikta' liktak. Moyens.*

Hughes, Monica. Au-delà de la rivière noire. Tr. par J. La Gravière. Duculot, 1981. 174 p. $7.95 collé [2-8011-0355-1]. (Travelling sur le futur)
En l'an 2025, quarante-cinq ans après l'explosion de la bombe atomique, deux jeunes survivants tentent de trouver une solution à l'épidémie mystérieuse qui a frappé les enfants hutterites. Traduction de *Beyond the dark river. Grands, aînés.*

Hughes, Monica. Le cerveau de la ville. Tr. par André Romain. Lidec-Duculot, 1979. 192 p. $7.00 collé [2-8011-0238-5]. (Travelling sur le futur)
Caro, la fille de l'ingénieur qui a conçu C-3, découvre que l'ordinateur essaie de controler toute la population. Avec l'aide de son ami David, elle essaie de mettre fin aux initiatives de l'ordinateur. Traduction de *The e Tomorrow city. Grands, aînés.*

Hughes, Monica. Mike, chasseur des ténèbres. Tr. par Paule Daveluy. Pierre Tisseyre, 1985. 189 p. $9.95 collé [2-89051-229-1]. (Deux solitudes, jeunesse)
Le rêve de Mike Rankin de partir seul en forêt l'aide dans sa bataille quotidienne contre la maladie incurable qui l'afflige. Traduction de *Hunter in the Dark. Grands, aînés.*

Hughes, Monica. Visiteurs extra-terrestres. Tr. par Marie-Andrée Clermont. Héritage, 1984. 142 p. $5.95 collé [0-7773-3404-6].
Télépathes de naissance, Julie et Jacques confrontent des extra-terrestres lors d'un séjour d'exploration scientifique dans les Rocheuses. Traduction de *Beckoning lights. Moyens, grands.*

Korman, Gordon. Bruno et Boots mènent le bal. Tr. par Christiane Duchesne. Scholastic-TAB, 1982. 136 p. $4.95 collé [0-590-71182-2].
Bruno et Boots mènent le bal au pensionnat avec leurs farces amusant tout le monde, sauf la direction. Traduction de *This can't be happening at Macdonald Hall. Moyens, grands.*

Kropp, Paul. Le cave. Tr. par Jean Simard. Fides, 1981. 139 p. $4.95 collé [2-7621-1138-2]. (Mille-îles)
Danny vit son adolescence dans un foyer où le père et la mère ne s'entendent plus, où la petite soeur fume du 'pot', et où l'argent manque sans cesse. Traduction de *Wilted. Aînés.*

Lachance, Jeanne. Le voyage de Lapin Noir. Ill. par France Bédard. Héritage, 1977. 125 p. $5.95 collé [0-7773-4406-8]. (Pour lire avec toi)
Dans ce roman de science-fiction, Lapin Noir et ses amis visitent une planète bien étrange après un voyage à bord d'une sphère qu'ils ont trouvée en forêt. *Débutants, moyens.*

Lafrenière, Joseph. Par delà le mur. Fides, 1986. 121 p. $8.50 collé [2-7621-1315-6]. (Mille-îles)
Une histoire d'amour entre un jeune chômeur et une jeune handicappée. *Aînés.*

Legault, Mimi. Le robot concierge. Ill. par Stéphane Poulin. Héritage, 1984. 124 p. $5.95 collé [2-7625-4445-9]. (Pour lire avec toi)
Lorsque Léo, le concierge de l'école Montplaisir, démissionne parce qu'il en a assez des traîneries des enfants, il est remplacé par un robot concierge programmable. *Moyens.*

Little, Jean. Ecoute, l'oiseau chantera. Tr. par Paule Daveluy. Pierre Tisseyre, 1980. 194 p. $9.95 collé [2-89051-028-X]. (Deux solitudes, jeunesse)
Roman attachant qui raconte les problèmes d'une jeune handicappée visuelle et son adaptation au milieu scolaire secondaire. Traduction de *Listen for the singing. Grands.*

Little, Jean. Maman va t'acheter un moqueur. Tr. par Paule Daveluy. Pierre Tisseyre, 1986. 260 p. $10.95 collé [2-89051-309-2]. (Deux solitudes, jeunesse)
Jérémie Talbot accepte finalement la mort de son père lorsqu'il réalise que ce dernier lui a laissé un trésor impérissable. Traduction de *Mama's going to buy you a mockingbird. Moyens, grands.*

Loranger, Francine. Chansons pour un ordinateur. Ill. par Laurent Bouchard. Fides, 1980. 101 p. $8.50 collé [2-7621-1001-7]. (Goéland)
Un vaisseau spacial change de trajectoire. Perdus dans le cosmos, ses occupants tentent de reprendre leur route. *Grands.*

Loranger, Francine. Le renard rose. Ill. par France Bédard. Héritage, 1976. 121 p. $5.95 collé [0-7773-4404-1]. (Pour lire avec toi)
Monsieur La Belette est chargé de retrouver le Renard Rose qui a disparu très mystérieusement lors de la présentation de la pièce de théâtre qu'il avait lui-même composée pour fêter le Carnaval d'hiver. *Moyens.*

Loranger, Francine. Tourbillon, le lutin de la Côte-Nord. Ill. par Danielle Shelton. Héritage, 1977. 121 p. $5.95 collé [0-7773-4407-6]. (Pour lire avec toi)

L'auteur sait parler des réalités d'aujourd'hui sans quitter le terrain onirique propre au conte. *Débutants.*

Lotteridge, Celia et Ochrymovych, Ariadne. Le jongleur. Tr. par Danielle Thaler. Scholastic-TAB, 1985. 38 p. $7.95 broché [0-590-71526-7].

Presque aveugle, André, fils d'un riche négociant en fourrures se lie d'amitié avec le pauvre jongleur et réussit à convaincre ses parents qu'il a besoin d'un peu de liberté. Traduction de *The Juggler. Débutants, moyens.*

Mackay, Claire. La fille à la mini-moto. Tr. par Michelle Tisseyre. Pierre Tisseyre, 1984. 144 p. $9.95 collé [2-89051-157-X]. (Deux solitudes, jeunesse)

C'est un été mouvementé pour Julie qui doit passer ses vacances chez sa tante sans sa mini-moto. Traduction de *Mini-bike rescue. Aînés.*

Mackay, Claire. La mini-moto héroïque. Ill. par Merle Smith. Tr. par Raymond Morissette et Thierry Hautem-Morissette. Héritage, 1981. 124 p. $5.95 collé [0-7773-3017-2].

Marc vient de s'acheter une mini-moto malgré l'opposition de son père. Traduction de *Mini-bike hero. Aînés.*

Mackenzie, Nadine. Le petit dinosaure d'Alberta. Des Plaines, 1980. 47 p. $3.95 broché [0-920944-07-0].

Deux enfants découvrent un dinosaure tout juste sorti de sa coquille. Ils l'adoptent et le logent dans une grange jusqu'au jour où il devient trop grand. La famille décide finalement de lui rendre sa liberté. *Débutants.*

Mackenzie, Nadine. Le prix du silence. Fides, 1980. 139 p. $6.95 collé [2-7621-1062-9]. (Intermondes)

Roman à caractère politique. Un journaliste tente de dénoncer le régime communiste qui entrave la liberté des gens de son pays. Arrêté par les hommes du Troisième Bureau, il réussit à s'évader, mais il est poursuivi jusqu'en Amérique. *Aînés.*

Major, Henriette. Le club des curieux. Fides, 1967. 122 p. $4.95 collé [2-7621-0210-3]. (Quatre vents)

Les aventures d'une bande de jeunes curieux qui arrive à percer le mystère de la disparition de l'oncle Horace. *Moyens.*

Major, Henriette. Les contes de l'arc-en-ciel. Ill. par Danielle Shelton. Héritage, 1976. 124 p. $5.95 collé [0-7773-4401-7]. (Pour lire avec toi)

Dix contes très courts pour ceux qui aiment le rêve et la fantaisie. *Débutants, moyens.*

Major, Henriette. Elise et l'oncle riche. Ill. par Michèle Devlin. Fides, 1979. 110 p. $8.50 collé [2-7621-0731-8]. (Goéland)

Une jeune adolescente rêve d'un oncle riche et d'une vie meilleure. *Grands.*

Major, Henriette. Sophie, l'apprentie sorcière. Ill. par Garnotte. Héritage, 1986. 125 p. $5.95 collé [2-7625-4453-X]. (Pour lire avec toi)

Dans son langage bien à elle, Sophie nous livre sa pensée sur sa famille et sur le monde. *Moyens.*

Major, Henriette. La ville fabuleuse. Héritage, 1982. $5.95 collé [0-7773-4429-7]. (Pour lire avec toi)

Passer des vacances ennuyeuses sur un balcon, quelle perspective. Mieux vaut les vivre à explorer une caverne et y découvrir une ville secrète! *Moyens, grands.*

Major, Kevin. Tiens bon! Tr. par Michelle Robinson. Pierre Tisseyre, 1984. 210 p. $9.95 collé [2-89051-108-1]. (Deux solitudes, jeunesse)

L'histoire de Michel qui, devenu orphelin, est envoyé vivre chez un oncle qu'il n'aime pas. Il se révolte et, accompagné de son cousin, il s'enfuit pour revenir à son village natal. Traduction de *Hold fast. Grands.*

Martel, Suzanne. Jeanne, fille du roy. Ill. par Michelle Poirier. Fides, 1974. 254 p. $7.95 collé [2-7621-1172-2]. (Mille-îles)

L'histoire de Jeanne, courageuse 'fille du roi,' qui débarque en Nouvelle-France, un pays où la vie est dure et isolée, où les Iroquois menacent et où l'hiver est rigoureux. *Grands.*

Martel, Suzanne. Les Montcorbier. v.1. -L'apprentissage d'Arahé. Fides, 1979. 368 p. $13.95 collé [2-7621-0781-4] v.2 - *Premières armes – 1918*. Fides, 1979. 432 p. $13.95 collé [2-7621-0782-2].

Ces deux récits dramatiques coupés d'incidents humoristiques et tragiques racontent les aventures d'Arnaud de Montcorbier, garçon attachant et casse-cou, et à la fois musicien et bagarreur. Sur un fond historique, celui de la guerre de 1914-1918, l'action se dessine dans une atmosphère mi-orientale, mi-européenne. *Aînés.*

Martel, Suzanne. Nos amis robots. Héritage, 1981. 241 p. $5.95 collé [0-7773-3402-X]. (Galaxie)

Les robots que Adam Colbert et Eve Kevin ont reçus de leurs parents astronautes sont des postes émetteurs qui permettront aux vaisseaux amandariens d'aider à repousser l'attaque des extra-terrestres 'Worlaks' et de sauver ainsi la planète Terre. *Moyens, grands.*

Martel, Suzanne. Un orchestre dans l'espace. Ill. par Georgeta Pusztai. Méridien, 1985. 284 p. $13.95 collé [2-920417-01-0].

Les exploits des Cinq Coeurs et 1/4, un groupe de jeunes musiciens de la Terre invité à donner des concerts sur Vania, redonneront l'eau et la liberté au peuple vanien. *Moyens, grands.*

Martel, Suzanne. Pi-oui. Héritage, 1974, 1979. 186 p. $5.95 collé [0-7773-3004-0]. (Katimavik) L'histoire de la vie quotidienne de Pi-oui, un jeune joueur de hockey. *Moyens.*

Martel, Suzanne. Surréal 3000. Héritage, 1981. 159 p. $5.95 collé [0-7773-340300]. (Galaxie) Mille ans après la destruction atomique, des enfants de Surréal, cité souterraine, se glissent en secret par une fissure pour monter à l'Air Libre et découvrent un monde qu'ils croyaient inhabité. *Moyens, grands.*

Martel, Suzanne. Titralak, cadet de l'espace. Héritage, 1974, 1979. 282 p. $5.95 collé [0-7773-3401-7]. (Galaxie) Un roman de science-fiction très animant dans lequel les héros voyagent à travers le temps et l'espace. *Moyens, grands.*

Massé, Johanne. De l'autre côté de l'avenir. Paulines, 1985. 102 p. $5.95 collé [2-89039-039-X]. Envoyés en mission sur orbite, trois astronautes survivent à la guerre nucléaire qui ravage la planète. Les radiations ont rendu la terre inhabitable et ses habitants ont tellement changé. *Aînés.*

Mativat, Daniel. Ram, le robot. Ill. par Michèle Perrault. Héritage, 1984. 117 p. $5.95 collé [2-7625-4442-4]. (Pour lire avec toi) Ram, un robot fabriqué par Electro, son père, est métamorphosé en un petit garçon après une succession de malheurs et de péripéties. Ce conte reprend les thèmes de *Pinocchio* par Collodi. *Débutants, moyens.*

Mativat, Marie-Andrée et Mativat, Daniel. Dos bleu, le phoque champion. Ill. par Evelyne Arcouette. Héritage, 1986. 125 p. $5.95 collé [2-7625-4452-1]. (Pour lire avec toi) Conte inspiré par l'épopée du véritable Dos Bleu, ce phoque à capuchon qui échoua le 18 août 1983 sur l'île Sainte-Hélène. *Moyens.*

Mélançon, André. Comme les six doigts de la main. Adaptée par Henriette Major. Ill. de photos. Héritage, 1986. 125 p. $5.95 collé. [2-7625-4454-8]. (Pour lire avec toi) Avec *Comme les six doigts de la main*, on entre dans l'univers des 'bandes' d'amis. Adaptation littéraire du film d'André Mélançon. *Moyens.*

Mitchell, W.O. Qui a vu le vent? Cercle du Livre de France, 1974. 294 p. $11.95 collé [0-7753-0038-1].

Une enfance en Saskatchewan au cours des années 1920-1930. Traduction de *Who has seen the wind*. *Aînés.*

Miville-Deschenes, Jean. La mafia du pensionnat. Fides, 1964. 106 p. $4.95 collé [2-7621-0144-1]. (Quatre vents) Dans un carnet, Jacques relate les activités et les ruses employées par la mafia en vue de combattre les injustices infligées aux pensionnaires. *Moyens.*

Montgomery, Lucy Maud. Anne, la maison aux pignons verts. Tr. par Henri-Dominique Paratte. Ragweed Press, 1986. 278 p. $12.95 collé [2-89037-295-2]. (Littérature d'Amérique) Une fille maigre aux cheveux roux et à la langue déliée est adoptée par deux célibataires qui s'attendaient à recevoir un garçon. Traduction de *Anne of Green Gables*. *Aînés.*

Montgomery, Lucy Maud. Emilie de la Nouvelle Lune. Tr. par Paule Daveluy. Pierre Tisseyre, 1983. 318 p. $11.95 collé [2-89051-090-5]. (Deux solitudes, jeunesse) Après la mort de son père, Emilie Star doit aller vivre à la ferme de la Nouvelle Lune avec les soeurs de sa mère défunte. C'est dans ce milieu rural et au sein d'une famille attachée à ses traditions qu' Emilie prépare sa carrière d'écrivain. Traduction de *Emily of New Moon*. *Aînés.*

Mowat, Farley. Deux grands ducs dans la famille. Tr. par Paule Daveluy. Pierre Tisseyre, 1980. 80 p. $8.95 collé [2-89051-032-8]. (Deux solitudes, jeunesse) Les deux hiboux, Ghibou et Geignard, viennent bouleverser la vie de la famille de Robert. Traduction de *Owls in the family*. *Moyens, grands.*

Mowat, Farley. Une goélette nommée Black Joke. Tr. par Michel Caillol. Pierre Tisseyre, 1982. 214 p. $9.95 collé [2-89051-071-9]. (Deux solitudes, jeunesse) Lors de la prohibition des années trente, deux garçons vont déjouer le plan de maître Simon qui essaie de s'approprier le Black Joke pour faire la contrebande de !'alcool. Traduction de *The Black Joke*. *Grands.*

Mowat, Farley. La malédiction du tombeau Viking. Tr. par Maryse Côté. Pierre Tisseyre, 1980. 194 p. $7.95 collé [2-89051-030-1]. (Deux solitudes, jeunesse) Une expédition audacieuse dans l'Arctique canadien est entreprise par quatre adolescents afin de résoudre l'énigme d'un tombeau viking. Traduction de *The Curse of the Viking grave*. *Grands, aînés.*

Noël, Michel. Les Papinachois. Ill. par Joanne Ouellet. Hurtubise HMH, 1981. 6v. $5.95 chac. (Contes amérindiens). v.1 L'origine [2-89045-502-5] v.2 Les voisins [2-89045-503-3] v.3 La cueillette [2-89045-504-1] v.4 Sagesse [2-89045-569-6] v.5 Exploits [2-89045-570-X] v.6 L'école [2-89045-571-8].

Contes qui traitent de la vie et des coutumes d'une famille amérindienne. *Débutants.*

Noël, Michel. Les Stadaconés. Ill. par Joanne Ouellet. Univ. du Québec, 1986. 24 p. chac. $3.95 chac ou 9 tomes $38.50 série. t.1 Les ancêtres [2-920073-37-0] t.2 L'éloquence [2-920073-38-9] t.3 L'héritage [2-920073-39-1] t.4 Le visiteur [2-920073-42-7] t.5 La coutume [2-920073-43-5] t.6 L'origine [2-920073-44-3] t.7 La peur noire [2-920073-45-1] t.8 La corvée [2-920073-46-X] t.9 Le grognon [2-920073-47-8].

Ces albums décrivent la vie traditionnelle des Stadaconés. *Débutants, moyens.*

Page, Marie. L'enfant venu d'ailleurs. Héritage, 1983. 115 p. $5.95 collé [0-7773-4431-9]. (Pour lire avec toi)

Un récit de science-fiction avec un enfant venu d'ailleurs qui bouleverse la vie d'une famille. *Moyens.*

Page, Marie. Vincent, Sylvie et les autres. Ill. par Stéphane Poulin. Héritage, 1985. 127 p. $5.95 collé [2-7625-4449-1]. (Pour lire avec toi)

Vincent, Sylvie et les autres vivent des aventures palpitantes grâce à une machine qui les transporte dans un fantastique voyage dans le temps. *Moyens.*

Pasquet, Jacques. Méli-Mélo. Québec/Amérique, 1986. 121 p. $4.95 collé [2-89037-314-2]. (Jeunesse-Romans)

Serait-il possible que leur voisin soit un vrai sorcier? Marine et Célia font justement une telle découverte. *Grands.*

Pasquet, Jacques. Mystère et boule de gomme. Ill. par Richard Parent. Québec/Amérique, 1985. 126 p. $4.95 collé [2-89037-251-0]. (Jeunesse-Romans)

Fantaisie qui met en vedette une école qui disparaît, Léopold, le premier suspect et Chloé, la tante qui décide de résoudre le mystère interplanétaire. *Moyens, grands.*

Pigeon, Pierre. L'ordinateur égaré. Québec/Amérique, 1985. 171 p. $4.95 collé [2-89037-266-9]. (Jeunesse-Romans)

Par erreur, la famille Blondeau acquiert un ordinateur aux possibilités fabuleuses recherché par l'Agence Abri. La tranquilité de la famille est menacée. *Grands.*

Piper, Eileen. Le piège du magicien. Ill. par Alan Daniel. Tr. par Christiane Duchesne. Scholastic-TAB, 1984. 60 p. $4.95 broché 0-590-71447-3].

Elsa, la jeune aveugle, descend au fond de la mer des Sargasses pour trouver la perle magique qui lui permettra de souhaiter le retour du prince transformé en tortue par Java le magicien. Traduction de *The Magician's trap. Débutants, moyens.*

Plante, Raymond. Le dernier des raisins. Québec/Amérique, 1986. 125 p. $4.95 collé [2-89037-312-6]. (Jeunesse/Romans)

L'histoire d'amour de deux adolescents d'une polyvalente. *Grands, aînés.*

Plante, Raymond. La machine à beauté. Québec/Amérique, 1982. 125 p. $4.95 collé [2-89037-141-7].

Pour les personnes qui veulent devenir les plus belles, une machine à beauté remplit sa promesse ... à sa façon. *Grands.*

Plante, Raymond. Minibus. Québec/Amérique, 1985. 126 p. $4.95 collé [2-89037-267-7].

Nouvelles inspirées de Minibus, une émission populaire de Radio-Canada. *Moyens.*

Plante, Raymond. Monsieur Genou. Ill. par Renée Veillet. Leméac, 1981. 156 p. $9.95 collé [2-7609-9839-8]. (Jours de fête)

Roman farfelu qui met en vedette Monsieur Genou, un drôle de bonhomme qui, dans sa tête d'oeuf, rêve d'être quelqu'un. *Grands.*

Plante, Raymond. Le record de Philibert Dupont. Ill. par Stéphane Poulin. Québec/Amérique, 1984. 125 p. $4.95 collé [2-89037-221-9].

Qui peut se vanter d'avoir son nom dans le célèbre Livre des records? C'est le rêve que caresse Philibert Dupont, l'oncle de Julie Cadieux qui nous raconte cette histoire folle. *Moyens, grands.*

Proulx, Jean-Baptiste. L'enfant perdu et retrouvé ou Pierre Cholet. Ill. par Suzanne Cholette-Longtin. Fides, 1982. 110 p. $5.95 collé [2-7621-1184-6]. (Mille-îles)

Ouvrage fictif ou réel, nul ne le sait. C'est une nouvelle édition dont la première datant de 1887 fut l'un des récits les plus populaires du Canada français. Il raconte les pérégrinations d'un homme kidnappé alors qu'il était enfant et maintenant à la recherche de ses parents. *Grands.*

Renaud, Bernadette. Bach et Bottine. Photos par Jean Demers. Québec/Amérique, 1986. 208 p. $4.95 collé [2-89037-313-4]. (Jeunesse-Romans)

A dix ans, Fanny arrive avec ses bagages, son rire et sa moufette chez un oncle solitaire qui se croit musicien. Roman inspiré du scénario du film 'Bach et Bottine' par la même auteure et réalisé par André Mélançon. *Moyens.*

Renaud, Bernadette. Le chat de l'oratoire. Ill. par Josette Michaud. Fides, 1978. 90 p. $8.50 collé [2-7621-0697-4]. (Goéland)

Une émouvante histoire d'amitié entre un chat et le jeune organiste de l'Oratoire St. Joseph. *Moyens, grands.*

Renaud, Bernadette. Emilie, la baignoire à pattes. Ill. par France Bédard. Héritage, 1976. 126 p. $5.95 collé [0-7773-4400-9]. (Pour lire avec toi)

Les aventures cocasses d'Emilie, la baignoire à pattes qui n'accepte pas facilement d'être rejetée au hangar par ses maîtres après les avoir servis si longtemps. *Débutants, moyens.*

Renaud, Bernadette. La grande question de Tomatelle. Ill. par Suzanne Langlois. Leméac, 1982. 100 p. $6.95 collé [2-7609-9848-7].

Tomatelle, une jeune tomate curieuse, part à l'aventure et à la recherche du sens de sa vie. *Moyens.*

Renaud, Bernadette. La maison tête de pioche. Ill. par Lucie Ledoux. Héritage, 1979. 124 p. $5.95 collé [0-7773-4415-7]. (Pour lire avec toi)

Une vieille maison vient d'être achetée par un jeune couple qui commence aussitôt à la restaurer. Interprétant mal ces bonnes intentions, elle leur en fait voir de toutes les couleurs. *Débutants, moyens.*

Renaud, Bernadette. La révolte de la courtepointe. Ill. par Lucie Ledoux. Fides, 1979. 95 p. $6.95 collé [2-7621-0961-2].

Julie reçoit une courtepointe à Noël. Très déçue de ces vieilles guenilles qu'elle juge inutiles, elle s'endort ce soir-là en pleurant ... Une histoire amusante et une héroïne bien sympathique. *Débutants, moyens.*

Richler, Mordecai. Jacob Deux-Deux et le vampire masqué. Ill. par Fritz Wegner. Tr. par Jean Simard. Pierre Tisseyre, 1977. 93 p. $5.95 collé [0-7753-0098-5]. (Deux solitudes – juvénile)

La manie de Jacob de répéter deux fois les choses pour que les adultes l'écoutent le mènera bien loin. Traduction de *Jacob Two-Two and the Hooded Fang. Moyens.*

Roberts, Ken. Les idées folles. Tr. par Jean-Pierre Fournier. Québec/Amérique, 1985. 120 p. $4.95 collé [2-89037-263-4].

En vue d'obtenir son diplome de l'école Max Barca, Christine doit trouver une idée folle mais ce n'est pas facile dans une ville où l'innovation est la plus grande richesse. Traduction de *Crazy ideas. Moyens.*

Rocher, Suzanne. Les Cailloux voient du pays. Ill. par Paule Girard. Fides, 1980. 157 p. $8.50 collé [2-7621-0974-4]. (Goéland)

Anne raconte les aventures cocasses et émouvantes vécues par sa famille lors d'un voyage en roulotte à travers le Canada et les Etats-Unis. *Grands.*

Rocher, Suzanne. Le dernier-né des Cailloux. Ill. par Guy Faucher. Fides, 1975. 95 p. $8.50 collé [2-7621-0546-3]. (Goéland)

A l'occasion d'un concours, Anne gagne un jeune épagneul qu'elle amène à la maison et qui bientôt est adopté par toute la famille. *Moyens.*

Rochon, Esther. L'étranger sous la ville. Paulines, 1986. 123 p. $5.95 collé [2-89039-086-1]. (Jeunesse-pop)

Une jeune fille destinée à devenir sorcière essaie de communiquer avec un étranger descendu vivre dans les caves de la Citadelle. *Moyens, grands.*

Roquebrune, Robert de. Les habits rouges. Ill. par Josée Guberek. Fides, 1978. 136 p. $8.50 collé [2-7621-0684-2]. (Goéland)

Quand la rébellion éclate en 1837, Henriette et son frère Jérôme se portent au secours de leurs compatriotes. *Grands.*

Roy, Gabrielle, Ces enfants de ma vie. Stanké, 1977. 212 p. $7.95 collé [2-7604-0211-8].

Récit qui évoque la vie de l'auteur comme jeune institutrice au Manitoba durant les années trente et ainsi que les enfants issus de cultures différentes avec des besoins de leur âge, de sécurité et d'amour. *Aînés.*

Roy, Gabrielle. L'Espagnole et la Pékinoise. Ill. par Jean-Yves Ahern. Boréal, 1986. 42 p. $8.95 collé [2-89052-171-0].

L'Espagnole et la Pékinoise s'entendent comme chien et chat jusqu'au jour où l'Espagnole met au monde trois petits chats. *Débutants, moyens.*

Rubbo, Michael. Opération beurre de pinottes. Ill. par Christian Bénard. Tr. par Viviane Julien. Québec/Amérique, 1985. 228 p. $5.95 collé [2-89037-278-8].

En visitant une maison incendiée, Michel a eu tellement peur qu'il a perdu tous ses cheveux. Heureusement, ils ont repoussé grâce à une pommade au beurre de pinottes. *Moyens.*

Sabella, Monique. L'inconnue des Laurentides. Paulines, 1972. 124 p. $4.95 collé [0-88840-351-8]. (Jeunesse-pop)

Un gentil livre simple, facile à lire. Aventure de vacances. *Moyens.*

Sanschagrin, Joceline. Atterrissage forcé. Ill. par Pierre Pratt. La Courte échelle, 1987. 94 p. $5.95 collé [2-89021-064-2]. (Roman-jeunesse)
Wonder, une fille de douze ans qui sait voler d'elle-même, tente de franchir un mur insurmontable pour retrouver son père. *Grands.*

Savard, Félix-Antoine. Menaud maître draveur. Fides, 1970. 214 p. $4.50 collé [2-7621-0162-X]. (Bibliothèque québécoise)
Roman-poème. Un plaidoyer vibrant pour la sauvegarde du patrimoine national et un hymne à la liberté. *Aînés.*

Schinkel, David et Beauchesne, Yves. Aller retour. Pierre Tisseyre, 1986. 144 p. $10.95 collé [2-89051-321-1]. (Conquêtes)
Ne pouvant plus supporter les abus physiques de son oncle qui l'avait adopté après la mort de ses parents, Martin se rend à Montréal où il espère convaincre sa tante qu'il ne peut retourner vivre avec son oncle. *Grands.*

Sernine, Daniel. Le cercle violet. Pierre Tisseyre, 1984. 231 p. $9.95 collé [2-89051-280-0]. (Conquêtes)
Après avoir appris le mystère qui entoure sa famille, Pierre Michay affronte les descendants des Davard en vue d'obtenir sa part du trésor et réussit à avorter l'incarnation d'Abaldurth. Cinquième et dernier volume de la saga des Davard et Michay. *Aînés.*

Sernine, Daniel. La cité inconnue. Paulines, 1982. 160 p. $5.95 collé [2-89039-885-4]. (Jeunesse-pop)
Premier volume de la saga des Davard et Michay mettant en jeu la sorcellerie et la haine entre ces deux familles. *Grands, aînés.*

Sernine, Daniel. Les envoûtements. Paulines, 1985. 109 p. $5.95 collé [2-89039-976-1]. (Jeunesse-pop)
La mort du père de Didier fait resurgir la haine entre les Davard et les Michay. *Grands, aînés.*

Sernine, Daniel. L'épée Arhapal. Paulines, 1981. 175 p. $5.95 collé [2-89039-859-5]. (Jeunesse-pop)
L'origine de la rancune de Luc-Alexandre Davard envers Didier Michay. *Grands, aînés.*

Sernine, Daniel. Ludovic. Pierre Tisseyre, 1983. 274 p. $9.95 collé [0-89051-091-3]. (Conquêtes)
Ludovic délivre la princesse Ligelia des mains du prince Drogomir et trouve enfin le grimoire qui va le libérer du maléfice de Drogomir. *Aînés.*

Sernine, Daniel. Organisation Argus. Ill. par Gabriel de Beney. Paulines, 1979. 113 p. $4.50 collé [2-89039-014-4]. (Jeunesse-pop)
Le jeune Marc Alix et son oncle le docteur Guillon sont mêlés à une affaire d'espionnage scientifique. Face à des adversaires impitoyables, Marc Alix recevra une révélation stupéfiante sur l'identité d'êtres extra-terrestres. *Grands.*

Sernine, Daniel. Le trésor du 'Scorpion'. Paulines, 1980. 144 p. $6.95 collé [2-89039-828-5]. (Jeunesse-pop)
Les crimes du légendaire sorcier Davard. *Grands, aînés.*

Smucker, Barbara. Les chemins secrets de la liberté. Tr. par Paule Daveluy. Pierre Tisseyre, 1978. 161 p. $8.95 collé [0-7753-0114-0]. (Deux solitudes, juvénile)
Julilly et Lisa, jeunes esclaves noires, tentent de s'enfuir vers le Canada où elles trouveront la liberté. Traduction de *Underground to Canada*. *Grands.*

Smucker, Barbara. Jours de Terreur. Tr. par Paule Daveluy. Pierre Tisseyre, 1981. 217 p. $7.95 collé [2-89051-057-3]. (Deux solitudes, jeunesse)
Au début du XX siècle, un jeune mennonite russe et sa famille vivent l'effondrement de l'univers paisible de l'Ukraine et les atrocités de la guerre avant de se réfugier au Canada. Traduction de *Days of Terror*. *Grands.*

Smucker, Barbara. Un monde hors du temps. Tr. par Paule Daveluy. Pierre Tisseyre, 1985. 224 p. $9.95 collé [2-89051-283-5]. (Deux solitudes, jeunesse)
En route vers Toronto où il devra passer six mois avec une tante rétrograde, Ian McDonald a un accident de voiture et il est accueilli par une famille amish qui s'occupera de lui temporairement. Traduction de *Amish adventure*. *Moyens, grands.*

Soulières, Robert. Casse-tête chinois. Pierre Tisseyre, 1985. 180 p. $9.95 collé [2-89051-287-8]. (Conquêtes)
Un detective privé part à la recherche d'un jeune homme disparu mystérieusement. *Grands, aînés.*

Soulières, Robert. Le visiteur du soir. Pierre Tisseyre, 1980. 147 p. $8.95 collé [2-89051-039-5]. (Conquêtes)
Dans l'espoir de remporter la meilleure prise de l'école, Charles et Vincent décident 'd'emprunter' un tableau exposé au musée des Beaux Arts. Simultanément, de véritables cambrioleurs recherchent le même tableau 'Le visiteur du soir'. *Grands.*

Sutal, Louis. Le piège à bateaux. Ill. par Gabriel de Beney. Paulines, 1973. 123 p. $6.95 relié [0-88840-400-X]. (Jeunesse-pop)

Un roman policier et d'anticipation. Trois personnages extra-terrestres visitent la Terre et enquêtent sur la disparition de bateaux dans le Golfe Saint-Laurent. *Grands*.

Tanguay, Bernard. La petite menteuse et le ciel. Ill. par Michael Fog. Québec/Amérique, 1985. 162 p. $4.95 collé [2-89037-264-2].

A onze ans, Mélanie prophétise la fin du monde à Saint-Euchariste-en-bas et, par ce fait, bouleverse le village. *Moyens, grands*.

Thériault, Yves. Ashini. Fides, 1981. 145 p. $3.50 collé [2-7621-0815-2]. (Bibliothèque québécoise)

Epopée de la liberté et de la grandeur, ce roman chante l'âme de la race montagnaise dans une langue majestueuse et riche de sonorités, *Aînés*.

Thériault, Yves. Kuanuten vent d'est. Paulines, 1981. 125 p. $5.95 collé [2-89039-858-7].

Un jeune métis marqué par la vie urbaine affronte les traditions montagnaises de son grand-père. *Grands, aînés*.

Thériault, Yves. L'or de la Felouque. Hurtubise HMH, 1981. 110 p. $6.50 collé [2-89045-495-9].

Près de Baie Comeau, quatre jeunes affrontent à bord d'un voilier les risques de la haute mer et prennent part à une aventure semblable à celles de la piraterie au XVIII siècle. *Aînés*.

Thériault, Yves. Popok, le petit esquimau. Ill. par Pierre Desrosiers. Québécor, 1980. 104 p. $7.95 collé [2-89089-102-X].

Grâce à sa bonté, Popok, un petit esquimau, se fait trois amis: un oiseau, un phoque et un ours blanc qui lui jurent une amitié éternelle. *Débutants, moyens*.

Thériault, Yves. Le ru d'Ikoué. Ill. par Michelle Poirier. Fides, 1977. 123 p. $8.50 collé [2-7621-0631-1]. (Goéland)

Ikoué, un jeune Algonquin, découvre un ruisselet qui lui apprend à devenir un homme. Ce roman empreint de nature et de poésie a d'abord paru chez le même éditeur en 1963. *Moyens, grands*.

Truss, Jan. Jasmine. Tr. par Marie-Andrée Clermont. Pierre Tisseyre, 1986. 247 p. $9.95 collé [2-89051-308-4]. (Deux solitudes, jeunesse)

Certaine d'un échec scolaire après que son projet scientifique est détruit par l'un de ses frères et ne pouvant plus supporter les responsabilités familiales, Marie-Antoinette-Jasmine se sauve vers les montagnes. Cette expérience lui enseigne plusieurs leçons. Traduction de *Jasmin*. *Moyens, grands*.

Turcotte, Diane. Les os de l'Anse-aux-Mouques. Ill. par Claude Côté. La Liberté, 1985. 154 p. $9.95 collé [2-89084-033-6]. (Apanage Jeunesse)

Que veut dire M. Simon quand il déclare à Jean-René et à Elise que l'immense est dans l'immensité? Ces mots stimulent et mettent à l'épreuve les jeunes du village. *Grands*.

Turcotte, Diane. La piste de l'encre. Paulines, 1986. 117 p. $5.95 collé [2-89039-052-7]. (Jeunesse-pop)

Récit d'aventures qui commence par la découverte d'un tatouage discret au bras d'un homme. *Grands*.

Villeneuve, Jocelyne. Contes des quatre saisons. Ill. par France Bédard. Héritage, 1978. 125 p. $5.95 collé [0-7773-4412-2]. (Pour lire avec toi)

Sept courtes histoires variées et joliment illustrées. *Débutants, moyens*.

Villeneuve, Jocelyne. La ménagerie. Des Plaines, 1985. 106 p. $4.95 collé [0-920944-57-4].

Cinq contes du monde merveilleux des enfants. *Moyens*.

Warnant-Côté, Marie-Andrée. Des dieux et des hommes. Ill. par Christine Dufour. Pierre Tisseyre, 1982. 163 p. $9.95 collé [2-89051-073-5]. (Conquêtes)

Neufs récits illustrant les mythes grecs les plus connus sont racontés d'une façon claire et vivante. *Moyens, grands*.

Warnant-Côté, Marie-Andrée. L'enchanteur du pays d'Oz. Ill. par Michèle Devlin. Héritage, 1977. 125 p. $5.95 collé [0-7773-4410-6]. (Pour lire avec toi)

Une adaptation intéressante d'un classique. La présentation est soignée et attrayante. *Débutants, moyens*.

Waterton, Betty. Moutarde. Ill. par Barbara Reid. Tr. par Françoise Marois. Scholastic-TAB, 1983. 40 p. $2.95 broché [0-590-71176-8].

Moutarde, la plus gentille des petites chiennes, est si grosse et si maladroite que personne ne veut d'elle. Traduction de *Mustard*. *Débutants, moyens*.

Wilscam, Lynda. Les mots ... de Picotine – L'homme aux ballons. Ill. par Cécile Gagnon. Héritage, 1977. 108 p. $5.95 collé [0-7773-4408-4]. (Pour lire avec toi)

Picotine et ses amis ont de la difficulté à comprendre un vendeur de ballons. *Débutants, moyens*.

Wilson, Serge. Fend-le-vent: Les bonhommes jaunes. Ill. par Claude Poirier. Héritage, 1986. 125 p. $5.95 collé [2-7625-3032-6]. (Aventures en tête)

Fend-le-vent et ses compagnons percent finalement le mystère des bonhommes jaunes aperçus dans un terrain de camping de la région du Saguenay. *Moyens*.

Wilson, Serge. Fend-le-vent et le visiteur mystérieux. Ill. par Claude Poirier. Héritage, 1980. 123 p. $5.95 collé [0-7773-3016-4]. (Aventures en tête)

Fend-le-vent, un ventard, sorte de fantôme spécialisé dans la science des vents, est invité à démasquer le visiteur nocturne qui dérange les livres de la bibliothèque de Mauriceville. *Moyens.*

Wilson, Serge. Marie-Mardi. Le secret d'Anthime. Ill. par Michèle Devlin. Héritage, 1978. 123 p. $5.95 collé [0-7773-4414-9]. (Pour lire avec toi)

Marie-Mardi, fée apprentie, doit accomplir une mission au pays des humains. C'est le début d'une aventure mouvementée. *Débutants, moyens.*

Wilson, Serge. Mimi Finfouin et le monstre du lac Saint-Ernest. Ill. par Claude Poirier. Héritage, 1984. 126 p. $5.95 collé [2-7625-3030-X].

Une créature mystérieuse apparue à la surface du lac Saint-Ernest attire la curiosité de Mimi Finfouin et ses amis. *Moyens.*

Yates, Elizabeth. En avant voyageurs! Ill. par Vincent Rio. Tr. par Paule Daveluy. Flammarion, 1981. 284 p. $3.95 collé [2-081617323]. (Castor-poche)

Une histoire sur les voyageurs du Canada français. Traduction de *With pipe, paddle and song. Grands.*

GEOGRAPHIE ET VOYAGES

Bherer, Harold. Regards sur le Canada.
Paulines, 1983. 80 p. $8.50 collé [2-89039-921-4].
(Documentation Vidéo-Presse)
L'auteur donne un bref aperçu historique,
géographique, économique et culturel pour
chacune des provinces et du Grand Nord. Photos
en couleurs et cartes géographiques. *Moyens,
grands.*

Bherer, Harold. Regards sur le Québec.
Paulines, 1982. 80 p. $8.50 collé [2-89039-894-3].
(Documentation Vidéo-Presse)
Information sur dix régions du Québec. Les
caractéristiques historiques, géographiques,
économiques et culturelles sont discutées pour
chaque région. Photos en couleurs et cartes
géographiques. *Moyens, grands.*

Hocking, Anthony. L'Ontario. McGraw, 1981.
95 p. $12.95 relié [0-07-092448].
Un aperçu de la province de l'Ontario couvrant
le gouvernement, les industries, les lieux
historiques, les personnalités et l'environnement
dans un style simple et clair. Traduction de
Ontario. Moyens, grands, aînés.

Lafortune, Ambroise. Le pays d'où je viens.
Héritage, 1977. 122 p. $5.95 collé
[0-7773-3013-X].
Des anecdotes personnelles et des légendes
recueillies par le père Ambroise font parcourir
les différentes régions du Québec: l'île
d'Orléans, Trois-Rivières, les Laurentides, la
Côte Nord, les Iles-de-la-Madeleine, la
Gaspésie, le Nouveau Québec et l'Abitibi.
Moyens, grands.

Lévesque, Gilbert. François de Laval, Seigneur
de la Côte. Leméac, 1979. 93 p. $4.95 collé
[0-7761-9426-7]. (Second regard)
Réflexions et reportage d'une marche organisée
par un scripteur-recherchiste pour suivre les
traces d'un fondateur. *Aînés.*

Québec. Le Ministère des Communications.
Le Québec sur le pouce. Editeur Officiel du
Québec, 1984. 188 p. $5.95 collé [EOQ21026-1].
Conseils pratiques et préventifs, itinéraires
variés, adresses et lieux d'hébergement. *Aînés.*

BIOGRAPHIES

voir
COLLECTIONS
Artistes Canadiens
Célébritiés canadiennes

Bonic, Tom. Sa sainteté le Pape Jean-Paul II. Tr. par Anne Minquet-Patocka. Grolier, 1984. $6.95 collé [2-89301-001-6].
Brève biographie relatant la jeunesse de Karol Wojtyla, un polonais, qui, en 1978, fut nommé pape. Traduction de *Pope John Paul II. Moyens.*

Lamarche, Hélène. Le Miro des enfants. Musée des Beaux-arts de Montréal, 1986. 26 p. $6.00 collé [2-89192-078-3].
Une excellente introduction sur ce peintre espagnol. Ouvrage qui brosse un tableau de l'époque et discute ses oeuvres. *Moyens, grands.*

Lamarche, Hélène. Le Morrice des enfants. Musée des Beaux-arts de Montréal, 1985. 24 p. $5.00 collé [2-89192-069-4].
Information sur ce peintre canadien-anglais du début du XXe siècle. *Moyens, grands.*

Lamarche, Hélène. Le Picasso des enfants. Musée des Beaux-arts de Montréal, 1985. 24 p. $5.00 collé [2-89192-061-9].
Information sur Picasso et son art. De nombreuses reproductions accompagnent le texte. *Moyens, grands.*

Leclerc, Félix. Pieds nus dans l'aube. Fides, 1969. 216 p. $4.50 collé [2-7621-0829-2]. (Bibliothèque québécoise)
Raconte la jeunesse de l'auteur, son milieu natal, la vallée du Saint-Maurice, ses amis, et son goût de l'aventure. *Aînés.*

Major, Henriette. François d'Assise. Ill. par Claude Lafortune. Fides, 1981. 80 p. $10.95 relié [2-7621-1126-9].
La vie de St François d'Assise, réformateur audacieux, qui fonda en 1208 l'ordre des Franciscains. Illustré de photographies de personnages et de maquettes en papier. *Débutants, moyens.*

Major, Henriette. Marguerite Bourgeoys. Ill. par Claude Lafortune. Hurtubise HMH, 1983. 55 p. $11.95 relié [2-89045-554-8].
La vie héroïque de Marguerite Bourgeoys, fondatrice de la Congrégation de Notre-Dame en Nouvelle-France. Illustré de photographies de personnages et de maquettes en papier. *Débutants, moyens.*

Martel, Suzanne. Au temps de Marguerite Bourgeoys quand Montréal était un village. Méridien, 1982. 333 p. $10.00 collé [2-920417-85-1].
La vie aventureuse et héroïque de Marguerite Bourgeoys, première femme à être cannonisée au Canada, qui, en 1653, vient s'établir à Ville-Marie. A la fin de chaque chapitre, l'auteur précise dans des notes ce qui est fictif et réel. *Moyens, grands.*

Scrivener, Leslie. Terry Fox. Tr. par Francine de Lorimier et Claude Béland. Héritage, 1981. 176 p. $12.95 relié [0-7773-553-4-5]. (Vis-a-vies)
La vie de Terry Fox qui, en 1980, commença un marathon pour solliciter de l'argent pour le cancer. Traduction de *Terry Fox: his story. Moyens.*

HISTOIRE

voir
COLLECTIONS
Une nation en marche
Les peuples autochtones du Canada
La préhistoire

Assiniwi, Bernard et Fadden, John. Les Cris des marais. Leméac, 1979. 44 p. $5.95 relié [2-7609-9881-9]. (Chicouté)
Vie et coutumes d'un peuple. *Débutants, moyens.*

Assiniwi, Bernard et Fadden, John. Le guerrier aux pieds agiles. Leméac, 1979. 47 p. $5.95 relié [2-7609-9880-0]. (Chicouté)
'Chez les Agniers des monts Adirondacks, les hommes étaient évalués selon leur véritable mérite.' *Débutants.*

Assiniwi, Bernard et Fadden, John. Les Montagnais et Naskapi. Leméac, 1979. 47 p. $5.95 relié [2-7609-9882-7]. (Chicouté)
Histoire sociale d'un peuple de chasseurs. *Débutants.*

Kurelek, William. Les bûcherons. Ill par William Kurelek. Tr. par Jacques de Roussan. Toundra, 1983. 48 p. $9.95 collé [2-88776-158-5].
Kurelek raconte en détail la vie dans un camp de bûcherons vers la fin des années quarante. Traduction de *Lumberjack. Moyens, grands.*

McConkey, Lois. La mer et le cèdre: Ainsi vivaient les Indiens de la Côte du Nord-Ouest. Ill. par Douglas Tait. Tr. par Danielle Thaler. Douglas & McIntyre, 1983. 31 p. $7.95 collé [0-88894-373-3]. (Ainsi vivaient les Indiens du Canada)
Une introduction à la vie des sept tribus indiennes qui vivaient sur la Côte du Nord-Ouest. Traduction de *Sea and cedar. Débutants, moyens.*

Mathieu-Loranger, Francine. Les mémoires de Jean Talon. Ill. par Pierre Decelles. Héritage, 1981. 122 p. $4.95 collé [0-7773-3301-5]. (Les bâtisseurs)
Récit des activités et des tâches remplies par l'intendant Talon en Nouvelle-France de 1665 à 1672. *Moyens, grands.*

Mathieu-Loranger, Francine. Les mémoires de Samuel de Champlain. Ill. par Pierre Decelles. Héritage, 1981. 125 p. $4.95 collé [0-7773-3300-7]. (Les bâtisseurs)
La vie de Samuel de Champlain et le récit de ses voyages et de la colonisation de Québec. *Moyens, grands.*

Monet, Jacques. La monarchie au Canada. Cercle du Livre de France, 1979. 96 p. $9.95 collé [2-89051-012-3].
L'évolution du rôle constitutionnel des représentants de l'Autorité Royale au Canada à partir des débuts où ces derniers gouvernaient véritablement le pays. *Grands, aînés.*

Nations autochtones de Québec. Gouvernement du Québec, 1984. 171 p. $6.95 collé [2-551-06307-8].
Description des origines du mode de vie ancestral, des mythes et des traditions des autochtones du Québec. *Grands, aînés.*

Pachano, Jane. Coutumes Cries: La cérémonie des premiers pas/Cree customs: walking out ceremony. Ill. par J. Pachano et R. Pachano. Tr. par Réjane Babin. Le Centre culturel et éducatif Cri de la Baie James, 1984. 24 p. $11.50 collé [0-920791-06-9].
Des enfants Cris participent à la cérémonie des Premiers Pas qui symbolise le premier jour d'un enfant Cri comme chasseur ou comme femme. *Débutants.*

Pachano, Jane. Les temps changent: Bébé William/Changing times: Baby William. Ill. par J. Eitzen et J. Rabbit Ozores. Tr. par Réjane Babin. Le Centre culturel et éducatif Cri de la Baie James, 1985. 18 p. $7.50 collé [0-920791-00-X].
Une comparaison entre la façon que les bébés Cris viennent au monde aujourd'hui et celle d'autrefois. *Débutants.*

Pachano, Jane. Les temps changent: Bobby et Mary chez eux/Changing times: Bobby and Mary at home. Ill. par J. Eitzen. Tr. par Jacqueline Gravelle. Le Centre culturel et éducatif Cri de la Baie James, 1985. 27 p. $9.00 collé [0-920791-04-2].

La façon que les enfants Cris vivent aujourd'hui est comparée à celle de leurs grand-parents. Illustré avec des photos et des dessins. *Débutants*.

Pachano, Jane. Les temps changent: Moyens de transport/Changing times: transportation. Le Centre culturel et éducatif Cri de la Baie James, 1985. 20 p. $11.00 collé [0-920791-14-X].

Une comparaison des moyens de transportation d'aujourd'hui et d'autrefois des Cris de la Baie James. *Débutants*.

Pachano, Jane. Les temps changent: Le vêtement/Changing times: clothing. Tr. par Renée Cartier. Le Centre culturel et éducatif Cri de la Baie James, 1985. 18 p. $11.50 collé [0-920791-02-6].

Une comparaison entre les vêtements que portent les Cris d'aujourd'hui et les vêtments qu'ils portaient du temps de leurs grand-parents. Le contraste nous est montré par des illustrations en couleurs pour le temps présent et des sépias pour le temps passé. *Débutants*.

Pigeon, Danielle et Charlebois-Dumais, Hélène. Un serrurier en Nouvelle-France. Ill. par Marie Trudel et Robert Lemire. Méridien, 1984. 91 p. $13.95 collé [2-920417-94-0]. (Arts et métiers anciens)

Conte historique d'Ambroise Casale, forgeron serrurier à Montréal, et de sa famille au début du XVIIIe siècle. *Moyens, grands*.

REFERENCE

Atlas du Canada. Reader's Digest, 1981. 220 p. $29.95 relié [0-88850-100-5].

Banfield, Alexandre. Les mammifères du Canada. Université Laval, 1974. 432 p. $27.50 relié [2-7637-6699-4].

Bélisle, Louis-Alexandre. Dictionnaire nord-américain de la langue française. Beauchemin, 1979. 1196 p. $52.45 relié [2-7616-0013-4].

Carrière, Jean. Atlas des jeunes québécois. Centre éducatif et culturel, 1985. 88 p. $16.95 relié [2-7617-0232-8].

Dagenais, Gérard. Dictionnaire des difficultés de la langue française au Canada. Editions Françaises, 1984. 679 p. $26.95 relié [2-7618-1037-6].

Des Ruisseaux, Pierre. Le livre des proverbes. Hurtubise, 1978. 220 p. $8.95 collé [0-7758-0132-1].

Dictionnaire biographique du Canada, volume 1. De l'an 1000 à 1700. Brown, George W. et Trudel, Marcel, éditeurs. Université Laval, 1966. 800 p. $35.00 relié [2-7637-6525-4].

Dictionnaire biographique du Canada, volume 2. De l'an 1701 à 1740. Hayne, David et Vachon, André, éditeurs. Université Laval, 1969. 792 p. $35.00 relié [2-7637-6459-2].

Dictionnaire biographique du Canada, volume 3. De l'an 1741 à 1770. Halpenny, Francess G., éd. Université Laval, 1974. 856 p. $35.00 relié [2-7637-6735-4].

Dictionnaire biographique du Canada, volume 4. De l'an 1771 à 1800. Halpenny, Francess G., éd. Université Laval, 1980. 1034 p. $35.00 relié [2-7637-6899-7].

Dictionnaire biographique du Canada, volume 5. De l'an 1801 à 1820. Halpenny, Francess G., éd. Université Laval, 1983. 1044 p. $45.00 relié [2-7637-7010-X].

Dictionnaire biographique du Canada, volume 8. De l'an 1851 à 1860. Halpenny, Francess G., éd. Université Laval, 1985. 1129 p. $60.00 relié [2-7637-7069-X].

Dictionnaire biographique du Canada, volume 9. De l'an 1861 à 1870. Halpenny, Francess G., éd. Université Laval, 1977. 1060 p. $35.00 relié [2-7637-6811-3].

Dictionnaire biographique du Canada, volume 10. De l'an 1871 à 1880. Halpenny, Francess G., éd. Université Laval, 1972. 844 p. $35.00 relié [2-7637-5278-9].

Dictionnaire biographique du Canada, volume 11. De l'an 1881 à 1890. Halpenny, Francess G., éd. Université Laval, 1982. 1092 p. $45.00 relié [2-7637-6951-9].

Dictionnaire CEC jeunesse. Centre Educatif et Culturel, inc, 1986. 1092 p. $18.95 relié [2-7617-0142-9].

Dupont, Jean-Claude. Histoire populaire de l'Acadie. Leméac, 1978. 440 p. $19.95 collé [2-7609-5278-9].

Dupuis, Hector et Légaré, Romain. Dictionnaire des synonymes et des antonymes. Fides, 1979. 606 p. $19.95 relié [2-7621-0971-X].

L'encyclopédie du Canada. Stanké, 1987. 3 vols. $248.00 relié.

Godfrey, W. Earl. Encyclopédie des oiseaux du Québec. Homme, 1972. 663 p. $24.00 relié [0-7759-0317-5].

Grand atlas du Canada et du monde. Editions Françaises, 1982. 96 p. $35.00 relié [2-7618-0999-X].

Hosie, R.C. Arbres indigènes du Canada. Fides, 1980. 383 p. $12.95 collé [2-7621-1061-8].

Kerr, Donald Gordon Grady. Atlas historique du Canada. Nelson, 1979. 100 p. $13.50 relié [0-17-600699-0].

Légaré, Yves. Dictionnaire des écrivains québécois contemporains. Québec/Amérique, 1983. 399 p. $19.95 relié [2-89037-158-1].

McQuarrie, Jane et Dubois, Diane. Canadian picture books/Livres d'images canadiens. Reference, 1986. 217 p. $24.00 relié [0-919981-12-7]; $18.00 collé [0-919981-09-7].

Michaud, Daniel. L'histoire du Canada et du Québec en quelques épisodes. Guérin, 1979. 86 p. $6.95 collé [2-7601-0040-5]. (Culture québécoise)

Préfontaine, Robert R. 'Demande à Isabelle,' dictionnaire descriptif, phonologique, analogique et orthographique du vocabulaire actif. Le Sablier, 1974. 395 p. $14.00 broché [2-89093-040-8].

Victorin, Louis-Marie. Flore Laurentienne. Université de Montréal, 1964. 925 p. $25.00 relié [0-8405-0018-1].

REVUES

Coulicou. Héritage, 300 avenue Arran, St. Lambert, Québec. J4R 1K5. Abonnement: 1 an (10 numéros): $17.50, 2 ans (20 numéros): $30.00. A l'étranger 1 an: $22.50.

Hibou. Héritage, 300 avenue Arran, St. Lambert, Québec. J4R 1K5. Abonnement: 1 an (10 numéros): $17.50, 2 ans (20 numéros): $28.00. A l'étranger 1 an: $22.50.

Je me petit débrouille. Service Hebdo-Science. Distribuée par le Conseil du développement du loisir scientifique, 4545 Pierre de Coubertin, C.P. 1000, Succursale M, Montréal, Québec. H1V 3R2. Abonnement: 1 an (11 numéros): $14.00.

La puce à l'oreille. Science Jeunesse Montréal, 2765 Chemin de la Côte Sainte-Catherine, Montréal, Québec. H3T 1B5. Abonnement:

Gratuit pour les écoles secondaires. 1 an (8 numéros): $10.00.

Québec Rock. Québec Rock Group, 3510 St. Laurent, Ste. 404, Montréal, Québec. H2X 2V2. Abonnement: 1 an (12 numéros): $26.00.

Québec-Science. Université du Québec, C.P. 250, Sillery, Québec. G1T 2R1. Abonnement: 1 an (12 numéros): $25.00.

Vidéo-Presse. Paulines, 3965 Henri-Bourassa Est, Montréal, Québec. H1H 1L1. Abonnement: 1 an (10 numéros): $16.00, 2 ans (20 numéros): $28.00. A l'étranger 1 an: $23.00, surface, $33.50 avion.

ZIP: Le magazine des jeunes. Le Magazine ZIP, C.P. 777, Succursale A, Montréal, Québec. H3C 2V2. Abonnement: 1 an (10 numéros): $20.00.

COLLECTIONS

CELEBRITES CANADIENNES

Lidec. $4.25 chacun. Courtes biographies de célébrités canadiennes à l'intention des étudiants. Accompagnées de photographies et de dessins.

Barnett, Donald C. Poundmaker. [21-59-30152].

Bassett, John M. Allan Napier MacNab. [21-59-30055].

Bassett, John M. Elisabeth Simcoe. [21-59-30080].

Bassett, John M. Laura Secord. [21-59-30063].

Bassett, John M. Samuel Cunard. [21-59-30152].

Bassett, John M. Timothy Eaton. [21-59-30071].

Bassett, John M. William Hamilton Merritt. [21-59-30039].

Benham, Mary Lile. La Vérendrye. [21-59-70049].

Bertrand, Réal. Alphonse Desjardins. [21-59-70103].

Bertrand, Réal. Emile Nelligan. [21-59-32490].

Bertrand, Réal. Thérèse Casgrain. [21-59-70014].

Damania, Laura. Egerton Ryerson. [21-59-30098].

Duggan, James. Paul-Emile Léger. [21-59-70057].

Frénette, Pierre. Napoléon Comeau. [21-59-70022].

Garrod, Stan. Samuel de Champlain. [21-59-70111].

Granatstein, J.L. Mackenzie King. [21-59-3-160].

Hacker, Carlotta. Crowfoot. [21-59-30136].

Jodoin, Rachel. Kateri Tékakwitha. [21-59-70120].

Mayles, Stephen. William Van Horne. [21-59-30128].

Neering, Rosemary. Emily Carr. [21-59-30110].

Neering, Rosemary. Louis Riel. [21-59-30179].

Pétrie, Auldham Roy. Alexander Graham Bell. [21-59-30012].

Pétrie, Auldham Roy. Henri Bourassa. [21-59-70030].

Pétrie, Auldham Roy. Sam McLaughlin. [21-59-30055].

Pickersgill, J.W. Louis St-Laurent. [21-59-70065].

Precious, Carole. J.A. Bombardier. [21-59-70170].

Smith, James K. David Thompson. [21-59-30101].

Spigelman, Martin. Sir Wilfrid Laurier. [21-59-30195].

Stewart, Roderick. Norman Bethune. [21-59-30039].

Woodcock, George. Gabriel Dumont. [21-59-32481].

COLLECTION ARTISTES CANADIENS

10 volumes publiés, mais seulement sept sont disponibles. La Galerie Nationale du Canada. Prix varient.

Une collection bien écrite et bien illustrée à la portée des adolescents sur différents peintres canadiens.

Dorais, Lucie. J.W. Morrice. $8.95 collé [0-88884-526-X], #8.

Harper, J. Russell. William G.R. Hind. $3.25 collé [0-8884-316-X], #2.

Ostiguy, Jean-René. Charles Huot. $8.95 collé [0-88884-376-3], #7.

Reid, Dennis. Bertram Brooker. $2.95 collé [0-88884-378-X], #1.

Reid, Dennis. Edwin H. Holgate. $5.95 collé [0-88884-317-8], #4.

Stacey, Robert. C.W. Jeffreys. $8.95 collé [0-88884-530-8], #10.

Varley, Christopher. Frederick H. Varley. $5.95 collé [0-88884-377-1], #6.

Zemans, Joyce. Jock MacDonald. $8.95 collé [0-88884-528-6], #9.

LE MONDE ANIMAL

12 volumes. Etudes Vivantes. $40.00 pour la série, broché [2-7607-0052-6]. $3.95 chacun.

Cette collection aide l'enfant à découvrir des animaux, tant dans leur environnement naturel qu'au jardin zoologique. Chaque volume est illustré de photographies en couleurs. Les volumes ont été écrits par Judy Ross et traduits par Marie-Hélène de la Chenelière.

Alfred, le manchot. [2-7607-0041-0].
Amok, le gorille. [2-7607-0051-8].
Bobosse, le chameau. [2-7607-0042-9].
Bozo, l'orang-outan. [2-7607-0040-2].
Inouk, l'ours polaire. [2-7607-0044-5].
Kamon, l'orignal. [2-7607-0049-6].
Khan, le tigre. [2-7607-0046-1].
Lobo, le loup. [2-7607-0047-X].
Manic, le castor. [2-7607-0048-8].
Moustache, l'otarie. [2-7607-0050-X].
Tango, l'hippopotame. [2-7607-0043-7].
Trompette, l'éléphant. [2-7607-0045-3]

LE MONDE MERVEILLEUX DES ANIMAUX

57 volumes. Grolier. $9.50 chacun, relié. La série complète: $499.50.

Une excellente série sur les animaux pour les jeunes. Chaque volume est illustré en couleurs et individuellement indexé.

Dingwall, Laima. Le bison. [0-7172-1961-5].

Dingwall, Laima. Les cerfs. [0-7172-4375-3].

Dingwall, Laima. La loutre de rivière. [0-7172-1963-1].

Dingwall, Laima. La marmotte. [0-7172-1983-6].

Dingwall, Laima. Le morse. [0-7172-1977-1].

Dingwall, Laima. La moufette rayée. [0-7172-1953-X].

Dingwall, Laima. L'opossum. [0-7172-1962-3].

Dingwall, Laima. Le porc-épic. [0-7172-1956-9].

Dingwall, Laima. Le rat musqué. [0-7172-1960-7].

Dingwall, Laima. Raton laveur. [0-7172-4378-8].

Greenland, Caroline. Le coyote. [0-7172-1997-6].

Greenland, Caroline. Les fourmis. [0-7172-1909-9].

Greenland, Caroline. L'ours blanc. [0-7172-1954-2].

Greenland, Caroline. L'ours grizzly. [0-7172-1958-5].

Greenland, Caroline. L'ours noir. [0-7172-1965-8].

Grier, Katherine. Le colibri. [0-7172-1606-3].

Grier, Katherine. Le cougar. [0-7172-1989-5].

Grier, Katherine. Le pic mineur. [0-7172-1987-9].

Harbury, Martin. Les chevaux sauvages. [0-7172-1995-X].

Ivy, Bill. Les araignées. [0-7172-1605-5].

Ivy, Bill. Les belettes. [0-7172-1991-7].

Ivy, Bill. Le canard malard. [0-7172-1955-0].

Ivy, Bill. Les goélands. [0-7172-2154-7].

Ivy, Bill. Les grenouilles. [0-7172-1984-4].

Ivy, Bill. Le monarque. [0-7172-1996-8].

Kelsey, Elin. Les abeilles. [0-7172-1968-2].

Kelsey, Elin. Le castor. [0-7172-4380-X].

Kelsey, Elin. Les hiboux. [0-7172-4377-X].

Lottridge, Celia. Le chien de prairie. [0-7172-1973-9].

Lottridge, Celia et Horner, Susan. Les souris. [0-7172-1993-3].

Peck, George K. L'écureuil. [0-7172-1985-2].

Ross, Judy. La bernache du Canada. [0-7172-1957-7].

Ross, Judy. Le caribou. [0-7172-1994-1].

Ross, Judy. Le huart. [0-7172-1966-6].

Ross, Judy. Le loup. [0-7172-1999-2].

Ross, Judy. L'orignal. [0-7172-1971-2].

Savage, Candace. Le pélican. [0-7172-1979-X].

Schemenauer, Elma. L'antilope d'Amérique. [0-7172-1981-X].

Schemenauer, Elma. Le saumon. [0-7172-1959-3].

Shawver, Mark. Les cétacés. [0-7172-1998-4].

Shawver, Mark. Les lions. [0-7172-1970-4].

Switzer, Merebeth. Les aigles. [0-7172-1988-7].

Switzer, Merebeth. Le boeuf musqué. [0-7172-1986-0].

Switzer, Merebeth. Les lapins. [0-7172-4376-1].

Switzer, Merebeth. Le lynx. [0-7172-1969-0].

Switzer, Merebeth. Le phoque. [0-7172-1980-1].

Switzer, Merebeth. Les rapaces diurnes. [0-7172-1976-3].

Switzer, Merebeth. Le renard roux. [0-7172-1964-X].

Switzer, Merebeth. Les tamias et le suisse. [0-7172-4379-6].

Switzer, Merebeth. Les tortues. [0-7172-1972-0].

Switzer, Merebeth et Grier, Katherine. Les serpents. [0-7172-1978-X].

Taylor, David. Les requins. [0-7172-2155-5].

L'index – guide. [0-7172-1604-7].

UNE NATION EN MARCHE

8 volumes. $4.75 chacun, broché.

A l'intention des écoles, cette collection recrée des péripéties de l'histoire canadienne. *Moyens.*

Neering, Rosemary. La colonisation de l'Ouest. Ill. par Richard Gregory. Tr. par Richard Bergeron. [2-7608-3023-3].

Neering, Rosemary. La construction du chemin de fer. Ill. par Richard Gregory. Tr. par Jean-Pierre Fournier. [2-7608-3025-0].

Neering, Rosemary. La police montée du Nord-Quest. Ill. par Richard Gregory. Tr. par Richard Bergeron. [2-7608-3024-1].

Neering, Rosemary. La ruée vers l'or. Ill. par Richard Gregory. Tr. par Richard Bergeron. [2-7608-3026-8].

Neering, Rosemary. La traite des fourrures. Ill. par Richard Gregory. Tr. par Jean-Pierre Fournier. [2-7608-3027-6].

Neering, Rosemary et Garrod, Stan. Les Loyalistes. Ill. par Merle Smith. Tr. par Jean-Pierre Fournier. [0-88902-482-0].

Neering, Rosemary et Garrod, Stan. La vie en Acadie. Ill. par Merle Smith. Tr. par Richard Bergeron. [0-7608-3020-9].

Neering, Rosemary et Garrod, Stan. La vie en Nouvelle-France. Ill. par J. Merle Smith. Tr. par Albert Ledoux. [2-7608-3021-7].

LES PEUPLES AUTOCHTONES DU CANADA

4 volumes. Etudes Vivantes. $4.95 chacun, broché.

Informations pertinentes sur les peuples autochtones du Canada, leur mode de vie, le partage du travail, leurs légendes et coutumes. Traduit par Serge-André Crète.

Cass, James. Ekahotan, la semeuse de maïs: Les Amérindiens des forêts de l'est. [2-7607-0186-7].

Cass, James. Mistatin, le chasseur de bison: Les Amérindiens des Plaines. [2-7607-0187-5].

Cass, James. Ochechak, le chasseur de caribou: Les Amérindiens de Subarctique. [2-7607-0188-3].

Cass, James, Oyai, le pêcheur de saumon et le sculpteur: Les Amérindiens de la Côte-Nord du Pacifique. [2-7607-0189-1].

LA PREHISTOIRE DU CANADA

6 volumes. Fides. Prix varient.

Cette collection présente les découvertes préhistoriques de chaque région du Canada avant l'arrivée de Jacques Cartier. *Grands, aînés.*

McGhee, Robert. La préhistoire de l'Arctique canadien. $7.95 collé [2-7621-1220-6].

Tuck, James A. La préhistoire de Terre-Neuve et du Labrador. $7.95 collé [2-7621-1219-2].

Tuck, James A. La préhistoire des provinces Maritimes. $12.95 collé [2-7621-1291-5].

Wright, J.V. La préhistoire de l'Ontario. $7.95 collé [2-7621-1037-8].

Wright, J.V. La préhistoire du Québec. $7.95 collé [2-7621-1027-0].

Wright, J.V. Visages de la préhistoire du Canada. $7.95 collé [2-7621-1042-4].

PRIX DE LITTERATURE DE JEUNESSE

CACL MEDAILLE DE BRONZE

Cette médaille de bronze était décernée par l'Association canadienne des bibliothécaires pour enfants (Canadian Association of Children's Librarians) aux livres pour enfants en français les plus marquants des années de 1954 à 1973.

1954 *Mgr. de Laval*, par Emile Gervais. S.J. Comité des Fondateurs de l'Eglise canadienne, 1954.

1955 Pas de prix

1956 Pas de prix

1957 Pas de prix

1958 *Le chevalier du roi*, par Béatrice Clément. Atelier, 1955.

1959 *Un drôle de petit cheval*, par Hélène Flamme. Leméac, 1957.

1960 *L'été enchanté*, par Paule Daveluy. Atelier, 1957.

1961 *Plantes vagabondes*, par Marcelle Gauvreau. Centre de Psychologie et de Pédagogie, 1959.

1962 *Les îles du Roi Maha Maha II*, par Claude Aubry. Pélican, 1960.

1963 *Drôle d'automne*, par Paule Daveluy. Pélican, 1963.

1964 *Férie*, par Cécile Chabot. Librairie Beauchemin, 1962.

1965 *Le loup de Noël*, par Claude Aubry. Centre de Psychologie et de Pédagogie, 1963.

1966 *Le Wapiti*, par Monique Corriveau. Jeunesse, 1964. *Le Chêne des tempêtes*, par Andrée Maillet. Fides, 1965.

1967 Pas de prix

1968 *Légendes indiennes du Canada*, par Claude Mélançon. Jour, 1967.

1969 Pas de prix

1970 *La merveilleuse histoire de la naissance*, par Lionel Gendron. Homme, 1969.

1971 *La surprise de dame chenille*, par Henriette Major. Centre de Psychologie et de Pédagogie, 1970.

1972 Pas de prix

1973 *Le petit sapin qui a poussé sur une étoile*, par Simone Bussières. Les Presses Laurentiennes, 1972.

PRIX ASTED-CLA

Prix offert en 1974 par l'Association pour l'avancement des sciences et des techniques de la documentation et la Canadian Library Association pour le meilleur livre de l'année pour enfants.

1974 *Ouram*, par Anne Vallières. Leméac, 1973.

PRIX ALVINE-BELISLE

Le prix ASTED-CLA devient en 1974 le prix Alvine-Bélisle. C'est à ce moment que l'Association pour l'avancement des sciences et des techniques de la documentation a pris la responsabilité du secteur français. Le prix est décerné à la meilleure oeuvre de littérature canadienne-française pour la jeunesse. Le prix est remis pendant le congrès annual de l'ASTED à l'automne.

1975 *Jeanne, fille du roy*, par Suzanne Martel. Fides, 1974.

1976 *Les saisons de la mer*, par Monique Corriveau. Fides, 1975.

1977 *Emilie, la baignoire à pattes*, par Bernadette Renaud. Héritage, 1976.

1978 *L'évangile en papier*, par Henriette Major. Ill. par Claude Lafortune. Fides, 1977.

1979 *La petite fille aux yeux rouges*, par Gabrielle Grandbois-Paquin. Fides, 1978.

1980 *Les quatre saisons de Piquot*, par Gilles Vigneault. Ill. par Hugh John Barrett. Nouvelles Editions de l'Arc, 1979.

1981 *Le visiteur du soir*, par Robert Soulières. Pierre Tisseyre, 1980.

1982 *Le voyage à la recherche du temps*, par Lucie Ledoux. Ill. par Philippe Béha. Mondia, 1981.

1983 Je deviens grand: *J'aime Claire, Pipi dans le pot, Les cheveux, Dors petit-ours*, par Sylvie Assathiany et Louise Pelletier. Ill. par Philippe Béha. Ovale, 1982.

1984 *La soeur de Robert*, par Marie-Louise Gay. Ill. par Marie-Louise Gay. La Courte échelle, 1983.

1985 *Zunik*, par Bertrand Gauthier. Ill. par Daniel Sylvestre. La Courte échelle, 1984.

1986 *Le complot*, par Chrystine Brouillet. La Courte échelle, 1985.

1987

PRIX MARIE-CLAIRE DAVELUY

Le prix est offert annuellement depuis 1969 par l'Association pour l'avancement des sciences et des techniques de la documentation pour l'oeuvre originale la plus marquante soumise dans le cadre d'un concours. Le concours s'adresse à toute personne de 15 à 20 ans, d'expression française, domiciliée au Canada. Deux prix sont attribués: un premier prix de $700 et un deuxième de $300.

1970 *Opium en fraude*, par Robert Chavarie. Paulines, 1971. (1er prix) *Miroir de l'âme*, par André Champagne. (2e prix)

1971 *L'inconnue des Laurentides*, par Monique Sabella. Paulines, 1972. (1er prix) *Raie de lumière*, par Aline Martinet. La Liberté, 1972. (2e prix)

1972 *Lavabosse ou légendes du pays perdu*, par Christian Desrosiers.

1973 *Le naufrage*, par Jean-Pierre Charland. Jour, 1975. (1er prix) *Les voyageurs du temps*, par Reynald Lefebvre. Fides, 1978. (2e prix)

1974 *Raminagradu: Histoires ordinaires pour enfants extraordinaires*, par Louise Aylwin. Jour, 1975.

1975 *L'éveil d'un somnambule*, par Laurier Côté.

1976 Pas de prix

1977 Pas de prix

1978 *Arabesque*, par Christina Sergi. (1er prix) *Le lion des mers*, par Isabelle Bérubé. (2e prix)

1979 *Dont acte*, par Jean-François Chassay.

1980 *Au-delà des rêves*, par Diane Bérard. (1er prix) *Photo périlleuse*, par Roger Lafrance. (2e prix)

1981 *Frédéric Lortie*, par François Pichette. (1er prix) *Un dernier souffle*, par Line Caouette. (2e prix)

1982 *Passages, poésie*, par Denis Filion. (1er prix) *La naissance d'une légende*, par Patrick David Campbell. (2e prix)

1983 *Métamorphose, nouvelle*, par Suzanne Latulippe. (1er prix) *Wandeln, poésie*, par Christopher Park. (2e prix)

1984 *Peaux-Aiment*, par Marc-André Latour.

1985 *Se meurent d'opium*, par Christiane Levesque (1er prix); *Les merveilleuses aventures de Ti-Nomme en pays d'Acadie*, par Norbert Robichard. (2e prix)

1986 *Tension*, par Geneviève Ribordy. (1er prix) *Froid au coeur*, par Daniel Bédard. (2e prix)

1987

PRIX DE LITTERATURE DE JEUNESSE DU CONSEIL DES ARTS DU CANADA

Ce prix a été établi en 1975 et est décerné annuellement par le Conseil des arts du Canada en reconnaissance d'une contribution marquante à la littérature de jeunesse. Deux prix de $5000 étaient offerts à l'auteur et/ou à l'illustrateur de langue française et de langue anglaise dont une oeuvre a été publiée au cours de l'année. Depuis 1980, afin de souligner officiellement l'importance de l'illustration dans la littérature pour la jeunesse, deux prix de $5000 sont attribués chaque année pour un illustrateur dans chaque catégorie. Il y a maintenant quatre prix de $5000 chacun, l'un pour le texte et l'autre pour l'illustration dans chaque catégorie. Les lauréats sont choisis par deux comités nommés par le Conseil des Arts. (Voir Award Winning Books pour les prix de langue anglaise)

1975 *Raminagradu: Histoires ordinaires pour enfants extraordinaires*, par Louise Aylwin. Jour, 1975.

1976 *Emilie, la baignoire à pattes*, par Bernadette Renaud. Héritage, 1976.

1977 Texte: *Lune de neige*, par Denise Houle. La société de belles-lettres, Guy Maheux, 1977. Illustration: *L'évangile en papier*, par Henriette Major. Ill. par Claude Lafortune. Fides, 1977.

1978 Texte et illustration. *La chicane*, par Ginette Anfousse. Ill. par Ginette Anfousse. La Courte échelle, 1978. *La varicelle*, par Ginette Anfousse. Ill. par Ginette Anfousse. La Courte échelle, 1978.

1979 Texte: *Courte-Queue*, par Gabrielle Roy. Ill. par François Olivier. Alain Stanké, 1979. Illustration: *Une fenêtre dans ma tête*, par Raymond Plante. Ill. par Roger Paré. La Courte échelle, 1979.

1980 Texte: *Hébert Luée*, par Bertrand Gauthier. Ill. par Marie-Louise Gay. La Courte échelle, 1980. Illustration: *Les gens de mon pays*, par Gilles Vigneault. Ill. par Miyuki Tanobe. La Courte échelle, 1980.

1981 Texte: *Nos amis robots*, par Suzanne Martel. Héritage, 1981. Illustration: *Les Papinachois*, par Michel Noël. Ill. par Joanne Ouellet. Hurtubise, HMH, 1981.

1982 Texte: *Fabien 1: Un loup pour Rose* et *Fabien 2: Une nuit au pays des malices*, par Ginette Anfousse. Leméac, 1982. Illustration: *Agnès et le singulier bestiaire*, par Marie José Thériault. Ill. par Darcia Labrosse. Pierre Tisseyre, 1982.

1983 Texte: *Hockeyeurs cybernétiques*, par Denis Côté. Paulines, 1983. Illustration: Petit ours: *Grand-maman, Où est ma tétine?*, *Mon bébé-soeur*, *Quand ça va mal*, par Sylvie Assathiany et Louise Pelletier. Ill. par Philippe Béha. Ovale, 1983.

1984 Texte: *Le cercle violet*, par Daniel Sernine. Pierre Tisseyre, 1984. Illustration: Drôle d'école: *Rond comme ton visage*, *Blanc comme neige*, *Petit et grand*, *Un léopard dans mon placard*, par Marie-Louise Gay. Ill. par Marie-Louise Gay. Ovale, 1984.

1985 Texte: *Casse-tête chinois*, par Robert Soulières. Pierre Tisseyre, 1985. Illustration: *L'alphabet*, par Roger Paré. Ill. par Roger Paré. La Courte échelle, 1985.

1986 Texte: *Le dernier des raisins*, par Raymond Plante. Québec/Amérique, 1986. Illustration: *Album de famille*, par Stéphane Poulin. Ill. par Stéphane Poulin. Michel Quintin, 1986; *As-tu vu Joséphine?*, par Stéphane Poulin. Ill. par Stéphane Poulin. Toundra, 1986.

1987 Texte:

Illustration:

LITTERATURE PROFESSIONNELLE

OUTILS PROFESSIONNELS

Animal world in Canadian books for children and young people/Le monde animal dans les livres de jeunesse canadiens. Liste préparée par Irene E. Aubrey. Bibliothèque nationale du Canada, 1983. 24 p. Gratuit.

Association des traducteurs littéraires/Literary translators association. Liste des membres et répertoire des oeuvres traduites/List of members and directory of translated works. $10.00. Pas de ISBN.

Aubrey, Irene E. Notable Canadian children's books: 1975-1979/Un choix de livres canadiens pour la jeunesse: 1975-1979. Bibliothèque nationale du Canada, 1985. 103 p. $8.95 collé [0-660-530040-6]; $10.75 à l'étranger.

Aubrey, Irene E. Pictures to share: illustration in Canadian children's books/Images pour tous: illustration de livres canadiens pour enfants. Bibliothèque nationale du Canada, 1987. 60 p. $4.95 broché [0-660-53763-X]; $5.95 à l'étranger.

Beauchamp, Hélène. Le théâtre pour enfants au Québec: 1950-1980. Hurtubise HMH. $19.95 collé [2-89045-782-6]. (Collection littérature).

Beauchesne, Yves. Animer la lecture pour faire lire ... Asted, 1985. 68 p. $27.00 reliure spirale [2-89055-067-2].

Bibliographie sélective commentée; mieux connaître les Amérindiens et les Inuits avec les enfants. Québec, Ministère de l'Education, 1987.

Canadian translations/Traductions canadiennes 1986. Bibliothèque nationale du Canada, 1987. 498 p. $36.25 [0-660-53802-4]; $43.50 à l'étranger.

Charbonneau, Hélène. Livres en langue française pour les jeunes. Bibliothèque de Montréal, 1985. 382 p. $35.00 relié [2-920374-00-1].

Un choix de livres canadiens pour la jeunesse. Compilée et préparée par Irene E. Aubrey. Bibliothèque nationale du Canada. Publié annuellement. Gratuit.

Gamache, Sylvie. Un, deux, trois, quatre, les tout-petits découvrent le livre. Communication-Jeunesse, 1983. 32 p. $5.00 broché [2-920453-01-7].

Lemieux, Louise. Pleins feux sur la littérature de jeunesse au Canada français. Leméac, 1972. 337 p. $15.95 collé [2-7609-9700-6].

Lire c'est voyager: Livres québécois pour enfants. Communication-Jeunesse, 1986. $2.00 broché. Pas de ISBN.

Livres québécois pour enfants: sélection de Communication-Jeunesse, publié annuellement. Dépliant, $1.00.

Les meilleurs films québécois pour les jeunes. Communication-Jeunesse, 1983. Dépliant, $1.00.

Mystery and adventure in Canadian books for children and young people/Romans policiers et histoires d'aventures canadiens pour la jeunesse. Liste préparée par Irene E. Aubrey. Bibliothèque nationale du Canada, 1983. 18 p. Gratuit.

Potvin, Claude. Le Canada français et sa littérature de jeunesse. Editions CRP, 1981. 185 p. $16.50 collé [0-9690939-0-X].

Rencontres avec les créateurs de livres pour enfants: Auteurs et illustrateurs. Communication-Jeunesse, 1982. $6.00 fiches-rencontres [2-920453-00-9].

Répertoire des prix littéraires 1986. Ministère des Affaires culturelles, 454, place Jacques Cartier, 3e étage, Montréal, Québec. H2Y 3B3. Gratuit. broché [2-550-16749-X].

Répertoire 1986-87. Association des illustrateurs et des illustratrices du Québec, 1986. $7.95. collé [2-9800522-0-5].

Sources of French Canadian children's and young people's books/Sources d'information sur les livres de jeunesse canadiens-français. Liste préparée par Irene E. Aubrey. Bibliothèque nationale du Canada, 1984. 18 p. Gratuit.

Sports and games in Canadian children's books/Livres canadiens sur les sports et les jeux pour la jeunesse. Liste préparée par Irene E. Aubrey. Bibliothèque nationale du Canada, 1982. 12 p. Gratuit.

Turgeon, Raymond, ed. Romans et contes pour les 12 à 17 ans. Editions du Trécarré, 1985. 126 p. $14.95 collé. [2-89249-129-0].

Warren, Louise. Répertoire des ressources en littérature de jeunesse. Le Marché de l'écriture Enr., 1982. 146 p. $12.95 collé [2-920330-02-0].

PERIODIQUES

Bibliographie du Québec. Ministère des Communications du Québec, C.P. 1005, Québec, Québec. G1K 7B5. Mensuel. $75.00.

The Book trade in Canada/L'industrie du livre au Canada. Ampersand Communication Services Inc. Annuel. $27.50.

Canadian children's literature/Littérature canadienne pour la jeunesse. A journal of criticism and review/Une revue de critiques et de comptes rendus. Canadian Children's Literature Association. University of Guelph, D Department of English, Guelph, Ontario. N1G 2W1. 4 nos. par année. $16.00.

Canadian publishers directory: including the names of foreign publishers and their representatives in Canada. Supplément à Quill and Quire, Avril et Octobre. Gratuit avec abonnement ou $15.00 chac.

Canadiana: La bibliographie nationale du Canada. Compilée sous la responsabilité de la Direction des acquisitions et des services bibliographiques de la Bibliothèque nationale du Canada. Bibliothèque nationale du Canada. Mensuel. $154.00; à l'étranger $184.80.

Choix jeunesse: Documentation imprimée. Ministère de l'Education. Centrale des bibliothèques, 1685 rue Fleury est, Montréal, Québec. H2C 1T1. 10 nos. par année. $45.00 inclus la refonte. $30.00 sans la refonte.

Documentation et bibliothèques. ASTED. 7243 rue Saint-Denis, Montréal, Québec. H2R 2E3. 4 nos. par année $28.00. Gratuit pour les membres de l'ASTED.

Government of Canada publications/ Publications du gouvernement du Canada. Centre d'édition du gouvernement du Canada. Approvisionnements et Services Canada, Ottawa, Ontario. K1A 0S9. Trimestriel avec un index annuel. $21.00 par année; à l'étranger $25.00.

La liste des livres disponibles en langue française des auteurs et des éditeurs canadiens. Bibliodata, 1155 avenue Ducharme, Outremont, Québec. H2V 1E2. Abonnement: Periodica Inc., C.P. 444, Outremont, Québec. H2V 4R6. 4 nos par année. $150.00.

Le livre d'ici. S.P.L. 445 rue Saint-François Xavier, Montréal, Québec. H2Y 2T1. 10 nos. par année. $12.00.

Livres et auteurs québécois: Revue critique de l'année littéraire. Université Laval. Annuel. $15.00.

Des livres et des jeunes. L'Association canadienne pour l'avancement de la littérature de jeunesse. C.P. 2152 Succursale Jacques-Cartier, Sherbrooke, Québec. J1J 3Y2. 3 nos. par année $9.50, 6 nos. pour deux ans $18.00.

Lurelu: La seule revue exclusivement consacrée à la littérature québécoise pour la jeunesse. L'Association Lurelu, C.P. 446, Succursale de Lorimier, Montréal, Québec. J7Y 5T7. 3 nos. par année. $7.50.

Nos livres: Revue d'analyse de l'édition nationale. Office des Communications sociales, 4005, rue de Bellechasse, Montréal, Québec. H1X 1J6. 10 nos. par année. $14.00.

Point de repère: Index analytique de périodiques québécois et étrangers. Montréal, Centrale des bibliothèques. 1685 rue Fleury est, Montréal, Québec. H2C 1T1. 6 nos. par année et refonte annuelle. $180.00.

Revue de presse jeunesse. Centre de consultation jeunesse, Bureau de consultation jeunesse, 420 rue Saint-Paul Est, Montréal. H2Y 1H4. Mensuel, $7.00 le numéro.

Vie pédagogique. Direction des ressources matérielles, Ministère de l'éducation, 1035 rue de la Chevrotière, 14e étage, Québec, Québec. G1R 5A5. 6 nos. par année. Gratuit.

AUTHORS / AUTEURS

Ainsley, Luc 123
Akrigg, G.P.V. 73
Akrigg, Helen B. 73
Alderson, Sue Ann 5, 43, 103
Alice, Mary 86
Allen, Robert Thomas 43, 89, 123
Allison, Rosemary 82
Amey, L.J. 92
Amstrong, Jeannette 82
Amtmann, Bernard 95
Anastasiu, Stéphane 3, 101
Andersen, Doris 88, 123
Andersen, Lorrie 96
Anderson, Alda M. 68
Anderson, Allen 70
Anderson, Anne 18
Anderson, Daniel 68
Anderson, Frank W. 70
Anderson, Valerie 35
Andrews, Jan 5
Anfousse, Ginette 5, 103, 123, 147
Angel, Barbara 85
Angel, Michael 85
Angell, Tony 28
Angus, Terry 80
Archer, P. Colleen 91
Armstrong, Audrey L. 65, 72
Arnold, Rist 6
Ashley, L.F. 95
Ashwell, Reg 68
Aska, Warabé 6
Assathiany, Sylvie 3, 101, 146, 147
Asselin, Claude 103
Assiniwi, Bernard 139
Atwood, Margaret 82
Aubert de Gaspé, Phillipe 123
Aubin, Michel 104
Aubrey, Irene E. 92, 96, 148
Aubry, Claude 18, 58, 123, 145
Austrom, Liz 92, 93
Avis, Walter S. 73
Aylwin, Louise 146, 147

Bailey, Lydia 25
Baltensperger, Peter 61
Banfield, A.F. 73, 140
Barbara Smucker 87, 88, 90
Barbeau, Marius 18, 88, 111
Barber, Lois 33
Barker, George 65
Barkhouse, Joyce 18, 65, 82
Barnett, Donald C. 79, 142
Barton, Bob 96
Bassett, John M. 79, 142
Batten, Jack 43
Beauchamp, Hélène 148
Beauchamp-Richards, Huguette 117
Beauchesne, Yves 134, 148
Beaudin, Louise 115
Beaugrand, Honoré 111
Beaulieu, Jacques 117
Bédard, Daniel 146
Béha, Philippe 3, 4, 101
Beissel, Henry 41
Bélisle, Louis-Alexandre 140
Bell, Bill 84
Bellingham, Brenda 43, 56
Bénard, Christian 104
Benham, Mary Lile 79, 142
Benn, Carl 70
Bennett, Paul W. 80
Benois, Alexandre 34
Benoit, François 110
Benoît, Jean 123
Bérard, Diane 146
Bercuson, David Jay 80
Bereiter, Carl 35
Bertelli, Mariella 90
Berton, Pierre 22
Bertrand, Réal 142
Bérubé, Isabelle 146
Betts, Jim 41
Bherer, Harold 137
Bianchi, John 6
Bilson, Geoffrey 43, 56, 123, 124

Bird, Michael 74
Bishop, Carroll Atwater 58
Black, Gerald J. 30
Blades, Ann 6, 43, 87, 88, 89
Blakely, Cindy 23, 114
Blakely, Phyllis Ruth 65
Blakeslee, Mary 44
Blanchet, M. Wylie 58
Bliss, Michael 80
Blohm, Hans 36
Blood, Don 26
Blostein, Fay 92
Bodger, Joan 6
Bolt, Carol 41
Bondy, Robert Joseph 79
Bonic, Thomas 84, 138
Borden, Darryl 6
Bosak, Susan 25
Bothwell, Robert 80
Boucher, Claudette 124
Boulanger, Claudette 24
Boulard, Roselyne 122
Boulton, Roger 32
Bourgeois, Paulette 6, 31, 104
Bourinot, John George 73
Bowers, Neal 73
Boy Scouts of Canada 37
Bradbury, Raymond 44
Bradford, Karleen 44, 56, 58, 59
Brandis, Marianne 56, 89, 91
Brasser, Ted J. 68
Bregman, Alvan 93
Brisebois, Raymond 114
Brochmann, Elizabeth 44
Brooks, Bill 26
Brooks, Martha 65
Brothers Grimm 19
Brouillet, Chrystine 124, 146
Brown, Cassie 71
Brown, George W. 74, 140
Brown, Graham Leslie 79
Brown, Jamie 44, 91
Brown, Susan 44
Brown, Thomas 73
Bruemmer, Fred 26, 63
Buchanan, Joan 6
Burnford, Sheila 44, 88
Bussières, Johanne 111
Bussières, Simone 104, 120, 145
Butchart, Jaylene 44
Butler, Edith 119
Butler, Marian 92
Butts, Ed 23
Cailloux, André 104, 119, 121, 124
Cailloux, Grand-père 121
Cairo, Jasmine 29
Cairo, Shelley 29
Cairo, Tara 29
Callaghan, Morley 44, 124
Calleja, Gina 6
Cameron, Anne 18

Cameron, Silver Donald 44
Camirand, François 121
Campbell, John Gounod 41
Campbell, Maria 65, 81
Campbell, Paddy 41
Campbell, Patrick David 146
Canada. Dept. of Fisheries and Oceans 73
Canada. Dept. of Indian Affairs and Northern Development 36
Canada. Statistics Canada. 73
Cantin, Roger 124
Caouette, Line 146
Carbet, Marie-Madeleine 124
Careless, J.M.S. 79
Cariou, Mavis 93
Carleton, Alex 23
Carr, Emily 65
Carrier, Roch 6, 87, 104, 124
Carrière, Jean 140
Carter, Floreen Ellen 74
Cashman, Tony 71
Cass, James 82, 144
Cass-Beggs, Barbara 33
Caswell, Maryanne 65
Chabot, Cécile 124, 145
Chafe, J.W. 71
Champagne, André 146
Champagne, Carole 124
Charbonneau, Hélène 148
Charland, Jean-Pierre 146
Charlebois-Dumais, Hélène 140
Chase, Edith 6
Chassay, Jean-François 146
Chavarie, Robert 146
Chénard, Madeleine 111
Chetin, Helen 44, 124
Children of La Loche and friends 6
Chislett, Gail 6, 7
Choquette, Adrienne 124
Choquette, Robert 111
Clark, Catherine Anthony 88
Clark, Ella E. 18
Clark, Joan 7, 44, 56, 59, 89, 124
Clark, Patti 29
Clarke, Arthur H. 115
Cleaver, Elizabeth 7, 18, 34, 87, 88
Cleaver, Nancy 18, 111
Clément, Béatrice 145
Clermont, Marie-Andrée 125
Clery, Val 63
Climo, Lindee 7, 27, 87, 118
Cloutier, Cécile 104
Clubb, Angela 31
Coady, Mary Frances 84
Cochrane, Jean 81
Collard, Eileen 71
Collins, David H. 22
Collins, Meghan 18
Collins, Paul 79
Collins, Robert 22, 65
Collura, Mary-Ellen Lang 44, 89, 91

Colombo, John Robert 38
Colter, Rob 38
Common, Dianne L. 68
Connor, Ralph 45
Constantineau, Céline 104
Coombs, Ernie 35
Corbeil, Jean-Claude 74
Corby, Lynda 29
Corrective Collective, The 71
Corrigan, Kathy 7
Corriveau, Bernadette 119
Corriveau, Monique 45, 125, 145
Cosentino, Frank 79
Côté, Denis 125, 147
Côté, Laurier 146
Côté, Marie-Josée 4, 101
Coulombe, Pauline 104
Coulombe-Côté, Pauline 125
Cowan, Doris 80
Cox, Sandra J. 93
Craig, John 45
Craven, Margaret 45
Crean, Patrick 24
Creighton, Helen 18, 33
Culleton, Beatrice 45, 56
Cumming, Peter 45
Cummings, Tom 62
Custode, Michael 22
Cutler, Ebbitt 126
Cutler, Michael 36
Cutt, W. Towrie 56
Cyr, Céline 126
Dabbs, Rickey 75
Dagenais, Gérard 140
Dagg, Anne Innis 27
Damania, Laura 79, 142
Daniel, Alan 26
Daniels, Betty Ternier 31
Darrach, Jim 23
Daveluy, Paule 126, 145
David, Normand 115
Davidson, Marion 56
Davies, Colin 85
Davies, Peter 45
Davis, Ascher 7
Davis, Calvin Lewis 29
Dawe, Tom 38
Day, David 59, 89
Day, Shirley 7
Décary, Marie 126
Demers, Patricia 95
Dempsey, Hugh A. 65, 68
Deprez, Marie Rose 108
Dereume, Angela 17, 85
Des Ruisseaux, Pierre 140
Desbarats, Peter 38
Deschênes, Josseline 126
Desjardins, Denis 126
Deslongchamps, Roxanne 126
Desrosiers, Christian 146
Desrosiers, Sylvie 126

Deverell, Rex 41
Dewdney, Selwyn 69, 82, 90
Dick, Judith 93
Dickinson, Terence 25
Dicks, Stewart Kinloch 79
Dickson, Barry 82, 90
Dingwall, Laima 27, 83, 143
Doan, Helen 29
Dobson, Clive 29
Dobson, Murray 82
Dobson, Vera 82
Doerksen, Nan 56
Dommasch, Hans 63
Dorais, Lucie 77, 143
Doucet, Paul 114
Doucet-Leduc, Hélène 118
Douglas, Charles 115
Douglas, W.A.B. 71
Dowler, Marion 66
Downie, John 56
Downie, Mary Alice 7, 19, 36, 38, 39, 56, 84, 86, 119
Doyle, Brian 45, 89, 126
D'Oyley, Enid F. 19
Dragland, Stan 59
Drawson, Blair 7
Drinkwater, Suzanne 23, 114
Driscoll, Dianne 93
Dubé, Jasmine 122
Dubois, Diane 74, 141
Duchesne, Christiane 104
Dufour, Josée 126
Duggan, James 142
Dumas, Jacqueline 7
Duncan, Frances 45, 59, 127
Dunham, Mabel 88
Dunlop, Marilyn 29
Dunn, Sonja 39
Dupont, Jean-Claude 111, 141
Dupuis, Hector 141
Egoff, Sheila 95
Einarsson, Magnus 71
Elbl, Martin 19
Ellis, Sarah 45
Endicott, Marion 65
Engel, Marian 90
Engelhart, Margaret S. 72
England, Claire 93
English, John 80
Evans, Denise 105
Evans, Hubert 45
Evans, Millie 63
Eyvindson, Peter 7
Fadden, John 139
Fairbairn, Douglas Hall 79
Fairfield, Lesley 7, 8
Fales, Douglas 36
Fardy, B.D. 66
Fasick, Adele M. 93
Faulknor, Cliff 45
Ferguson, Mary 27

Fernandes, Eugenie 8, 105
Ferrier, Shannon 31
Field, Eugene 39
Filion, Denis 146
Fine, Diane 31
Fine, Judylaine 29
Finley, Gerald 77
Finnigan, Joan 19, 111
Fitch, Sheree 39
Fitzharris, Tim 27, 36
Flamme, Hélène 145
Flanagan, Thomas 80
Fleischman, Paul 39
Foon, Dennis 8, 23, 41
Forcade, Robert J. 45
Ford, Joan E. 46
Ford, Karen 66
Forrest, Diane 66
Forsyth, Adrian 27
Fossey, S. Joan Danielson 46
Foster, Janet 27
Fowke, Edith 19, 33, 88
Fox, Mary Lou 19
Franklyn, Mary Eliza 32, 36
Franko, Ivan 19
Freeman, Bill 57, 87, 127
French, Alice 66
Frénette, Pierre 142
Froom, Barbara 27
Fryer, Mary Beacock 57
Fuerstenberg, Anna 41
Fulford, Robert 32
Gaboury, Serge 110
Gaetz, Dayle 59
Gagnon, André 93
Gagnon, Ann 93
Gagnon, Cécile 8, 105, 127
Gagnon, François 78
Gagnon, Gilles 127
Gagnon, Madeleine 127
Gagnon, Maurice 127
Gaitskell, Susan 66
Gallant, Melvin 111
Galloway, Priscilla 8
Gamache, Sylvie 148
Gardner, Alison 79
Garrett, Jennifer 8, 105
Garrod, Stan 81, 142, 144
Gaudreault-Labrecque, Madeleine 127
Gauthier, Bertrand 105, 127, 146, 147
Gautreau, Evalyn 19
Gauvreau, Marcelle 145
Gay, Marie-Louise 4, 8, 87, 102, 105, 106, 146, 147
Gendron, Lionel 118, 145
George, Dan 69
Germain, Georges-Hébert 121
German, Tony 57, 128
Gervais, Emile 145
Gill, Gail 8
Gillen, Mollie 79
Gilliland, Jillian Hulme 36, 119
Gilman, Phoebe 8, 106
Gilroy, Doug 26
Girard, Suzanne 31
Glatt, Louise 33
Godfrey, Martyn 46, 61, 84, 85, 91
Godfrey, W. Earl 29, 141
Goldstyn, Jacques 110
Goller, Claudine 83
Goman, Joan R. 9
Gorosh, Esther 75
Gough, Barry 80
Granatstein, J.L. 80, 142
Grandbois-Paquin, Gabrielle 128, 146
Grant, Janet 80
Greater Vancouver Library Federation 93
Green, Carrolle 9
Green, John F. 9, 106
Green, Lorne 80
Greene, Elizabeth 38
Greenland, Caroline 83, 143
Greenwood, Barbara 57, 91
Gregor, Alexander D. 85
Grey Owl 46, 66
Grier, Katherine 83, 143, 144
Grieve, Walter 42
Grisé, Yolande 113, 120
Grosbois, Paul de 128
Gross, George 66
Gross, Renie 25
Gryski, Camilla 35
Guay, Georgette 42
Guèvremont, Germaine 128
Guillet, Edwin C. 22, 71
Gunnery, Sylvia 46
Haas, Rudi 36
Hacker, Carlotta 66, 142
Hadden Mole, Elsie 9
Haegert, Dorothy 64
Hahn, Sylvia 39
Haig-Brown, Roderick 88
Hall, D.J. 80
Hall, Pam 106
Hall, Pamela 59
Hall, Tom W. 26
Halpenny, Francess G. 74, 94, 140, 141
Halpin, Marjorie M. 69
Halvorson, Marilyn 46, 89, 128
Hamilton, Mary 19, 57, 84
Hamilton, Robert M. 74
Hammond, Franklin 9
Hancock, David A. 29
Hancock, Lyn 66
Hancock, Susan 29
Handman, Fran 9
Hanson, Christilot 66
Harber, Frances 19, 106
Harbury, Martin 83, 143
Harel, Louise 118

Harper, J. Russell 78, 143
Harper, Kenn 24
Harris, Christie 19, 20, 46, 57, 59, 86, 87, 88
Harris, Dorothy Joan 9, 46, 106
Harris, Lawren 33
Harris, R. Cole 64
Harrison, Ted 9, 64, 87
Harvey, Wendy 23
Haseley, Dennis 9
Hasler, Eveline 9
Hattori, Gene 64
Hawkins, Elizabeth M. 69
Haycock, Carol-Ann 94
Haycock, Ken 94
Hayes, John F. 88
Hayne, David 74, 140
Hazbry, Nancy 9, 106
Head, Sandra 42
Heaps, Leo 66
Hearn, Emily 9
Hearn, John 36
Heath, Jeffrey M. 84
Hébert, Françoise 94
Hehner, Barbara 27, 28, 30, 36, 117, 118
Heidbreder, Robert 39
Hémon, Louis 128
Henderson, Gordon 66
Hewitt, Garnet 20, 87, 87, 89
Hewitt, Marsha 57, 90, 128
Hiebert, Susan 46
Hill, Douglas 61
Hill, Kay 20, 66, 88
Hocking, Anthony 77, 137
Hoffman, E.T.A. 34
Hogan, Homer 39
Holgmren, Eric 74
Holmgren, Patricia 74
Hood, Kit 47
Horn, Michael 80
Horner, Susan 83, 143
Hornstein, Reuben A. 25
Hornyansky, Michael 88
Horrall, Stanley 23
Horwood, Harold 23, 71
Hosie, R.C. 26, 141
Houde, Pierre 106
Houle, Denise 111, 147
Houston, James 47, 88, 89, 91, 128, 129
Howard, Richard 23
Howarth, Mary 47
Hudson, Jan 57, 87, 89
Hughes, Monica 47, 48, 59, 61, 62, 87, 91, 129
Hull, Raymond 71
Hunter, Bernice Thurman 48, 90
Huot, Guy 115
Hutchins, Hazel J. 9, 10, 59
Ian Wallace 87, 90
Ibbitson, John 84, 85
Ilmokari, Irina 20
Inglis, R.I. 78

Irvine, Joan 36
Italiano, Carlo 86
Ivy, Bill 83, 143
Jacob, Jo-Anne 118
James, Donna 80
James, Ross 29
Jameson, Anna B. 72
Jefferys, C.W. 71
Jenness, Diamond 69
Jenness, Eileen 69
Jennings, Eve 47
Jesseau, Patricia 27
Jodoin, Rachel 142
Johnson, Philip E. 23
Johnston, Basil 20, 69
Johnston, Jean 66
Johnston, Patronella 20
Johnston, Richard 33
Johnston, Simon 59
Jones, Mary Fallis 71
Jordan, Wendy Adler 69
Jowsey, J.R. 27
Julandré 106
Kahn, Charles 23, 80
Kahn, Maureen 80
Kaiper, Dan 69
Kaiper, Nan 69
Kalbfleisch, Susan 35
Kallman, Helmut 74
Kalman, Rolf 42
Kane, Alice 96
Kaplan, Bess 48
Karstad, Aleta 26
Kassian, Olena 10, 115
Katz, Welwyn 59, 60, 89
Kellerhals-Stewart, Heather 10
Kelly, Nora 71
Kelly, William 71
Kelsey, Elin 83, 143
Kemball, Walter G. 64
Kerr, D.G.G. 64
Kerr, Donald Gordon Grady 141
Khalsa, Dayal Kaur 4, 10
Kidd, Bruce 82
Kidd, Kenneth E. 69
Kilbourne, Frances 10
King, Dennis 85
Kirkness, Verna 83
Kleitsch, Christel 48
Klippenstein, Lawrence 85
Knap, Jerome 37
Knight, Brenda 23
Kobayashi, Terry 74
Kogan, Marilyn H. 94
Kogawa, Joy 57
Kong, Shiu L. 20
Korman, Gordon 48, 49, 129
Kouhi, Elizabeth 39
Kovalski, Maryann 10, 106
Kropp, Paul 49, 84, 85, 129

Kurelek, William 24, 32, 66, 72, 86, 88, 90, 119, 139
Kurius, Professor 25
Kushner, Donn 60, 88
Labrosse, Darcia 106
Lachance, Jeanne 129
Lacoursière, Estelle 115, 116
Laforge, M. 116
Lafortune, Ambroise 137
Lafortune, Claude 24
Lafrance, Roger 146
Lafrenière, Joseph 129
Laganière, Benoît 116
Lahaie, Pierre 116
Lai, Elizabeth 25
Lamarche, Hélène 138
Lambert, Richard S. 88
Lamoureux, Gisèle 116
Landry, Louis 111
Landsberg, Michele 95
Lane, John 39
Lane, Peter 116
Langford, Cameron 49
Laquerre, Dominique 112
Laracque, Bernard 116
Larkin, Bill 81
Larose, Céline 106
LaRouche, Adelle 10
Lasker, David 10
La Terreur, Mara 74
Latour, Marc-André 146
Latulippe, Suzanne 146
Laughton, Barrie 35
Laurence, Margaret 60, 82, 86, 88
Lauvaux, Yves 121
Layton, Aviva 90
Layton, Irving 39
Le Blanc, Monique 114
Leacock, Stephen 49
Leaden, Bruce W. 37
Lear, Edward 39, 87
Lebailly, Andrée 112
Lebeau, Suzanne 122
Leclerc, Félix 121, 138
Ledoux, Lucie 107, 146
Lee, Dennis 39, 40, 86, 87, 88, 89, 90, 91
Lefebvre, Reynald 146
Légaré, Romain 141
Légaré, Yves 141
Legault, Mimi 129
Leibel, B.S. 30
Lemieux, Germain 112
Lemieux, Louise 148
Lemieux, Michèle 10
Lemna, Don 49
Lepage, Roland 122
Lessard, Marie 107
Levchuk, Helen 10
Levert, Mireille 4, 102
Levesque, Christiane 146

Lévesque, Gilbert 137
Levetzow, Joanna von 94
Levine, Dr. Saul 30
Lewis, Robin Baird 10
Lewis, Shirley 95
L'Heureux, Christine 107
Lim, John 64, 67, 86
Lim, Sing 67
Linton, Marilyn 32
Little, Harry Lee 28
Little, Jean 40, 49, 87, 89, 90, 129
Loates, Glen 29
Loewen, Iris 10
Loranger, Francine 129
Lorimer, Rowland M. 94
Lottridge, Celia 11, 57, 83, 130, 143
Lunn, Janet 20, 50, 58, 60, 86, 87, 89, 90, 91
Lussier, Antoine S. 69
MacDonald, George F. 69, 78
Macdonald, Janet 95
Macdonald, Kate 32
Macdonald, R.H. 64
MacEwan, Grant 28, 67
MacEwen, Gwendolyn 20
Mackay, Claire 23, 50, 57, 90, 128, 130
MacKay, Jed 11
Mackenzie, Nadine 130
Mackenzie-Porter, Patricia 50
MacLean, Harrison John 71
MacLean, Janet 66
MacLennan, Hugh 64
Macleod, R.C. 81
MacMechan, Archibald 71
Macmillan, Cyrus 88
MacNeil, Joe Neil 96
Magadini, Peter 33
Maillet, Andrée 145
Major, Henriette 107, 113, 130, 138, 145, 146, 147
Major, Kevin 50, 87, 88, 90, 91, 130
Maloney, Margaret Crawford 20, 87
Manny, Louise 33
Manuel, Ella 50
Marcotte, Danielle 107, 112
Marcus, Susan 11
Markoosie 50
Marquis, Helen 50
Marsh, Audrey 56
Marsh, Winifred Petchey 69
Marshall, Ingeborg 81
Martel, Suzanne 50, 58, 62, 90, 114, 118, 130, 131, 138, 145, 147
Martin, Eva 20
Martin, Pamela 83
Martinet, Aline 146
Massé, Johanne 131
Matas, Carol 62
Matheson, Edward 95
Mathieu-Loranger, Francine 139
Mativat, Daniel 131

Mativat, Marie-Andrée 131
Matresky, Jim 81
Matthews, Geoffrey 64
Mattys, William Charles 79
Maxine 112
Mayles, Stephen 80, 142
Maynard, Fredelle Bruser 67
Mazalto, Maurice 118
Mazalto, Michèle 118
McArthur, Wenda 38
McCarrick, Ismay 37
McConkey, Lois 81, 139
McCutcheon, Jane 35
McDiarmid, Louise 96
McDonough, Irma 74
McDougall, Bruce 80
McDougall, Marina 91
McFarlane, Brian 36, 120
McGee, Harold 70
McGhee, Robert 68, 78, 144
McKeever, Katherine 29
McKenzie, Ruth 67
McLean, J.S. 27
McLean, T.W. 71
McMaster, Beth 42
McNaught, Kenneth 80
McNeil, Florence 50, 60
McNeill, James 88
McQuarrie, Jane 74, 141
McSweeney, Susanne 84
Meeker, Howie 120
Melady, John 67
Mélançon, André 131
Melançon, Claude 116, 145
Mellen, Peter 75
Melling, O.R. 60, 91
Melzack, Ronald 90
Mendelson, Susan 32
Mennil, Paul Delmar 79
Menotti, Gian Carlo 60
Mercer, Anne 75
Mérinat, Eric 119
Metayer, Maurice 20, 112
Méthé, Louise 119
Metson, Graham 71
Mia/Klaus 107
Michailiuk, George 11
Michailiuk, Richard 11
Michaud, Daniel 141
Michaud, Josette 119
Mignault, Guy 122
Mika, Helma 23, 71
Mika, Nick 23, 71
Milks, Robert E. 37
Millard, Nicky 50
Mills, Alan 33
Milnes, Herbert 72
Mintzberg, Yvette 11
Mitchell, W.O. 131
Miville-Deschenes, Jean 131

Moak, Allen 11
Molnar, Gwen 40
Monet, Jacques 139
Monet, Jacques S.J. 81
Monica Hughes 87, 91
Montero, Gloria 50, 51
Montgomery, Lucy M. 51, 52, 67, 131
Montpetit, Raymond 114
Moodie, Susanna 72
Moody, Barry 81
Moore, Christopher 72, 78
Morency, Pierre 122
Morgan, Allen 11, 52, 107
Morgan, Frances 125
Morgan, Murray 72
Morgan, Nicola 12
Morin, Paule-Nicole 122
Morriseau, Norval 20
Morrison, A.L. 32
Morrow, Patrick 37
Morrow, Robert, Jr. 64
Morse, Janice M. 29
Morton, Desmond 80, 81
Motheral, Elva 41
Mowat, Farley 28, 52, 88, 131
Moyles, Gordon 95
Muir, Mary Jane 12
Mullen, Eric 63
Muller, Robin 21, 87, 90, 112
Munsch, Robert 12, 90, 91, 107
Munsil, Janet 12
Munson, Harold 110
Murphy, Joanne Brisson 13
Murphy, Larry 80
Murray, Joan 32, 33
Musgrave, Susan 40
Nanogak, Agnes 21
Neatby, Leslie H. 72
Neering, Rosemary 80, 81, 142, 144
Newfeld, Frank 88
Newman, Fran 24, 40
nichol, b.p. 13
Nichols, Ruth 60, 88
Nicol, Eric 42
Noël, Michel 112, 121, 122, 132, 147
Novelli, Florence 42
Nyberg, Morgan 60
o huigin, sean 40, 87
Obed, Ellen Bryan 13
O'Byrne, Lorainne 38
Ochrymovych, Ariadne 130
O'Hearn, Audrey 52
Oickle, Don 13
O'Keefe, Frank 52
Ondaatje, Christopher 67
Oppenheim, Joanne 13, 87, 89, 90
Osborne, Kenneth 79
Osborne, K.W. 85
Ostiguy, Jean-René 78, 143
Ouellet, Joanne 122

Owens, Judy 24
O'Young, Leoung 82
Ozores, J. Rabbit 13, 114
Pachano, Jane 13, 69, 70, 114, 139, 140
Page, Marie 132
Palmer, Howard 80
Pamenter, Lou 39
Paperny, Myra 52, 87
Paquette, Gaétan 115
Paré, Roger 13, 108, 147
Park, Christopher 146
Parry, Caroline 24
Pasnak, William 60
Pasquet, Jacques 121, 132
Passe-Partout 119
Pasternak, Carol 13
Patenaude, Danyèle 124
Patterson, E. Palmer 81, 83
Patterson, Nancy-Lou 83
Patton, Janice 72
Pavlick, Leon E. 26
Pearse, Jack 35
Pearson, Kit 53, 60
Peck, George K. 83, 144
Pecknold, Adrian 34
Pelletier, Francine 125
Pelletier, Louise 3, 101, 146, 147
Penrose, Gordon 25
Peters, James 82
Peters, Julie 82
Peterson, Len 41
Petrie, A. Roy 79, 80, 142
Petrie, Francis J. 36
Pichette, François 146
Pickersgill, J.W. 142
Pierce, Patricia 72
Piette, Robert 112
Piette, Suzanne 113
Pigeon, Danielle 140
Pigeon, Pierre 132
Piper, Eileen 61, 132
Pirot, Alison Lohans 53
Pitseolak, Peter 67
Pittman, Al 13, 40, 86
Plant, Maria R. 61
Plante, Raymond 53, 121, 132, 147
Poe, Edgar Allan 40, 121
Pomminville, Louise 108
Porsild, A.E. 27, 116
Potvin, Claude 148
Potvin, Gilles 74
Poulin, Stéphane 13, 108, 147
Poulsen, David A. 53
Poupart, Jean-Marie 108
Pratt, Pierre 4
Precious, Carole 142
Préfontaine, Robert R. 141
Prescott, Jacques 116
Prévost, Bernard 116
Prouche 110

Proulx, Jean-Baptiste 132
Provencher, Paul 117
Ptak, Andrew 34
Purich, Donald 70
Québec. Le Ministère des Communications. 137
Québec. Ministère de l'Agriculture des Pêcheries et de l'Alimentation 117
Québec. Ministère des Terres et Forêts 117
Quinlan, Patricia 13
Quintin, Michel 115
Raffi 34
Ramsay, Marion 13
Rancourt, Roger 120
Rawlyk, George A. 56, 84
Ray, Janet 81
Razzell, Mary 30, 53
Reaney, James 42, 58
Redekop, Magdalene 80
Redsky, James 67
Reid, Barbara 13, 108
Reid, Dennis 78, 143
Reid, Dorothy M. 88
Reid, Malcolm 53
Reimer, Isabel 91
Renaud, Bernadette 53, 122, 132, 133, 146, 147
Ribordy, Geneviève 146
Richard, Pierre 116
Richards, Jack 14
Richards, Nancy Wilcox 14, 108
Richards, Robert 117, 118
Richardson, Gillian 53
Richler, Mordecai 61, 88, 89, 133
Richmond, Sandra 53
Ridington, Jillian 82
Ridington, Robin 82
Riley, Louise 88
Rioux, Monique 121
Ripley, Catherine 28
Ripley, Gordon 75
Rising, Jim 29
Rising, Trudy 29
Roache, Gordon 14
Robart, Rose 14
Robert, Jocelyne 118
Roberts, Charles G.D. 53
Roberts, Ken 53, 133
Robertson, Barbara 39, 86
Robichard, Norbert 146
Robinson, Gail 21
Robinson, Helen Caister 67
Robinson, Larry 120
Robinson, Marita 37
Robinson, Sinclair 75
Rocan, Claude 80
Rocher, Suzanne 133
Rochon, Esther 133
Roquebrune, Robert de 133
Ross, Judy 83, 85, 143, 144
Rosser, Eric 14

Rothstein, Etho 14
Roussan, Jacques de 14, 86
Rousseau-Darnell, L. 36
Rowe, Erna Dirks 26
Roy, Gabrielle 53, 108, 133, 147
Roy, Raoul 120
Rubbo, Michael 133
Rubin, Mark 34
Russell, Andy 28, 64
Russell, E.T. 75
Ryan, Judith 81
Ryder, Dorothy E. 94
Ryder, Huia G. 73
Sabella, Monique 133, 146
Sabourin, Marcel 122
Sadiq, Nazneen 54
Saint-Pierre, Christiane 122
St-Pierre, Paul 54
Salata, Estelle 91
Salt, Jim R. 29
Salt, W. Ray 29
Saltman, Judith 14, 95
San Souci, Robert D. 21
Sanschagrin, Joceline 134
Santor, Donald Murray 79
Sarrazin, Johan 14
Sass, Gregory 58, 80
Saunders, Richard 27
Saunders, Robert 80
Savage, Candace 67, 83, 144
Savard, Félix-Antoine 134
Sawicki, Leo 62
Scalabrini, Rita 108
Schemenauer, Elma 78, 83, 144
Schinkel, David 134
Schmidt, René 72
Schuessler, Karl 23
Schuessler, Mary 23
Schultz, Mike 81
Schuyler, George 72
Schuyler, Linda 47
Schwalbe, Monica 25
Schwarz, Herbert T. 21
Scientifix, Professeur 116
Scott, W.B. 28
Scribe, Murdo 21, 87
Scrivener, Leslie 67, 138
Sealey, D. Bruce 69, 80, 85
Sergi, Christina 146
Semine, Daniel 125, 134, 147
Service, Robert W. 40
Seton, Ernest Thompson 28, 54
Sharon, Lois & Bram 34
Sharp, Edith Lambert 58
Shaw, Barbara 14
Shaw, Margaret M. 80
Shawver, Mark 83, 144
Sheffe, Norman 80
Shields, Dorothy 74
Shields, Patricia 93

Shilling, Arthur 70
Shuh, John Hennigar 28
Shuttleworth, Tamara 31
Siamon, Sharon 54
Sillers, Pat 14
Simard, Claire 117
Simard, Rémy 110
Simmie, Lois 14, 40
Siska, Heather Smith 82
Skeoch, Alan 80, 81
Skeoch, Eric 81
Slaight, Annabel 27
Smith, David Allenby 28
Smith, Donald 75
Smith, James K. 142
Smith, T.H. 58
Smucker, Barbara 54, 58, 61, 87, 88, 90, 134
Sneyd, Lola 41
Snow, Kathleen M. 75
Soules, Christine 71
Soules, Gordon 71
Soulières, Robert 108, 109, 113, 134, 146, 147
Souster, Raymond 41
Speare, Jean E. 14
Speirs, J. Murray 29
Spigelman, Martin 142
Spray, Carole 21, 86
Stacey, Robert 78, 143
Stafford, Terry 14
Stanley, George F.G. 23
Stanton, James B. 72
Staunton, Ted 14, 15, 54, 109
Steen, David 30
Steltzer, Ulli 33, 64, 70
Stephens, Paul 48
Stewart, Hilary 70
Stewart, Roderick 142
Stinson, Kathy 15, 90, 109
St. John, Judith 96
Stravinsky, Igor 34
Stren, Patti 15, 54
Stubbs, Gordon, T. 95
Stump, Sarain 41
Sturgis, James 80
Such, Peter 70
Sullivan, Nick 61
Surette, Roy 42
Sutal, Louis 134
Sutterfield, Allen 13
Suzanne Martel 90, 145, 147
Suzuki, David 27, 28, 30, 117, 118
Swainson, Donald 84, 86
Swainson, Eleanor 84, 86
Swede, George 15, 41
Switzer, Merebeth 83, 144
Sylvestre, Daniel 102
Symchych, Victoria 21
Symons, R.D. 73
Takashima, Shizuye 67, 86
Tanaka, Shelley 35, 84, 86

Tanguay, Bernard 135
Tanobe, Miyuki 64, 86
Tappage, Mary Augusta 15
Taylor, Barbara 61
Taylor, Cora 54, 87, 89
Taylor, David 84, 144
Taylor, Lee 54
Teale, Ria 31
Telford, W.P. 79
Tennant, Veronica 54
Tetso, John 67
Theberge, John B. 84
Theberge, Mary T. 84
Thériault, Marie Jose 147
Thériault, Yves 135
Therrien, J. 116
Thomas, Colin 42
Thompson, M.A. 38
Thompson, Richard 15
Thorne, Eunice A. 95
Thurman, Mark 15, 16, 109
Tibo 109
Tomlinson, Betty 70
Tomlinson, Mary 23
Tonnerova, Maria 113
Toronto Public Libraries 96
Town, Florida 78
Toye, William 21, 22, 72, 75, 86, 87, 90
Trelawny, John G. 27
Troendle, Yves 61
Trudel, Marcel 74, 140
Trueman, Stuart 22, 28, 68
Trump, Christopher 81
Truss, Jan 42, 54, 89, 90, 135
Tuck, James A. 78, 144
Turcotte, Diane 135
Turgeon, Raymond 149
Turnbull, Elsie G. 70
Turner, D. Harold 58
Turner, Wesley 81
Updike, Lee R. 70
Ursell, Geoffrey 38
Vachon, André 74, 140
Vachon, Hélène 119
Vallières, Anne 145
Van Camp, J.L. 26
Van Kampen, Vlasta 16, 87
Vance, F.R. 27
Vanhee-Nelson, Louise 109
Varley, Christopher 78, 143
Vesey, Olga 21
Viau, Normand 110
Victorin, Louis-Marie 141
Vigneault, Gilles 109, 121, 146, 147
Villeneuve, Jocelyne 113, 135
Vineberg, Ethel 68
Von Königslöw, Andrea Wayne 16
Vowles, Andrew 26
Waite, P.B. 80
Waite, Peter 80

Wallace, Ian 16, 87, 90
Wallas, James 22
Walsh, Ann 61
Wansbrough, Michael 66
Warnant-Côté, Marie-Andrée 113, 125, 135
Warren, Louise 149
Waterton, Betty 16, 54, 55, 86, 87, 88, 135
Watson-Russell, Anne 23
Watt, Tom 36
Watts, Irene N. 42, 43
Weber, Ken 35, 75, 80
Weihs, Jean 95
Weir, Joan S. 55
Whale Research Group, The 28
Whalen, George 94
Wheeler, Bernelda 16
Whitaker, Muriel 17, 63, 86
Whitaker, Pamela 22
White, Ellen 22
White, Shirley 80
Whitehead, Ruth Holmes 70
Wieler, Diana J. 55, 91
Wilcox, Dr. Kathleen 30
Wilkins, Charles 36
Williams, Saul 70
Williams, Sophia 70
Willing, Kathlene R. 31
Willoughby, Brenda 78
Wilscam, Lynda 135
Wilson, Barbara 17
Wilson, Bruce 72
Wilson, Budge 55
Wilson, Desmond 81
Wilson, Eric 55
Wilson, Jeffery 23
Wilson, Keith 41, 81, 85
Wilson, Mary C. 80
Wilson, Serge 113, 135, 136
Wink, J.T. 19
Winters, Kenneth 74
Wolfson, Steve 17
Wong, Elizabeth K. 20
Wood, Angela 16
Woodcock, George 68, 142
Wooding, Frederick H. 28
Woods, Shirley E. 28
Wrenshall, G.A. 30
Wright, Helen K. 85
Wright, J.V. 78, 144
Wright, R.H. 30
Wrigley, Robert E. 28
Wynne-Jones, Tim 17, 41, 87, 90, 109
Yates, Elizabeth 136
Yee, Paul 55, 58
Young, Scott 55, 56
Zalan, Magda 56
Zemans, Joyce 78, 143
Zinnemann-Hope, Pam 17
Zola, Meguido 17, 78, 84, 85
Zola, Melanie 84

TITLES / TITRES

ABC 7
ABC & 123 17
ABC/123: the Canadian alphabet and counting book 16, 87
ABC du hockey, L' 120
Abécédaire de Pitatou, L' 108
Abeilles, Les 143
Acadians, The 81
Acadie sans frontières, L' 119
Achimoona 38
Adagio 121
Adam Beck 80
Adèle Mystère et Clément Secret 118
Adieu, Sarah! 123
Adventure of nature photography, The 36
Adventurers, The: ordinary people with special callings 66
Adventures with wild animals 28
Aerobic fun for kids 30
Afraid of the dark 82, 90
Afraid to ask: a book about cancer 29
Agnès et le singulier bestiaire 147
Agouhanna 123
Ah! belle cité!/A Beautiful city ABC 13, 108
Ah, ces oiseaux! 104
Aigles, Les 144
Ain't lookin' 45
Akavak 128
Alberta 77
Album de famille 108, 147
Album of New France 81
Album of the Great War 81
Album of Western settlement 81
Alerte au lac des loups 125
Alexander Graham Bell 78, 80, 142
Alfred dans le métro 105, 127
Alfred, le manchot 143
Algonkian hunters of the Eastern Woodlands 83
Alice: a wonderland 42
Alien war games 61
All kinds of magic 60
Allan Napier MacNab 142

Allegro 121
Aller retour 134
Alligator pie 39, 88, 90
Alligators 84
Alphabet, L' 108
Alphonse Desjardins 142
Alphonse has an accident 46
Alpine path, The: the story of my career 67
Am I the only one?: a young people's book about sex abuse 23
Amahl and the night visitors 60
Amanda et le génie 127
Amanda, the gorilla 85
Amazing apple book, The 31
Amie and Anika 14
Amish adventure 54
Amok, le gorille 143
Amour, réglisse et chocolat 126
Amphibians of Canada, The 27
Amy's wish 84
Anastasia Morningstar and the crystal butterfly 59
Anciens canadiens, Les 123
Ancient ships on American shores 22
And I'm never coming back 7
And to-morrow the stars: the story of John Cabot 88
Andante 121
Angel square 45
Ani Croche 127
Animal fables and other tales retold 19
Animal parade: a children's musical 42
Animal tracks and hunter signs 28
Animal world in Canadian books for children and young people/Le monde animal dans les livres de jeunesse canadiens 92, 148
Animalerie des petits débrouillards, L' 118
Animer la lecture pour faire lire ... 148
Annabel Lee 40, 121
Anna's pet 82
Anne, la maison aux pignons verts 131
Anne of Avonlea 51

Anne of Green Gables 51
Anne of Green Gables cookbook, The 32
Anne of Ingleside 51
Anne of the Island 51
Anne of Windy Poplars 51
Anne-Marie Maginol tu me rends folle 103
Anne's house of dreams 51
Anniversaire de Douglas, L' 109
Antilope d'Amérique, L' 144
Antique furniture by New Brunswick craftsmen 73
Antoine, le grognon 108
Ants 83
Anytime stories 62
Apple butter 42
Appleseed: the newsletter of The Storytellers School of Toronto 96
April Raintree 45
Arabesque 146
Araignées, Les 143
Arbre aux ballons, L' 106
Arbre, L' 101
Arbres indigènes du Canada 141
Arbrier québécois, L' 115
Archer blanc, L' 128
Archibaldo le dragon 109
Arctic animals: a celebration of survival 26
Arctic, The 26
Armadillo is not a pillow, An 40
Arms, flags and emblems of Canada, The 23
Artisan de la nature 119
As ever, Booky 48
As she began: an illustrated introduction to Loyalist Ontario 72
Ascenseur d'Adrien, L' 127
Ashini 135
Asphalt octopus, The: a child's world in poetry 41
Association des traducteurs littéraires/Literary translators association. Liste des membres et répertoire des oeuvres traduites/List of members and directory of translated works 148
As-tu vu Joséphine? 108, 147
At grandmother's house 67
Atlas des jeunes québécois 140
Atlas du Canada 140
Atlas historique du Canada 141
Atlas of Canada 64
Atterrissage forcé 134
Au revoir cauchemars! 106
Au temps de Marguerite Bourgeoys quand Montréal était un village 138
Au-delà de la rivière noire 129
Au-delà des rêves 146
Au-delà du soleil/Beyond the sun 14, 86
Audio-visual media for children in the public library 94
Aunt Armadillo 10
Auntie's knitting a baby 40

Autobus à Margo, L' 126
Automne 101
Aventures de Frizelis, Les 124
Aventures de la canicule, Les 125
Aventures des petits débrouillards, Les 110
Baabee books, The. Series I 4
Baabee books, The. Series II 4
Baabee books, The. Series III 4
Baby, Baby 84
Baby Beluga book 34
Baby project, The 45
Bach et Bottine 132
Bad day, The 3
Baiser maléfique, Le 113
Baitchopper, The 44
Bal des chenilles, Le 108
Baleines viennent-elles dans le golfe Saint-Laurent? Sont-elles de gros poissons?, Les 116
Ballade de Monsieur Bedon, La 106
Ballet book, The: a young dancer's guide 34
Balloon tree, The 8
Bare naked book, The 15
Barnaby and Mr. Ling 11
Bath, The 5
Battle of York, The 70
Beast, The 84
Beau soleil, Un 103
Beaver, The: exploring Canada's history 75
Beavers 83
Bébé, Le 107
Beckoning lights 61
Bees 83
Bel Ria 44
Belettes, Les 143
Belinda's ball 6
Benjamin et la nuit 104
Ben's snow song: a winter picnic 9
Bernache du Canada, La 144
Bertram Brooker 78, 143
Best of the Group of Seven, The 33
Best of Tom Thomson, The 33
Beware the Fish! 48
Beyond Everest: quest for the seven summits 37
Bible en papier, La 113
Bibliographie du Québec 149
Bibliographie sélective commentée; mieux connaître les Amérindiens et les Inuits avec les enfants 148
Bibliography of Canadian children's books and books for young people 1841-1867/Livres de l'enfance et livres de la jeunesse au Canada 1841-1867 95
Bicycle camping in Canada 37
Bicyclette neuve, La 109
Bien mauvaise grippe, Une 108
Big bang, The: the creation of the universe 25
Big city ABC, A 11
Big or little? 15
Big Sarah's little boots 6

Big secret, The 11
Big tree and the little tree, The 15
Bighorn sheep 83
Billy Bishop & the Red Baron 41
Billy Higgins rides the freights 50
Binky and the bamboo brush 10
Birds of Alberta with their ranges in Saskatchewan and Manitoba, The 29
Birds of Canada, The 29
Birds of Ontario: Volumes I and II 29
Bison 83
Bison, Le 143
Black bears 83
Black diamonds: a search for Arctic treasure 47
Black joke, The 52
Blacksmith of Fallbrook, The: the story of Walter Cameron – blacksmith, woodcarver, raconteur 65
Blaine's way 47
Blanc comme neige 102, 147
Blind date 91
Blind dates 41
Bling said hello, The 42
Blink: a strange book for children 40
Blizzard leaves no footprints, A 42
Blue castle 51
Bluenose ghosts 18
Bobosse, le chameau 143
Boeuf musqué, Le 144
Boîte magique très embêtante, Une 122
Bo'jou, Nejee!: profiles of Canadian Indian art 68
Bon voyage, Baabee 4
Bonhomme d'Hélène, Le 107
Bonjour l'arbre 105
Bonjour, Monsieur de La Fontaine 122
Bonnie McSmithers is at it again! 5
Bonnie McSmithers (you're driving me dithers) 5
Book dragon, A 60
Book of Canadian fishes, The 28
Book of Grey Owl, A: pages from the writings of Wa-Sha-Quon-Asin 46
Book of Small, The 65
Book trade in Canada, The/L'industrie du livre au Canada 95, 149
Books for young people 96
Books in Canada 96
Boss of the Namko Drive 54
Bouches décousues 122
Bourinot's rules of order 73
Boy at Leafs' camp, A 55
Boy called Nam, A: the true story of how one little boy came to Canada 66
Boy of Taché, A 43
Boy on defense 56
Boy who loved music, The 10
Boy who walked backwards, The 91
Boy with an R in his hand, The 58
Bozo, l'orang-outan 143

Brave petit Tamia, Le 111
Breaking Smith's quarter horse 54
Breed apart, A 57
Brenda and Edward 10
Brian McFarlane's NHL hockey 36
British Columbia 77
British Columbia place names 73
Brownies around the world, Book 1 37
Brownies around the world, Book 2 37
Brownies around the world, Book 3 37
Brownies around the world, Book 4 37
Brum, the Siberian tiger 85
Bruno et Boots mènent le bal 129
Bûcherons, Les 139
Budgeting for children's services 94
Buffalo hunt, The 84, 86
Bugs Potter live at Nickaninny 48
Building a new life 81
Building an igloo 64
Building of the railway 81
Bungalo boys, The: last of the tree ranchers 6
Burial at L'Anse-Amour, The 68
Burn out 84
Busy nights 6
Butter down the well: reflections of a Canadian childhood 65
Butterscotch dreams: chants for fun and learning 39
Buzz 75
By the light of the Quilliq: Eskimo life in the Canadian Arctic 69
By the sea: an alphabet book 6, 87, 89
Byron and his balloon/Byrón chu bets'i balloón: an English-Chipewyan counting book 6
C.W. Jeffreys 78, 143
Cachette, La 103
Cailloux voient du pays, Les 133
Cake that Mack ate, The 14
Camels can make you homesick and other stories 54
Camion, Le 107
Campfire programs 35
Can you catch Josephine? 13
Can you promise me spring? 53
Canada 77
Canada and the world 76
Canada and the world: an atlas resource 64
Canada coast to coast 32
Canada français et sa littérature de jeunesse, Le 148
Canada goose 83
Canada handbook, The 73
Canada in colour 63
Canada in space 81
Canada, the missing years: the lost images of our heritage, 1895-1924 72
Canada: windows on the world 79
Canada's native people 79
Canadian almanac & directory 1987 73
Canadian-American relations 79

164 TITLES / TITRES

Canadian Arctic prehistory 78
Canadian books for older children 93
Canadian books for younger children 92
Canadian books in print: author and title index 92
Canadian books in print: subject index 92
Canadian children's literature/Littérature canadienne pour la jeunesse 96, 149
Canadian collections in public libraries 94
Canadian dictionary for children, The 73
Canadian disasters 72
Canadian encyclopedia, The 73
Canadian entry 66
Canadian fairy tales 20
Canadian films for children and young adults 93
Canadian folk songs for the very young 33
Canadian geographic 76
Canadian nature notebook 26
Canadian Oxford intermediate atlas 64
Canadian periodical index 96
Canadian picture books/Livres d'images canadiens 74, 141
Canadian publishers directory: including the names of foreign publishers and their representatives in Canada 149
Canadian reference sources 94
Canadian school housed-public library, The 92
Canadian selection: books and periodicals for libraries 93
Canadian songbirds and their ways 29
Canadian students' dictionary 73
Canadian translations/Traductions canadiennes 1986 93, 148
Canadian wildflowers 27
Canadian world almanac and book of facts 1987, The 73
Canadian yuletide treasury, A 24
Canadiana: La bibliographie nationale du Canada 149
Canadians all: portraits of our people 80
Canadians all 2: portraits of our people 80
Canadians all 3: portraits of our people 80
Canadians all 4: portraits of our people 80
Canadians all 5: portraits of our people 80
Canadians all 6: portraits of our people 80
Canadians at war 1914-1918 79
Canadians at war 1939-1945 79
Canadians at work: labour, unions and industry 79
Canadians of long ago 69
Canadiens, Les: the French in Canada 1600-1867 79
Canard malard, Le 143
Candle for Christmas, A 14
CANSCAIP membership directory 1987 73
Caribou 83
Caribou, Le 144
Carnets d'histoire naturelle 115
Carry my bones northwest 56
Cartier discovers the St. Lawrence 72, 88

Casey visits the doctor 11
Casimir Gzowski 80
Casse-cou de la rivière Koksoak, Les 128
Casse-tête chinois 134, 147
Castor, Le 143
Castor, the beaver 85
Cat in the cathedral, The 53
Catastrophes de Rosalie, Les 123
Cat's cradle, owl's eyes: a book of string games 35
Cave, Le 129
Cave of snores, The 9
Celebration: 75 years of challenge and change 37
Cercle violet, Le 134, 147
Cerfs, Les 143
Cerveau de la ville, Le 129
Ces enfants de ma vie 133
C'est ta fête 120
Cet hiver-là 126
Cétacés, Les 144
Chain of words, A 43
Chandail de hockey, Le 104
Changing times: Baby William/Les temps changent: Bébé William 69
Changing times: Bobby and Mary at home/Les temps changent: Bobby et Mary chez eux 69
Changing times: clothing/Les temps changent: Le vêtement 70
Changing times: transportation/Les temps changent: moyens de transport 70
Chansons et comptines 119
Chansons pour un ordinateur 129
Chant de l'alouette, Le 120
Charles Huot 78, 143
Charles Mair 80
Chas de l'aiguille, Le 119
Chasse-galerie, La (Beaugrand) 111
Chasse-galerie, La (Chénard) 111
Chat de l'oratoire, Le 133
Chemins secrets de la liberté, Les 134
Chêne des tempêtes, Le 145
Cher printemps 126
Chester's barn 27, 87
Cheval de plume, Le 126
Cheval du nord, Le 112
Chevalier du roi, Le 145
Chevaux sauvages, Les 143
Cheveux, Les 146
Chez moi 101
Chicane, La 103, 147
Chickadee 76
Chicken pox 5
Chien de prairie, Le 143
Chien d'or, Le 113
Child in prison camp, A 67, 86
Children and the law 23
Children of the first people 64
Children of the North 63
Children of the Yukon 64

Children's book news, The 76, 96
Children's choices of Canadian books 93
Childview: evaluating and reviewing materials for children 93
Chin Chiang and the dragon's dance 16, 87, 90
Chinook 41
Chipmunks 83
Choix de livres canadiens pour la jeunesse, Un 148
Choix jeunesse: Documentation imprimée 149
Chouchou, Le 105
Christmas in the big igloo 24
Christmas tree from Puddin' Stone Hill, A 9
Christmas wolf, The 58
Christopher and the dream dragon 11
Christopher and the elevator closet 11
Chronicles of Avonlea 51
Cibles; esprit et techniques des scouts et guides 120
Cité inconnue, La 134
City scrapes 15
City under ground, The 62
Claire-de-la-lune et Barbarou 107
Clam made a face, The: a play for children 42
Click 82
Clifford Sifton 80
Clins d'oeil & pieds de nez 121
Cliptail 53
Clothing in English Canada circa 1867 to 1907 71
Clouds on the clothesline & 200 other great games 35
Club des curieux, Le 130
Clyde 7
CM: a reviewing journal of Canadian materials for young people 96
Coast Salish: their art, culture and legends 68
Colibri, Le 143
Collected poems of Robert Service, The 40
Collection development 94
Collection of Canadian plays, Volume IV, A 42
Colonisation de l'Ouest, La 144
Comet's tale 43
Comme les six doigts de la main 131
Comment nourrir les oiseaux autour de chez-soi? 115
Community outreach and publicity 94
Compagnons du soleil, Les 125
Compendium of Canadian folk artists, A 74
Complete outdoorsman's handbook, The: a guide to outdoor living and wilderness survival 37
Complot, Le 124, 146
Comptines traditionnelles du Canada français 121
Computers in the library 94
Concise dictionary of Canadianisms 73
Confederation 81
Confederation: a new nationality 80
Confederation generation, The 71

Confident years, The: Canada in the 1920's 79
Connections two: writers and the land 74
Construction du chemin de fer, La 144
Contes de Bohème 113
Contes de bûcherons 111
Contes de l'arc-en-ciel, Les 130
Contes de ma ville 125
Contes de mon igloo 112
Contes de mon pays 112
Contes de Tantana 124
Contes des quatre saisons 135
Contes du Chalin aux îles Saint-Pierre et Miquelon, Les 112
Contes québécois 111
Cookie bookie, The 31
Costume guide and suggestions, 1848-1868 36
Cougar, Le 143
Cougars 83
Could Dracula live in Woodford? 47
Coulicou 141
Courte-Queue 108, 147
Coutumes Cris: La cérémonie des premiers pas/ Cree customs: walking out ceremony 139
Cowboy Kid, The 53
Cowboys don't cry 46, 89
Coyote 83
Coyote, Le 143
Crabs wear their skeletons on the outside 28
Crapauds et autres animaux 121
Crazy ideas 53
Cree customs: Walking-Out Ceremony/ Coutumes Cries: la cérémonie des premiers pas 70
Cremation of Sam McGee, The 40
Cricket Christmas 10
Cris des marais, Les 139
Crisis on Conshelf Ten 62
Croque-notes 121
Cross of Valour 67
Crowfoot 142
Cry to the night wind 58
CSLA policy statement: a recommended curriculum for education for school librarianship 93
Curse of the Viking grave, The 52
Curses of Third Uncle, The 58
Cuthbert Grant and the Métis 85
Cycle Canada 76
Cyclone Jack 41
Dame épouvantail, La 124
Dancing feathers 48
Danger on the tracks 57
Dangerous cove, The: a story of early days in Newfoundland 88
Dans mon petit violon 120
Daring game, The 53
Dark, The 12
Darnell stamps of Canada catalogue 36
Dassen, the penguin 85
David Klassen and the Mennonites 85

David Suzuki talks about AIDS 30
David Thompson 142
David's father 12
Days of terror 58, 87, 88, 90
De l'autre côté de l'avenir 131
De vieux amis, de nouveaux amis 109
De zéro à minuit 106
Dead on 84
Dear Bruce Springsteen 50
Dear Doctor: teenagers ask about ... 30
Dear mom, dear dad: poems for everyone 38
Death on the ice 71
Death over Montreal 56
Death ride 85
Deer 83
Déguisements d'Amélie, Les 107
Demande à Isabelle: dictionnaire descriptif, phonologique, analogique et orthographique du vocabulaire actif 141
Depression, The 81
Depression years, The: Canada in the 1930's 79
Dernier des raisins, Le 132, 147
Dernier souffle, Un 146
Dernier voyage du Scotian, Le 127
Dernier-né des Cailloux, Le 133
Des animaux pour rire 121
Des bleus et des bosses 126
Des dieux et des hommes 135
Des livres et des jeunes 149
Des mots pour se connaître 120
Deux grands ducs dans la famille 131
Devil on my back 62
Devil's diamond, The 58
Dialogues d'hommes et de bêtes 121
Dictionary of Canadian biography. Index. Volume I-IV. 1000-1800 74
Dictionary of Canadian biography. Volume I. 1000-1700 74
Dictionary of Canadian biography. Volume II. 1701-1740 74
Dictionary of Canadian biography. Volume III. 1741-1770 74
Dictionary of Canadian biography. Volume IV. 1771-1800 74
Dictionary of Canadian biography. Volume V. 1801-1820 74
Dictionary of Canadian biography. Volume VI. 1821-1835 74
Dictionary of Canadian biography. Volume VIII. 1851-1860 74
Dictionary of Canadian biography. Volume IX. 1861-1870 74
Dictionary of Canadian biography. Volume X. 1871-1880 74
Dictionary of Canadian biography. Volume XI. 1881-1890 74
Dictionary of Canadian quotations and phrases, The 74
Dictionary of literary biographies 74
Dictionnaire biographique du Canada, volume I 140
Dictionnaire biographique du Canada, volume II 140
Dictionnaire biographique du Canada, volume III 140
Dictionnaire biographique du Canada, volume IV 140
Dictionnaire biographique du Canada, volume V 141
Dictionnaire biographique du Canada, volume VIII 141
Dictionnaire biographique du Canada, volume IX 141
Dictionnaire biographique du Canada, volume X 141
Dictionnaire biographique du Canada, volume XI 141
Dictionnaire CEC jeunesse 141
Dictionnaire des difficultés de la langue française au Canada 140
Dictionnaire des écrivains québécois contemporains 141
Dictionnaire des synonymes et des antonymes 141
Dictionnaire nord-américain de la langue française 140
Different dragons 49
Difficult day, A 8
Dig, The 78
Dingles, The 10
Dinner at Auntie Rose's 12
Dinner party, The 40
Dinosaur country: unearthing the Badlands' prehistoric past 25
Dirt bike 84
Dirtbikes at hangman's clubhouse 54
Discovery and exploration: a Canadian adventure 79
Disneyland hostage 55
Doctor's sweetheart, The and other stories 51
Documentation et bibliothèques 149
Dodo, Le 107
Dog who stopped the war, The 54
Dog who wanted to die, The 91
Dog who wouldn't be, The 52
Donald Jackson, king of the blades 66
Donald Smith and the Canadian Pacific Railway 85
Dont acte 146
Don't call me Sugar Baby! 46
Don't Care High 48
Don't cut my hair 3
Don't eat spiders 39
Dope deal 84
Dors petit-ours 101, 146
Dos bleu, le phoque champion 131
Double knights, The: more tales from round the world 88
Double spell 50

Douze saynètes de Noël 122
Down by Jim Long's stage: rhymes for children and young fish 40, 86
Downy woodpecker 83
Dr. Zed's dazzling book of science activities 25
Dragon dans la garde-robe, Un 106
Dragon on parade 7
Dream catcher, The 62
Drôle d'automne 126, 145
Drôle de petit cheval, Un 145
Druid's tune, The 60, 91
Dudley and the birdman 15
Early Canadian children's books 1763-1840: a bibliographical investigation into the nature of early Canadian children's books and books for young people/Livres de l'enfance et livres de la jeunesse au Canada 1763-1840: étude bibliographique 95
Earthdark 62
École, L' 103
Ecoute, l'oiseau chantera 129
Ecoute, mon ami 121
Écureuil, L' 144
Edgar Potato 13
Edwin H. Holgate 78, 143
Edythe with a Y 44
Egerton Ryerson 79, 142
Egg-carton zoo 36
Eight plays for young people: prairie performance II 41
Ekahotan, la semeuse de maïs: Les Amérindiens des forêts de l'est 144
Ekahotan, the corn grower: Indians of the eastern woodlands 82
Elephant jam 34
Elephant's cold, The 15
Elik and other stories 21
Elisabeth Simcoe 142
Elise et l'oncle riche 130
Elitekey: Micmac material culture from 1600 A.D. to the present 70
Elk 83
Emergency librarian 96
Emile Nelligan 142
Emilie de la Nouvelle Lune 131
Emilie, la baignoire à pattes 133, 146, 147
Emily 66
Emily Carr 80, 142
Emily Carr: the story of an artist 65
Emily climbs 51
Emily Murphy 80
Emily of New Moon 51
Emily Umily 7
Emily's quest 51
Emperor's panda, The 59, 89
Empty chair, The 48
En avant voyageurs! 136
En été 104
En hiver 107

En montant à Low 126
En pleine terre 128
En toute liberté 128
Enchanted caribou, The 18
Enchanted tapestry, The 21
Enchanteur du pays d'Oz, L' 135
Encore des expériences 116
Encyclopedia of music in Canada 74
Encyclopédie des oiseaux du Québec 141
Encyclopédie du Canada, L' 141
Energy 81
Enfant de la maison folle, L' 104
Enfant perdu et retrouvé, L' 132
Enfant venu d'ailleurs, L' 132
Enfants du bonhomme dans la lune, Les 124
Ensemble, si on chantait 120
Envoûtements, Les 134
Épée Arhapal, L' 134
Épouvantail et le champignon, L' 127
Ernest Thompson Seton 80
Escape: adventures of a Loyalist family 57
Esclave des Haïdas 123
Espagnole et la Pékinoise, L' 133
Et la vie par devant 126
Et le cheval vert 124
Étang apprivoisé, L' 116
Été 102
Été enchanté, L' 126, 145
Été inoubliable, Un 128
Étranger sous la ville, L' 133
Évangile en papier, L' 113, 146, 147
Éveil d'un somnambule, L' 146
Every girl: learning about menstruation 29
Everyman's heritage: an album of Canadian folk life 71
Exit Barney McGee 50
Exodus of the Japanese, The 72
Expériences scientifiques du Centre des sciences de l'Ontario 115
Exploring the night sky: the equinox astronomy guide for beginners 25
Extraordinary tales from Manitoba's history 71
Fabien 1: Un loup pour Rose 123, 147
Fabien 2: Une nuit au pays des malices 123, 147
Fables and legends from ancient China 20
Fables des trois commères, Les 104
Fair play 84
Falcon bow, The: an Arctic legend 47
Fall 4
False face 59
Falstaff, the hippopotamus 85
Famille Citrouillard aux poissons des chenaux, La 108
Fantôme à bicyclette, Un 127
Far from shore 50, 91
Farmer Joe's hot day 14
Farmyard, The 3
Fate of the Griffon, The 71
Feeding wild birds in winter 29

Feelings 13
Fend-le-vent et le visiteur mystérieux 136
Fend-le-vent: Les bonhommes jaunes 135
Fenêtre dans ma tête, Une 147
Férie 145
Fête, La 103
Feux follets, Les 111
Fieldbook for Canadian Scouting 37
50 below zero 12
50 more things to make and do: year-round activities from Mr. Dressup 35
Fifty trees of Canada east of the Rockies 26
Fight, The 5
Fille à la mini-moto, La 130
Find your coat Ned 17
Fingerprinting: a science at your fingertips 23
Finnish fairy tales and stories for children 20
Fire! Fire! 84
Fire stealer, The 21
Firefighter, The 82
Fireside book of Canadian Christmas, The 24
First spring on the Grand Banks 57
Flabbergast 76
Flare 76
Flashback 82
Fleur et autres personnages, La 124
Flight of the roller-coaster: poems for younger readers 41
Flip the dolphin saves the day 10
Flore Laurentienne 141
Fly away Paul 45
Flying and swimming creatures from the time of the dinosaurs 26
Flying ship, The. ... and other Ukrainian folk tales 21
Folk songs of Canada 33
Folk songs of Quebec (Chansons de Québec) 33
Folktales of French Canada 19
Foodworks: an Ontario Science Centre book 32
Forêt derrière les arbres, La 116
Forty years a chief 65
Four seasons for Toby 9
Four seasons west 64
Fourmis, Les 143
Fox Mykta 19
Fox of a thousand faces 41
François d'Assise 138
François de Laval, Seigneur de la Côte 137
François et l'oiseau du Brésil 121
Franklin in the dark 6
Franklin of the Arctic 88
Fraude électrique 110
Frédéric Lortie 146
Frederick Banting 80
Frederick H. Varley 78, 143
Free stuff for kids 36
Free! The Newsletter of free materials and services 96
Freshwater fishes of Canada 73

Freshwater fishes of eastern Canada 28
Fridge, The 4
Friend called 'Chum', A 16
Friend just like you, A 13
Frogs 83
Froid au coeur 146
From Anna 49
From instruction to delight: an anthology of children's literature to 1850 95
Frozen fire 47
Fuel for change: cooperative program planning and teaching 93
Fun in the kitchen 31
Fur trade 81
Fur trade in Canada 81
Fur trade in Canada, The 81
Fusion factor, The 62
Gabriel Dumont 142
Gage intermediate dictionary 73
Galahad Schwartz and the Cockroach Army 60
Gang war 84
Garbage delight 39, 86, 88, 90
Garçon au cerf-volant, Le 125
Garden, The 4
Géants de Blizzard, Les 125
Gens de mon pays, Les 147
Gentle persuader, The: a biography of James Gladstone, Indian senator 65
Geography match 42
George Brown 79
George Heriot 77
George Simpson and the Hudson's Bay Company 85
Get lost 84
Getting along: fish, whales, and fishermen 28
Ghost horse of the Mounties, The 40, 87
Ghost of Lunenburg Manor 55
Giant dinosaurs 26
Giraffe, La 104
Glausgab, créateur du monde: La véritable histoire du Grand Manitou algonquin 112
Glausgab, le protecteur: La véritable histoire du Grand Manitou algonquin 112
Glen Loates birds of North America 29
Glengarry school days 45
Glooscap and his magic: legends of the Wabanaki Indians 20
Glooskap's country and other Indian tales 88
Go jump in the pool 48
Goélands, Les 143
Goelette nommée Black Joke, Une 131
Gold Rush! 80
Gold Rush 81
Golden phoenix, and other fairy tales from Quebec, The 18
Golden phoenix and other French-Canadian fairy tales, The 88
Golden road, The 51
Goldie by the sea 14
Goldwin Smith 80

Good morning Franny, goodnight Franny 9
Good news in paper 24
Good times, bad times, Mummy and me 8
Goodbye mom, goodbye 23
Goodbye Sarah 56
Goodman of Ballengiech, The 20
Goodnight Jeffrey 9
Gopher Hills 62
Goûte à tout 118
Government 81
Government and you 23
Government of Canada publications/ Publications du gouvernement du Canada 97, 149
Graffiti 76
Grammar to go 38
Grand atlas du Canada et du monde 141
Grand cerf-volant, Le; poèmes, contes et chansons 121
Grande question de Tomatelle, La 133
Grandfather Heron finds a friend 59
Grandfather Symons' homestead book 73
Grand-maman 101, 147
Grandma's visit 3
Grandmother came from Dworitz 68
Grange aux lutins, La 112
Grange de Chester, La 118
Granny's gang: life with the most unusual family of owls 29
Great Canadian adventure stories 86
Great Canadian animal stories 63, 86
Great Canadian lives: portraits in heroism to 1867 66
Great hockey masks/Grands masques de hockey 36
Great Klondike gold rush 1896-1904, The 79
Great leader of the Ojibway: Mis-Quona-Queb 67
Great railway, The 22
Green Angels, The 50
Greetings from Canada: an album of unique Canadian postcards from the Edwardian era 1900-1916 70
Grenouilles, Les 143
Gretzky! Gretzky! Gretzky! 84
Grey Nuns and the Red River settlement, The 85
Griff gets a hand and other stories 47
Griff makes a date and other stories 47
Grizzly bears 83
Groaning ups 82
Group of Seven, The 75
Grouse 84
Guardian of Isis, The 62, 87
Guardians of time 61
Guerre des tuques, La 124
Guerrier aux pieds agiles, Le 139
Gueule-de-loup 127
Guide des mammifères terrestres du Québec, de l'Ontario et des Maritimes 115

Guide du botaniste amateur 115, 117
Guide to basic reference materials for Canadian libraries 93
Guide to western wildlife 29
Guidelines for children's services 94
Gullband 40
Gulls 83
Gunfire on the lakes; the naval war of 1812-1814 on the Great Lakes and Lake Champlain/ Cannonnades sur les lacs; la guerre navale de 1812-1814 sur les Grands Lacs et le lac Champlain 71
Guppy love, or, the day the fish tank exploded 52
Gynn 12
Habit de neige, L' 107
Habits rouges, Les 133
Haida potlatch, A 70
Halfbacks don't wear pearls 44
Halfbreed 65
Halifax ABC, A 14
Halifax Explosion, The: December 6, 1917 71
Hallowe'en 85
Hallowe'en fun 24
Hand of Robin Squires, The 56
Handbook for school library organization 94
Handful of time, A 60
Happy birthday, Baabee 4
Harbour thieves 57
Hardcastle legacy, The 82
Harness in the parlour: a book of early Canadian fact & folklore 72
Harpoon of the hunter 50
Hart Massey 79
Harvest yet to reap, A; a history of Prairie women 71
Haunted castle, The 42
Haunting of Cliff House, The 44
Have you seen birds? 13, 87, 89, 90
Have you seen Josephine? 13
Hawks 83
Hayes book of amazing experiments you can do at home, The 26
Heavy horses: highlights of their history 28
Hébert, Luée 147
Hello Calgary 78
Hello Charlottetown 78
Hello Edmonton 78
Hello Fredericton 78
Hello Halifax 78
Hello Montreal 78
Hello Ottawa 78
Hello Quebec City 78
Hello Regina 78
Hello St. John's 78
Hello Toronto 78
Hello Vancouver 78
Hello Victoria 78
Hello Whitehorse 78
Hello Winnipeg 78

Hello Yellowknife 78
Henri Bourassa 142
Henry Larsen 79
Heracles 41
Herbier québécois, L' 115
Here she is, Ms. Teeny Wonderful! 46, 91
Here's how it happens 23
Hey, Chicken Man 44
Hey, dad! 45
Hey world, here I am! 40
Hibou 141
Hiboux, Les 143
Hide and seek 5
High wire spider 41
Hill for looking, A 65
Histoire d'Adèle Viau et de Fabien Petit 105
Histoire du Canada et du Québec en quelques épisodes, L' 141
Histoire populaire de l'Acadie 141
Historical atlas of Canada (Harris) 64
Historical atlas of Canada (Kerr) 64
Hiver 102
Hiver ou le bonhomme sept heures, L' 103
Ho for the Klondike 72
Hockey showdown 82
Hockey sweater, The 6, 87
Hockey: the illustrated history 36
Hockeybat Harris 43
Hockeyeurs cybernétiques 125, 147
Hold fast 50, 87, 88, 90
Homme aux oiseaux, L' 108
Hommes du chantier, Les 127
Honey drum, The 20
Honor bound 56
Hooray for today 24
Horse called Farmer, A 45
Horses of the Royal Canadian Mounted Police, The: a pictorial history 71
Hot cars 84
House far from home, A 55
House mouse, The 9
How food was given 82
How names were given 82
How Raven freed the moon 18
How summer came to Canada 21
How the chipmunk got its stripes 18
How the kookaburra got his laugh 90
How the Loon lost her voice 18
How to get rid of bad dreams 9
How to make pop-ups 36
How to play hockey 36
How to start and maintain a toy library 94
How turtles set the animals free 82
Huart, Le 144
Hug me 15
8e merveille, La 107
Hummingbirds 83
Humphrey Beauregard dans Eliess Nut l'incorrigible 110
Hungry time, The 82, 90

Hunter in the dark 47, 87, 91
Huntsman, The 61
Hurry up, Bonnie 5
I am Phoenix: poems for two voices 39
I can't have bannock, but the beaver has a dam 16
I have to go! 12
I heard the owl call my name 45
I like birds 6
I like hats 7
I love my babysitter 3
I said to Sam 40
I want a dog 10
I want to go home! 48
I was a 15-year-old blimp 54
I wish there were unicorns 44
Icare 122
Ice hawk 84
Ice swords: an undersea adventure 47
Ida and the wool smugglers 5
Idées folles, Les 133
If I came from Mars/Si j'étais Martien 14
Ignoramus 42
Il était une fois 111
Îles du Roi Maha Maha II, Les 145
I'll make you small 17
I'm Locker 145, who are you? 46
Images des Cris de la Baie James 114
In a big ugly house far from here 56
In the city of the king 60
In the pioneer home 81
Inconnue des Laurentides, L' 133, 146
Incredible journey, The: a tale of three animals 88
Index/Guide (Nature's children series) 84
Index to Canadian children's records 73
Index – guide, L' (Le monde merveilleux des animaux) 144
Indian artists at work 33
Indian fishing: early methods on the Northwest coast 70
Indian legends of Canada 18
Indian peoples of Canada 81
Indian summer of Arty Bigjim and Johnny Jack, The 46
Indian tribes of Alberta 68
Indian tribes of Canada, The 69
Indian tribes of the Northwest 68
Indian weaving, knitting, basketry of the Northwest 69
Indians of Canada, The 69
Indians of the Plains 83
Indomitable lady doctors, The 66
Initiés de la Pointe-aux-cageux, Les 128
Inook and the sun 41
Inouk, l'ours polaire 143
Insect alert: a layman's guide to insect safety 29
Insect zoo and the wildcat hero, The 54
Insectes, Les 117
Insulin 30

Introducing ... Canadian children's authors and illustrators 74
Introduction to the arts in Canada, An 32
Invitations, celebrations: a handbook of ideas and techniques for book talks to junior and senior high school students 92
Iron barred door, The 91
Iroquoians of the Eastern Woodlands 83
Isis peddlar, The 62
It isn't easy being Ms. Teeny Wonderful 46
It's a good thing 6
J.A. Bombardier 142
J.S. Woodsworth 80
J.W. Morrice 77, 143
Jacob Deux-Deux et le vampire masqué 133
Jacob Two-Two and the dinosaur 61
Jacob Two-Two meets the Hooded Fang 61, 88, 89
J'ai chaud 105
J'ai faim 105
J'aime Claire 101, 146
Jamais plus les chevaux 124
James Bay Cree ABC in song and picture 13
James Douglas 79
Jane of Lantern Hill 51
Jardinez avec le professeur Scientifix: Des expériences pour toutes les saisons 117
Jasmin 54, 89, 90
Jasmine 135
Jason's quest 60
Je boude 103
Je m'appelle Pax: Histoire d'un chien heureux qui médite sur son bonheur 124
Je me petit débrouille 141
Je t'attends à Peggy's Cove 126
Je te laisse une caresse 121
Jean-Claude et Béatrice 118
Jeanne, fille du roy 130, 145
Jelly Belly 39, 89
Jennifer has two daddies 8
Jenny Greenteeth 7
Jenny's neighbours 15
Jerry Potts 80
Jerry Potts: Paladin of the plains 66
Jill and the big cat 14
Jillian Jiggs 8
Jock MacDonald 78, 143
Joe Howe: the man who was Nova Scotia 66
Johann's gift to Christmas 14
John A. Macdonald 78, 80
John Wilson 80
'Johnny' Eagleclaw 45
Jonathan cleaned up – then he heard a sound, or blackberry subway jam 12
Jongleur, Le 130
Jos Montferrand, le géant de l'Outaouais 112
Jo's search 85
Joseph Brant: a man for his people 67
Jour blanc 125
Journal intime d'Ani Croche, Le 127

Journey through a shadow 44
Journeys of exploration 81
Jours de terreur 134
Juggler, The 57
Julie 54, 87, 89
Junior computer dictionary, The 31
Just desserts and other treats for kids to make 32
Justin, Jay-Jay and the juvenile dinkent 49
Kadel 123
Kamon, l'orignal 143
Kap-Sung Ferris 45
Karen Kain 84
Kateri Tékakwitha 142
Keeper of the Isis light 62
Khan, le tigre 143
Khan, the camel 85
Kids and libraries: selections from Emergency Librarian 94
Kids' bakebook, The 31
Kids' cat book, The 27
Kids' dog book, The 27
Kids from B.A.D, The 52
Kids in the kitchen 31
KidsFood cookbook, The 31
Kiki of Kingfisher Cove: a tale of a Nova Scotia cat 14
Kilmeny of the orchard 51
King of the Thousand Islands, The 58
Kingdom of riddles, The 91
King's daughter, The 58, 90
Kite on the wind, A 36
Koli 110
Kristli's trees 88
Kuanuten vent d'est 135
Kurelek's vision of Canada 32
Kwakiutl legends 22
Kwulasulwut: stories from the Coast Salish 22
Kyle's bath 7
Labour in Canada 81
Lady of the strawberries, The 44
Land called morning, The: three plays 42
Landwash days: Newfoundland folklore, sketches and verse for youngsters 38
Lapins, Les 144
Larry Robinson le jeu défensif 120
Last chance summer 55
Last ship, The 84
Last voyage of the Scotian, The 57
Last war, The 84
Laura Secord 79, 142
Laura Secord: the lady and the legend 67
Lavabosse ou légendes du pays perdu 146
Lazaros Olibrius 104
Leanna builds a genie trap 10
Learning about ... Alberta 79
Learning about ... British Columbia 79
Learning about ... Canada 79
Learning about ... Manitoba 79
Learning about ... New Brunswick 79
Learning about ... Newfoundland 79

Learning about ... Nova Scotia 79
Learning about ... Ontario 79
Learning about ... Prince Edward Island 79
Learning about ... Quebec 79
Learning about ... Saskatchewan 79
Learning about ... The Canadian North 79
Légendes indiennes du Canada 145
Legends of my people, the great Ojibway 20
Legends of Wesakecha 18
Leopard and the lily, The 7
Léopard dans mon placard, Un 102, 147
Let it go 46
Let me in the kitchen!: a cookbook for kids & other first-timers 32
Letitia Hargrave and life in the fur trade 85
Let's celebrate! 24
Let's eat!/Allons manger! 7
Let's go!/Allons-y 8
Let's go shopping Ned 17
Let's hear it for Christmas 42
Let's play ball Ned 17
Letter carrier, The 82
Library service to children: CACL pamphlet series 94
Lie that grew and grew, The 15
Life in Acadia 81
Life in New France 81
Life in Upper Canada 81
Life of the Loyalist 81
Link between the oceans 72
Lion des mers, Le 146
Lions, Les 144
Lire c'est voyager: Livres québécois pour enfants 148
Lisa makes the headlines and other stories 47
Liste des livres disponibles en langue française des auteurs et des éditeurs canadiens, La 149
Listen for the singing 49, 87
Listen! Songs and poems of Canada 39
Little Bear can't sleep 3
Little Blue Ben 8
Little boy who cried himself to sea, The 8
Little Loon and the Sun Dance 68
Little mermaid, The 20, 87
Little Snowshoe 13
Little Wild Onion of the Lillooet 68
Livre des proverbes, Le 140
Livre d'ici, Le 149
Livre tout nu, Le 109
Livres à fabriquer soi-même 119
Livres en langue française pour les jeunes 148
Livres et auteurs québécois: Revue critique de l'année littéraire 149
Livres québécois pour enfants: sélection de Communication-Jeunesse 148
Lizzy's lion 40, 87
Lobo, le loup 143
Lobo, the timber wolf 85
Log jam 47
Long claws 47, 89, 91

Longest day of the year, The 50
Look out book!, The: a child's guide to street safety 23
Look! The land is growing giants: a very Canadian legend 19
Looking at insects 28
Looking at plants 27
Looking at senses 30
Loons 83
Loon's necklace, The 21, 86, 90
Lost and found 49
Lost in the barrens 52, 88
Lost treasure of Casa Loma, The 55
Louis Riel 80, 142
Louis Riel and the new nation 85
Louis St-Laurent 142
Loup de Noël, Le 145
Loup, Le 144
Loutre de rivière, La 143
Loyalistes, Les 144
Loyalists, The: revolution, exile, settlement 72
Lucky Hans 19
Lucky old woman, The 21
Lucy Maud Montgomery 79
Ludovic 134
Luke Baldwin's vow 44
Lumberjack 66
Lune de neige 147
Lurelu: La seule revue exclusivement consacrée à la littérature québécoise pour la jeunesse 149
Lynx 83
Lynx, Le 144
Ma rue 101
Ma sexualité 118
Ma vache Bossie 108
Macail 106
Machine à beauté, La 132
Mackenzie King 80, 142
Mafia du pensionnat, La 131
Maggie and me 54
Magic fiddler and other legends of French Canada, The 18
Magic for Marigold 52
Magic pears, The 20
Magician's trap, The 61
Main de Robin Squires, La: Le mystère de l'île aux Chênes 124
Maison des vacances, La: Une année du tonnerre 1 126
Maison Miousse ou les bienfaits d'une tempête, La 127
Maison tête de pioche, La 133
Major resolution, A 91
Malédiction de Tchékapesh, La 122
Malédiction du tombeau Viking, La 131
Mallard ducks 83
Maman 105
Maman va t'acheter un moqueur 129
Mama's going to buy you a mockingbird 49, 89, 90

Mammals in North America 28
Mammals of Canada, The 73
Mammals of Ontario 27
Mammals of the Canadian wild 27
Mammifères du Canada, Les 140
Mammifères du Québec et de l'est du Canada 116
Man who stole dreams, The 61
Mangeur d'étoiles, Le 110
Manic, le castor 143
Manitoba 77
Many stars and more string games 35
Maple syrup book, The 32
Mare's egg, The: a new world folk tale 21, 86
Margaret in the middle 48
Marguerite Bourgeoys 138
Maria Chapdelaine 128
Marie Anne: the frontier adventures of Marie Anne Lagimodière 67
Marie of the Metis 68
Marie-Mardi. Le secret d'Anthime 136
Marion Hilliard 80
Marionnettes de papier, Les 119
Marlot dans les merveilles 122
Marmotte, La 143
Marrow of the world, The 60, 88
Martha et Edouard 106
Mary of Mile 18 6, 88
Mask 'n melody: drama and music for Canadian schools (K-8) 97
Matou marin, Le 109
Matt et Kayak: Une aventure du Grand Nord 128
Matthew and the midnight money van 11
Matthew and the midnight tow truck 11
Matthew and the midnight turkeys 11
Max 125
Me and Luke 52
Meet the author: poster kits 74
Meet the author: sound filmstrips or video format 94
Meeting the challenge: library service to young adults 93
Meilleurs films québécois pour les jeunes, Les 148
Méli-Mélo 132
Mémoires de Jean Talon, Les 139
Mémoires de Samuel de Champlain, Les 139
Men of the last frontier, The 46
Ménagerie, La 135
Menaud maître draveur 134
Mensonge, Le 109
Mental gymnastics for trivia freaks and puzzle nuts 35
Mer et le cèdre, La: Ainsi vivaient les Indiens de la Côte du Nord-Ouest 139
Merchants of the mysterious East 64, 86
Merry Christmas, Baabee 4
Merveilleuse histoire de la naissance, La 118, 145

Merveilleuses aventures de Ti-Nomme en pays d'Acadie, Les 146
Mes cheveux 101
Mes observations sur les insectes 117
Mes observations sur les mammifèeres 117
Mes observations sur les poissons 117
Metal head 84
Métamorphose, nouvelle 146
Métis, Canada's forgotten people, The 69
Métis people of Canada, The: a history 68
Métro caverne 128
Métro en folie, Le 107
Mgr. de Laval 145
Mias, the orangutan 85
Mice 83
Michele Landsberg's guide to children's books: with a treasury of more than 350 great children's books 95
Michi's New Year 84, 86
Micmac, The: how their ancestors lived five hundred years ago 70
Micro man 84
Mike and the bike 82
Mike, chasseur des ténèbres 129
Millicent and the wind 12
Mime: the step beyond words 34
Mimi Finfouin et le monstre du lac Saint-Ernest 136
Mine, The 81
Minerva program, The 50
Mini-bike hero 50
Mini-bike racer 50
Mini-bike rescue 50
Minibus 132
Mini-moto héroïque, La 130
Miraculous hind, The 88
Miro des enfants, Le 138
Miroir de l'âme 146
Mischief city 41
Miss P and me 50
Mista Amisk de Piekouagami, Les: Les castors géants du Lac Saint-Jean 112
Mistatin, le chasseur de bison: Les Amérindiens des Plaines 144
Mistatin, the buffalo hunter: Indians of the plains 82
Mr. Dressup's book of things to make and do 35
Mr. John Bertrand Nijinsky and Charlie 55
Mistress Molly, the brown lady: a portrait of Molly Brant 67
Mistress Pat: a novel of Silver Bush 52
Modern Canadian children's books 95
Mollie Whuppie and the giant 21
Mollie Whuppie et l'ogre de la forêt 112
Mollusques d'eau douce du Canada, Les 115
Molly and Mr. Maloney 11
Mom and Dad don't live together anymore 15
Mon ami parmi les oiseaux 104
Mon ami Pichou 103
Mon bébé-soeur 101, 147

Mon grand-père a un jardin 121
Mon petit frère Bertrand 104
Monarch butterfly 83
Monarchie au Canada, La 139
Monarque, Le 143
Monde des dieux, Le 113
Monde hors de temps, Un 134
Monsieur Genou 132
Monster cheese 17
Montagnais et Naskapi, Les 139
Montcorbier, Les 130
Moonbeam on a cat's ear 8, 87
Moons of Madeleine, The 59
Moose 83
More Glooscap stories 20
More kids in the kitchen: metric munchies for junior cooks 31
More tales from the igloo 21
More than weird 85
Morgan the Magnificent 16
Morrice des enfants, Le 138
Morse, Le 143
Mort sur Montréal 124
Mortimer 12
Mots ... de Picotine, Les. – L'homme aux ballons 135
Moufette rayée, La 143
Mountain goats of Temlaham, The 22
Mounties and law enforcement, The 85
Mounties, The 81
Mouse Woman and the mischief-makers 19
Mouse Woman and the muddleheads 19
Mouse Woman and the vanished princesses 19, 88
Moustache, l'otarie 143
Moutarde 135
Mud puddle 12
Multicultural programming 94
Murder on the Canadian 55
Murdo's story: a legend from northern Manitoba 21, 87
Murmel, murmel, murmel 12
Music we can see and hear 33
Muskox 83
Muskrats 83
Mustard 16
MVP: Canada's sports magazine 76
My baby sister 3
My dad takes care of me 13
My first French-English word book 8
My friend Pichou 5
My Grandma the monster 7
My heart soars 69
My house 3
My impossible uncle 53
My Island pictures: the story of Prince Edward Island 32
My kind of pup 17
My king has donkey ears 19
My mom is so unusual 10
My name is Masak 66
My name is not Odessa Yarker 90
My name is Paula Popowich! 47
My street 4
Mystère et boule de gomme 132
Mystery and adventure in Canadian books for children and young people/Romans policiers et histoires d'aventures canadiens pour la jeunesse 94, 148
Mystery at the edge of two worlds 46
Mystery of the Oak Island treasure, The 41
Naciwonki cap 42
Naissance d'une légende, La 146
Name for himself, A: a biography of Thomas Head Raddall 65
Names and nicknames 42
Nanna Bijou: Le géant endormi 113
Naomi's road 57
Napoléon Comeau 142
Nation beckons, A: Canada 1896-1914 79
Nation in the schools, The 94
Nation launched, A: Macdonald's dominion 1867-1896 79
Nations autochtones de Québec 139
Native trees of Canada 26
Natural history notebook No. 1 83
Natural history notebook No. 2 83
Natural history notebook No. 3 83
Natural history notebook No. 4 83
Natural history notebook No. 5 83
Nature amie; sciences de la nature 117
Nature Canada 76
Naufrage, Le 146
Ne faites pas mal à l'avenir 124
Ned Hanlan 79
Neeka and Chemai 82
Nellie McClung 79
Nellie McClung and women's rights 85
Never cry wolf 28
Never done: three centuries of women's work in Canada 71
New baby calf, The 6
New Brunswick 77
New Canadian Oxford atlas, The 64
New France and war 81
New wind has wings, The 39
New world bestiary, A 19
Newfoundland 77
Newfoundland and Labrador prehistory 78
Nicole's boat 11
Night and day 28
Night the city sang, The 38
Night watch: the equinox guide to viewing the universe 25
Nine days queen, The 56
Ninstints: Haida world heritage site 69
Nkwala 58
No coins, please 48
No ordinary pig 13
No way 84
No word for good-bye 45

Nobody 17
Nobody asked me 44
Nobody said it would be easy 46
Noël de Savarin, Le 112
Noël de Zéphirin, Le 104
Noëls nordiques: Les rêves de Noël d'un garçon des Prairies 119
Non book materials: the organization of integrated collections 95
Norman Bethune 142
North/Nord 76
North country spring: a book of verse for children 39
North, The 81
North West Mounted Police 81
Northern alphabet, A 9, 87
Northern nativity, A 24
Northern survival 36
Nos amis robots 130, 147
Nos livres: Revue d'analyse de l'édition nationale 149
Nose is for smelling, A 30
Not impossible summer, The 43
Not in our schools?!!! School book censorship in Canada: a discussion guide 93
Not only me 85
Notable Canadian children's books, 1975-1979/ Un choix de livres canadiens pour la jeunesse 1975-1979 92, 148
Nova Scotia 77
Nova Scotia's Oak Island: the world's greatest treasure hunt 63
Nova Scotia's two remarkable giants 65
Nuit du grand coucou, La 109
Nuits d'Arthur, Les 107
Nuits magiques 108
Nutcracker, The 34
Observation des oiseaux, L' 115
Ochechak, le chasseur de caribou: Les Amérindiens de Subarctique 144
Ochechak, the caribou hunter: Indians of the Subarctic 82
Ogre de Niagara, L' 112
Oiseaux d'hiver au Québec, Les 116
Ojibway ceremonies 69
Ojibway dream, The 70
Old enough 7
Old friends, new friends 15
Olden days coat, The 60, 86, 88
Olivier le forgeron 104
On stage, please 54
On the edge of the eastern ocean 59
Once: a lullaby 13
Once more upon a totem 19
One chance to win 53
100 great Canadians 68
One man's gold rush 72
One ocean touching: papers from the first Pacific Rim Conference on children's literature 95
One proud summer 57, 90
One thousand cranes 42
One watermelon seed 11
One wonderful fine day for a sculpin named Sam 13
Only connect: readings on children's literature 95
Ontario 77
Ontario, L' 137
Ontario prehistory 78
Oomeraghi oh 42
Opération beurre de pinottes 133
Opération herbe à puces 109
Opération marmotte 127
Opium en fraude 146
Opossum 83
Opossum, L' 143
Or de la Felouque, L' 135
Orchestra, The 34
Orchestre dans l'espace, Un 130
Ordeal of John Gyles, The 68
Ordinateur égaré, L' 132
Orff, 27 dragons (and a snarkel!) 16
Organisation Argus 134
Orignal, L' 144
Os de l'Anse-aux-Mouques, Les 135
Osborne collection of early children's books, 1566-1910, The: a catalogue 96
Oscar, le cheval à la queue tressée 112
Other Elizabeth, The 58
Où est le chat? 106
Où est le ver? 106
Où est ma tétine? 101, 147
Our brother has Down's Syndrome 29
Our choice/your choice catalogue 94
Our land: native rights in Canada 70
Our man Weston 48
Our Nell: a scrapbook biography of Nellie L. McClung 67
Our people: Indians of the Plains 70
Ouram 145
Ours blanc, L' 143
Ours grizzly, L' 143
Ours noir, L' 143
Outdoor Canada 76
Over 2000 place names of Alberta 74
Overnight adventure 10
Owl 76
Owl and the pussycat, The (Berg) 39, 87
Owl and the pussycat, The (Rutherford) 39
Owls 28, 83
Owls in the family 52
Owl's question and answer book #1 26
Owl's question and answer book #2 26
Oxford companion to Canadian literature, The 75
Oyai, le pêcheur de saumon et le sculpteur: Les Amérindiens de la Côte-Nord du Pacifique 144
Oyai, the salmon fisherman and woodworker: Indians of the north Pacific coast 82

Ozerov – v.1 L'héritier, Les 126
Papa, réveille-toi 107
Paperbag princess, The 12
Papillons du Québec, Les 116
Papinachois, Les 132, 147
Par delà le mur 129
Par la bave de mon crapaud 112
Pardon me, Mom 7
Parkland portraits: some natural history of the prairie parklands 26
Parle-moi de la ceinture fléchée! 114
Parli, parlo, parlons 120
Pas encore seize ans ... 126
Passage des loups, Le 128
Passages, poésie 146
Pat of Silver Bush 52
Patrick et Sophie en fusée 125
Patte dans le sac, La 126
Paul-Emile Borduas 78
Paul-Emile Léger 142
Pauline Johnson 78
Pay cheques & picket lines: all about unions in Canada 23
Pays d'où je viens, Le 137
Peaux-Aiment 146
Peepee in the potty 3
Peewee 50
Pélican, Le 144
Pelicans 83
Penguin book of Canadian folk songs, The 33
Pénombre jaune, La 125
People of the buffalo: how the Plains Indians lived 81
People of the ice: how the Inuit lived 82
People of the long house: how the Iroquoian tribes lived 82
People of the trail: how the northern forest Indians lived 82
People of the Willow: the Padlimiut tribe of the Caribou Eskimo 69
Pepper makes me sneeze 32
Perdriole, La 119
Perfect day for kites, A 45
Pernilla in the perilous forest 17
Peter Pitseolak's escape from death 67
Petit débrouillard, Le 116
Petit dinosaure d'Alberta, Le 130
Petit et grand 102, 147
Petit fabriquant de jouets, Le 105
Petit nuage, Un 103
Petit sapin qui a poussé sur une étoile, Le 145
Petit soulier 106
Petite fille aux yeux rouges, La 128, 146
Petite fille du printemps, La 125
Petite flore forestière du Québec 117
Petite menteuse et le ciel, La 135
Petite soeur, La 103
Petites bottes de la grande Sarah, Les 104
Petits marmitons, Les 117
Petits pouvoirs, Les 122

Petrouchka 34, 87
Pettranella 16
Peux-tu attraper Joséphine 108
Phantom sailors, The 82
Phoque, Le 144
Photo périlleuse 146
Pic mineur, Le 143
Picasso des enfants, Le 138
Pictorial history of the Royal Canadian Mounted Police, The 23
Picture gallery of Canadian history, The 71
Picture history of Alberta, A 71
Pictures to share: illustration in Canadian children's books/Images pour tous: illustration de livres canadiens pour enfants 92, 148
Pieds nus dans l'aube 138
Piège à bateaux, Le 134
Piège du magicien, Le 132
Pierrot de Monsieur Autrefois, Le 105
Pilgrims of the wild 66
Pillow, The 82
Pioneer girl 65
Pioneer settlement in Canada 1763-1895 79
Pioneer travel in Upper Canada 22
Pi-oui 131
Pipi dans le pot 101, 146
Pirates & outlaws of Canada 1610-1932 23
Piste de l'encre, La 135
Pitatou et la neige 108
Place for Margaret, A 48
Place names of Ontario 74
Place names of the province of Nova Scotia, The 73
Plaisirs de chat 108
Plan B is total panic 46
Planéria: Anthologie de science-fiction 125
Plantes, Les 117
Plantes sauvages des montagnes Rocheuses 116
Plantes sauvages des villes, des champs et en bordure des chemins 116
Plantes sauvages du bord de la mer 116
Plantes sauvages printanières 116
Plantes vagabondes 145
Please don't interrupt 13
Pleins feux sur la littérature de jeunesse au Canada français 148
Pleurer pour rire 122
Plouf le dauphin passe à l'action 115
Plumeneige 105, 127
Poems of the Inuit 38
Poets' record, The: verses on Canadian history 41
Point de repère: Index analytique de périodiques québécois et étrangers 149
Poissons de nos eaux, Les 116
Polar bears 83
Police montée du Nord-Quest, La 144
Policeman, The 82

Pop bottles 53
Pope John Paul II 84
Popok, le petit esquimau 135
Porc-épic, Le 143
Porcupines 83
Poulette grise, La 119
Poundmaker 79, 142
Pour se faire un nom 120
Practical handbook of Quebec and Acadian French/Manuel pratique du français québécois et acadien 75
Prairie boy's summer, A 66, 86, 88
Prairie boy's winter, A 66, 86, 90
Prairie dogs 83
Prairie giants 63
Prairie jungle: songs, poems and stories for children 38
Prairie kid's cook book, The 31
Prairie wildlife: the best of Doug Gilroy's nature photography 26
Préhistoire de l'Arctique canadien, La 144
Préhistoire de l'Ontario, La 144
Préhistoire de Terre-Neuve et du Labrador, La 144
Préhistoire des provinces Maritimes, La 144
Préhistoire du Québec, La 144
Premier printemps sur le grand Banc de Terre-Neuve 127
Preschool storytimes 94
Pride of lions 12
Primary computer dictionary, The 31
Prime ministers of Canada, The: Macdonald to Mulroney 67
Prince Edward Island 77
Princess, the hockey player, magic and ghosts, The: Canadian stories for children 63
Princesse à la mante verte, La 113
Princesse à la robe de papier, La 107
Princesse Souillon, La 112
Principaux insectes défoliateurs des arbres du Québec, Les 116
Printemps 102
Prisonniers de Monsieur Alphonse, Les 126
Prix du silence, Le 130
Profiles 74
Profiles 2: authors and illustrators: children's literature in Canada 74
Profiles in Canadian literature 84
Programming for school-aged children 94
Promesse de Luke Baldwin, La 124
Pronghorns 83
Proper Acadian, A 56
Prophecy of Tau Ridoo, The 59
Prudence! Le guide de sécurité pour les enfants 114
Puce à l'oreille, La 141
Puce dans l'espace, Une 106
Puddleman 14
Puffin Canadian beginner's dictionary 75
Put on the spot 42

Quand ça va mal 101, 147
Quarter-pie window, The 56, 89, 91
Quatre saisons de Piquot, Les 109, 146
Quebec 77
Québec je t'aime/I love you 64, 86
Quebec prehistory 78
Québec Rock 141
Québec sur le pouce, Le 137
Québec-Science 141
Queen Cat of Furbit 42
Queen who stole the sky, The 8
Quel beau petit! 104
Quelle journée 105
Qu'est-ce qui mijote 118
Question of loyalty, A 57
Qui a vu le vent? 131
Quill & quire 97
Quincy Rumpel 54
R.B. Bennett 80
R.B. Russell and the labor movement 85
Rabbits 83
Raccoons 83
Race you Franny 9
Raffi singable songbook, The 34
Raft baby 41
Raie de lumière 146
Railways in Canada: the iron link 81
Railways of Canada: a pictorial history 23
Rainbow Valley 52
Rainy day magic 8
Raisins and almonds 67
Ram, le robot 131
Raminagradu: Histoires ordinaires pour enfants extraordinaires 146, 147
Rapaces diurnes, Les 144
Rat musqué, Le 143
Raton laveur 143
Rats in the sloop 56
Raven the trickster: legends of the North American Indians 21
Raven's children 61
Raven's cry 57, 88
Read to me: libraries, books and your baby 93
Rebecca's Nancy: a story of a little Mennonite girl 9
Rebel yell 84
Rebellion in the Northwest: Louis Riel and the Métis people 80
Record de Philibert Dupont, Le 132
Recyclers, The 10
Red Fox 53
Red fox 83
Red is best 15, 90
Red ochre people, The: how Newfoundland's Beothuck Indians lived 81
Red pines on the ridge 26
Red River Settlement 81
Redcoat 58
Regarde, il y a des géants partout! 111
Regards sur le Canada 137

Regards sur le Québec 137
Reine qui avait volé le ciel, La 105
Remembrance Day 85
Renard rose, Le 129
Renard roux, Le 144
Rencontres avec les créateurs de livres pour enfants: Auteurs et illustrateurs 148
Répertoire 1986-87 149
Répertoire des prix littéraires 1986 148
Répertoire des ressources en littérature de jeunesse 149
Report on photocopying in Canadian libraries 94
Republic of childhood, The: a critical guide to Canadian children's literature in English 95
Requins, Les 144
Révolte de la courtepointe, La 133
Revue de presse jeunesse 149
Rhume d'éléphant, Un 109
Riel's people: how the Métis lived 81
Rilla of Ingleside 52
Rima: the monkey's child 28
Ring-rise, ring-set 62
Ringtail 14
River otter 83
River runners: a tale of hardship and bravery 47, 88
Riverside anthology of children's literature, The 95
Road to yesterday, The 52
Robena's rose-colored glasses 42
Robin and the rainbow 61
Robot alert 62
Robot concierge, Le 129
Rock express 76
Rockies, The 64
Rocky Mountain wild flowers 27
Rocky Mountain wildlife 26
Roi a des oreilles d'âne, Le 106
Roi de Novilande, Le 105
Roll out the barrel: the story of Niagara's daredevils 36
Romans et contes pour les 12 à 17 ans 149
Rond comme ton visage 102, 147
Root cellar, The 60, 89
Rosanne et la vie: Une année du tonnerre 2 126
Rouge c'est bien mieux, Le 109
Roughing it in the bush 72
Round slice of moon and other poems for Canadian kids 40
Ru d'Ikoué, Le 135
Rude visitors, The 7
Ruée vers l'or, La 144
Runaway 84
Ruthie's big tree 7
Sa sainteté le Pape Jean-Paul II 138
Sadie and the snowman 11
Saint John: scenes from a popular history 72
Saint Lawrence, The 88
Saisons de la mer, Les 125, 145
Sajo and the beaver people 46

Sally go round the sun 33, 88
Sally, where are you? 11
Salmon 83
Salmon for Simon, A 16, 86, 87, 88
Salmonberry wine 53
Salut, Gadou! 53
Sam McLaughlin 80, 142
Samedis fantastiques, Les 127
Samuel Cunard 79, 142
Samuel de Champlain 78, 142
Sandford Fleming 80
Sandwich, The 16
Sandwriter 59
Sandy Mackenzie, why look so glum? 66
Saskatchewan: the colour of a province 64
Saumon, Le 144
Savon, Le 103
Scary poems for rotten kids 40
School libraries in Canada: the journal of the Canadian School Library Association 97
School on wheels: reading and teaching the isolated children of the North 23
School, The 81
Science activities for young people 25
Science is ... 25
Scienceworks: an Ontario Science Centre book of experiments 26
Scrub on skates 56
Se meurent d'opium 146
Sea and cedar: how the North West Coast Indians lived 81
Sea lions 83
Sea, The 3
Seals 83
Seasons of Canada 63
Secret code of DNA, The 30
Secret de Vanille, Le 125
Secret formula, The 82
Seeds and weeds: a book of country crafts 36
Selected stories of Ernest Thompson Seton 54
Semester in the life of a garbage bag, A 49
Sens, Les 118
Serpent vert, Le 104
Serpents, Les 144
Serrurier en Nouvelle-France, Un 140
Settlement of the West 81
Settlers' traditions 72
Settling the Canadian West 80
Seul au monde 108
Seven bears 53
Seven rivers of Canada 64
Seventh princess, The 61
75 years of Scouting in Canada 37
Shadow cat 39
Shadow in Hawthorn Bay 58, 87, 89, 91
Shantymen of Cache Lake 57, 87
Sharks 84
Sharon, Lois & Bram 84
Sharon, Lois & Bram's Mother Goose 34
Sharptooth: a year of the beaver 28

Shirt of the happy man, The 90
Shivers in your nightshirt: eerie stories to read in bed 63
Short stop 82
Short tree and the bird that could not sing, The 8
Si l'herbe poussait sur les toits 107
Sieges of Quebec 81
Simon 127
Simon and the golden sword 88
Simon Jesse's journey 59
Simon's surprise 14
Sing a song of Mother Goose 13
Singing our history 33
Singing stone, The 60
Sir Wilfrid Laurier 142
Sirène de Percé, La 112
Six chapters of Canada's prehistory 78
Six darn cows 82
Skate like the wind 46
Ski Canada 77
Ski for your mountain 54
Skip to it! the new skipping book 35
Skunks 83
Sky caribou, The 84
Sky full of babies 15
Sky man on the totem pole? 59
Slave of the Haida 88
Sleighs of my childhood, The/Les traîneaux de mon enfance 86
Slip the otter finds a home 10
Small talk 82
Smoke over Grand Pré 56
Snakes 83
Snakes of Canada, The 27
Snow apples 53
Snow babies 14
Snow ghost 84
Snowfeather 8
Snowflake, the polar bear 85
So, I'm different 55
So, you have to go to court!: a child's guide to testifying as a witness in child abuse cases 23
Soeur de Robert, La 105, 146
66 nouvelles expériences pour les petits débrouillards 116
Son of Interflux 49
Son of the Salmon People 45
Song for Harmonica, A 59
Songs and ballads from Nova Scotia 33
Songs and sayings of an Ulster childhood 96
Songs of Miramichi 33
Sophie, l'apprentie sorcière 130
Sorcerer's apprentice, The 21, 87, 90
Sorcier d'Anticosti et autres légendes canadiennes, Le 111
Sources of French-Canadian children's and young people's books/Sources d'information sur les livres de jeunesse canadiens-français 149

Souris, Les 143
Space trap 59
Sparrow's song, The 16
Spider danced a cosy jig, A 39
Spiders 83
Spin out 84
Spindlerion and the princess 42
Spirit in the rainforest 55
Spirit of the white bison 56
Sports and games in Canadian children's books/ Livres canadiens sur les sports et jeux pour la jeunesse 94, 149
Spring 4
Squirrels 83
Squirrels of Canada, The 28
Stadaconés, Les 132
Starbuck Valley winter 88
Starring Quincy Rumpel 55
Steve Podborski 84
Stoddart visual dictionary, The 74
Stone in the meadow, The 59
Stone soup 13
Stones and cones 36
Store, The 81
Stories from the Canadian North 63
Storm Child 56
Story girl, The 52
Story of Canada's flag, The 23
Story of Canadian roads, The 71
Storytellers' encore: more Canadian stories to tell to children 96
Storytellers' rendezvous: Canadian stories to tell to children 96
Streets of gold 84
Subject index to Canadian poetry in English for children and young people 75
Sulphur and molasses: home remedies and other echoes of the Canadian past 72
Summer 4
Summer goes riding 54
Summer the whales sang, The 51
Sun god, moon witch 59, 89
Sun horse, The 88
Sunflakes and snowshine 40
Sunshine sketches of a little town 49
Super science discovery book, The: easy-to-do experiments that really work! 25
Super string games 35
Superbike! 44, 91
Sur les îles des pierres dansantes 106
Surprise de dame chenille, La 145
Surréal 3000 131
Survenant, Le 128
Sweetgrass 57, 87, 89
Système métrique apprivoisé, Le 114
Take a giant step 52
Take off 84
Taking care of Crumley 15
Tale spinners in a spruce tipi 19
Tales from the Amazon 19

Tales from the igloo 20
Tales of a gambling grandma 10
Tales of an empty cabin 46
Tales of Nanabozho 88
Tales of Nokomis 20
Tales the elders told: Ojibway legends 20
Tales told in Canada 19
Tales until dawn: the world of a Cape Breton Gaelic story-teller 96
Tall tales and true tales from down east 22
Tamias et le suisse, Les 144
Tangled web 52
Tango, l'hippopotame 143
Tatterhood 21
Teach me to fly, Skyfighter! and other stories 55
Techniques d'impression 119
Tell me another: storytelling and reading aloud at home, at school and in the community 96
Tell me, grandmother 66
Temps changent, Les: Bébé William/Changing times: Baby William 139
Temps changent, Les: Bobby et Mary chez eux/Changing times: Bobby and Mary at home 139
Temps changent, Les: Moyens de transport/Changing times: transportation 140
Temps changent, Les: Le vêtement/Changing times: clothing 140
Temps des fêtes au Québec, Le 114
Ten little ducks 9
Tension 146
Tequila, the African elephant 85
Terror in Winnipeg 55
Terry Fox 84, 138
Terry Fox: his story 67
Testament de Madame Legendre, Le 126
TG: Teen generation 77
Thanksgiving 85
That fine summer 50
That scatterbrain Booky 48, 90
Théâtre mot magique; marionnettes, jeux scéniques, ombres chinoises 122
Théâtre pour enfants au Québec, Le: 1950-1980 148
Théo et les quatre saisons 106
There is my people sleeping 41
There's a dragon in my closet 9
There's an alligator under my bed 8
Thérèse Casgrain 142
They shared to survive 69
They sought a new world: the story of European immigrants to North America 72
Thinking games 35
Thinking metric for Canadians 30
Thirty-six exposures 50
This can't be happening at Macdonald Hall 49
Thomas Keefer 80
Thomas' snowsuit 12, 90
Those green things 15

Three and many wishes of Jason Reid, The 59
Thursday's child: trends and patterns in contemporary children's literature 95
Tick bird 41
Tie-breaker 43
Tiens bon! 130
Ti-Jean: Contes acadiens 111
Ti-Jean et le gros roi 113
Ti-Jean voudrait ben s'marier mais ... 122
Tikta'liktak 129
Tikta'liktak: an Eskimo legend 88
Time for bed Ned 17
Time for tots: library service to toddlers 94
Time is flies 41
Time to be brave, A 48
Timothy Eaton 79, 142
Tinderbox, The 56
Tin-lined trunk, The 57
Titralak, cadet de l'espace 131
Tlingit: their art, culture and legends 69
To hang a rebel 58
To the end of the block 13
Tobi et le gardien du lac 124
Tobo hates purple 6
Toes in my nose 39
Toilet tales 16
Tom Penny 57, 128
Tomate inquiète, Une 106
Tom Penny and the Grand Canal 57
Tom Penny et les géants de l'Outaouais 128
Tombé des étoiles 121
Tomorrow city, The 62
Tonto, the South African fur seal 85
Tony et Vladimir 109
Too busy day, The 9
Too many kings 41
Toothpaste genie, The 59
Tootle 14
Tortues, Les 144
Totem poles: an illustrated guide 69
Tourbillon, le lutin de la Côte-Nord 129
Tournoi, Le 123
Tours de Maître Lapin, Les 113
Tout sur Noël 114
Towards women's rights 81
Tragedies of the Crowsnest Pass 70
Train for Tiger Lily 88
Train, Le 102
Train, The 4
Traite des fourrures, La 144
Trapping is my life 67
Treasure of the Long Sault 48
Treasures: Canadian children's book illustration 75
Tree, The 4
Trésor du 'Scorpion', Le 134
Trips 82
Triste dragon, Le 104
Trompette, l'éléphant 143

Trouble at Lachine Mill 57
Trouble with adventurers, The 20
Trouble with princesses, The 86, 87, 88
Trouble with stitches, The 40
Turk, the moose 85
Turkey pops 82
Turtles 83
Turtles of Canada, The 27
Twelve dancing princesses, The 20, 86, 87, 90
Twelve days of Christmas north 33
Two pals on an adventure 16
Two parents too many 43
Umiak, L' 121
Un beau soleil 103
Un, deux, trois, quatre, les tout-petits découvrent le livre 148
Un, deux, trois, voilà la mère l'oie 108
Uncle Jacob's ghost story 60
Under cover 85
Underground to Canada 58, 88
Understanding cancer: an invaluable book for cancer patients and their families 29
Une ... Deux ... Trois prises. T'es mort 123
Union of the Canadas: 1840-1867 81
United Empire Loyalists and the American Revolution 81
United Empire Loyalists, pioneers of Upper Canada 71
Universe, The ... and beyond 25
Unmasking of 'Ksan, The 55
Up to Low 45, 89
Upside-down king of Minnikin, The 9
Vacances d'Amélie, Les 107
Vache et d'autres animaux, La 121
Vampires of Ottawa 55
Vancouver nightmare 55
Vancouver's past 71
Vandarian incident, The 61
Vanished peoples: the Archaic, Dorset and Beothuk peoples of Newfoundland 70
Varicelle, La 147
Vérendrye, La 142
Very last first time 5
Very small rebellion, A 42
Vidéo-Presse 141
Vie de nos ancêtres en Acadie: Coutumes, croyances et religion populaire 114
Vie de nos ancêtres en Acadie: Le vêtement 114
Vie en Acadie, La 144
Vie en Nouvelle-France, La 144
Vie pédagogique 149
Vieille dame et le chaudron magique, La 112
Vieille sauvage, La 126
Viking dagger, The 91
Vilhajalmur Stefansson and the Arctic 85
Ville fabuleuse, La 130
Vincent, Sylvie et les autres 132
Violin maker's gift, The 60, 88
Violin, The 43, 89

Violon, Le 123
Virginie chante ... la locomotion 119
Virginie chante ... les instruments de musique 119
Visages de la préhistoire du Canada 144
Visit from Mr. Lucifer, A 49
Visiteur du soir, Le 134, 146
Visiteurs extra-terrestres 129
Voice from afar; the history of telecommunications in Canada, A 22
Vol à retardement 126
Voyage à la recherche du temps, Le 107, 146
Voyage au claire de lune 106
Voyage de Lapin Noir, Le 129
Voyages fantastiques de Globulo, Les 117
Voyages of discovery 81
Voyageurs de l'arc-en-ciel, Les 124
Voyageurs du temps, Les 146
Voyaginaires 102
Waldo's back yard 7
Walk out of the world, A 60
Wallpaper 82
Walrus 83
Wandeln, poésie 146
Wapiti, Le 125, 145
War at Fort Maggie, The 44
War with Mr. Wizzle, The 49
Warriors of the wasteland 61
Watch for the breaking of day 45
Wayne's wagon 11
We make Canada shine: poems by children 82
Weagamow notebook 70
Weasels 83
Weather book, The 25
Welcome, twins 4
We're friends, aren't we? 46
West coast Chinese boy 67
Westwoods monster, The 82
Whale for the killing, A 28
Whale named Henry, A 58
Whale people, The 88
Whales 83
What are uncles for? 39
What holds up the moon? 14
What is it?: a gallery of historic phrases 38
What is that noise? 10
What to do until the music teacher comes 33
What's in a name: the story behind Saskatchewan place names 75
What's the matter girl? 44
What's the word/Cherchez le mot 8
Wheels for walking 53
Wheels on the bus, The 10
When an osprey sails 50
When everybody cares 42
When you were little and I was big 8
Where books come from 95
Where did you get your moccasins? 16
Where is my dummy? 3

White archer, The: an Eskimo legend 88
White mist 61
Who cares about Karen? 53
Who goes to the park 6
Who hides in the park/Les mystères du parc 6
Who is Bugs Potter? 49
Who's a soccer player 82
Who's who in Canadian literature 1985-86 75
Why the beaver has a broad tale 19
Why the man in the moon is happy 90
Wicked fairy-wife, The 19
Wild animals I have known 54
Wild horses 83
Wild life I've led, The 28
Wild mammals of Canada 28
Wild man of the woods 44, 89
Wild night 84
Wild one 84
Wilderness women: Canada's forgotten history 66
Wildflowers across the prairies 27
Wildflowers of Canada 27
Wildflowers of the Yukon and Northwestern Canada, including adjacent Alaska 27
Wildlife of Canada 26
Wilds of Whip-poor-will Farm, The: true animal stories 27
Will o' the wisp: folk tales and legends from New Brunswick 21
William Cornelius Van Horne 78
William G.R. Hind 78, 143
William Hamilton Merritt 79, 142
William Van Horne 80, 142
Willow maiden, The 18
Willow: the story of an Arabian foal 27
Wimp and easy money, The 85
Wimp and the jock, The 85
Wimp, The 84
Wind has wings, The 86
Wind, The 11
Window of dreams, The: new Canadian writing for children 38
Wings across time: the story of Air Canada 22
Winners 44, 89, 91
Winter 4
Winter magic 9
Winter of the fisher, The 49
Winter studies and summer rambles in Canada 72
Winter: the bogey-man-twice-seven 5
Witch of Port LaJoye, The 18
Witch of the North, The 86

Witchery Hill 60, 89
With love from Booky 48
Wolves 83
Woodchucks 83
Wooden people, The 87
Woodozz et le robot sculpteur 110
Woosh! I hear a sound 9
World War I 81
Worst Christmas present ever, The 55
Wynken, Blynken and Nod 39
Yeah, I'm just a kid 6
Years of change: 1967-1985 80
Years of conflict: 1911-1921 80
Years of despair: 1929-1939 80
Years of growth: 1948-1967 80
Years of hope: 1921-1929 80
Years of promise: 1896-1911 80
Years of promise: Canada 1945-1963 79
Years of struggle: 1867-1879 80
Years of victory: 1939-1949 80
Yellow flag, The 84
Yeux en fête, Les 120
You bug me 16
You can pick me up at Peggy's Cove 45
You want me to be grown up, don't I? 41
You'll never be the same 42
Young collector, The 36
Young relationships: a booktalk guide to novels for Grades 6 through 9 92
Your baby needs music 33
Your time, my time 61
You're someBODY: how to be a slim kid 29
Youth science news 77
Ytek and the Arctic orchid: an Inuit legend 20, 86, 87, 89
Yukon and Northwest Territories, The 77
Zap eating 85
Zap fire 85
Zap flying 85
Zap hockey 85
Zap magic 85
Zap monsters 85
Zap music 85
Zap underground 85
Zap water 85
ZIP: Le magazine des jeunes 141
Zoom at sea 17, 87, 90
Zoom away 17, 87
Zou la loutre trouve une maison 115
Zunik 105, 146
Zunik dans le championnat 105

ILLUSTRATORS / ILLUSTRATEURS

Aguanno, Leonard 9
Ahern, Jean-Yves 133
Aislin 14
Alexander, Roslyn A. 27
Allerston, John 24
Anastasiu, Stéphane 3, 101
Anfousse, Ginette 5, 103, 123, 147
Arbuckle, Franklin 69
Arcouette, Evelyne 131
Arnold, Rist 6
Aska, Warabé 6
Asselin, Claude 103
Auml, Ana 8
Baker, Mary Lynn 7
Barker, Paul 24
Barrett, Hugh John 109, 146
Baumgarten, Susan Im 26
Bédard, France 129, 133, 135
Bédard, Laurent 104
Beddows, Eric (see also Nutt, Ken) 9, 59
Béha, Philippe 3, 4, 101, 107, 108, 109, 112, 121, 146, 147
Bekkering, Herman 16
Bénard, Christian 104, 133
Beney, Gabriel de 134
Benham, Paddy 31
Benoît, Nicole 121
Berg, Ron 39, 56, 57, 84, 86, 87
Berger, Bob 36
Bergeron, André 125, 128
Bianchi, John 6, 8, 10, 25
Blades, Ann 5, 6, 14, 16, 43, 86, 87, 89
Blanchard, Louise 105
Bobak, Molly Lamb 39
Bouchard, Laurent 129
Bouchard, Yvon 112
Boucher, Terry Roscoe 55
Boulanger, Claudette 40
Brender à Brandis, G. 56
Briansky, Rita 54, 68
Brooks, Bill 63
Brooks, Terry 24

Brown, Robert 30
Bruemmer, Fred 26, 63
Bucholtz-Ross, Linda 25
Burden, P. John 45
Calleja, Gina 6
Calvert, Lissa 8, 26, 84
Campbell, Hedy 13
Chapleau, Serge 125
Chaplin, Carl 33
Charles, Veronika Martenova 8, 61
Chatillon, Yolande 121
Cheechoo, Shirley 20
Cholette-Longtin, Suzanne 132
Clark, Brenda 6, 11, 28, 54, 84, 104, 107
Clark, Phil 66
Clarke, Stephen 57
Cleaver, Elizabeth 7, 18, 21, 22, 34, 39, 86, 87
Climo, Lindee 7, 27, 87, 118
Cobiness, Eddy 46
Cockburn, Kitty 33
Cohen, Sheldon 6, 87, 104
Cole, Kathryn 24
Collins, Heather 8, 9, 11, 13, 15, 47, 109
Condy, Roy 106
Conroy, Richard A. 45, 48, 61
Cooney, Barbara 9
Côté, Claude 135
Côté, Marie-Josée 4, 101
Cranston, Toller 34
Crespo, Colette 125
Crockett, Lou 46
Crosby, John A. 29
Cserepy, Mary 54
Custode, Michael 22
Daigle, Gisèle 17
Daigneault, Sylvie 14
Dancho, Beverly 65
Daniel, Alan 34, 44, 61, 132
Daniel, Lea 48, 49
Dawe, Tom 38
Day, Shirley 7, 13
Decelles, Pierre 113, 139

Della-Vedova, Rod 35
Denton, Kady MacDonald 17
Desbarats, Michelle 59
Desputeaux, Hélène 104
Desrosiers, Pierre 135
Devlin, Michèle 112, 127, 130, 135, 136
Devos-Miller, Kathryn 29
Di Lella, Barbara 6, 7, 32, 40
Dobson, Clive 29
Dombrowski, Josée 111, 112
Douglas, Charles 83
Drawson, Blair 7
Drew-Brook, Deborah 11, 58
Duchesne, Christiane 104
Dufour, Christine 135
Dufour, Marcellin 121
Dunnigan, Huguette 104
Duranceau, Suzanne 8, 12, 105, 108, 126
Edwards, Ken 82
Eitzen, J. 13, 69, 114, 139
Eitzen, T. 69
Ense, Don 48
Eyolfson, Norman 61
Fairfield, Lesley 7, 8, 32
Faucher, Guy 133
Fernandes, Eugenie 8, 15, 105
Fernandes, Jane 34
Ferron, Yseult 111
Field, Saul 18
Fine, Diane 31
Fitzgerald, Joanne 7
Fleury, Jean-Denis 117
Fog, Michael 135
Foote-Jones, Pat 58
Ford, Eric 37
Foster, Velma 7
Frankenberg, Robert 20, 52
Freire, Carlos 40
Frischeteau, Gérard 127
Gaboury, Serge 110
GAD, VictoR 41, 59
Gagnon, Cécile 118, 127, 135
Gal, Laszlo 18, 20, 21, 72, 86, 87, 90, 111
Gallagher, Terry 15, 21, 87
Garnotte 130
Garrick, Fiona 5, 103
Gay, Marie-Louise 4, 8, 40, 87, 102, 105, 106, 146, 147
Germain, Philippe 127
Gilman, Phoebe 8, 106
Girard, Paule 126, 133
Glyde, H.G. 28
Goldstyn, Jacques 25, 110, 116, 117, 118
Goman, Joan R. 9
Gould, Matt 57
Gower, Anthony 25
Graham, Georgia Pow 43
Grau, Peter 30, 118
Grégoire, Renée 121
Gregory, Richard 144

Gruda, Anna Maria 58
Guberec, Josée 114
Guberek, Josée 133
Hahn, Sylvia 9, 39
Hall, Pam 40, 86, 106
Hall, Pamela 59
Hamberger, John 20
Hammond, Franklin 9, 11, 34
Hanley, Wanda 31
Hannans, Nancy 9
Harris, Dorothy Joan 9
Harrison, Ted 9, 40, 64, 87
Harty, Dwayne 28
Hayes, Chris 24
Hayes, Melanie 31
Helmer, Katherine 41
Hendry, Linda 8, 9, 24, 31, 32, 105, 106
Hirnschall, Helmut 69
Hodgson, Barbara 30
Hoey, Elizabeth Wilkes 33
Holdcroft, Tina 15, 26, 109, 115
Houde, Pierre 106
Houston, James 47, 129
Hyman, Trina Schart 60
Ironside, Jetske 17
Irving, Daphne 18
Italiano, Carlo 86
Jobson, Kellie 66
Johnson, Bill 17, 56
Johnson, Bruce 126
Jorisch, Stéphane 113
Julien, Henri 19
Kagige, Francis 20
Kakaygeesick, Robert 56
Kassian, Olena 10, 14, 27, 29, 50, 90, 115
Kaulbach, Kathy 63, 70
Kauperman, Larissa 19
Kebic, Bob 28
Kemp, Carol A. 68
Khalsa, Dayal Kaur 4, 10
Klumder, Barbara 114
Klunder, Barbara 23
Knaff, Jean-Christian 121
Königslöw, Andrea Wayne von 16
Kotopoulis, Dino 49
Kovalski, Maryann 10, 11, 14, 17, 19, 34, 106
Krstanovich, Vesna 58
Krykarka, Vladyana 34
Kuch, Peter 21
Kulyk, Karen 16
Kunz, Anita 44
Kurelek, William 19, 24, 32, 66, 72, 86, 119, 139
La Perrière, Josée 105
Labrosse, Darcia 41, 105, 106, 147
Lachance, Em 53
Ladouceur, François 119
LaFave, Kim 14, 19, 21, 86
Lafortune, Claude 113, 138, 146, 147
Langlois, Claire 126

Langlois, Suzanne 107, 133
Laquerre, Dominique 104, 112
Laroche, Gaétan 112
Larose, Pierre 106
LaRouche, Adelle 10
Larouche, Henri 116
Lasker, Joe 10
Lauzon, A. 116
Lawrason, June 105
Le Baron, Anthony 40
Leblanc, Bernard 111
Leblanc, Renée 120
Lebon, France 111, 113
Leclerc, Michèle 121
Ledoux, Lucie 107, 133
Leduc, Pierre 115
Lee, Ina K. 13
Lefebvre, Fernande 125
Lemieux, Michèle 9, 10, 19, 60, 108
Lemire, Robert 140
Lessard, Marie 107
Léveillé, Jacques 122, 124
Leventhal, Ian 36
Levert, Mireille 4, 102, 104, 107
Lévesque, Nicole 124
Lewis, Robin Baird 9, 10, 15, 109
Lid, Dagny Tande 27, 116
Lightwood, Jeannette 27
Lim, John 64, 67, 86
Lim, Sing 67
Lobel, Anita 13
Loranger, Francine 106
Louie, BoKim 96
Lunn, Jenni 50
MacDonald, S.D. 29
MacDougall, Ken 53
Mah, Anna 59
Malish, Miro 39
Marchiori, Carlos 33
Martchenko, Michael 11, 12, 107
Marton, Jirina 11
Mathews, Jacqueline McKay 58
Matthews, Sharon 24
McGugan, Laurie 35
McLeod, Phil 40
McLoughlin, Mary 15
McNeely, Tom 58
McNeil, Irene 29
Menarick, R. 13, 114
Mérinat, Eric 119
Mérola, Caroline 126
Méthé, Louise 119, 121, 125
Michailiuk, George 11
Michailiuk, Richard 11
Michaud, Josette 53, 119, 133
Miller, Tara 18
Milnes, Herbert 72
Mintzberg, Yvette 11
Moak, Allan 11
Moore, Harold M. 46

Morgan, Nicola 12
Morrill, Leslie 60
Morrison, A.L. 32
Muir, Mary Jane 12
Muller, Robin 21, 87, 112
Nanogak, Agnes 20, 21, 112
Nault, Francine 124
Neubacher, Gerda 19
Newfeld, Frank 38, 39, 86
Nicholls, Chuck 120
Nidenoff, Michele 20
Nokony, Denis 38
Norris, Len 14
Nutt, Ken (see also Beddows, Eric) 17, 39, 87, 109
O'Halloran, Tim 26
Ohoveluk, Mona 21
Olivier, François 53, 108, 124, 147
O'Neill, Catharine 10
Orr, M. 13, 114
Ouellet, Joanne 112, 132, 147
O'Young, Leoung 47, 49, 84
Ozores, J. Rabbit 69, 139
Paabo, Iris 7
Pachano, J. 70, 139
Pachano, R. 70, 139
Pakarnyk, Alan 10
Panamik, Martin 19
Panton, Doug 60
Paré, Roger 13, 108, 147
Parent, Richard 132
Parker, Lewis 73
Parsons, Michèle 113
Pastic, George 43, 123
Patkau, Karen 11, 14, 39
Paxton, Maureen 13, 14, 40
Peacock, David 23
Pelham, Richard 19, 111
Pelletier, Micheline 108
Pennanen, J.O. 30
Pépin, Johanne 121
Perna, Debi 28, 84
Perrault, Michèle 131
Perron 110
Pik 66
Pitsolak, Peter 67
Poirier, Claude 111, 113, 135, 136
Poirier, Michelle 130, 135
Poisson, Danielle 104
Pomminville, Louise 108, 125
Poulin, Stéphane 13, 108, 129, 132, 147
Poulton, Michael 44
Powell, Ann 7, 10
Pratt, Pierre 4, 134
Precious, Carole 33
Price, Arthur 18
Price, Kim 19
Pruden, Greg 68
Pusztai, Georgeta 130
Rampen, Leo 58

, Barbara 6, 7, 13, 16, 32, 34, 36, 87, 89, 90, 104, 108, 135
id, Bill 57
empel, Judith Anne 65
eynolds, Nancy Lou 15
Richards, Lori 25
Richmond, John 59
Rickels, Robert 39
Rikki 40
Rio, Vincent 136
Ritchie, Scot 12
Ritchie, William 13
Roache, Gordon 14
Robert, Luc 113
Robinson, Michael 62
Robitaille, Denis 120
Rother, Christina 43
Roussan, Jacques de 14, 86
Rousseau, Albert 121
Ruhl, Greg 44, 46, 54, 59
Rutherford, Erica 39
Sankey, Tom 35
Sapon, Datherien 111
Sarrazin, Marisol 123
Savage, Harry 28
Scalabrini, Rita 108
Schaller, Adolf 25
Schoenherr, John 53
Schwartz, Roslyn 24
Sedgewick, Carol 32
Senécal, Marc 123
Shadbolt, Frances 37
Shapira, Sheila 31
Shaw, Barbara 14
Shelton, Danielle 129, 130
Sheridan, David 42
Shilling, Arthur 70
Shoemaker, Kathryn E. 15
Shore, J.L. 58
Shore, Judie 61
Simard, Rémy 110
Simmie, Anne 14, 40
Simpson, David 50
Sinclair, Valerie 38
Skaalen, Sue 13
Smith, Lisa 9
Smith, Lynn 6
Smith, Mark 84
Smith, Merle 26, 50, 58, 72, 130, 144
Sneyd, Doug 41
Stafford, Terry 14
Steffler, Shawn 13
Steltzer, Ulli 64
Stobie, Nancy 28
Stout, Andy 16
Stren, Patti 15
Suomalainen, Sami 12
Sylvestre, Daniel 102, 105, 124, 126, 146
Symons, R.D. 73
Tait, Douglas 19, 20, 66, 86, 139
Takashima, Shizuye 67, 86
Talbot, Sylvie 4, 101, 102, 112
Tanobe, Miyuki 64, 86, 147
Taylor, William 56
Théorêt, Michèle 111
Thérien, Lise 126
Thomas, André 114
Thomas, Eric 114
Thomson, Tom 33
Thornton, J.M. 68
Thurman, Mark 6, 9, 15, 16, 109
Tibo 109, 118, 119
Tibo, Gilles 40, 121
Todeo, Adriana 42
Tremblay, C. 116
Troughton, Joanna 21
Trower, Barry 59
Trudel, Marie 140
Trueman, Stuart 28
Tuckerman, Robert 28, 117
Tughan, James 34, 86
Twigg, Jeremy 39
Van Kampen, Vlasta 7, 9, 13, 16, 63, 86, 87, 106
Varga, Julius 56
Veillet, Renée 132
Verdaguer, Raymond 61
Verret, Suzanne 116
Wallace, Ian 5, 16, 87
Warner, Nancie 25
Wegner, Fritz 61, 133
White, Silas 39
Wijngaard, Juan 39
Wilson, Mélinda 125
Winik, Terry 26
Wolsak, Wendy 7, 17
Wood, Muriel 60, 86
Woodall, Heather 20, 86, 87
Wright, Don 28
Yamamoto, Joyce 34
Yaryomich, Lucya 10
Yee, Paul 55
Ying, Wong 20
Zander, Hans 31
Zgodzinski, Rose 53
Zimmerman, Werner 14, 108